A New Documentary History of Hong Kong, 1945–1997

Edited by Florence Mok and Fung Chi Keung Charles

T0396666

HKU PRESS
香港大學出版社

Hong Kong University Press
The University of Hong Kong
Pok Fu Lam Road
Hong Kong
https://hkupress.hku.hk

ISBN 978-988-8876-82-2 (*Paperback*)

British Library Cataloguing-in-Publication Data
A catalogue record for this book is available from the British Library.

Digitally printed

Contents

Foreword by John M. Carroll

Why a new documentary history of Hong Kong? As each of the fourteen chapters in this pioneering book shows, it is not only Hong Kong that changed from 1945 to 1997; it is also how we *study* Hong Kong's history over this period that has changed, especially in the past few decades. This is partly because of sources that have become available or easier to access, but it is also because historians have asked different questions and approached their topics in new ways. The chapters here are by twelve young scholars who are all conducting cutting-edge research on Hong Kong history.

A key theme in the book is politics. Florence Mok and Fung Chi Keung Charles's chapter on governance and Matthew Hurst's on constitutional change show how, despite minor adjustments, Hong Kong's non-democratic political structure remained remarkably similar – 'largely and stubbornly unchanged' as Hurst puts it – with little resulting from the sweeping reforms proposed in the 1940s. Challenging notions of Hong Kong's supposed political apathy, Mok's chapter on political culture reveals how the colonial government responded and adapted to pressures from civil society to introduce reforms. As the chapter by Fung on fiscal and budgetary policy shows, both were always political and help us understand how state and society interacted. Jack Greatrex's chapter on environment and natural disasters demonstrates how environmental issues were never separate from politics, including efforts to protect dolphins and green space.

Allan T. F. Pang's first chapter shows how education became a key element in Hong Kong's Cold War politics and its gradual decolonisation – a process that for education began shortly after the Sino-British negotiations over Hong Kong's post-1997 future. Pang's second chapter, on policies for popular culture, reveals how they could be a way to attract public support. These policies involved both censorship and control, but also collaboration and appropriation. The arts, Reynold K. W. Tsang's chapter shows, played an important role in Hong Kong's post-war recovery and in its politics. More support for the arts was one of the many demands made by the Reform Club, one of the colony's oldest political groups. The documents in this chapter cover both official initiatives such as the Arts Festival and unofficial ones such as those by the colourful impresario Harry Odell. And if cultural policies could be political, so too could medicine and healthcare. Kelvin Chan expands these to include mental health, drug addiction, and disability. Moreover, he illustrates how traditional Chinese medicine thrived in Hong Kong, partly because it was unregulated by the colonial regime, and partly because of Hong Kong's geopolitical position, which helped it circulate among Chinese communities in Southeast Asia and North America.

Hong Kong was a colony in flux, affected always by changes in mainland China and across the region. The 'China factor' looms large in almost every chapter, but particularly in James Fellows's chapter on economy and trade. Even while showing the importance of colonial and regional connections, this chapter reveals how so much of Hong Kong's economic history was shaped by developments across the border. In Adonis M. Y. Li's chapter on transport and communication, we see not only a 'city constantly on the move' but also one where transport and mobility became part of local identity and Hong Kong's relationship with the outside world. Mobility is also the theme of Doris Y. S. Chan's chapter on migration, both inward and outward. The chapter shows how fears of a 'brain drain' emerged well before the signing of the Sino-British Joint Declaration in 1984 and reminds us that concerns about migration were not always directly related to China, as seen in the influx of Vietnamese refugees after 1975.

The documents analysed here often take us into the minds of Hong Kong's colonial administrators, but they also reveal how local people reacted to and challenged colonial governance. Carol C. L. Tsang's chapter on the politics of gender and family shows how the two interacted, sometimes in complementary ways but also in opposition. Here we see not only efforts by the government and NGOs, but also by ordinary people, who had their own ideas about family, and how notions of gender equality were challenged in both cultural and political terms. And whereas most scholars have approached race and racism mainly through laws and regulations, Vivian Kong's chapter demonstrates how race shaped social hierarchies, but also how these hierarchies could be challenged at the personal level (through autobiographies and other writings, for example) and by groups such as the Sino-British Club. Moreover, while racial divides and boundaries could be rigid, they could also be porous.

This book is far more than a collection of historical documents; it is a new history of Hong Kong from 1945 to 1997. As useful as these sources are for telling the history of Hong Kong during this period, just as valuable are the introductions and commentaries by the contributors. For while these sources tell us much about Hong Kong, this book is a powerful testament to the fact that it is historians who make historical documents speak and who give them meaning.

Foreword by Tai-lok Lui

The idea of editing a volume of documentary history is admirable. Firstly, the outcome is most unlikely to please its readers. Many of them, especially those who are new to archival research, would find it more of a 'tasting menu', only allowing them to have an initial glimpse of what would be a long and tiring process of submerging themselves in the sea of documentary materials, than really a start of the serious business of mining of archival sources. For those who know enough about historical research, what is shown in front of them is merely a selection of some relevant pieces of archival material. In the case of either group of readers, they would ask for more.

Secondly, no matter how voluminous the documentary history text is, it cannot be exhaustive. Perhaps no readers would ask for a thorough collection of documents. Archival search is, by definition, an unending quest, with the researcher always looking for new sources and/or previously unavailable pieces. In this regard, some kind of disappointment is almost a built-in feature of a documentary history sourcebook. Many readers would find the selection not enough – not enough in the sense that the set of selected documents does not quite suit their own research purpose. Almost inevitably, there would be questions about the selection decisions made by editors and contributors.

I want to make the point that editing a documentary history is probably the least appreciated effort in our contemporary academic world. As stated above, it would not easily please its readers. Furthermore, nowadays, the role of editorship is rapidly depreciated, seen as minimally pertinent, if not outright negligible, in the evaluation of academic contributions. Against such a backdrop, I find a commitment to academic sharing and altruism among the editors and contributors of this sourcebook. They shared with us the documents they covered in their own research. They identified those that were most relevant to capturing the essential features of Hong Kong society in their chosen areas of study. They started their chapters with a brief introduction, informing the readers about how those selected documents would enable them to grasp the main issues of the topic of discussion. To some extent, what the contributors have offered is more than giving us their selection of relevant documents. They also provide their own interpretation of what constitutes the main themes and/or the critical issues in the respective domain of enquiry. They bring us closer to Hong Kong society in a particular historical context.

While most history students would probably find an emphasis on the historical context, social processes leading to historical change, and the historical configuration of social institutions as something they have long taken for granted, this is not necessarily so for students and researchers practising sociology. Many sociologists take variable-based analysis as the starting point of their sociological analysis. Though most of them would not write off the pertinence of historical context, their analysis often shows limited sensitivity to the effects of historical change on the social fabric. The social setting is treated as if it is abstracted from historical changes. The meanings of social variables are assumed to be constant, leaving little room for imagining how social life is historically constituted. It is, therefore, important to recognise the significance and implications of connecting sociology and history to enrich the complexities of our sociological analysis.

In fact, sociological studies of Hong Kong society have a long-established intellectual linkage, though increasingly unduly neglected, with a historical perspective. H. J. Lethbridge's Hong Kong: Stability and Change, a collection of articles published between 1970 and 1975, alerts younger sociologists of a need to grapple with the historical configuration of the political and social institutions in pre-1941 Hong Kong, shaping the interface between the colonial governance on the one side and the Chinese community on the other, that promoted social stability.[1] Janet W. Salaff, based on her ethnographic fieldwork from 1971 to 1976, examined why and how Hong Kong's working daughters, despite their participation in economic activity and growing contributions to their family economy, continued to see themselves subordinated to the patriarchal Chinese family tradition.[2] Industrialisation enabled a new generation of young women to earn and gain more control over some aspects of their social lives. Yet their family obligations and the need to pool family resources significantly restricted the independence of the working daughters in a period when Hong Kong's industry and economy took off. W. K. Chan took up the concept of social class and analysed the making of Hong Kong society between 1841 and 1922 in the light of the formation of the British merchant class, the Chinese merchant class, and Chinese labourers.[3] Just to quote a few examples. Sociological studies of

---

1. H. J. Lethbridge, *Hong Kong: Stability and Change* (Hong Kong: Oxford University Press, 1978).
2. Janet W. Salaff, *Working Daughters of Hong Kong: Filial Piety or Power in the Family?* (Cambridge: Cambridge University Press, 1981).
3. W. K. Chan, *The Making of Hong Kong Society: Three Studies of Class Formation in Early Hong Kong* (Oxford: Clarendon Press, 1991).

Hong Kong society need a good sense of historical sensitivity in order to show how the sociological question is embedded in a particular historical context.

This volume of a documentary history of Hong Kong covers fourteen areas of study. As I said earlier, readers would not find the coverage and the selection of documentary materials enough for their research interests. But they would be given the pointers and handles for further explorations. They will learn to navigate Hong Kong studies with an awareness of the richness of documentary sources and the pathways of social and political developments in different historical periods. Sociology students will benefit from their exposure to archival materials. A stronger sense of historical sensitivity will enable them to debunk some of the established analyses and to look for fresh perspectives and interpretations.

Acknowledgements

The idea of this project first started with a few of us attending a lecture on the new edition of the *Cambridge History of Southeast Asia* at Nanyang Technological University in 2022. It has been a long but productive and fruitful journey since then.

The editors would like to thank the following individuals/organisations for granting permission to include materials in this volume: the Hong Kong Public Records Office, the National Archives in Kew, *South China Morning Post*, the Constitutional and Mainland Affairs Bureau (the government of the Hong Kong Special Administrative Region), Article 19, the Hong Kong Journalists Association, Lord Patten of Barnes, the Hong Kong General Chamber of Commerce, the Modern Records Centre at the University of Warwick, the Hong Kong Heritage Project, the Bodleian Libraries at the University of Oxford, University Archives at the University of Hong Kong, History Society A.A.H.K.U., the Editorial Board (Session 2022) of the *Undergrad* student newsletter of the Hong Kong University, the Family Planning Association of Hong Kong, the Hong Kong Family Welfare Society, and the Hong Kong Society for the Protection of Children. All these organisations/individuals have provided kind assistance and clarified issues over copyright during the undertaking of our research. We are also grateful that this book is supported by the generous NAP-SUG grant by Nanyang Technological University.

We are also grateful that the Hong Kong University Library has granted us permission to use an image from its Special Collections as the cover of this volume. In addition, we would like to thank Prof. John M. Carroll and Prof. Tai-lok Lui for providing advice and feedback on this project and writing the forewords for this volume. The feedback and suggestions given by the two anonymous reviewers have improved the manuscript significantly. And to all members of the Study Group and contributors to this documentary, this project would never have been possible without your consistent support and input – we are in debt to all of you. All remaining errors remain our responsibility.

Abbreviations

BL: Basic Law
CCP: Chinese Communist Party
CLP: Hong Kong and China Electric Power Co., Ltd.
CMA: Chinese Manufacturers' Association of Hong Kong
CO: Colonial Office
CPG: Central People's Government of the People's Republic of China
DCNT: District Commissioner, New Territories
EEC: European Economic Community
FCO: Foreign and Commonwealth Office
FPAHK: Family Planning Association of Hong Kong
HKCW: Hong Kong Council of Women
HKFS: Hong Kong Federation of Students
HKFWS: Hong Kong Family Welfare Society
HKG: Hong Kong Government
HKGCC: Hong Kong General Chamber of Commerce
HKPRO: Hong Kong Public Record Office
HKRS: Hong Kong Record Series
HKSPC: Hong Kong Society for the Protection of Children
HKU: The University of Hong Kong
HMG: Her Majesty's Government
IPPF: International Planned Parenthood Federation
IVF: In-vitro fertilisation
KCR: Kowloon–Canton Railway
KMT: Kuomintang

MINT: Royal Mint (file series at the National Archives, UK)
MTR: Mass Transit Railway
NGO: Non-governmental organisation
NSPCC: National Society for the Prevention of Cruelty to Children
PRC: People's Republic of China
PREM: Prime Minister's Office (file series at the National Archives, UK)
SAR: Special Administrative Region
TB: Tuberculosis
TNA: The National Archives, London
UK: United Kingdom

Contributors

Doris Y. S. Chan is a PhD student in history at Nanyang Technological University, Singapore. Her current research studies Chinese migration in the post–Second World War British Empire, primarily focusing on Hong Kong and Southeast Asia and the colonial control over migration. She previously obtained her BA and MA from the University of Hong Kong and King's College London. She can be reached at CHAN1018@e.ntu.edu.sg.

Kelvin Chan is a post-doctoral research associate at the Hong Kong History Centre at the University of Bristol. He received his PhD from McGill University. His PhD research focuses on the history of colonial psychiatry in Hong Kong during the mid and late-twentieth centuries, exploring the relationship between decolonisation and psychiatry. Part of his PhD research has been published in *China Information* and *Medical History*.

Fung Chi Keung Charles received his MPhil in government and public administration from the Chinese University of Hong Kong and is a PhD student in sociology at the State University of New York, Stony Brook. His research interests include state (trans)formation, fiscal politics, identity-making, geopolitics, and governance, focusing on how these processes unfold in the context of colonial/imperial rule. He is the co-author of *Hong Kong Public and Squatter Housing: Geopolitics and Informality, 1963–1985* (Hong Kong University Press, 2023), and has contributed articles to journals such as *Asian Perspective, Social Transformations in Chinese Societies*, and *East Asia*. He can be reached at charlesfung1990@gmail.com.

James Fellows obtained a PhD in history from Lingnan University in Hong Kong and later held a postdoctoral fellowship at Sun Yat-sen University in Guangzhou. His PhD thesis concerned the changing trade relationship between Hong Kong and Britain in the second half of the twentieth century, in areas such as trade restrictions on textiles, British entry into the European Economic Community, and commercial diplomacy and public relations. He has published articles in *Historical Research* and

The International History Review. He is currently employed at Oxford University Press.

Jack Greatrex is a postdoctoral research fellow at Nanyang Technological University, Singapore. He completed a PhD on the bodily, discursive, economic, and infrastructural histories of 'pests' in colonial Hong Kong and Malaya, undertaken at the University of Hong Kong. Before this, he read the world history MPhil and the undergraduate history tripos at the University of Cambridge. His research is located at the conjunctions of colonial, environmental, medical, and multi-species histories in Southeast Asia and the South Pacific. He can be reached at jack.greatrex@ntu.edu.sg.

Matthew Hurst is a PhD student at the History Department, University of York, UK, funded by the White Rose College of the Arts and Humanities, a UK Research and Innovation consortium. He is currently researching how Hong Kong people influenced the handover negotiations. Matthew received a master's degree in Contemporary Chinese Studies from the University of Oxford. His research papers have been published in the journals *East Asia* and *The International History Review*, and he received the PSA Conservatism Studies Group 2022 Research Prize. He can be reached at matthew.hurst@york.ac.uk.

Vivian Kong is senior lecturer in modern Chinese history and founding co-director of Hong Kong History Centre at the University of Bristol. Vivian is a social historian of colonial Hong Kong, and her work to date has focused largely on the city and its global connections. She is the author of *Multiracial Britishness: Global Networks in Hong Kong 1910–45* (2023) and has published articles on migration, press debates, and civil society in interwar Hong Kong in *Historical Journal*, *Journal of British Studies*, and *Journal of Imperial and Commonwealth History*.

Adonis M. Y. Li is lecturer in East Asian history at the University of Lincoln, UK. He holds a PhD from the University of Hong Kong, where he conducted research on the history of the Kowloon–Canton Railway. His work has been published in *The International History Review* and *Urban History*. His research and teaching interests include Hong Kong in Sino-British relations, mobility and transport history, and migration history. He received his BA and MA from the University of York, UK.

Florence Mok is a Nanyang Assistant Professor of History at Nanyang Technological University. She is a historian of colonial Hong Kong and modern China, with an interest in environmental history, the Cold War, and state–society relations. She completed her PhD in history at the University of York in 2019. Florence is one of the founders of the Hong Kong Research Hub (HKRH) at NTU and an Executive Board member of the Society for Hong Kong Studies (SHKS). She has published peer-reviewed articles in well-respected interdisciplinary and historical journals; the *China Information* article won the Eduard B. Vermeer Best Article Prize in 2019 and ICAS Best Article Prize on Global Hong Kong Studies in 2021. Her first monograph, *Covert Colonialism: Governance, Surveillance and Political Culture in British Hong Kong, c. 1966–97,* has just been published by Manchester University Press (Studies in Imperialism series). She is also the series editor of the *Cold War in Asia and Beyond* book series published by Amsterdam University Press.

Allan T. F. Pang is a postdoctoral research associate at the Hong Kong History Centre and Department of History, University of Bristol. He is a historian of Hong Kong, Chinese overseas, and Southeast Asia. His research engages with themes such as history education, popular music, and decolonisation from a transregional perspective across East and Southeast Asia. He completed his PhD at the University of Cambridge, where he examined history education in Hong Kong, Malaysia, and Singapore in the second half of the twentieth century. His ongoing research investigates Chinese popular music in Hong Kong and Southeast Asia from the 1950s onwards. He received his BA and MPhil in History at the University of Hong Kong and has published in the *Journal of Imperial and Commonwealth History* and *Historical Journal.*

Carol C. L. Tsang is lecturer in the Department of History at the University of Hong Kong. She is a historian of gender and reproductive health in Hong Kong and has published articles on prostitution and women's medicine. She coordinates and teaches courses on gender studies, motherhood, and family. Her works on family planning in Cold War Hong Kong and hormone pregnancy test in East Asia will appear in *Cold War History* and *Global Studies in Medicine, Science, Race, and Colonialism* respectively. She can be reached at cctsang1@hku.hk.

Reynold K. W. Tsang is a DPhil student in history at the University of Oxford. He currently holds the position of visiting fellow (2023–2024) in the Department of Chinese and History at City University of Hong Kong. Reynold's DPhil research looks at the development of museums in British colonial East and Southeast Asia during the nineteenth and twentieth centuries. He is interested in a wide range of historical topics, including British imperialism in Asia, museums and material culture, arts and cultural development, and modern Hong Kong. Reynold received his BA and MPhil from the University of Hong Kong. He can be reached at kaiwontsang@yahoo.com.hk.

Introduction

Hong Kong's History Redux: Recent Trends and New Departures[1]

Florence Mok and Fung Chi Keung Charles

The 'Hong Kong Story' Exhibition

In Hong Kong recently, there has been a revival of interest in history. Not only have activists and politicians invoked historical narratives to justify their political agendas, but ordinary people have also demonstrated increased interest in Hong Kong's colonial past.[2] Some of us may still remember the unusually long queues outside the Hong Kong Museum of History in October 2020. Those people were there to visit the permanent 'Hong Kong Story' exhibition, which displayed Hong Kong's development from the prehistoric period up to its handover in 1997. Because the Leisure and Cultural Services Department of the HKSAR Government had decided to undertake a revamp to update the 'Hong Kong Story', there were widespread anxieties that 'controversial' parts of its history would be removed and that the information presented in the new exhibition would be biased and fragmentary. This popular concern could be explained by the prevailing notion that the Beijing government was increasingly trying to interfere in Hong Kong's politics, education, and media. There was therefore a pervasive fear that historical narratives would be revised and misrepresented in the new exhibition. In particular, there were suspicions that the government would suppress colonial nostalgia by downplaying the role of the British in Hong Kong history. Letters to the editor, for example in the *South China Morning Post*, condemned the revamp as 'pointless' and 'unacceptable'

---

1. Both authors would like to express their gratitude to John Carroll as well as the two anonymous reviewers for their detailed comments on the earlier versions of this Introduction. All errors remain the authors' responsibility.
2. Mark Hampton and Florence Mok, 'Remembering British Rule: The Use of Colonial Memory in Hong Kong Protest Movements, 1997–2019', in *Memory and Modern British Politics: Commemoration, Tradition, Legacy*, ed. Matthew Roberts (London: Bloomsbury, 2023), 257–73.

as it would only 'hide the truth'.[3] Parents brought their children to the exhibition hoping that the next generation could witness the 'genuine Hong Kong story' before the exhibition was closed.[4] Many tried to preserve the 'original exhibition' with photographs. This sense of uneasiness caused by the ongoing developments facilitated the reinvigoration of the discourse of historical memories.

However, history is different from memories. Historical memories often affect the cultural process of identity formation in a society and play an important role in shaping the general political culture. As John Tosh has rightly argued, even our political judgements are 'permeated by a sense of the past'.[5] However, the way memories are formed is often related to people's current consciousness and needs. In other words, collective memories can be fluid and fallible. Even in public discourse, popular memories constantly shift in response to contemporary political developments. In the words of Geoffrey Cubitt, it is 'the present that produces the past, through an effort of the creative and analytical imagination'.[6]

This phenomenon is particularly common in today's Hong Kong – historical narratives are revised and bent to serve present political, economic, and social needs.[7] This misuse of history can range from presenting inaccurate and partial information and misrepresenting historical accounts to neglecting the context and selecting primary sources in a biased manner. One notable example is how some activists painted a rosy picture of British colonialism in Hong Kong, describing the colonial regime as enlightened and progressive without demonstrating a thorough historical understanding of the situation.[8] In fact, the colonial state was not always benevolent and hands-off but was sometimes repressive, as we will discuss in the following section. In contrast, former Chief Executive Carrie Lam made a statement in September 2020 suggesting that 'separation of power' had never existed in

3. 'Revamp of Hong Kong Story in History Museum Must Not Be a Rewrite', *South China Morning Post*, 23 October 2020.
4. '"Story" to Add New Chapters after a Break', *The Standard*, 19 October 2020.
5. John Tosh, *The Pursuit of History* (London: Longman, 1984), 2.
6. Geoffrey Cubitt, *History and Memory* (Manchester: Manchester University Press, 2007), 31.
7. See Hampton and Mok, 'Remembering British Rule'.
8. This misuse of history does not only happen in Hong Kong. A most recent example outside Hong Kong that happened in the social science field is the 'Bruce Gilley Controversy'. The controversy began when a political scientist published an article titled 'The Case for Colonialism' in the journal *Third World Quarterly* in 2017, arguing colonialisation also has good sides. The publication of the article soon attracted global attention and widespread criticism as Gilley had ignored the fact that colonisation was based on brutal force and unequal power relations. The article was subsequently retracted. For a critical discussion and review of the controversy, see Pepijn Brandon and Aditya Sarkar, 'Labour History and the Case against Colonialism', *International Review of Social History* 64, no. 1 (2019): 73–109. For British imperialism and colonisation as a global/coercive phenomenon, see Caroline Elkins, *Legacy of Violence: A History of the British Empire* (London: Bodley Head, 2022).

Hong Kong, showing only a partial understanding of Hong Kong's colonial past.[9] Although there might not have been a 'separation of power in the Western sense', 'checks and balances between three branches of government are a reality', as journalist Gary Cheung has pointed out.[10] The misuse of history can be particularly dangerous when it is used to justify unethical practices, provoke popular sentiment, and encourage radicalism. It is therefore crucial for us to understand history as a 'systematic discipline' that relies on specific 'mechanisms and controls';[11] and one important 'control' is the meticulous examination of empirical evidence and close analysis of context when constructing historical narratives.

This documentary history seeks to produce both original and revised historical knowledge for Hong Kong studies. Since the late 1990s, academics have made huge efforts to provide a substantially revised understanding of Hong Kong's history. These revisions are essential: they not only shed light on how complex Hong Kong history is in terms of economic development, the Cold War, and decolonisation, but they also raise important questions vis-à-vis our established understanding of Hong Kong, opening new realms for researchers. In this book, we contribute to the existing historical discourse by revisiting some of the familiar topics using newly uncovered or underexplored primary sources and examining previously under-researched areas in Hong Kong's historiography. With improved technologies and increased digitalisation of primary sources, researchers, students, and teachers can now access both official and unofficial data online. For example, Gale has recently developed two archival databases that focus on Hong Kong: 'China and the Modern World: Hong Kong, Britain, and China, Part I: 1841–1951' and 'Part II: 1965–1993'; Proquest's Historical Collections provide important primary sources on global history from both national and international governments and agencies, which sometimes touch upon Hong Kong; and the Multimedia Information Service and Hong Kong Memory are both useful websites that contain relevant unofficial data, such as old newspapers clippings and oral testimonies.

As Hong Kong studies have become increasingly globalised, these latest developments undoubtedly benefit historical research, especially for researchers and learners who are not located near archives which have abundant Hong Kong records. Indeed, since the mid-2010s, we have witnessed a surge in Hong Kong studies networks and centres across the world, such as the Hong Kong Studies Initiatives at the University of British Columbia (Canada), Hong Kong History Centre at the University of Bristol (United Kingdom), Hong Kong Research Hub

9. 'Why Escalating Row over Whether Hong Kong Has "Separation of Powers" in Its Political System Is Not Just a Fight over Words', *South China Morning Post*, 3 September 2020.
10. 'Escalating Row', *South China Morning Post*.
11. Michael Bentley, *Modern Historiography: An Introduction* (London: Routledge 1999), 155.

at Nanyang Technological University (Singapore), and Global Hong Kong Studies at the University of California (United States). And we will probably see even more initiatives in future years.

However, these online databases also have their drawbacks. Databases such as Gale and Proquest are extremely expensive. Taking the new Hong Kong series created by Gale as an example, it can cost up to US$49,000, which is unaffordable to many small to medium-sized humanities departments. More importantly, while the online catalogues are easy to navigate (one can enter keywords and specify the time period/years using a search engine), all these databases provide no or little contextual information which helps users read the sources against the grain or in appropriate context. Since large quantities of information are included, users must go through all the records with the same keywords in a time-consuming and laborious manner before they can get a sense of how history developed and select the more important sources as empirical evidence. In addition, these materials themselves provide no explanation of how they engage with the existing literature.

This sourcebook therefore seeks to fill the voids in these research and teaching aids, providing users in different geographical locations with a relatively affordable and accessible option that is easy to navigate, even for researchers who are beginners in Hong Kong studies. It provides readers with useful primary materials, both official and unofficial, and maps them with key moments in Hong Kong history and the evolving historiography. Many of these primary sources were released in the 2010s and 2020s, decades after the publication of the three documentaries by Hong Kong University Press in the 1990s and early 2000s.[12] These sources will stimulate new discussions and debates and advance the study of Hong Kong history.

A New Documentary History

For these reasons, a new documentary sourcebook is needed to provide an updated and improved understanding of the city and its history. Through analysing either sources that have been 'newly' released, that is, since the publication of the previous three sourcebooks (since the 2000s), or underexplored archival records from the Hong Kong Public Records Office, the National Archives in London, and other overseas archives, and unofficial records, such as newspapers and private papers, this sourcebook fills a long-standing void in the existing scholarship by providing an expanded understanding of the history of post-war Hong Kong. It highlights how

12. The documentary histories are Steve Tsang, ed., *A Documentary History of Hong Kong: Government and Politics* (Hong Kong: Hong Kong University Press, 1995); David Faure, ed., *A Documentary History of Hong Kong: Society* (Hong Kong: Hong Kong University Press, 1997); David Faure and Lee Pui-tak, eds, *A Documentary History of Hong Kong: Economy* (Hong Kong: Hong Kong University Press, 2004).

a reformist colonial administration governed Hong Kong while being influenced by factors such as widespread decolonisation across the globe, increased economic development, changing Sino-British relations, and Cold War dynamics. It also explores how Hong Kong's society, culture, infrastructures, and landscapes shifted in response to these internal and external changes. It does not only address familiar topics but, more importantly, investigates topics that are original and underexplored. It addresses the immediate post-war period, which has been studied extensively by scholars, but also investigates the late colonial period, from the 1970s to 1990s – precursors of important changes in post-colonial Hong Kong. Each contributor briefly sketches what has been done with respect to the chapter's topic and then contextualises the primary sources through short abstracts. This arrangement enables us to delve into the relationship between sources and methods, and demonstrate why historians would interpret a primary source in a particular way.

Nonetheless, readers must bear in mind a cautionary note. The sourcebook includes more official sources (notably government reports and declassified archival records) than unofficial sources (private papers, diaries, internal company records, amateur photography, newspaper clippings, and oral histories). The contributors tried to incorporate more unofficial sources into the documentary. However, in the course of preparing this documentary, due to copyright issues, we were unable to include some of the privately owned sources. This may not affect chapters such as those on governance and fiscal policy, which are 'official in nature'. However, it is with regret that the volume is unable to present some of the unofficial sources, which we must acknowledge is a practical limitation.

Historiographical Methods

This documentary aims to provide original knowledge on new topics and a revised understanding of the existing historical discourse through primary sources. The use of formerly classified archival documents and private personal records enables readers to gain new and comprehensive insights into the study of Hong Kong history. To apply these records appropriately in our research, we must understand the historiographical methods used by professional historians to revise and generate knowledge. Very often, historians' research builds upon existing work and is revisionist. In other words, scholars usually start by engaging with the accepted understanding, conventional interpretation, and orthodox views of the past.[13] This often takes place

13. See, for example, Marnie Hughes-Warrington, *Revisionist Histories* (London, Routledge: 2013), 9–13; Sarah Maza, *Thinking about History* (Chicago: University of Chicago Press, 2017), 137–46; Gabrielle Spiegel, 'Revising the Past/Revisiting the Present: How Change Happens in Historiography', *History and Theory* 46, no. 4 (2007): 4; James M. Banner, *The Ever-Changing Past: Why All History Is Revisionist History* (New Haven, CT: Yale University Press, 2021), chapter 4.

in the form of debates, disputes, and disagreements among historians.[14] As James Banner has pointed out, there are a number of 'varieties of revisionist history', such as 'transformative', 'philosophical', 'conceptual', 'evidence-based', 'method-driven', and 'normal' revisionism.[15]

This part of the method is demonstrated and explained in the introduction in each chapter that analyses the existing debates and revisionist work. The author then explains how the primary sources presented in the chapter responded to these debates. This is especially the case in chapters that revisit familiar topics, such as 'Governance', 'Constitutional Change', and 'Political Culture', which refine our historical understanding by examining previously underexplored sources and informing us about the limitations of the existing scholarship. Constant revisions are important because, as Banner and Lucy Salmon have argued, only in this way can newly discovered/underutilised materials be considered.[16] In doing so, existing beliefs that are false, biased, or partial can be scrutinised and rectified. New historical interpretations can also be generated, taking the less articulated voices into consideration.[17] This process often involves moving away from orthodox historical studies that centred around a particular power bloc, race, gender, or class and creates new focuses,[18] such as marginalised historical actors, who also made a significant impact on the development of history, and under-researched themes, such as the chapters on medicine and healthcare, environment and natural disasters, gender and family, and race and diasporas in this book.

This book also seeks to show the deep connections between sources and historiographical methods. Primary sources are often considered by historians to be the 'holy grail' of history writing,[19] not only because they exert evidentiary weight to adjudicate competing interpretations of historical events,[20] but also because they constitute the basis of historical knowledge and historical method.[21] In particular, outside academia, it is commonly viewed that historical records, such as internal correspondence between bureaucrats and political intelligence reports, are 'facts'

---

14. Maza, *Thinking about History*, 142.
15. Banner, *The Ever-Changing Past*, 144, 150, 162, 171.
16. Banner, *The Ever-Changing Past*, 7; Lucy M. Salmon, 'Why Is History Rewritten?', *The North American Review* 195, no. 675 (1912): 225–37, 255.
17. Robert Carlton Clark, 'Why History Needs to Be Rewritten', *Oregon Historical Quarterly* 33, no. 4 (1932): 295–310.
18. Spiegel, 'Revising the Past/Revisiting the Present'; Ethan Kleinberg, *Haunting History: For a Deconstructive Approach to the Past* (Stanford, CA: Stanford University Press, 2017).
19. Banner, *The Ever-Changing Past*, 162.
20. Carl N. Degler, 'Why Historians Change Their Minds', *Pacific Historical Review* 45, no. 2 (1976): 167–84; Jonathan Gorman, 'The Commonplaces of "Revision" and Their Implications for Historiographical Understanding', *History and Theory* 46, no. 4 (2007): 20–44.
21. See, for example, Martha Howell and Walter Prevenier, *From Reliable Sources: An Introduction to Historical Methods* (Ithaca, NY: Cornell University Press, 2001).

that can speak for themselves. This, however, is certainly not an accurate description of historiographical methods.

By providing adequate contextual understanding, this book aims to aid researchers, students, and teachers to select their sources carefully based on their reliability and credibility and draw accurate analytical and descriptive inferences. It supports the consensus that is commonly shared by historians: records, no matter how factual they are, do not speak for themselves.[22] Therefore, it is crucial to situate history in the appropriate context; historians must put the primary sources within a 'framework', which may be a particular theoretical/empirical understanding of a specific historical dynamic, or a cluster of archival findings from which one can derive knowledge to explain the situation of a society within a given time period. This framework can give meanings to the content of the records and helps us construct accurate, coherent, and unbiased narratives of the past. In short, the research context has significant ramifications in shaping how the sources should be approached and analysed. It also influences how research question(s) should be formed and determines what counts as 'relevant' evidence. In sum, sources and historiographical methods are closely intertwined with each other, shaping how historical narrative is constructed and revised, producing 'novel' historical knowledge.

Revised Understanding of Colonial Power in Hong Kong History

Similar to many other fields, Hong Kong historiography has undergone revisions in recent decades. Christopher Munn has called this revisionist wave the 'Hong Kong school of history' which 'takes Hong Kong and its people as its central subject of study'.[23] He regards scholars such as Henry Lethbridge, Carl Smith, Elizabeth Sinn, Chan Wai Kwan, and Jung-fang Tsai as the pioneering revisionists. To Munn, this revisionist scholarship tries to study 'the dynamics of society and politics within Hong Kong' by bringing in the problems of 'race, class, and gender difference' to the discussion.

This revisionist scholarship is remarkable because it departs from the predominant historiographies that tended to neglect developments within and the roles played by the Hong Kong society.[24] For instance, the colonial narrative that dominated the discourse is largely a linear story, focusing on British colonial efforts to modernise Hong Kong society and depicting how Hong Kong developed from a

22. Maza, *Thinking about History*, 199.
23. Christopher Munn, *Chinese People and British Rule in Hong Kong, 1841–1880* (Hong Kong: Hong Kong University Press, 2009), 8–9.
24. See, for example, Jung-Fang Tsai, *Hong Kong in Chinese History: Community and Social Unrest in the British Colony, 1842–1913* (New York: Columbia University Press, 1993), 3.

'barren rock' to a capitalist metropolis.[25] The British colonisers, especially the governors, were often portrayed as the major historical actors in Hong Kong history; without their 'good intention' and policies (i.e., the so-called benevolent governance), Hong Kong might not have been the same. Another example is the nationalistic narrative propagated by the Chinese government in Beijing. This scholarship tended to reduce the multifaceted nature of British colonialism to a matter of imperial domination and exploitation.[26] Instead, it stressed the tight, if not inalienable, Hong Kong–mainland connections since ancient times and emphasised anti-colonial struggles to portray the British colonial power as 'oppressive'. These two strands of scholarship resemble what Rosie Bsheer has called 'disciplinary historiography', which rests on, structures, and promotes a distinctive state-sanctioned reading of the past.[27] But as Tak-wing Ngo has argued, these narratives significantly downplayed the 'complexity of colonial rule' by painting a unitary and static picture of Hong Kong society.[28]

These revisionist pioneers of the 'Hong Kong school' provided an alternative reading of Hong Kong's history and challenged some of the conventional colonial and nationalistic beliefs about Hong Kong and its history. While these earlier endeavours mostly focused on re-examining the history of the late nineteenth century, subsequent revisionists tapped into various unexplored/underexplored primary sources to rewrite the history of Hong Kong.[29] The limited space we have in this introduction will not do Hong Kong revisionist scholarship justice: it is a vibrant and dynamic field that generates vast original historical knowledge, which provides important insights not only for understanding Hong Kong but also other themes and regions, such as decolonisation, the Cold War, and Asia as a whole. While it is impossible to provide a full account of the revised Hong Kong history, we highlight some new empirical findings and insights that have been addressed by revisionists recently. Though selective and limited in scope, this introduction illustrates how revision as such provides a more nuanced and comprehensive historical understanding of Hong Kong.

Firstly, previous scholarship describes the state–society relations as a 'minimally integrated social-political system' where the colonial state was characterised as 'laissez-faire' and non-interventionist, governing a Chinese society that was

25. See, for example, Frank Welsh, *A History of Hong Kong* (London: HarperCollins 1997).
26. See, for example, Liu Shuyong, 'Hong Kong: A Survey of Its Political and Economic Development over the Past 150 Years', *The China Quarterly* 151 (1997): 583–92.
27. Rosie Bsheer, *Archive Wars: The Politics of History in Saudi Arabia* (Stanford, CA: Stanford University Press, 2020), 11.
28. Tak-Wing Ngo, 'Colonialism in Hong Kong Revisited', in *Hong Kong's History: State and Society under Colonial Rule*, ed. Tak-Wing Ngo (London: Routledge, 1999), 1–12, at 2.
29. Munn, *Chinese People and British Rule in Hong Kong*, 11.

apolitical, influenced by the ethos of 'utilitarianistic familism'.[30] The revisionist scholarship, however, has showed that these characteristics are a misrepresentation and a gross simplification of the relationships between the colonial government and the Chinese communities in Hong Kong. The contribution of Lui Tai-lok and Stephen Chiu, for example, has depicted the emergence of social activism in the 1970s, revealing that the Chinese communities were not politically aloof.[31] Lam Wai-man offers the most critical response to Lau Siu-kai's thesis of a 'minimally integrated social-political system'.[32] Through the use of published sources, such as newspapers, Lam reconstructed how activists organised protests between the 1950s and 1970s and argued that Hong Kong Chinese could be mobilised politically if their interests were at stake. While the existence of politically apathetic groups has not been dismissed entirely, revisionism offers a more complex picture of Hong Kong's political culture: the politically apathetic image was an outcome of the activists' tactics to avoid being jeopardised within a local 'culture of depoliticisation'.[33]

Secondly, previous scholarship on colonial rule in Hong Kong often portrayed the colonial state as a competent governing organisation. The conventional wisdom had two components. On the one hand, the colonial state was able to co-opt the Chinese elites into the administrative structure to legitimatise the undemocratic colonial government. Ambrose King refers to this colonial statecraft as 'administrative absorption of politics'.[34] On the other hand, such colonial statecraft failed, as indicated by the two major riots that occurred in the 1960s: the Star Ferry riots in 1966 and the leftist-inspired riots in 1967. The colonial state therefore adjusted its ruling strategies by increasing its reach into Chinese society through the City District Officer Scheme that co-opted the grassroots members of Hong Kong. Through these reforms, the colonial government sought to become more responsive, hoping to shore up popular support.[35] One particular problem for this existing narrative is that, as Florence Mok has argued, it is too impressionistic and fails to specify the mechanism(s) through which colonial statecraft actually took place.[36]

30. Lau Siu-kai, *Society and Politics in Hong Kong* (Hong Kong: Chinese University of Hong Kong Press, 1982), 72–85, 154–63.
31. Tai-lok Lui and Stephen W. K. Chiu, 'Social Movements and Public Discourse on Politics', in *Hong Kong's History: State and Society under Colonial Rule*, ed. Tak-Wing Ngo (London: Routledge, 1999), 101–18.
32. Wai-man Lam, *Understanding the Political Culture of Hong Kong: The Paradox of Activism and Depoliticization* (Armonk, NY: M.E. Sharpe, 2004).
33. Lam, *Understanding the Political Culture of Hong Kong*, 211–16, 218.
34. Ambrose Yeo-chi King, 'Administrative Absorption of Politics in Hong Kong: Emphasis on the Grass Roots Level', *Asian Survey* 15, no. 5 (1975): 422–39.
35. Ian Scott, *Political Change and the Crisis of Legitimacy in Hong Kong* (Hong Kong: Oxford University Press, 1989), 106–10, 163–70; see also Chapter 1 of this book.
36. Florence Mok, 'Public Opinion Polls and Covert Colonialism in British Hong Kong', *China Information* 33, no. 1 (2019): 66–87, especially 67.

On this question, John Carroll has argued that the functioning of colonial order and the maintenance of social stability cannot be understood without looking at the collaborations between the colonial state and the Chinese elites.[37] Through re-examining these Chinese elites' contribution to the preservation of colonial order, Carroll demonstrates that the colonial government was far from an 'all-powerful colonial state' and that the colonised Chinese were not entirely passive.[38] The effectiveness of such collaboration – a form of indirect rule – declined in the post-war era. Mok has illustrated how the colonial state started to realise this collaboration was becoming inefficient in the late 1950s.[39] Her research on Town Talk and Movement of Opinion Direction (also known as MOOD) – techniques of soliciting popular opinion via covert opinion polling exercises embedded in the City District Officer Scheme – provides clear evidence that surveillance, as well as co-optation of constructed 'public opinion' into the policymaking system, must also be considered to be one of the political mechanisms that helps to explain how the late colonial state could govern a rapidly changing Hong Kong society without democratisation.[40]

This, however, does not mean the colonial state did not use coercive means to check its rivals. During the 1967 riots, the colonial state was ready to compromise the due process of rule of law and leverage colonial emergency powers to deport and detain 'political undesirables' to restore colonial order.[41] One might think that the 1967 riots were a special occasion that called for exceptional treatment. However, Michael Ng's recent work on political censorship provides further evidence of how, since the pre-war period, the colonial state had used various censorship regimes to suppress criticisms in order to secure Britain's geopolitical interests in the region, particular in relation to China.[42] While the rule of law has long been regarded as a vital British contribution to Hong Kong's development,[43] these revisionist studies

37. John M. Carroll, *Edge of Empires: Chinese Elites and British Colonials in Hong Kong* (Cambridge, MA: Harvard University Press, 2005); John M. Carroll, 'Chinese Collaboration in the Making of British Hong Kong', in *Hong Kong's History: State and Society under Colonial Rule*, ed. Tak-Wing Ngo (London: Routledge, 1999), 13–29.

38. Carroll, 'Chinese Collaboration in the Making of British Hong Kong', 25.

39. Florence Mok, 'Town Talk: Enhancing the "Eyes and Ears" of the Colonial State in British Hong Kong, 1950s–1975', *Historical Research* 95, no. 268 (2022): 287–308.

40. Florence Mok, *Covert Colonialism: Governance, Surveillance and Political Culture in British Hong Kong, 1966–97* (Manchester: Manchester University Press, 2023).

41. Ray Yep, '"Cultural Revolution in Hong Kong": Emergency Powers, Administration of Justice and the Turbulent Year of 1967', *Modern Asian Studies* 46, no. 4 (2012): 1007–32.

42. Michael Ng, *Political Censorship in British Hong Kong: Freedom of Expression and the Law (1842–1997)* (Cambridge: Cambridge University Press, 2022). See also Stephen W. K. Chiu and Ho-Fung Hung, 'State Building and Rural Stability', in *Hong Kong's History: State and Society under Colonial Rule*, ed. Tak-Wing Ngo (London: Routledge, 1999), 74–100.

43. See Ming K. Chan, 1994. 'Introduction: Hong Kong's Precarious Balance – 150 Years in a Historic Triangle', in *Precarious Balance: Hong Kong between China and Britain, 1842–1992*, ed. Ming K. Chan and John Young (New York: M.E. Sharpe, 1994), 3–6, at 6.

have demonstrated that the consolidation of rule of law was not a linear and smooth process. This does not mean the principle of rule of law is simply a myth, but that the colonial state often found ways to circumvent the legal restrictions which might otherwise obstruct itself from exercising power to maintain social order.

Thirdly, understandings of state–society interactions in colonial Hong Kong have long been confined to a framework that is characterised as 'power dependence'.[44] Historians also used a similar triangular framework to describe the situation of Hong Kong and suggest that stability of the colony was largely dependent on the 'precarious balance' between China and Britain.[45] These works depicted British Hong Kong as being 'squeezed between the two powers', signifying how domestic developments and state–society interactions were conditioned by external factors, notably the geostrategic environment. The underlying logic is a unilateral direction of influences along the global/metropole–local nexus, moving top-down. While the importance of geopolitics in the Cold War should be acknowledged, revisionists have pointed out that local actors always managed to find ways to alter the trajectory of changes, contributing to unintended consequences. Steve Tsang has argued that the colonial state adopted an approach of 'non-involvement' in political issues while leveraging restrictive legal measures to contain the ideological and political struggle between the Chinese Communist Party and the Kuomintang.[46] In doing so, the colonial state was able to maintain a neutral position while preventing these conflicts from turning the colony into a flashpoint. However, Christopher Sutton has disagreed with Tsang, arguing that his assessment overstates the colonial state's degree of neutrality.[47]

Ng adds weight to Sutton's argument as his study of political censorship also found that the colonial state leveraged *administrative* measures to check the expanding communist influence.[48] The colonial state overtly presented itself as neutral, but by no means should this be taken at face value: its policies were still driven by anti-communism covertly. Nonetheless, all these works on the colonial state's geostrategic responses concur that the threat of communism was a crucial trigger. And Chi-kwan Mark's study underscoring Hong Kong's geopolitical and military vulnerability during the Cold War usefully pointed out that the British had to be cautious

44. Hsin-chi Kuan, 'Power Dependence and Democratic Transition: The Case of Hong Kong', *The China Quarterly* 128 (1991): 774–93.
45. For example, Chan, 'Introduction', 5.
46. Steve Tsang, 'Strategy for Survival: The Cold War and Hong Kong's Policy towards Kuomintang and Chinese Communist Activities in the 1950s', *Journal of Imperial and Commonwealth History* 25, no. 2 (1997): 294–317.
47. Christopher Sutton, *Britain's Cold War in Cyprus and Hong Kong: A Conflict of Empires* (London: Palgrave Macmillan, 2016), 85–99.
48. Ng, *Political Censorship in British Hong Kong*, chapters 3 and 4. See also Chapter 7 of this book.

about communist challenges and remain unprovocative.[49] The geopolitical ramifications were multifaceted. The recent study by Alan Smart and Charles Fung well illustrates this point, as they argue that the changes to geopolitical conditions marked by the signing of the Sino-British Joint Declaration in 1984 created an opportunity for the colonial government to institute the Squatter Occupancy Survey to end new urban squatting, which is consequential for understanding the contemporary urban landscape and public housing policy.[50] It would be a mistake to consider that geopolitics only matters to government policies, however. As John Wong vividly shows in his recent study of commercial aviation through the case of Cathay Pacific, a private corporation also had to be attentive to the changing geopolitical situation so as to adjust its business strategy to survive and thrive.[51]

Historiographical Revision and Extension

Building on this revisionist work and drawing on previously underexplored sources, some of our chapters aim to offer fresh insights into old questions and help explain various changes and developments that might be unique to Hong Kong. Others are revisionist, building upon and responding to the existing historiographical debates. The temporal framework of this volume starts from 1945, the year when the Second World War ended and Britain reoccupied Hong Kong, and ends in 1997, the year when Hong Kong was returned to China. This period witnessed a number of pivotal changes, ranging from a widening channel of political participation and emergence of Hong Kong identity to changing gender and racial relations and remarkable economic growth. By understanding this, we can comprehend why and how the city was transformed into the current Hong Kong that we know.

The chapter on governance by Florence Mok and Charles Fung examines previously unknown archival sources which give a deeper understanding of state–society relations in post-war Hong Kong. It illustrates not only why the colonial government adjusted its policies to govern a rapidly changing Hong Kong society, but also how it reformulated its colonial statecraft through learning from civil unrest. One

49. Chi-kwan Mark, *Hong Kong and the Cold War: Anglo-American Relations, 1949–1957* (Oxford: Oxford University Press, 2004).

50. Alan Smart and Chi Keung Charles Fung, *Hong Kong Public and Squatter Housing: Geopolitics and Informality, 1963–1985* (Hong Kong: Hong Kong University Press, 2023). See also Chi Keung Charles Fung, 'Colonial Governance and State Incorporation of Chinese Language: The Case of the First Chinese Language Movement in Hong Kong', *Social Transformations in Chinese Societies* 18, no. 1 (2022): 59–74; Chi Keung Charles Fung and Chi Shun Fong, 'The 1967 Riots and Hong Kong's Tortuous Internationalization', *East Asia* 37, no. 4 (2020): 89–105; Allan T. F. Pang, 'Stamping "Imagination and Sensibility": Objects, Culture, and Governance in Late Colonial Hong Kong', *The Journal of Imperial and Commonwealth History* 50, no. 4 (2022): 789–816.

51. John D. Wong, *Hong Kong Takes Flight: Commercial Aviation and the Making of a Global Hub, 1930s–1998* (Cambridge, MA: Harvard University Asia Center, 2022).

contribution of the chapter is that it shows how the colonial state was indeed very cautious of its failings and vulnerability. Town Talk and MOOD were two sides of the same mechanism (i.e., surveillance) that buttressed colonial rule and, to be sure, there were other means (such as the Mutual Aid Committee) that the colonial state leveraged to accomplish the same agenda. The key lesson is that future research should go beyond the notion of 'administrative absorption' which is too impressionistic to be useful and begin with a more concrete examination of colonial statecraft.

In a similar vein, Charles Fung's chapter contends that previous economic narratives of the colony's fiscal and budgetary policy fail to acknowledge the political nature of colonial taxation and budgeting. Building on revisionist studies that underscored how the making of the fiscal institution and processes of budgeting were functions of negotiation between the colonial state and elites, the chapter traces the behind-the-scenes processes and shows how the colonial state juggled its alliances and London to preserve the famously light and simple tax system which shaped the subsequent social development of contemporary Hong Kong. The main contribution here is that 'laissez-faire' and positive interventionism – two notions that are often associated with the economic role of the colonial state – are too simplistic for comprehending the colonial decision-making processes regarding resource extraction and distribution.

Existing works on Hong Kong's constitutional history have focused on particular episodes or been limited by the continued classification of primary sources.[52] In contrast, Matthew Hurst's chapter extends across the entire time period, from the end of the Second World War in 1945 through to the handover in 1997. It is enriched by recently declassified official sources that are also contrasted with non-official and public-facing sources. His chapter contributes to contemporary efforts that aimed at re-evaluating the colonial years,[53] offering a verdict on the administration drawn from its broad-sweep analysis of Hong Kong's post-war constitutional history.

Florence Mok's chapter is based on revisionist arguments that rejected the myth that Hong Kong's political culture was politically apathetic.[54] Instead, she

52. For example, G. B. Endacott, *Government and People in Hong Kong, 1841–1962: A Constitutional History* (Hong Kong: Hong Kong University Press, 1964); Brian Hook, 'The Government of Hong Kong: Change within Tradition', *The China Quarterly* 95 (1983): 491–511; Steve Tsang, *Democracy Shelved: Great Britain, China, and Attempts at Constitutional Reform in Hong Kong, 1945–1952* (Hong Kong: Oxford University Press, 1988).

53. Ray Yep and Tai-lok Lui, 'Revisiting the Golden Era of MacLehose and the Dynamics of Social Reforms', *China information* 24, no. 3 (2010): 249-72; Ng, *Political Censorship in British Hong Kong*.

54. Lau, *Society and Politics in Hong Kong*; J. S. Hoadley, 'Hong Kong Is the Lifeboat: Notes on Political Culture and Socialization', *Journal of Oriental Studies* 8 (1970): 206–18. For revisionist work, see Lam, *Understanding the Political Culture of Hong Kong*; and Thomas Wong and Tai-lok Lui, *From One Brand of Politics to One Brand of Political Culture* (Hong Kong: Occasional Paper 10, Hong Kong Institute of Asia-Pacific Studies, 1992).

points out that the political attitudes and orientations of the general public experienced changes during different periods of the late colonial era, and political culture varied in accordance with class and age. Her chapter also traces how public opinion regarding constitutional changes shifted, how political reforms affected public confidence, and how various political parties emerged from the mid-1980s, influenced by contemporary geopolitics.

The Hong Kong 'economic miracle' in the second half of the twentieth century received global attention and acclaim, giving rise to a substantial literature that sought to conceptualise Hong Kong's economic model. James Fellows's chapter provides an introduction to some of the main themes of Hong Kong's post-war economic trajectory. It draws on a diverse source base and engages with modern scholarship that adds nuance to (and often challenges) certain dominant myths and narratives of the period.

Allan Pang's chapter illustrates how education was part of governance in late colonial Hong Kong. It proceeds chronologically, first following Florence Mok's idea of Hong Kong as a 'Cold War pivot' and then showing how education in Hong Kong became a contentious issue across East and Southeast Asia.[55] The second section responds to the revisionist approach proposed by Ray Yep and Lui Tai-lok.[56] It showcases the problems of colonial governance in the 1970s and emphasises the emergence of social activism. The final section focuses on the unexplored politicisation of education by the colonial government during the 1980s and 1990s.

In his other chapter, instead of focusing on cultural texts, Pang examines the relationship between culture and governance in Hong Kong history. He follows recent works by Po-shek Fu, Jeremy Taylor, and himself and illustrates the construction of culture in different political contexts.[57] The first section develops on recent scholarship on Cold War culture and shows how Hong Kong functioned as a 'Cold War pivot' across China and Chinese overseas in Southeast Asia.[58] The later sections showcase the politics of culture from the Chinese, British, and local perspectives. They illustrate how, in the late twentieth century, the colonial administrators, instead of simply censoring cultural development or promoting British culture, preserved and promoted what the local population preferred.

55. See Florence Mok, 'Disseminating and Containing Communist Propaganda to Overseas Chinese in Southeast Asia through Hong Kong, the Cold War Pivot, 1949–1960', *The Historical Journal* 65, no. 5 (2022): 1397–417.
56. Yep and Lui, 'Revisiting the Golden Era'.
57. See Po-Shek Fu, *Hong Kong Media and Asia's Cold War* (New York: Oxford University Press, 2023); Jeremy E. Taylor and Lanjun Xu, eds., *Chineseness and the Cold War: Contested Cultures and Diaspora in Southeast Asia and Hong Kong* (New York: Routledge, 2021); Pang, 'Stamping "Imagination and Sensibility"'.
58. Mok, 'Disseminating and Containing Communist Propaganda'.

Doris Chan's chapter follows the recent international approach which highlights not only the China factor but also the changing Cold War and colonial dynamics in shaping the flow of people entering and departing Hong Kong. It first responds to the existing scholarship on the immigration history of Hong Kong, including the influx of Chinese immigrants after the Second World War and the arrival of Vietnamese refugees in the late 1970s. Then, it explores the emigration history of Hong Kong after the Second World War from the 1950s to the 1960s, and the more recent wave of emigration in the 1980s and 1990s, which have been understudied in previous historical literature. By incorporating both immigration and emigration in her chapter, Chan attempts to provide a more balanced picture of Hong Kong's migration history after the Second World War.

However, not all the chapters are revisionist. In fact, many chapters are important original topics that have previously been neglected by historians and scholars. Though amateur historians and enthusiasts have had a sustained interest in Hong Kong's transport history, academic historians have somewhat neglected this field. Adonis Li's chapter is the first work to look at the former colony's post-war transport development holistically, in a multi-modal fashion, and using documentary evidence. Through looking at a patchwork of case studies and evidence, it scrutinises Hong Kong's transport history at key junctures and shows how the city's internal mobility was as significant as its external mobility.

Regarding the arts, existing scholarship on Hong Kong history primarily focuses on their development after the 1967 riots in the context of the government's reform efforts. Although some studies look at specific art genres for an extended period, they tend to isolate their discussions and neglect the broader historical background. Reynold Tsang's chapter therefore bridges the two distinct approaches and offers a new perspective to examine the general development of the arts sector in Hong Kong. Moreover, few sourcebooks on Hong Kong history address the arts and arts policies, except for a handful of oral history collections. Thus, this chapter introduces a curated selection of textual documents.

Kelvin Chan's chapter makes two original contributions to the historiography of Hong Kong. Firstly, it integrates the growing literature on the medical and social welfare history of Hong Kong. It offers a comprehensive account of colonial medical policies from the 1950s, when the colonial state invested in medical services to integrate Chinese refugees as healthy and productive workers, to the 1970s, when social reforms took place to legitimise colonial governance and therefore emphasised previously overlooked medical problems, such as rehabilitation of the mentally and physically disabled. Secondly, it engages with a recent turn in the history of medicine by examining the globalisation of traditional Chinese medicine during the Cold War. It reveals how the colonial government strategically prioritised biomedicine in government-funded hospitals and, at the same time, avoided regulating traditional Chinese medicine. Combined with the refugee crisis, the ambivalent colonial attitude towards traditional Chinese medicine led to an unintended consequence: it turned Hong Kong into an 'in-between place' for circulating Chinese medical materials, personnel, and technology to Southeast Asia and North America.

Jack Greatrex's chapter connects developments which might appear incongruous or counter-intuitive, such as changes in landscape and the emergence of disease, or nature conservation and urban development. In doing so, it creates a fuller impression of Hong Kong's development across the second half of the twentieth century. Hong Kong's miraculous growth and transformation, this chapter helps to show, was paralleled and followed by other developments which were perhaps unexpected: an airport and dead dolphins. Hong Kong's globalised economy of flowing capital was accompanied by flows of zoonotic disease.

Carol Tsang's chapter shows how Hong Kong's post-war reconstruction and welfare provision altered gender relations and family dynamics. Gender norms changed drastically within the confines of family, specifically marriage, fertility, and the division of household labour. But it took legal reforms between the 1970s and 1990s to secure women's rights to jobs, wages, and property, a privilege that vested individuals defended as 'family tradition'. Easier access to medical technologies including abortion and in-vitro fertilisation (IVF) also transformed the way ordinary people maintain families, challenging the heteronormative nuclear family structure that prevails in Hong Kong.

Lastly, Vivian Kong's chapter explores the diversity of Hong Kong's population and the enduring impact of race and racism in colonial Hong Kong. Although racism played a pivotal role in structuring social hierarchies and divisions there, most historical research on race and racism in the city focuses mostly on the pre-war era. This may have much to do with the fact that Hong Kong was indeed becoming less racially segregated in the years following the Second World War. The historical reality remains, however, that racism, and racial hierarchies, still lingered. In her chapter, Kong assembles a wide array of sources, ranging from official documents and laws to newspapers and autobiographical writings, to help us understand the implications of 'race' in colonial governance, and how the city's multiracial residents experienced and interacted with systemic racism.

Suggested Readings

Banner, James M. *The Ever-Changing Past: Why All History Is Revisionist History*. New Haven, CT: Yale University Press, 2021.

Bentley, Michael. *Modern Historiography: An Introduction*. London: Routledge, 1999.

Bickers, Robert. 'Loose Ties that Bound: British Empire, Colonial Authority and Hong Kong'. In *Negotiating Autonomy in Greater China: Hong Kong and Its Sovereign Before and After 1997*, edited by Ray Yep, 29–54. Copenhagen: NIAS Press, 2013.

Bickers, Robert, and Ray Yep, eds. *May Days in Hong Kong: Riot and Emergency in 1967*. Hong Kong: Hong Kong University Press, 2009.

Brandon, Pepijn, and Aditya Sarkar. 'Labour History and the Case against Colonialism'. *International Review of Social History* 64, no. 1 (2019): 73–109.

Bsheer, Rosie. *Archive Wars: The Politics of History in Saudi Arabia*. Stanford, CA: Stanford University Press, 2020.

Carroll, John M. *Edge of Empires: Chinese Elites and British Colonials in Hong Kong*. Cambridge, MA: Harvard University Press, 2005.

Carroll, John M. 'Chinese Collaboration in the Making of British Hong Kong'. In *Hong Kong's History: State and Society Under Colonial Rule*, edited by Tak-Wing Ngo, 13–29. London: Routledge: 1999.

Chan, Ming K. 'Introduction: Hong Kong's Precarious Balance – 150 Years in an Historic Triangle'. In *Precarious Balance: Hong Kong between China and Britain, 1842–1992*, edited by Ming K. Chan and John Young, 3–6. New York: Routledge, 1994.

Cheung, Gary Ka-wai. *Hong Kong's Watershed: The 1967 Riots*. Hong Kong: Hong Kong University Press, 2009.

Chiu, Stephen W. K., and Ho-Fung Hung. 'State Building and Rural Stability'. In *Hong Kong's History: State and Society under Colonial Rule*, edited by Tak-Wing Ngo, 74–100. London: Routledge, 1999.

Clark, Robert Carlton. 'Why History Needs to Be Rewritten'. *Oregon Historical Quarterly* 33, no. 4 (1932): 295–310.

Cubitt, Geoffrey. *History and Memory*. Manchester and New York: Manchester University Press, 2007.

Degler, Carl N. 'Why Historians Change Their Minds'. *Pacific Historical Review* 45, no. 2 (1976): 167–84.

Elkins, Caroline. *Legacy of Violence: A History of the British Empire*. London: Bodley Head, 2022.

Endacott, G. B. *Government and People in Hong Kong, 1841–1962: A Constitutional History*. Hong Kong: Hong Kong University Press, 1964.

Faure, David. ed. *A Documentary History of Hong Kong: Society*. Hong Kong: Hong Kong University Press, 1997.

Faure, David., and Pui-tak Lee, eds. *A Documentary History of Hong Kong: Economy*. Hong Kong: Hong Kong University Press, 2004.

Fu, Po-Shek. *Hong Kong Media and Asia's Cold War*. New York: Oxford University Press, 2023.

Fung, Chi Keung Charles. 'Colonial Governance and State Incorporation of Chinese Language: The Case of the First Chinese Language Movement in Hong Kong'. *Social Transformations in Chinese Societies* 18, no. 1 (2022): 59–74.

Fung, Chi Keung Charles, and Chi Shun Fong. 'The 1967 Riots and Hong Kong's Tortuous Internationalization'. *East Asia* 37, no. 4 (2020): 89–105.

Gorman, Jonathan. 'The Commonplaces of "Revision" and Their Implications for Historiographical Understanding'. *History and Theory* 46, no. 4 (2007): 20–44.

Hampton, Mark, and Florence Mok. 'Remembering British Rule: The Uses of Colonial Memory in Hong Kong Protest Movements, 1997–2019'. In *Memory and Modern British Politics: Commemoration, Tradition, Legacy*, edited by Matthew Roberts, 257–73. London: Bloomsbury, 2023.

Hoadley, J. S. 'Hong Kong Is the Lifeboat: Notes on Political Culture and Socialization'. *Journal of Oriental Studies* 8 (1970): 206–18.

Hook, Brian. 'The Government of Hong Kong: Change within Tradition'. *The China Quarterly* 95 (1983): 491–511.

Howell, Martha, and Walter Prevenier. *From Reliable Sources: An Introduction to Historical Methods*. Ithaca, NY: Cornell University Press, 2001.

Hughes-Warrington, Marnie. *Revisionist Histories*. London: Routledge, 2013.

King, Ambrose Yeo-chi. 'Administrative Absorption of Politics in Hong Kong: Emphasis on the Grass Roots Level'. *Asian Survey* 15, no. 5 (1975): 422–39.

Kleinberg, Ethan. *Haunting History: For a Deconstructive Approach to the Past*. Stanford, CA: Stanford University Press, 2017.

Kuan, Hsin-chi. 'Power Dependence and Democratic Transition: The Case of Hong Kong'. *The China Quarterly* 128 (1991): 774–93.

Lam, Wai-man. *Understanding the Political Culture of Hong Kong: The Paradox of Activism and Depoliticization*. Armonk, NY: M.E. Sharpe, 2004.

Lau, Siu-kai. *Society and Politics in Hong Kong*. Hong Kong: Chinese University of Hong Kong Press, 1982.

Liu, Shuyong. 'Hong Kong: A Survey of Its Political and Economic Development over the Past 150 Years'. *The China Quarterly* 151 (1997): 583–92.

Lui, Tai-lok, and Stephen W. K. Chiu. 'Social Movements and Public Discourse on Politics'. In *Hong Kong's History: State and Society under Colonial Rule*, edited by Tak-Wing Ngo, 101–18. London: Routledge, 1999.

Mark, Chi-kwan. *Hong Kong and the Cold War: Anglo-American Relations, 1949–1957*. Oxford: Clarendon Press, 2004.

Maza, Sarah. *Thinking about History*. Chicago: University of Chicago Press, 2017.

Mok, Florence. *Covert Colonialism: Governance, Surveillance and Political Culture in British Hong Kong, 1966–97*. Manchester: Manchester University Press, 2023.

Mok, Florence. 'Disseminating and Containing Communist Propaganda to Overseas Chinese in Southeast Asia through Hong Kong, the Cold War Pivot, 1949–1960'. *The Historical Journal* 65, no. 5 (2022): 1397–417.

Mok, Florence. 'Town Talk: Enhancing the "Eyes and Ears" of the Colonial State in British Hong Kong, 1950s–1975'. *Historical Research* 95, no. 268 (2022): 287–308.

Mok, Florence. 'Public Opinion Polls and Covert Colonialism in British Hong Kong'. *China Information* 33, no. 1 (2019): 66–87.

Munn, Christopher. *Chinese People and British Rule in Hong Kong, 1841–1880*. Hong Kong: Hong Kong University Press, 2009.

Ng, Michael. *Political Censorship in British Hong Kong: Freedom of Expression and the Law (1842–1997)*. Cambridge: Cambridge University Press, 2022.

Ngo, Tak-Wing. 'Colonialism in Hong Kong Revisited'. In *Hong Kong's History: State and Society under Colonial Rule*, edited by Tak-Wing Ngo, 1–12. London: Routledge, 1999.

Pang, Allan T. F. 'Stamping "Imagination and Sensibility": Objects, Culture, and Governance in Late Colonial Hong Kong.' *The Journal of Imperial and Commonwealth History* 50, no. 4 (2022): 789–816.

Salmon, Lucy M. 'Why Is History Rewritten?' *The North American Review* 195, no. 675 (1912): 225–37.

Scott, Ian. *Political Change and the Crisis of Legitimacy in Hong Kong*. Hong Kong: Oxford University Press, 1989.

Smart, Alan. *The Shek Kip Mei Myth: Squatters, Fires and Colonial Rulers in Hong Kong, 1950–1963*. Hong Kong: Hong Kong University Press, 2006.

Smart, Alan, and Chi Keung Charles Fung. *Hong Kong Public and Squatter Housing: Geopolitics and Informality, 1963–1985*. Hong Kong: Hong Kong University Press, 2023.

Smart, Alan, and Tai-lok Lui. 'Learning from Civil Unrest: State/Society Relations in Hong Kong Before and After the 1967 Disturbances'. In *May Days in Hong Kong: Riot and Emergency in 1967*, edited by Robert A. Bickers and Ray Yep, 145–60. Hong Kong: Hong Kong University Press, 2009.

Spiegel, Gabrielle M. 'Revising the Past/Revisiting the Present: How Change Happens in Historiography.' *History and Theory* 46, no. 4 (2007): 1–19.

Sutton, Christopher. *Britain's Cold War in Cyprus and Hong Kong: A Conflict of Empires*. Cham, CH: Palgrave Macmillan, 2016.

Taylor, Jeremy E., and Lanjun Xu, eds. *Chineseness and the Cold War: Contested Cultures and Diaspora in Southeast Asia and Hong Kong*. New York: Routledge, 2021.

Tosh, John. *The Pursuit of History*. London: Longman, 1984.

Tsai, Jung-Fang. *Hong Kong in Chinese History: Community and Social Unrest in the British Colony, 1842–1913*. New York: Columbia University Press, 1993.

Tsang, Steve. *Democracy Shelved: Great Britain, China, and Attempts at Constitutional Reform in Hong Kong, 1945–1952*. Hong Kong: Oxford University Press, 1988.

Tsang, Steve. 'Strategy for Survival: The Cold War and Hong Kong's Policy towards Kuomintang and Chinese Communist Activities in the 1950s'. *The Journal of Imperial and Commonwealth History* 25, no. 2 (1997): 294–317.

Tsang, Steve, ed. *A Documentary History of Hong Kong: Government and Politics*. Hong Kong: Hong Kong University Press, 1995.

Welsh, Frank. *A History of Hong Kong*. London: HarperCollins, 1997.

Wong, John D. *Hong Kong Takes Flight: Commercial Aviation and the Making of a Global Hub, 1930s–1998*. Cambridge, MA: Harvard University Asia Center, 2022.

Wong, Lawrence Wang-chi. 'Narrating Hong Kong History: A Critical Study of Mainland China's Historical Discourse from a Hong Kong Perspective'. In *Read the Cultural Other: Forms of Otherness in the Discourses of Hong Kong's Decolonization*, edited by Shi-xu, Manfred Kienpointner, and Jan Servaes, 197–210. Berlin: Mouton de Gruyter, 2005.

Wong, Thomas, and Tai-lok Lui. *From One Brand of Politics to One Brand of Political Culture*. Hong Kong: Occasional Paper 10, Hong Kong Institute of Asia-Pacific Studies, 1992.

Yep, Ray. '"Cultural Revolution in Hong Kong": Emergency Powers, Administration of Justice and the Turbulent Year of 1967'. *Modern Asian Studies* 46, no. 4 (2012): 1007–32.

Yep, Ray, and Tai-Lok Lui. 'Revisiting the Golden Era of MacLehose and the Dynamics of Social Reforms'. *China Information* 24, no. 3 (2010): 249–72.

1
Governance[1]

Fung Chi Keung Charles and Florence Mok

After the end of the Second World War, limited political reforms were introduced in Hong Kong. The colonial government continued to practise indirect rule, a system of control exercised primarily through intermediaries such as prominent elites who had influence over the wider population, in governing Hong Kong society.[2] This of course does not mean that direct contact between the colonial government and the governed as well as active state intervention were non-existent, as discussed in the introductory chapter. But the statecraft that the colonial government used to

1. The term 'governance' carries broad and diverse meanings. It can refer to the institutional (formal and informal) arrangement, process, mechanism, and strategy that actors leverage to realise their own objectives. Politically, it can mean securing compliance of the governed and control of the wider population through means that fall inside as well as outside the government. In the context of colonial rule, it means securing compliance of the colonised through (re)creating a system of rule that maintains the socio-political order. Thus, it can encompass a wide range of phenomena, as one of the anonymous reviewers of this volume pointed out, including the ideology, organisation, operation, conduct, and effectiveness of government. Nonetheless, it is impossible to cover all these aspects in a single chapter. Instead, this chapter focuses on one tenet that has to do with state–society relations through the lens of political communications, surveillance, and intelligence. Readers should keep in mind that there are alternative means that the colonial state used to secure control over the colonised (e.g., the use of civic and grassroots organisations such as the Mutual Aid Committees) and there are other relevant topics such as corruption. Thus, we include other revisionist studies in the suggested readings for those who would like to further explore this genre of research. For a discussion of the definition of governance, see David Levi-Faur, 'From "Big Government" to "Big Governance"?', in *The Oxford Handbook of Governance*, ed. David Levi-Faur (Oxford: Oxford University Press, 2012), 3–18. For governance in the context of colonial rule, see Jürgen Osterhammel, *Colonialism: A Theoretical Overview*, trans. Shelley L. Frisch (Princeton, NJ: Princeton University Press, 1997).
2. For a classic discussion of how indirect rule renders colonial ruling, see Ronald Robinson, 'Non-European Foundations of European Imperialism: Sketch for a Theory of Collaboration', in *Studies in the Theory of Imperialism*, ed. Roger Owen and Bob Sutcliffe (London: Longman, 1972), 117–42.

govern Hong Kong society still largely adhered to what George Endacott called 'government by discussion', which 'ensure[d] that difficulties' were 'ironed out at an early stage', minimising the risk of social unrest.[3] Apart from Chinese elites in the Legislative and Executive Councils and leaders in community organisations, such as Kaifong associations, the Secretary for Chinese Affairs and Public Relations Office were the main channels for state–society communications.

The absence of constitutional reforms can be explained by Britain's assumption that the People's Republic of China would oppose Hong Kong's democratisation.[4] While acknowledging that Hong Kong was administered by Britain for economic and strategic reasons, China refused to recognise the unequal treaties that formed the basis for Hong Kong's status as a colony and insisted that the problem of its sovereignty should be 'resolved through negotiations when the conditions were ripe'.[5] In the 1950s, British officials remained uncertain whether the Chinese government would object to Hong Kong's democratisation.[6] By the mid-1960s, the notion that China would not accept any attempts to democratise Hong Kong became widely accepted by senior bureaucrats in Britain and Hong Kong.[7]

However, this indirect rule was challenged by Hong Kong's changing demographics and the Cold War. Hong Kong society mainly comprised refugees from various parts of Guangdong.[8] From the late 1950s, the sojourner mentality held by recent migrants started to fade, and more people began to accept that they were permanent residents of Hong Kong.[9] The 1966 riots in particular revealed there was a 'gap' between the colonial government and the Chinese communities.[10] As a result, in 1968 the colonial government introduced the City District Officer Scheme, what Ambrose King called 'administrative absorption of politics'. The Scheme was perceived by scholars as an official attempt at decentralisation and de-bureaucratisation which evaluated and addressed popular grievances.[11] However, recent scholarship

3. George B. Endacott, *Government and People in Hong Kong, 1841–1962: A Constitutional History* (Hong Kong: Hong Kong University Press, 1964), 229 and 239.
4. Steve Tsang, *Hong Kong: An Appointment with China* (London: I.B. Tauris, 1997), 69.
5. Tsang, *An Appointment with China*, 69–71; *People's Daily*, 8 March 1963.
6. Steve Tsang, *A Modern History of Hong Kong* (London: I.B. Tauris, 2004), 206.
7. Tsang, *A Modern History*, 207.
8. Chi-kwan Mark, 'The "Problem of People": British Colonials, Cold War Powers, and the Chinese Refugees in Hong Kong, 1949–62', *Modern Asian Studies* 41 (2007): 1145–81; J. S. Hoadley, 'Hong Kong Is the Lifeboat: Notes on Political Culture and Socialisation', *Journal of Oriental Studies* 8 (1970): 206–18; Florence Mok, 'Chinese Illicit Immigration into Colonial Hong Kong, c. 1970–1980', *Journal of Imperial and Commonwealth History* 49, no. 2 (2021): 339–67.
9. Tsang, *A Modern History*, 180–82.
10. Ian Scott, 'Bridging the Gap: Hong Kong Senior Civil Servants and the 1966 Riots', *Journal of Imperial and Commonwealth History* 45, no. 1 (2017): 131–48.
11. Ambrose Yeo-chi King, 'Administrative Absorption of Politics in Hong Kong: Emphasis on the Grass Roots Level', *Asian Survey*, 15, no. 5 (1975): 422–39.

has shown that covert mechanisms embedded in the scheme, namely Town Talk and the Movement of Opinion Direction (MOOD), provided the undemocratic colonial government with increased capacity to gather valuable intelligence on public opinion and widened the channels of 'political participation' for the Chinese society without introducing democratic reforms and provoking China.[12] The covert exercises' function as an intelligence device was prioritised; this reform therefore both enhanced and limited the ability of the public to influence the policymaking process.

Section 1. Governing Hong Kong with an Unreformed Political System, 1945–1965

The unreformed political system's inadequate political communication channels began to frustrate the Chinese communities, in particular the younger generation in the late 1950s. The colonial government was aware that this would constitute a problem of governance and legitimacy, and they started considering improving political communication channels with the public, as the following extract reveals.

Document 1.1: HKPRO, HKRS 163/1/2176, 'S.C.A.', Memo from J. C. McDouall, Secretary for Chinese Affairs to Colonial Secretary, 10 April 1958.

2. First, there is unanimous, not to say vehement agreement that the S.C.A. [Secretary for Chinese Affairs]should be government's main official channel for two-way communication with the Chinese population of Hong Kong. In practice, this should mean maintaining continuous contacts with and through the Chinese Members of the Councils, the traditionally accepted Chinese bodies such as the Tung Wah 'Hospitals', Kaifong Associations and other social organisations, and the leaders of non-New Territories village communities . . .

3. The second point of agreed policy was the desirability of the S.C.A. continuing, with the help of other departments where appropriate, to build up among the Chinese residents of Hong Kong, a feeling of local citizenship, founded on the two essential ingredients of profitable self-interest and selected and sectional traditional

12. Florence Mok, 'Public Opinion Polls and Covert Colonialism in British Hong Kong', *China Information* 33, no. 1 (2019): 66–87; Florence Mok, 'Town Talk: Enhancing the "Eyes and Ears" of the Colonial State in British Hong Kong, 1950s–1975', *Historical Research* 95, no. 268 (2022): 287–308. We must acknowledge that the people still possessed far less agency compared with the traditional means of political participation in a democratic society: they were not aware that they were 'participating' in the policy formulation process and the colonial state had the leeway to decide when to listen to public opinion.

loyalties. I should add that I discussed the practical and political implications of this at some length with the Chinese Members of Councils. They unanimously conceded the desirability of this work, but were more pessimistic than I have reason to be about its effective success.

4. The third point of policy, already touched on at the end of paragraph 2 above, was that the S.C.A.'s membership of Executive and Legislative Councils and of any other statutory bodies are or should be designed primarily to assist in the discharge of his two principal sets of duties.

5. I have only three other comments to submit-
1) I believe that government is very much out of touch with public opinion, except when a sometimes very small section of that opinion is vociferously expressed in the newspapers, by agitators or demagogues, or through vested interests' pressure groups. I believe that the S.C.A.'s inadequate direct and indirect contacts with the bulk of usually inarticulate population (inarticulate as far as public affairs are concerned) can be increasingly dangerous.

Section 2. Waves of Civil Unrest and Innovation of Governance Strategy, 1966–1980

As the Chinese population of Hong Kong gradually turned into 'a settled one' and the sojourner mentality dissipated, political culture shifted, as the Star Ferry riots in 1966 showed. In 1965, the colonial government announced that the Star Ferry Company had applied for a fare increase of between 50 and 100 per cent (though only in first class). The Transport Advisory Committee approved the increase in March 1966. A protest initiated by So Sau-chung and Lo Kei took place in early April 1966 but was suppressed by the colonial government. Subsequently, the peaceful demonstrations turned into a violent riot, in which vehicles were burnt and shops were looted. One person died in the riots and many more were injured. More than 1,800 people were arrested. This demonstrated to the colonial government that the existing political communication channels were inadequate and further reforms had to be introduced to bridge the communication gap between it and the public.

Document 1.2: Hong Kong Government Printer, 'VI. The Immediate Cause of the Disturbances and Alleged Cause of Underlying Unrest or Discontent', *Kowloon Disturbance 1966: Report of Commission of Inquiry* (Hong Kong, 1967), pp. 127–28.

468. In recounting these views, we are very conscious that none of these factors were specifically mentioned by any of the demonstrators and rioters as a motive for his

participation in the disturbances. Nevertheless, the evidence relating to the ferry fare issue and the outbreak of disturbances had led us to the conclusion that there was, to some extent, a failure in communication between government, the press, and the general public and, consequently, that there is need to take particular note of any factor which is put forward as a contributory or likely cause of such failure.

469. The emergence or existence of a gap between the government and the people is a continual danger and anxiety for any form of administration, whilst a colonial or bureaucratic government tends to be at a disadvantage in evoking or securing the support of its people, even though it may provide the most efficient administration and offer the best chances for their economic and social progress. But, the evidence before us did not indicate that the vast majority of the population would welcome any fundamental change in the constitutional form of the Government or that this was a material factor in causing the riots. We were left with the impression that those who complain are seeking not so much a change in government, as readier access to the government.

470. In this connection, however, two matters emerged as tending to create a gap between Government and the people which might well merit closer attention in the future: a) difficulties arising from the fact that the language of the law and of much of the administration is not understood by the bulk of the population; and b) the centralisation, both physical and organisational, of the government which has been conductive in the past to efficiency and economy in the provision of services but which has tended to create an image of detachment from the actual problems of the man in the street. But again we believe that few would welcome the complete reversal of the present approach in the interest of bringing the government closer to the people without any guarantee that this would have a marked beneficial effect on general attitudes.

The 1966 riots signified the beginning of a new era. Identity politics faded and political demands were now 'spontaneous, issue-driven and non-ideological'. This 'new political and social climate' encouraged discussions about political affairs in public discourse.[13] *The emergence of political consciousness and the legitimacy crisis encouraged colonial bureaucrats to reform the existing political communication channels to obtain political information which was critical to sustaining the legitimacy of the colonial state in Hong Kong. This trend coincided with the conclusion of the 'Hong Kong Long Term Study' reached by the British Cabinet after the 1967 riots which suggested that, while 'Hong Kong's future must eventually lie in China', the colonial government had to demonstrate*

13. Tai-lok Lui and Stephen W. K. Chiu, 'Social Movements and Public Discourse on Politics', in *Hong Kong's History: State and Society under Colonial Rule*, ed. Tak-Wing Ngo (London: Routledge, 1999), 105–6.

its intention to maintain its political position of Hong Kong.[14] *In this vein, the colonial government introduced the City District Officer Scheme in 1968. The City District Office was 'a communication agent, a community organiser and a trouble-shooter for the people'.*[15] *On the one hand, it facilitated communications between the government and the Hong Kong Chinese and explained policies to the public; on the other hand, it addressed people's grievances and fed 'public opinions' to the policymakers in the bureaucracy.*

Document 1.3: TNA, FCO 40/79, 'Hong Kong: Long Term Study, Defence and Oversea Policy (Official) Committee Defence Review Working Party', Commonwealth Office, 23 April 1968.

A. Introduction

Our terms of reference were to examine policy in respect of Hong Kong in the long term, on the basis that we could not rely on remaining in Hong Kong on present terms until the lease of the New Territories lapsed and should therefore consider what adaptations of its status might be possible and desirable after the conclusion of the present conflict in Vietnam . . .

B. British Interests

Political

3. Hong Kong is of political benefit to us as a Free World enclave on the mainland of China, demonstrating that a "free" society, even (of necessity) without representative government, is preferable in the eyes of many Chinese to communist society of China. Chinese influence has ensured that its retention by us has not been a target of the anti-colonial lobby at the United Nations. Its loss to China would be a severe blow to Free World prestige in Asia and would correspondingly in South East Asia. Our presence there is a British contribution to inter-dependence. The Americans recognise its usefulness.

4. There are on the other hand a number of political disadvantages in our position. Our inability to develop representative institutions in the Colony is a startling anomaly in our post-war record of colonial administration; while this has not so far embarrassed us in the international field . . . Difficult problems may lie ahead

14. Chi-kwan Mark, 'Development without Decolonisation? Hong Kong's Future and Relations with Britain and China, 1967–1972', *Journal of the Royal Asiatic Society* 24, no. 2 (2014): 315–35.

15. King, 'Administrative Absorption of Politics in Hong Kong: Emphasis on the Grass Roots Level', 432.

as there emerges a generation brought up and educated in Hong Kong in Western ways for whose energies there can be no outlet in political activities and for whose aspirations for a secure national identity there can be no solution other than China. Moreover our position in Hong Kong clouds our relations with China and might stand in the way of their improvement . . .

The Effect of China's Attitude on Policy in Hong Kong

45. The lesson of the 1967 confrontation is that we need to show firmly and resolutely it is our intention to hold our position in Hong Kong; to do otherwise would convey to the Chinese the impression that Hong Kong is a ripe plum which will fall into their hands at the slightest disturbance of the three . . . it is always necessary for the Hong Kong Government to maintain a balance between the necessity to preserve its own authority in Hong Kong and the need not to antagonise China to such an extent that the latter is driven to change her policy of tacit acceptance of the status quo . . .

J. Recommendations

(1) We should recognise that Hong Kong's future must eventually lie in China and that our objective must be to attempt to negotiate its return, at a favourable opportunity, on the best terms obtainable for its people and for our material interests there.

(2) Withdrawal should not be contemplated while present conditions in China persist. We could not now negotiate terms that would take care of our responsibilities towards the people of our material interests.

(3) We should look for a suitable opportunity to negotiate or reach some understanding with them on our withdrawal with China, as soon as a more moderate regime emerges there. It is important to do this when not under Chinese pressure and before the economy of the Colony starts to run down in the 1980s.

(4) Meanwhile we should show firmly that we intend to maintain our position there, giving no indication that we contemplate withdrawal. We should examine interdepartmentally what means we have (if any) of exercising effective economic pressure upon China . . .

(5) At regular intervals and at any time the Chinese regime or attitude towards the Colony change significantly future policy towards the Colony should be reviewed, in consultation with the Governor.

Document 1.4: TNA, FCO 40/235, 'City District Officer Scheme Hong Kong: Progress Report to 10th October, 1968', by D. R. Holmes, Secretary for Chinese Affairs, 10 October 1968.

The Concept of the Scheme

The C.D.O. [City District Officer Scheme] represents more the ultimate development of the District Officer concept than the all-round judicial and executive authority of the traditional District Officers. The New Territories District Officers have shed all judicial and many executive functions since the war, the only important executive powers remaining being those concerned with land. The C.D.O. has no important executive powers but he is expected to have an interest in all government activities and policies as they make their impact on ordinary people. He is an agent both for the explanation of government policies and activities and for the collection of information about the needs and aspirations of ordinary people. He is expected to supply a new element of informal coordination for the activities of departments at District level and to assess local social needs and political under-currents.

Interdepartmental Meetings and Public Consultation

Interdepartmental liaison takes the form of District meetings, where the C.D.O.s chair regular meetings of officials and local leaders, and there is also ad hoc consultation on special subjects. As garbled version of District meetings occasionally found their way into the press the press is now often invited to attend, with gratifying results. The composition of District meetings is not uniform and changing, so that they are not ready for formal constitution as advisory committee. This informality enabled varied attendance by officials and unofficials to suit the subject and avoids many issues of status that would arise from formal appointments, constitutions and terms of reference. Other meetings called study groups meet to discuss a wide range of local matters and may lead to a more active interest in affairs by responsible citizens who for various reasons are not attracted by Kaifong Association and the like.

Accessibility

In an attempt to make the District Office be seen to be accessible the permanent offices are accommodated in ordinary shop premises. Three such offices, complete with shop windows, counters for public enquiries and the more conventional offices and conference rooms in the background have been opened. There is a traditional shrinking from the yamen which is still strong among many people. Only a prolonged effort to put attractive displays in the shop windows and the continuous encouragement of callers can do anything to counteract this.

As well as trying to attract people into their offices C.D.O.s and their staff go out to meet people at work and in their homes. This is particularly important where a government activity impinges on some small local groups, for instance, in a hawker operation, in the construction of a flyover affecting near-by building, or the reclamation of a strip of busy water front. By showing concern for those directly affected C.D.O.s are slowly beginning to be accepted as men interested to ensure that public interest is not used as an excuse to ride roughshod over real local problems.

To strengthen colonial rule, the public's grievances had to be identified and their aspirations for political participation had to be fulfilled, as seen in the extract of a correspondence from the Deputy Colonial Secretary to the heads of departments and branches. The colonial administration therefore departed from its indirect ruling strategies and in 1968 introduced the City District Officer Scheme, the first direct state–society communication channel which aimed to increase 'political participation' without implementing democratic reforms or enhancing the power of the Urban Council. Apart from these incremental changes, the colonial government also introduced administrative reforms, such as the McKinsey Review, that aimed to strengthen the government's capacity in delivering public services and articulating public opinion through a rationalised advisory system. Even with these reforms, the colonial government was still alert to institutional faults, as seen in Governor MacLehose's despatch to London. Reform of the Legislative Council was considered in the early 1970s but was seen as politically risky and therefore ultimately yielded nothing.

Document 1.5: HKPRO, HKRS 742/15/22, 'Aims and Policies of the Hong Kong Government: Text of an Address by the Defence Secretary at a Seminar, September 1970', attached to 'Aims and Policies of the Hong Kong Government', from M. D. A. Clinton to Heads of Departments and Secretariat Branch Heads, 7 October 1970.

9. Our policies have really three aspects, each one contributing to the maintenance of confidence, which is as much the key of our future as it has always been. The first aspect is the framework of law and order, under which law-abiding people need to be afraid of neither criminal nor subversive elements; the second is the maintenance of sound economic and financial policies, which will result in a steady improvement of the standard of living of our people; and the third is a soundly based programme of social development, using this term in a wide sense to embrace not merely such as housing, education, health and welfare, but also the development of a sound sense of community . . .

18. In terms of performance, very great achievements have been made there and there is every intention that they should continue to be made, though some of our

critics seem to think, in a confused way, that when we publicise what we have done and are doing, this implied an intention to rest on our laurels. Nothing could be farther from the truth. We know very well that there are aspects of our administration – law and order, economic and social – that cause individuals or groups to feel in some measures aggrieved or disappointed or neglected. It is a matter of government policy to bring these to light, to correct them where possible and to prevent their recurrence and to learn by experience. It is a very distinct feature of government policy to promote this kind of communication, and while we are sometimes criticized for the lack of constitutional development in Hong Kong, I venture to suggest that our performance, when it comes to entertaining complaints and consulting opinion, compares reasonably well with that achieved by the more formal democratic processes that exist in the west.

19. A variety of methods exists for these purposes. The columns of the Press are studied daily with care, and here one should remember that the Chinese papers with their 2 million readers are more important than English language dailies with their 100,000. The District Administration is in closer and regular contact with the rural committees and village representatives and there is no issue or development of importance which affects them that does not come under discussion. In the urban area the City District Officers are developing rapidly a whole range of new contacts and, as almost any Department can testify, are proving to be a much more effective means of ascertaining public views and reactions than we have ever had before. Then there are our often-maligned committees. There is scarcely any important departmental activity that does not have its advisory committee of unofficials, professional and lay . . .

21. Many people will tell us – and often do – that none of this is as effective in promoting the rights of the citizen as democratic self-government but it is commonly held that the Chinese government will accept the status of Hong Kong only for as long as there are no constitutional developments which might be interpreted as pointing towards self-government – anything in fact which would alter the status of Hong Kong under the so-called unequal treaties. Two Chinas are displeasing enough to them without our trying to add a third. Any electoral processes which would lead to a genuine control of the affairs of government would open the door to an uncontrollable confrontation between left-wing and right-wing supporters. This is well recognised by the majority of our people and no doubt greatly contributes to the lack of any genuine popular demand for and elected Legislative Council. You will therefore not find in government policy any intention to promote sophisticated western democratic institutions. We have to get our public participation in other ways, and this we do; indeed probably more effectively than in constitutionally more advanced countries. The progressive development of a settled middle class

should make it possible and necessary for us to broaden our base of community participation.

Document 1.6: TNA, FCO 40/410, Strengthening the Machinery of Government: Summary, McKinsey & Company, Inc. November 1972.

Measured in terms either of its population or of its economy, Hong Kong has one of the highest growth rates in the world – a situation that imposes heavy pressure on Government to expand the scale and scope of the services it provides. It must respond to the demand to increase the volume of existing services. It must satisfy the rising expectations of the population by improving the quality of these services and by introducing new ones. And because the services are becoming increasingly complex in themselves, Government may require increasingly sophisticated methods of providing them . . .

We found a variety of problems, all of them symptoms of one underlying problem – the Hong Kong Government's fundamental difficulty of trying to expand services in the face of a continuing decline in numbers of skilled and experienced staff, and the resulting dilution of their efforts. Our task, therefore, was to identify and recommend ways of improving the machinery of Government so as to increase its capacity to expand with the present limitations on the supply of skilled staff. We were asked to advise on how these improvements could be achieved without, in the first instance, significantly changing the system – that is, without significantly changing organisational relationships, main areas of responsibility or constitutional requirements.

We believe that, within these limits, improvements can be achieved by adopting the three approaches described in the full report. Some further opportunities for improvement undoubtedly exist beyond the limits, and those that merit early attention are outlined at the end of the report. However, the issues they raise will require considerable study before changes can be demonstrated as being both desirable and feasible; it is intended that the more important of them shall be the subject of a further report. The three approaches that can be adopted now are as follows:

1. Strengthen the existing machinery without making radical changes. This could give significant but limited improvements

2. Introduce new machinery so that executive activities, which are performed mainly by the decentralised Government departments, could be managed more in terms of the results they produce than, as at present, in terms of the resources they use. This change would allow greater central control to be exercised while substantially reducing the administrative load, and would give the Government a greater capability to deal with continuing growth

3. Improve personnel management so that more skilled staff are made available and the potential of those already in service is more fully developed . . .

Rationalise and Change the Roles of Advisory Committees

The number of advisory bodies is large and is growing. Clearly these bodies perform a valuable and essential function, but frequently the benefits they produce hardly seem to merit the demands they make on the time of top-level staff and busy private citizens. We believe that more benefits could be obtained, first by rationalising the roles of these committees and reducing their numbers; second by adapting the existing machinery and the proposed new machinery to give committees a more positive and more clearly defined role in policy formulation.

Document 1.7: TNA, FCO 40/547, Despatch from Governor Murray MacLehose to James Callaghan, 30 May 1974.

2. The constitution of Hong Kong is archaic and looks very odd to visitors from England. What is not so generally recognized is how odd the local situation is that has produced it – or rather failed to produce anything else. Constitutional advance in Colonies has normally been made in response to a demand for self-government by local parties and with the object of achieving a viable administration which might assume power upon independence. There has been an obvious and popular goal – independence or self-government – and at least one political party with sufficient support available to work towards it. But in Hong Kong neither of these elements exist. On the contrary any hint of independence would be completely unacceptable to the Chinese People's Government (CPG) and though there are various groups and centres of influence in Hong Kong there is nothing approaching a political party except for the Communist party of China and the Kuomintang. Both of which would be equally unsuitable as a basis for more democratic movement. Moreover if the latent split in Hong Kong between the pro and anti-communist sympathisers were to become overt in election, the situation created would be intolerable.

3. The present traditional form of government is well understood and is accepted here, and I believe we could perfectly well carry on without changing the principles embodied in it. It certainly works sufficiently well to require us to be very sure indeed that any change would represent a genuine and above all viable improvement before making any move.

4. I myself am in two minds about the merits of change . . . In my first year here I still believed it would be possible, without constitutional change, to hold the loyalty and attention of the population and build up a sense of local identity based on civic pride. I thought this could be done by the implementation of extensive programmes

of social reform, by greater responsiveness on the part of Government, and by organising extensive grass-roots participation in neighbourhood affairs on the model of Singapore. The moves that have been made in these directions have had their impact and improved the relationship of government and governed, and I think that we could continue quite well on this basis. Nevertheless I now believe that Hong Kong would have a better chance of retaining its cohesion and sense of identity in the difficult period that will start with the '80s if it had a more obviously local and less obviously alien government.

5. The most natural way of achieving this would be by proceeding by stages to elected and, within defined limits, responsible government. Such a form of government, if it could once be successfully established, and we could be satisfied that it was viable and commanded general confidence, would have obvious merit. But experience elsewhere suggests that once embarked on such a course it would probably develop fast and be hard to stop, and we know that the special circumstances of Hong Kong would make it very risky indeed. The difficulties are so obvious I will not set them out at length here, but certainly I imagine we would not contemplate such a course unless assured that it would be acceptable to - and would not be abused by - the CPG, and would not upset the confidence of either the population or business in the Colony's future. These would be hard conditions to meet.

6. Conventional wisdom has been that the way to normal elected responsible government is blocked in Hong Kong. With some reluctance I conclude that this is right, at any rate at present . . .

8. After much consideration I conclude that the best way of meeting these local wishes and requirements would be by the appointment of some local unofficials as responsible ministers. If men of sufficient calibre could be found to fill such posts - and it might not be easy to persuade the right men or women to forsake more lucrative occupations - it would greatly improve the Government's standing with the people and I think also with the Chinese members of the civil service . . . It would also end the present situation in which criticism of the Government generally go[es] unanswered except by officials . . . The shift of power to local hands would have been significant, and insofar as the present administration is tainted as 'alien' or 'out of touch' the taint would have been removed. The Unofficial Ministers should also have contributed to a more responsive government machine and perhaps a faster-moving one. With careful handling neither business confidence nor CPG suspicion of a move towards independence would be involved . . .

18. To sum up, this despatch favours a move to what is conventionally called a 'member' system. That is to say the appointment of some local responsible ministers. A move towards a fully elected and responsible government, if successfully handled,

could have real merit, but it would also entail so many dangers that I do not think it should be contemplated in present circumstances. A move towards a Legislative Council that contained a small elected element would not be subject to any of these dangers but would have little local appeal and would be hard to combine with the present constructive partnership between UMELCO [Unofficial Members of the Executive and Legislative Councils] and officials, which is a special and valuable feature of the present situation, and would be of no significance in putting power into local hands.

The City District Officer Scheme incorporated the lower strata of society into the administrative system and policymaking process through a new direct mechanism named Town Talk. Town Talk was a covert opinion monitoring exercise that served as a substitute for representative democracy. Its objective was to capture opinions of ordinary Chinese of different educational levels, social classes, and age groups in 'town', Kowloon, and Hong Kong Island, the colony's urban areas. It was embedded in the City District Officer Scheme under the supervision of the Secretariat for Chinese Affairs. It summarised the public opinion of ordinary Chinese and was used by high-ranking colonial bureaucrats in policymaking.

Document 1.8: HKPRO, HKRS 413/1/2, 'The Preparation and Significance of Town Talk', Town Talk, 15 April 1969.

Background:

For some years, it has been the practice for the Secretary for Chinese Affairs, as he then was, to make a brief weekly up-to-date verbal report at Government House each Friday morning on what people have been talking about in the city. Collection of material for this report was done verbally at weekly departmental meetings in the S.C.A. until the expansion of the department for the City District Officer Scheme made it necessary to adopt a less cumbersome and more formal procedure. Officers at various levels in the Secretariat for Home Affairs are now required to reduce their reports to writing and this process culminated at the end of September 1968 in the weekly production of Town Talk.

The purpose of this note is to explain the nature, aims and limitations of Town Talk.

Public Opinion:

In so far as public opinion has any precise meaning it would probably be a majority opinion of adults. Town Talk does not purport to represent public opinion in this sense, for only a carefully conducted public opinion poll could come anywhere near this. Hong Kong people are said to be uninterested in public affairs unless they are personally affected . . . Town Talk then tends to comprise an extensive miscellany of almost random comment and opinion . . .

Sources and Contacts:

. . . The contacts are of course limited. At present we believe they are mostly effective among the more public spirited middle-class men, older students, housewives, the white collar class and well-to-do men whose English is very limited or non-existent. We are making some progress in establishing contacts with factory workers, hawkers and poorer people.

We aim to exclude our opinions. When Town Talk is critical this is what we hear – not what we think. Nor do we include an account of our advocacy of government policies when we hear contrary opinions. We do not usually ask for views on any particular topic though we can do if given, at present, about one week's notice. We shall usually have more information available on any topic included in Town Talk and this can be forward [*sic*] on request.

Under Town Talk, a more representative sample of public opinion was acquired, aiding the colonial government to respond to popular demands and devise strategies to strengthen the colonial rule. Town Talk was used until March 1975, after which it was replaced by MOOD, which employed more systematic sampling methods. The mechanism closely monitored changing public views of the government and evaluated its performances. MOOD at first had an expanded sample size of 2,500. It then adopted a quota sampling method with a sample size of 993 in 1980, covering both urban areas and the New Territories. The continual refinement of these polling mechanisms, along with other official reporting channels and surveillance devices, for example GIST and Press Review, which monitored the issues reported by the media; intelligence reports generated by the Hong Kong Police Special Branch, which informed high-ranking officials of the activities of potentially seditious groups, such as leftists, in Hong Kong; and regular information reports generated by the District Officers that captured changing sentiments in the New Territories, demonstrated the colonial government's commitment to understanding changing public opinion and its importance in policymaking. As the government became increasingly responsive to popular demands on issues such as corruption and changes in utility prices, public confidence increased, as the first extract below shows. Through the monitoring and surveying mechanisms, the colonial government was able to obtain increased intelligence on the opinion of the Chinese communities.

Document 1.9: HKPRO, HKRS 925/1/1, 'Changes in Public Attitudes towards the Hong Kong Government', MOOD, 18 September 1975.

Over the past three years, the Government has initiated significant changes in its policies and *modus operandi*, partly in response to social developments, emerging problems and challenges, but particularly with a view to winning the support of the public. It has adopted a vigorous style of leadership and an increasingly open stance. Many important events during this period have had a far-reaching impact on life in Hong Kong: the oil crisis, the downturn in the world economy, the stock market plunge, the rising incidence of crime etc. Through these challenges and trials, the new style of Government leadership manifested itself all the more effectively. In response, the important change in public attitudes towards the Government have become more discernible.

a) The Government greatly intensified its efforts in publicising and explaining its policies, achievements and difficulties, through increasingly powerful mass media and widely extended personal contact. It encouraged public discussion on major policies and current issues. It launched large scale campaigns such as Clean Hong Kong and Fight Violent Crime. More frequent appearances on the ground by the Governor, top-level civil servants and prominent unofficials to study problems in the fields and discuss them with ordinary people all helped to bridge the proverbial gap between the Government and the people. As a result, public knowledge[,] interest and involvement in current affairs increased considerably at all levels of society. Many more people now feel confident to approach the Government not only for help and advice, but also to offer suggestion and criticisms. The traditional fear of authority or officialdom reflected in the adage that one should 'keep away from officialdom when alive and from hell after death' has been greatly reduced. Today, the humblest labourer or hawker has no inhibitions about going to a City District Office, or even to Government House if and when his interest is at stake. Frequent meetings, discussions, seminars, visits, interviews through voluntary organisations, mutual aid committees and informal 'communication' efforts at the personal level greatly facilitated the inflow and outflow of information and ideas.

b) Previously, people were very cautious about saying anything adverse about the Government in public, let alone voice criticisms. Complaints to the press, especially in the Chinese papers, were mostly anonymous. Today, people have much less inhibition about criticising the Government in public. An articulate and ambitious few even hoped to create a public image for themselves by so doing. Although the traditional distrust of authority has by no means been completely removed, even the most hostile critics cannot deny that there is genuine freedom of speech in Hong Kong, and are in fact the first to take advantage of it. Many more people are now lodging complaints in their true name to government departments, to ICAC [Independent Commission Against Corruption] and the Consumer Council...

c) People are more inclined to believe that public criticism and the pressure of public opinion can produce results as Government is seen to be more sensitive and responsive. The statutory proclamation of Chinese as an official language, the establishment of the ICAC, the discussions on the Committee Exchange, the official stand taken against the China Light and Power's application for increase of charges, the Objectionable Publications Bill, the rejection of the 1% turnover tax proposal, and many other examples have gradually built up public confidence in the Government's open minded attitude and sincere interest in public reactions. Admittedly the Government is still being criticized by the advocates whose views have not been accepted in the decisions taken, and consequently feel frustrated, but that is inevitable and no decision can ever please all public sectors.

d) Many more people feel that the Government is prepared to take a fair and honest attitude about its own failings and shortcomings, and is not afraid of washing dirty linen in public. The publication in full of the Blair-Kerr Reports on Corruption may be cited as a classic example. Many critics gave credit to the Government for its courage in unearthing even the most devasting corruption scandals, in full anticipation of the widespread repercussions likely to result.

Document 1.10: HKPRO, HKRS 471/3/2, MOOD Methodology, 19 April 1980.

MOOD is written for senior officers who are familiar with the general background of life in Hong Kong, who have experience of contact with the public themselves, and who are familiar with up-to-date news of the Government interest. Its objectives are the sounding of public opinion and the assessment of public reactions, attitudes and feelings in appropriate instances. Heads of Departments were asked to ensure that their copies of MOOD are circulated selectively and stored securely at all times.

Starting with this issue of MOOD, the quota sampling method is adopted in the selection of respondents- i.e. that the number and distribution of the respondents is based on the percentage distribution, in terms of sex, age and occupation of the general population to ensure a truer representation of cross-section of the community... It works out that a total of 993 respondents should be contacted.

The distribution of the 993 respondents is equally spread out amongst the ten urban districts in Tsuen Wan/Kwai Chung in the New Territories; and the breakdown of the number of respondents that each district is to cover agreed.

Section 3. Incremental Modifications of Governance Strategy, 1981–1984

Incorporating public opinion into the decision-making process was an innovative strategy of the colonial government to strengthen its rule throughout the 1970s. However, it was increasingly clear to the colonial government that such a governance strategy was far from perfect. Several incremental modifications were made in the early 1980s. Nonetheless, the key aim was still to be more sensitive and responsive to public opinion and demands. One way to do so was to relegate the task of survey public opinion to independent organisations so that a more representative and hence accurate picture could be obtained. Another was the District Administration reform implemented in 1981 that, as revealed in the Kwun Tong District Pilot Study Report, could enhance the colonial government's monitoring and coordinating capacity.

Document 1.11: HKPRO, HKRS 476/6/28, 'Report on the Kwun Tong District Pilot Study' by A. G. Eason C.D.C. (Kwun Tong), 27 June 1979.

Improving the Government's Response

6. The key to improving the Government's response to district needs through the processes identified in the terms of reference lies in:

(a) the further regionalisation of functional departments,
(b) improving district administration, and
(c) placing more emphasis on district programmes.

The greater involvement of residents is also important but this matter is dealt with in Part II of the report . . .

District Administration

11. Even if the full regionalisation of all departments were achieved and senior supervisory staff became fully effective in exercising the powers and fulfilling the functions described in paragraph 8 above, there would still be a need for departmental activities in districts to be independently monitored and co-ordinated and for district priorities to be determined and resources allocated. There would be a need, in other words, for district administration. Given the present irregular pattern of regionalisation and the limitations placed on district staff, the need for district administration is even greater . . .

12. District administration exists on only a limited scale in the urban area at present . . . In fact the City District Officer has a responsibility superimposed on that of individual functional departments to monitor the situation in his district, draw

attention to any shortcomings apparent in departments' services, identify any district needs not being met and co-ordinate the activities of departments where necessary. However, City District Office staff are relatively young and inexperienced in government service and the main thrust of the Home Affairs Department's effort is directed towards community building activity and issue-oriented public opinion feedback exercises. The department's monitoring and co-ordinating capacity is insufficient therefore and because of the considerable extent and variety of government activity in a district neither systematic and comprehensive monitoring nor fully effective co-ordination is possible at present. Nevertheless, significant progress in these fields is being made and given the necessary organisation and staff much more could be done . . .

Document 1.12: HKPRO, HKRS 934/10/43, 'Points for Discussion' written by the Home Affairs Branch in October 1980, attached in Letter from Secretary for Home Affairs to Directors of Home Affairs concerning 'Role of Community Information Unit Home Affairs Branch', 17 November 1980.

<u>MOOD as a means of reflecting public opinion</u>

3. Despite criticisms leveled at its choice of subjects and methodology, MOOD represents "a gallant attempt to find out what the people think about various issues." The success or otherwise of this gallant attempt is debatable, depending on one's standpoint but few would suggest that the attempt should be abandoned and none has suggested any alternatives. MOOD must therefore remain the major vehicle for reflecting public opinion to the central government . . . Nevertheless, to maximise the effectiveness of MOOD, some modifications to the current approach should be considered . . .

<u>MOOD machinery</u>

5. The MOOD machinery is particularly suitable for reflecting in some depth the opinions and feelings of people on issues that are of immediate concern or have stimulated spontaneous interest . . . However, these strong points of the MOOD team would disappear or even become counter-productive if the MOOD machinery is used for surveying opinions on subjects which the people know very little about or on controversial issues in respect of which the people have yet to form an opinion. The reason being that in order to obtain reliable results, opinion surveys of this type should normally be carried out by independent organisations with a randomly selected sample of the population as respondents . . .

Document 1.13: HKPRO, HKRS 934/10/43, 'Notes of a discussion between HAB [Home Affairs Branch] and HAD [Home Affairs Department] on 21st November 1980' prepared by the Home Affairs Branch on 26 November 1980.

1. Flash-points should continue as at present. A more detailed presentation serves little useful purpose. There is no need to circulate Flash-points to UMELCO.

2. The title "MOOD" should be dropped and surveys should be referred to as public opinion survey with an indication of the sampling method . . .

4. Subjects which are considered suitable for an opinion survey by quota sampling should be carried out by HAD. Such surveys to be limited.

5. Surveys by random sampling should be carried out by independent research organisations with money coming from the Public Opinion surveys subhead now under the control of HAB . . .

Our understanding of this period would be incomplete without mentioning the Standing Committee on Pressure Groups (SCOPG). In February 1978, the colonial government formed a secret committee to monitor the activities of pressure groups. Document 1.14 is a report written by the Home Affairs Branch. It indicates that a local civil society was emerging and social movement mobilisation was becoming a part of Hong Kong life. On the one hand, it illustrates how being responsive enabled the colonial government to face criticisms from these pressure groups. On the other hand, the colonial government was ready to extend its surveillance network and co-opt dissidents into its consultative bodies.

Document 1.14: TNA, FCO 40/1264, 'Report of the Standing Committee of Pressure Group' written by Home Affairs Branch in July 1979.

Introduction

On 27th February 1978 . . . the Chief Secretary's Committee decided that a small standing group . . . should be set up to review and monitor the activities of pressure groups which use group mobilisation and propaganda techniques to highlight Government deficiencies in order to press for changes in Government policies. 2. The Standing Committee on Pressure Groups (SCOPG) was subsequently formed . . .

Counteracting Strategy

26. Pressure groups are now part of Hong Kong life. Some may become dormant, or even disappear, with the achievement of their objective, withdrawal of financial

support or the fading of current leaders. But as the community as a whole is becoming more vocal and demanding of the Government, pressure group activities are likely to grow in complexity and magnitude. The Government and individual members of the civil service, like their counterparts in most developed countries, must therefore accept this as a feature in their work.

27. Given the diversity of pressure group activities and the individual characteristics and background of their leaders, it is extremely difficult, if not entirely impossible, to devise a single strategy to deal with them. The guidelines must be flexibility and common sense, with different approaches of detail to deal with different pressure group activities. In general, the following principles appear valid:

(a) Responsive Government

28. As long as good and reasonable government exists, and as long as policies are formulated in accordance with the wishes of the majority of the community, the Government is in a good position to resist unreasonable pressure. With its various long term plans formulated in recent years in the fields of housing, new towns, social welfare, education and rehabilitation and the improvements brought by labour legislation and in the standard of living and quality of life in general, the Government is now better able to face criticism than in the past. One of the by-products of such progress policies is that Government is less vulnerable to criticism by pressure groups.

29. However, Government must not be complacent over achievements so far; programmes and policies must be constantly up-dated and refined to meet the rising expectations of the community . . .

(b) Publicity

31. As pressure groups generally thrive on publicity it is essential that special emphasis be given to publicising Government policies and actions. This should obviously not be done either with a sledgehammer or a whitewash brush. Acknowledgement of drawbacks and weaknesses in performance is at times just as important as the promotion of achievements and the sale of glossy brochures . . . Equally Government's case must not go by default and there is plenty of room for positive hard-sell publicity to build up a background of an active, energetic but caring Government . . .

(c) Handling of Pressure Groups

34. Departments should be encouraged to deal with pressure groups in consultation with the Secretariat where necessary and respond promptly to any specific issue raised. Whenever appropriate, a dialogue should be established with groups but they should not necessarily be regarded as the sole representatives on any issue; efforts should be made to deal direct with, and inform, the people affected.

35. Requests for information by pressure groups should be met, as far as possible, by providing information already available in Government published material or along the line of answers to pressure queries or letters. Requests for interviews should not be automatically rejected since they can provide an opportunity to dispel misconceptions . . .

(d) Intensification of Community Building Efforts

37. One of the reasons why pressure groups thrive is the belief widely held by social work graduates that confrontation and propaganda are the most effective means of achieving social advance . . . It is recommended that the number of community development projects presently being operated by reliable voluntary agencies in the 'identified areas' . . . should be increased. Because of the reliance on voluntary agencies who are in turn subject to influence or even direction by pressure groups, care should be taken to screen the projects and the sponsor selected. The increase in the number of community development projects should be subject to the ability of the District Social Welfare Officers to supervise, control and, if necessary, intervene.

38. At times it is possible to divert some of the group's efforts into more useful channels by bringing active members into contact with or even directly on existing boards and committees. This brings the individual and in some cases the group into the established system, helps them to obtain a more balanced picture of the Government and its policies and can remove them from extremist influence . . .

(e) Closer Liaison with Students and Tertiary Education Institutions

39. Students in tertiary educational institutions have become increasingly involved with the activities of pressure groups . . . they in turn seek the support of pressure groups in further their own causes. Whilst this can be seen as a legitimate increase in students' concern for the community, there are signs that, if not guided in the right direction, this development might result in further misunderstanding and mistrust of Government policies. The Hong Kong Week organised in 1978 by students of Hong Kong University indicates that students are generally concerned with the well-being of Hong Kong community and efforts should be made to channel their aspirations to useful ends.

By 1981, as indicated in the Annual Review of 1981 written by Governor MacLehose, 'a new Hong Kong is steadily being built'. Maintaining confidence was still admittedly difficult but the colonial government did achieve some progress based on the modified governing strategy and social reforms. MacLehose departed in May 1982 and Sino-British negotiations began when Margaret Thatcher visited China in September 1982. Despite these changes, the colonial government under the governorship of Edward Youde carried over the modified governing strategy and social reforms implemented in the 1970s. This continuity can be seen in Governor Youde's despatch below.

Document 1.15: TNA, FCO 40/1417, 'Hong Kong – Annual Review 1981', from Governor C. M. MacLehose to Secretary of State for Foreign and Commonwealth Affairs, 18 February 1982.

Hong Kong Domestic

11. With revenue buoyant on both current and capital account, the Hong Kong Government was . . . able to press on with its published programmes of expansion of works, housing and public and social services. I will not rehearse the details, which were generally satisfactory, but a new Hong Kong is steadily being built . . .

[Relations with China]

16. While confidence is an unpredictable commodity, and some new development could either buttress or undermine it . . . In these circumstances, and given the immense preoccupations of the Chinese Government, it would be a mistake to try and force the pace on grounds of imminent catastrophe. This is consistent with our present policy of quiet but firm insistence that the problem exists and must be solved soon if much that is of great mutual benefit is not to be set at risk. There are signs of this policy having some limited success. It will be for consideration when and how to add momentum by hinting at what we might give for a settlement.

Document 1.16: TNA, FCO 40/1532, 'Annual Review 1982–83: Hong Kong', from Governor Edward Youde to Secretary of State for Foreign and Commonwealth Affairs, 9 May 1983.

[Chinese Activities after the Prime Minister's Visit to Peking]

8. It became a prime aim of the Hong Kong Government to sustain that confidence. Accordingly, in speaking to the Legislative council on October 6, I emphasised the faith of the Government in the future of the territory and its intention to continue to invest vigorously in it. Towards the end of the year a number of banks and other companies announced plans for new investment and for longer periods of credit for home ownership extending beyond 1997 which were helpful to the same end . . .

10. Even so, the underlying risks remain. It has proved very difficult to draw the Chinese into substantive talks except on their terms . . . Anxieties among the population remain deep and very real. The vast majority know that they will have to stay here and face what comes . . .

Progress in other Fields

13. Concern about the economy and the future should not obscure the fact that the period under review was far from lacking in achievements or promise for the coming years . . .

14. It is issues such as these which are the bread and butter of the work of the Hong Kong Government. They will need to be dealt with in the face of an increasingly articulate population and well organised pressure groups who are learning fast how to use the media to promote their cause. Although Hong Kong's professional classes recognise what has been achieved and do not seek fundamental change, they will not remain satisfied with the governmental system as it is today. Changes will have to be made to give them a greater sense of participation and more visible role in government: and yet change will have to come in a way consonant with the stability which has underlain the success of Hong Kong and with the need not to provoke Peking into interfering with the process . . .

15. These then are the tasks that I see ahead for the coming year; to maintain the confidence of the business community and the competitiveness of the Hong Kong economy; to continue to manage its affairs in a manner which stand scrutiny by an increasingly articulate population and to continue to increase their participation in the processes of government: and first and foremost to negotiate on their behalf, and in consultation with them, an agreement with China which will preserve their identity and lifestyle and give them confidence to the future. It promises to be a busy year.

Section 4. Political Continuity and Change towards the End of Colonial Rule, 1984–1997

The 1984 Sino-British Joint Declaration concluded that Hong Kong would cease to be a British colony after 1997. For the colonial government, the Declaration was the first stage in the process of clarifying and determining the future of this territory. During the transition (1984–97), it would be necessary to accomplish several essential tasks, as underscored by Governor Youde's 'Change of Destiny' despatch. Governing Hong Kong's society, as the British anticipated, would be more complicated than before. One reason for this complication was the increasingly salient role of the China factor. This could be seen in the issue of political reforms, especially on whether direct election should be introduced in the 1987 Review and the drafting of the Basic Law, which defined Hong Kong's long-term future as well as how it would be governed (see also Chapter 3). It is worth noting that the colonial government continued to practise surveillance as a way to tap into public opinion in order to measure its performance. This could be seen in the mentioning of 'district feedbacks' and 'views from our contacts' during the internal discussion of the pace and scope of political change. The colonial government initially preferred an incremental approach, but that changed after the 1989 June Fourth incident as Hong Kong people became more attentive to the prospect of democratic development.

Document 1.17: TNA, FCO 40/1887, 'Hong Kong: A Change of Destiny', from Governor Edward Youde to Sir Geoffrey Howe, Secretary of State for Foreign and Commonwealth Affairs, 3 July 1985.

The Future

29. The ratification and registration of the Joint Declaration will complete the first stage in the process of securing the future of this territory. But that future cannot be assured by the agreement alone . . .

30. First it will be important never to lose sight of the constant factors in the wholly unorthodox equation which has maintained the equilibrium of Hong Kong throughout the past 35 years. These have not been fundamentally altered by the negotiation of the agreement . . .

33. The second essential is that there must be no attempt by the Chinese to encroach on the administration of Hong Kong through the operations of the Joint Liaison Group or the Land Commission . . . If the Chinese do not refrain from interference and do not respect the promise in the agreement that the United Kingdom will be responsible for the administration of Hong Kong up to 1997 . . . there will be no confidence in their willingness to respect the autonomy of Hong Kong thereafter . . . In this period, the maintenance of the morale of the Civil Service and of the Police will be vital . . .

34. The third essential task will be to establish a more visibly representative form of government in which . . . "the system of government is firmly rooted in the community". This process will inevitably be accompanied by a more highly charged political atmosphere in Hong Kong. Any new government structure which emerges is very unlikely to be on the Westminster model. It is not to be expected that the Chinese will tolerate after 1997 confrontational politics in Hong Kong; and in any case the people of Hong Kong do not want them. In the review promised for 1987 we shall need to address difficult and controversial issues . . . The attitudes of the Chinese who are highly suspicious already of our moves towards representative government will be crucial. Things are already moving fast on their side too. They have established a Committee to draft the Basic Law (in effect the mini-constitution) for the Special Administrative Region, and promised that it will be completed by 1990 . . . The problem is that they do not recognise any role for the UK in drafting that law.

Keeping the political development processes in line on their side and ours will not be an easy task.

35. The fourth essential need will be to achieve international acceptance of the practical arrangements which will be required to sustain Hong Kong's autonomous status . . . Means will have to be found to maintain the applicability of those arrangements . . .

36. Finally, the role of the British Government will be a delicate and demanding one. There will be a constant need to think ahead to the transition which is now only 12 years away. Hong Kong will change, particularly in its relationship with China, as that transition becomes closer. In the early 1990's there will almost certainly be a new period of doubt and anxiety . . . The transitional arrangements will need to be complete well before 1997 in order to reduce the impact of that date. In the meantime, while showing no diminution of interest in or concern for the interests of the people of Hong Kong, HMG will have to trust Hong Kong with an increasing degree of autonomy because if the UK does not show faith in Hong Kong's ability to exercise that autonomy responsibly before 1997, the Chinese will have no incentive to do so afterwards. We shall have to do all we can to preserve, not only the stability, but the economic success of Hong Kong if only because that is the prime factor in securing Chinese tolerance of its special status.

Document 1.18: HKPRO, HKRS 394/29/53, 'General Mood in Hong Kong' attached in draft of 'scene setting passage' to the Governor written by Alan J. Scott (Deputy Chief Secretary), 26 September 1986.

Public confidence though still delicate, appears to be picking up considerably from the low point in late 85/early 86, particularly as a result of Hong Kong's strong economic performance lately and the bullish stock market which has reached record levels. Confidence in the long term political future however is still shaky and people are maintaining a "wait and see" attitude. Those with the means to do so are still making arrangements to get overseas status . . .

<u>Political</u>

3. Confidence in the immediate and short term prospects in the economic field is not matched in the political. There is intense public and media interest in the drafting of the Basic Law and the prospects for the 1987 Review arising from concern over the long term future of Hong Kong. Discussions on the content of the Basic Law and particularly on the political structure and the relationship between the CPG and the SAR [Special Administrative Region] after 1997 are proceeding amid a blaze

of publicity. The CPG appears flexible and co-operative but there are nevertheless suspicions that it is steering the BLDC [Basic Law Drafting Committee] too much its own way. Public interest in the 1987 Review mainly centres around the possible introduction of a directly elected element into the Legislative Council and whether the Governor should withdraw from the presidency of the Council . . . The issue of direct elections is seen by some as an indicator of whether the Chinese will allow Hong Kong the autonomy promised in the JD [Joint Declaration] . . .

Document 1.19: HKPRO, HKRS 394/29/53, 'Contribution to Security Branch's Report on Hong Kong Opinion and Mood', attached in Memo by Secretary for District Administration to Principal Assistant Secretary (Security) Assessments of the Security Branch, 12 January 1987.

Public mood

Despite the untimely death of the late Governor, district feedbacks indicate that public confidence in Hong Kong's prosperity and stability in the short term continues to strengthen. Although the recent outbreak of student unrest in China is seen by some as a cause of concern, it has not generally caused any unnecessary jitters. It is suggested that the growing confidence is due essentially to Hong Kong's robust economic outlook, the bullish stock market with the Hang Seng Index rocketing to a record-high and the harmonious Sino-British relations . . .

Reaction to Basic Law drafting and political reform

4. The drafting of the Basic Law has not generally captured much attention from the grassroots who are genuinely uninterested in the matter. However, some of the better-informed contacts follow closely the progress and deliberations of the Basic Law drafting. The recent decision by the BLDC to defer its discussion on political structure for the future Hong Kong SAR has been well-received and is regarded as a wise and prudent move. It is believed that this would avoid the risk of dividing the BLDC over the thorny question of political structure and help pave the way for a convergence of the Basic Law with the 1987 Review.

5. Local political reforms continue to attract divergent views from our contacts. It is expected that the cut and thrust of the arguments involved would continue to rage. There is a tendency for the opposing views particularly those on the question of direct elections to polarize even further, but there is no indication to suggest which side has gained more popular support . . .

Document 1.20: HKPRO, HKRS 394/29/204, 'Minutes of the Special CSC Meeting Held on 27 May 1989', written by Chief Secretary's Office, Government Secretariat, 30 May 1989.

PA [Political Adviser] briefed Members on the latest situation in China and its implications for HK: there would be more attention on and increasing questioning of the JD and BL [Basic Law]. The Chinese decision-making process would no doubt be disrupted and it was not yet sure to what extent the BL consultation exercise was going to be affected, although the Chinese Authorities would be expected to emphasize the continuity of their policy on HK . . .

[Implications for HK]

5. AG pointed out that although the demonstrations so far had been benign as they were not directed at HK, there could be sensitive local issues on which the crowds might behave with much less discipline and brought the Administration into a very difficult position . . . The Administration would need to be even more alert and sensitive to public reactions on sensitive issues . . .

8. STI commented that there was a positive angle to the events in that the general public would value HK's systems and success even more than before. They had demonstrated their willingness to be self-disciplined for a cause. Provided that the Administration was prepared to be open and fair, there was no need to be over-concerned. Members noted that the circumstances giving rise to the mass march were very unique. The reactions were spontaneous and it was the issue and the strong sense of nationalism that brought out the crowds, and not the local politicians. There was unlikely to be many other public issues which could arouse such universal feelings.

[HKG and HMG' s Public Response]

10. In reply to the IC on whether Members felt that the Governor should say more than what he had already said or give a special media briefing, SES said that although it would be popular for the Governor to say more in public, she considered that he could not really go beyond what had already been said. S for T and SASI agreed.

11. As regards the extent to which individual civil servants should be allowed to express their personal views in public, CS(Ag) said that it was a very delicate issue: civil servants must remain apolitical and must not allow their personal stand be misinterpreted. On the other hand, they should not be barred from making known their views provided that they would be careful in presenting their views as personal ones.

Implications on the Basic Law

12. S for S(Ag) said that HK people would now expect a more democratic BL, but it could be at variance with the Chinese as they might be even more cautious in dealing with democratisation demands. He wondered whether this would be a source of conflict. PA agreed that there was such a risk at least initially. If HK was seen by the Chinese Authorities as a focus of discontent against their Regime, they might resort to a hard line approach. On the other hand, they would still need to reassure the international community if they wanted to maintain the present policy. Their Administration would also not be homogenous: there should continue to be a proportion of moderates and reform-oriented officials in the day-to-day dealings with HK. However, it did mean that HKG could face a difficult time ahead. CS(Ag) observed that recent events underlined that it was even more important now to make sure that the BL would be wholly satisfactory to HK. There would be advantage to push for bolder constitutional reforms in the BL, but we should refrain from mobilising or stimulating mass demonstrations in pursuing our case as this could be counter-productive. The balance was very fine indeed.

Document 1.21: TNA, FCO 40/4054, 'Hong Kong Political Situation', Letter from Alan R. Paul (British Senior Representative of the Sino-British Joint Liaison Group) to Peter F. Ricketts (Hong Kong Department, FCO), 1 April 1993.

[The Public Mood]

3. It is worth recalling that despite, or perhaps because of, the sustained attacks by the Chinese on the political reforms package, public support for it remained fairly constant for many months – at around 30% – and supporters outnumbered opponents by a ratio of about 2:1. In recent weeks, however, two related strands of opinion have become dominant . . . (b) the overwhelming view in the community is that there should be talks and that the necessary compromises should be made – by one side or the other – to ensure that a solution is reached. How this is to be done, and at what price in terms of diluting the package, is an unanswered question. But very few people indeed would still argue that the package as a whole is worth defending at any cost . . .

14. We should not have illusions about this: the task of deciding quickly upon a compromise set of proposals might in any case be one which proved to be beyond the capacity of a LegCo [Legislative Council] which embraces a variety of differing views, has no single predominant party and no pre-eminent personalities. Added to this would be the need to take account of pressures from China while attempting to

retain credibility in the community. A protracted process, or even deadlock, could not be excluded.

15. For all these reasons, the predominant mood in LegCo is in favour of talks, although as has been noted elsewhere, that route raises just as many, if not more, difficulties and is unlikely to lead to any solutions to our problems.

16. I should stress that the above represents my own views based on my own contacts with the community and the political forces in question. There are many here who would take a different view.

Suggested Readings

King, Ambrose Y. 'Administrative Absorption of Politics in Hong Kong: Emphasis on the Grass Roots Level'. *Asian Survey* 15, no. 5 (1975): 422–39.

Lau, Siu-kai. *Society and Politics in Hong Kong*. Hong Kong: Chinese University of Hong Kong Press, 1982.

Lui, Tai-lok. '"Flying MPs" and Political Change in a Colonial Setting Political Reform under MacLehose's Governorship of Hong Kong'. In *Civil Unrest and Governance in Hong Kong: Law and Order from Historical and Cultural Perspectives*, ed. Michael H. K. Ng and John D. Wong, 76–96. London: Routledge, 2017.

Lui, Tai-lok. *The Story of Hong Kong in the 1970s Retold*, revised and expanded edition. [那似曾相識的七十年代, *Na Si Ceng Xiang Shi De Qi Shi Nian Dai*]. Hong Kong: Chung Hwa Books, 2020.

Mok, Florence. *Covert Colonialism: Governance, Surveillance and Policymaking in British Hong Kong, c. 1966–1997*. Manchester: Manchester University Press, 2023.

Scott, Ian. *Political Change and the Crisis of Legitimacy in Hong Kong*. Hong Kong: Oxford University Press, 1989.

Scott, Ian. 'Hong Kong Senior Civil Servants and the 1966 Riots'. *The Journal of Imperial and Commonwealth History* 45, no. 1 (2016): 131–48.

Smart, Alan, and Lui Tai-lok. 'Learning from Civil Unrest: State/Society Relations Before and After the 1967 Disturbances'. In *May Days in Hong Kong: Riots and Emergency in 1967*, edited by Robert Bickers and Ray Yep, 145–60. Hong Kong: Hong Kong University Press, 2009.

Yep, Ray. Man in a Hurry: *Murray MacLehose and Colonial Autonomy in Hong Kong*. Hong Kong: Hong Kong University Press, 2024.

Yep, Ray. 'The Crusade against Corruption in Hong Kong in the 1970s: Governor MacLehose as a Zealous Reformer or Reluctant Hero?' *China Information* 32, no. 3 (2013): 197–221.

Yep, Ray, ed. *Negotiating Autonomy in Greater China: Hong Kong and Its Sovereign Before and After 1997*. Copenhagen: Nordic Institute of Asian Studies, 2013.

Yep, Ray, and Lui Tai-lok. 'Revisiting the Golden Era of MacLehose and the Dynamics of Social Reforms'. *China Information* 24, no. 3 (2010): 249–72.

2
Constitutional Change

Matthew Hurst

Hong Kong's colonial constitution consisted of the Letters Patent and the Royal Instructions. The Letters Patent outlined the organs and functions of government while the Royal Instructions gave more specific orders to the Governor. After the Second World War, both documents were amended from time to time but never in such a way that fundamentally altered the structure, scope, or remit of the colonial government. Although wide-ranging changes were considered in the 1940s, it was not until the 1980s that an entirely new constitution was drafted which would come into force in 1997.

Literature published before the mid-1980s was written without access to many archival sources that have since been declassified. Scholars relied instead on published materials supported by first-hand knowledge of how the constitution was implemented and perceived at the time. Consequently, some scholars simply accepted the official line.[1] As Hong Kong's future was debated in the 1980s, this inspired a new wave of scholarship that benefitted from access to newly declassified primary sources. For instance, Tsang drew on such materials to revise long-held assumptions about the extent to which authorities were committed to reforms tabled in the 1940s and their motivations for shelving those plans in the 1950s.[2]

1. For instance, writing about the Young Plan, Endacott unquestioningly adopted Westminster's view that it was an 'inopportune' time to pursue change (G. B. Endacott, *Government and People in Hong Kong, 1841–1962: A Constitutional History* (Hong Kong: Hong Kong University Press, 1964)). Similarly, Hook recounted without contest conclusions drawn in official reports of the 1960s (Brian Hook, 'The Government of Hong Kong: Change within Tradition', *The China Quarterly* 95 (1983): 491–511).
2. Steve Yui-Sang Tsang, *Democracy Shelved: Great Britain, China, and Attempts at Constitutional Reform in Hong Kong, 1945–1952* (Hong Kong: Oxford University Press, 1988).

More recent declassification has enabled scholars to re-examine the fateful final two decades of colonial rule, when Hong Kong's postcolonial constitution was written.[3]

This chapter reproduces primary sources and places them alongside public-facing documents to provide an overview history of Hong Kong's colonial constitution. It extends its scope from 1945 to the very end of British administration in 1997, enabling the reader to consider how the constitution was incrementally amended and why it remained largely and stubbornly unchanged across the entire period. This chapter proceeds chronologically, beginning with extracts of the Letters Patent and Royal Instructions as they would have read in 1945. It then reviews Governor Young's recommendations for constitutional reform, which were abandoned in 1952. Prior to the mid-1980s, the few changes of any significance affected only the composition of the Legislative Council and informal constitutional conventions, which are explored. Then, the Joint Declaration and the Basic Law of the 1980s are discussed. Lastly, the eleventh-hour reforms made in the final years of British administration are reviewed.

Section 1. The Letters Patent and Royal Instructions by 1945

The Letters Patent and the Royal Instructions formed Hong Kong's written constitution. The Letters Patent established the Governor's office, Executive Council, and Legislative Council while the Royal Instructions gave specific commands to the Governor. These two documents formed a constitution that was brief when compared with other written constitutions. This is reflective of Westminster's limited level of interference in the daily affairs of the colony and the high degree of responsibility vested in the Governor. Both documents were issued first in 1843, amended from time to time, and, after thorough re-examination during the First World War, reissued in full in 1917.[4]

In the extracts reproduced as Documents 2.1 and 2.2, the text of the 1917 Letters Patent and Royal Instructions has been synthesised with all relevant amendments up to 1945. This allows the reader to appreciate the constitution as it read by the close of the Second World War complete with amendments.

---

3. For example: Milia Hau, 'The Official Mind of British Post-Imperialism: Influencing Parliamentary Opinions during the Anglo-Chinese Negotiations on the Future of Hong Kong, 1982–84', *The International History Review* 43, no. 6 (2021): 1198–216; Matthew Hurst, 'Britain's Approach to the Negotiations over the Future of Hong Kong, 1979–1982', *The International History Review* 44, no. 6 (2022): 1386–401; Yui Chim Lo, 'The Last Stand of Colonialism? The Unofficial Members of the Executive and Legislative Councils and the Sino-British Negotiations over Hong Kong, 1982–1984', *The Journal of Imperial and Commonwealth History* 48, no. 2 (2020): 370–94.
4. Tsang, *Democracy Shelved*, 4.

Document 2.1: TNA, CO 132/58, Hongkong Letters Patent, 20 April 1917.

I. There shall be a Governor and Commander-in-Chief in and over Our Colony of Hongkong . . .

V. There shall be an Executive Council in and for the Colony . . .

VI. There shall be a Legislative Council in and for the Colony . . .

VII. The Governor, by and with the advice and consent of the Legislative Council, may make laws for the peace, order and good government of the Colony.

VIII. We do hereby reserve to Ourselves, Our heirs and successors, full power and authority to disallow, through one of Our Principal Secretaries of State, any such law as aforesaid. . . .

IX. We do also reserve to Ourselves, Our heirs and successors, Our and their undoubted right, with the advice of Our or their Privy Council, to make all such laws as may appear necessary for the peace, order, and good government of the Colony.

Document 2.2: TNA, CO 132/58, Royal Instructions, 20 April 1917.

II. The Executive Council of the Colony shall consist of the Senior Military Officer . . . the persons for the time being lawfully discharging the functions of Colonial Secretary, of Attorney-General, of Secretary for Chinese Affairs, and of Financial Secretary of the Colony, who are hereinafter referred to as *ex officio* Members, and of such other persons as We may from time to time appoint . . . or as the Governor in pursuance of Instructions from Us through one of Our Principal Secretaries of State may from time to time appoint . . . Persons so appointed are hereinafter referred to as Official Members or Unofficial Members according as they hold, or do not hold, office under the Crown in the Colony at the time of appointment. . . .

X. In the execution of the powers and authorities granted to the Governor by Our said recited Letters Patent, he shall in all cases consult with the Executive Council, excepting only in cases which may be of such a nature that, in his judgment, Our service would sustain material prejudice by consulting the Council thereupon, or when the matters to be decided shall be too unimportant to require their advice, or too urgent to admit of their advice being given by the time within which it may be necessary for him to act in respect of any such matters. In all such urgent cases he shall, at the earliest practicable period, communicate to the Executive Council the measures which he may so have adopted, with the reasons therefor.

XI. The Governor shall alone be entitled to submit questions to the Executive Council for their advice or decision; but if the Governor decline to submit any question to the Council when requested in writing by any Member so to do, it shall be competent to such Member to require that there be recorded upon the Minutes his written application, together with the answer returned by the Governor to the same.

XII. The Governor may, in the exercise of the powers and authorities granted to him by Our said recited Letters Patent, act in opposition to the advice given to him by the Members of the Executive Council, if he shall in any case deem it right to do so; but in any such case he shall fully report the matter to Us by the first convenient opportunity, with the grounds and reasons of his action. . . .

XIII. The Legislative Council of the Colony shall consist of the Governor, the Senior Military Officer . . . the persons for the time being lawfully discharging the functions of Colonial Secretary, Attorney-General, Secretary for Chinese Affairs, and Financial Secretary of the Colony, and such other persons holding office under the Crown in the Colony, and not exceeding four in number at any one time . . . all such persons shall be styled Official Members of the Legislative Council; and further of such persons, not exceeding eight in number at any one time . . . shall be styled Unofficial Members of the Legislative Council. . . .

XXII. All questions proposed for debate in the Legislative Council shall be decided by the majority of votes, and the Governor or the Member presiding shall have an original vote in common with the other Members of the Council, and also a casting vote, if upon any question the votes shall be equal. . . .

XXIV. It shall be competent for any Member of the Legislative Council to propose any question for debate therein; and such question, if seconded by any other Member, shall be debated and disposed of according to the standing rules and orders. Provided always that every ordinance, vote, resolution, or question, the object or effect of which may be to dispose of or charge any part of Our revenue arising within the Colony, shall be proposed by the Governor, unless the proposal of the same shall have been expressly allowed or directed by him.

Although on paper the Crown retained the power to appoint Members to both of the Councils, in practice this responsibility was entrusted to the Governor and thus became a constitutional norm. Another significant convention was that the Hong Kong Chamber of Commerce and Justices of the Peace were allowed to nominate one Legislative Council Member each whom the Governor would then appoint.

Section 2. The Young Plan, 1946–1952

As anti-imperialist movements worldwide pushed for self-governance after the Second World War, British colonial Governors were instructed to liberalise their administrations.[5] *Within this context, on 1 May 1946 Hong Kong's Governor Sir Mark Young announced the intention to give the colony's inhabitants more responsibility in managing their own affairs. After nearly six months of consultation, Young sent his proposals to London, as summarised in Document 2.3.*

Document 2.3: TNA, CO 537/1651, briefing document 'Summary of Proposals in [Despatch] No. 69 for Establishment of Hong Kong Municipality', unknown author, *c.* October 1946.

1. One Municipality.

A single Municipality to be established to cover Hong Kong Island, Kowloon and that part of the New Territories known as New Kowloon, the remainder of the New Territories, which consists mainly of rural districts, being left to administration under District Officers.

2. Composition of Council.

The Municipal Council to consist of thirty members of whom twenty would be directly elected on a moderately wide franchise and ten would be nominated. Half of both the elected and nominated members to be Chinese. . . .

6. Nominated Members.

The registered Trade Unions, the Hong Kong General Chamber of Commerce and the unofficial Justices of the Peace each to nominate two members. The Chinese Chamber of Commerce, the University, the Hong Kong Residents Association and the Kowloon Residents Association each to nominate one member. . . .

7. Proposed Functions of Council.

Initially the Council would take over the responsibilities of the existing Urban Council and control of the fire brigade, parks, gardens, recreation grounds and certain licensing powers. A Commission would be appointed (and would include the members of the Municipal Council) to consider the transfer of other functions.

5. Leo F. Goodstadt, 'The Rise and Fall of Social, Economic and Political Reforms in Hong Kong, 1930–1955', *Journal of the Royal Asiatic Society Hong Kong Branch* 44 (2004): 58; Steve Tsang, ed., *A Documentary History of Hong Kong: Government and Politics* (Hong Kong: Hong Kong University Press, 2006 [1995]), 21.

The ultimate list . . . includes such matters as education, social welfare, town planning and public works.

8. Finance.

The underlying principle is that the Council should be given the fullest possible control over municipal finance. Loan proposals should, however, be subject to the sanction of the Central Government and, it is suggested, to that of the Secretary of State. . . .

10. Control.

No power of veto or certification to be retained but Government to rely on its ability to control the Municipality (a) by Order rescinding or varying the list of services transferred and (b) by legislation amending the Municipal Ordinance. It to be [*sic*] an instruction to the Governor to obtain the Secretary of State's prior approval before proceeding with either (a) or (b) above.

London approved Young's proposals with only minor changes. Young was replaced by Sir Alexander Grantham in July 1947. Under Governor Grantham's leadership, progress on executing these reforms continued in fits and starts before slowing to a virtual stop. In June 1952, Unofficial Members of the Executive Council informed Grantham that they felt reforms at that time would be dangerous. They asked the Governor to convince London to drop the idea entirely. Grantham 'did not disagree'[6] and a few days later sent the following secret telegram to Secretary of State for the Colonies Oliver Lyttelton.

Document 2.4: TNA, CO 1023/41, secret telegram, Governor Sir Alexander Grantham to Secretary of State for the Colonies Oliver Lyttelton, 26 June 1952.

Members of the Executive Council now feel apprehensive regarding any major constitutional changes at the present time. I share their fears, but have not yet made up my mind whether the proposals . . . are of such a far reaching nature as to constitute a danger.

2. Members of Executive Council would prefer constitutional changes to be limited at present to increasing number of Elected Members on Urban Council from two to four and reduction of ex-officio members from four to two. At same time Urban Council should be given greater financial autonomy.

6. Alexander Grantham, *Via Ports: From Hong Kong to Hong Kong* (Hong Kong: Hong Kong University Press, 2012 [1965]), 112.

3. One advantage of limiting constitutional changes to minor modifications to Urban Council is that this could be done by a short final decision of Secretary of State . . . on grounds that the present was not the time for major changes.

Lyttelton promptly addressed the House of Commons. Grantham's excuse that 'the present was not the time for major changes' was echoed in Lyttelton's choice of words: 'the present time is inopportune'.[7] *This would become a common refrain for Governors, ministers, and scholars alike. In the same, brief speech, Lyttelton announced the increase from two to four in the number of elected Urban Council members that Grantham had asked for. By conflating constitutional reform with changes to the Urban Council – a municipal services body that appears nowhere in the constitution – attentions were diverted away from the matter of serious constitutional reform. The Young Plan was shelved and the decades that followed saw only relatively minor changes until the governorship of Governor MacLehose.*

Section 3. The MacLehose Years, 1971–1982, and the Legislative Council

Governor MacLehose has been lauded as a great reformer and the period of his governorship considered a 'golden age' with improvements spanning the social and political realms. But recent literature has questioned this legacy, arguing that many of MacLehose's initiatives were built upon foundations laid by his predecessors, that he in fact resisted changes recommended by London, and that the Governor was motivated more by Britain's long-term geopolitical concerns than by the interests of Hong Kong.[8] *A policy paper that MacLehose submitted a month before assuming office offers evidence that could be used to support both interpretations: reformer and reluctance. The document reveals the incoming Governor's belief that a move towards a more representative government was prohibited by the potentially damaging reaction of Beijing and that there was little local demand for constitutional change. Yet MacLehose also states that exploring proposals for change is his 'top priority'.*

---

7. House of Commons (London) Hansard, Written Answers to Questions Col. 70, Secretary of State for the Colonies Oliver Lyttelton, 20 October 1952.
8. Ray Yep and Tai-lok Lui, 'Revisiting the Golden Era of MacLehose and the Dynamics of Social Reforms', in *Negotiating Autonomy in Greater China: Hong Kong and Its Sovereign Before and After 1997*, ed. Ray Yep (Copenhagen: NIAS Press, 2013), 110–41; Michael Ng, *Political Censorship in British Hong Kong: Freedom of Expression and the Law (1842–1997)* (Cambridge: Cambridge University Press, 2022), chapter 5.

Document 2.5: TNA, FCO 40/329, 'Guidelines for the Governor Designate of Hong Kong: Paper B' enclosed in top secret letter, Sir Murray MacLehose to various recipients, 18 October 1971.

4. The bar to representative government maintained by the CPG [Chinese People's Government] is fully understood in Hong Kong, and is in any case of little interest to most of the Chinese population with its authoritarian tradition of government. Given this situation there is little scope for making government more acceptable by tinkering with the composition or activities of the Legislative and Executive Councils, though probably a certain amount can still be done. But there might be more scope and chance of success for an effort at a lower level aimed at giving residents of neighbourhoods a greater sense of participation in and identification with the administration where it touches their day to day lives. . . . As I see it people should be identified with government by a move towards recognition of responsible citizenship rather than towards representative government. Closely related with this is the problem of how to improve communication between government and population and population and government. . . .

10. I have read the papers in the Department setting out various proposals for reform of the structure of government . . . All I can say at this stage is that I accept this whole field as one of top priority for consideration.

Despite accusations of reluctance, under Governor MacLehose significant changes to the conventions surrounding the constitution took place.[9] *In 1973, MacLehose stopped the custom of allowing Unofficial Justices of the Peace and the Hong Kong General Chamber of Commerce to nominate one Unofficial Member of the Legislative Council each. MacLehose also appointed to the Legislative Council people from underrepresented quarters of the community. By purposefully appointing to the Legislative Council fewer Official Members than was permitted under the constitution, he introduced a* de facto *majority of Unofficial Members.*[10] *More generally, MacLehose sought to extend the responsibilities, responsiveness, and reach of government to address a growing range of issues.*[11] *Lastly, although Governor MacLehose did not table plans for constitutional reforms analogous to those of Governor Young,*[12] *in 1979 he began Sino-British negotiations that led to an entirely new constitution for Hong Kong, examined in the next section.*

9. Norman Miners, *The Government and Politics of Hong Kong*, 4th edition (Hong Kong: Oxford University Press, 1986), 58.
10. Steve Tsang, 'China and Political Reform in Hong Kong', *The Pacific Review* 2, no. 1 (1989): 70.
11. James T. H. Tang and Frank Ching, 'The MacLehose–Youde Years: Balancing the "Three-Legged Stool", 1971–86', in *Precarious Balance: Hong Kong between China and Britain, 1842–1992*, ed. Ming K. Chan (Hong Kong: Hong Kong University Press, 1994), 160.
12. MacLehose did, however, commission the consultancy company McKinsey to recommend improvements to the machinery of government. The McKinsey Report and a 1966 inquiry known

MacLehose also oversaw formal amendments to the constitution. While some were administrative in nature or seemingly minor in significance, others served to increase the number of Unofficial Members of the Legislative Council, thereby enhancing the Council's capacity for representation. Table 2.1 displays changes to the Legislative Council that were introduced both before and after MacLehose, highlighting the exponential growth in Unofficial Members under MacLehose. Table 2.1 also captures how nomenclature was updated over time.

Table 2.1: Changes to the Legislative Council, 1945–1984, compiled by the author based on the Royal Instructions and amendments[13]

Governor	Amendment	**Official Members** (including the Governor)	Unofficial Members
Young	(Resumption of Legislative Council 1 May 1946)	10: Governor, Senior Military Officer, Colonial Secretary, Attorney-General, Financial Secretary, and 'such other persons holding office . . . not exceeding four in number'	8
Trench	1964	13: the number of 'other' Official Members increased to up to seven	13: the same number as Official Members for the first time
	1966	13: Senior Military Officer removed; 'other' increased to up to eight (leaving the balance unchanged)	No change
	1969	'Secretary for Chinese Affairs' renamed 'Secretary for Home Affairs' (balance unchanged)	No change

(continued on p. 60)

as the Dickinson Report, conducted during Governor Trench's administration, have both been compared by some to the Young Plan (Hook, 'Government of Hong Kong', 500–1). Yet this comparison is flawed because McKinsey's terms of reference disbarred them from submitting recommendations that would have significantly encroached upon the central government or the existing colonial constitution (see also Trevor Clark, 'The Dickinson Report: An Account of the Background to, and Preparation of, the 1966 "Working Group Report on Local Administration"', *Journal of the Hong Kong Branch of the Royal Asiatic Society* 37 (1998): 1–17). As Lo observed, where some scholars talk of 'constitutional reforms', it is often more appropriate to instead say 'institutional reform' (Shiu-hing Lo, *The Politics of Democratization in Hong Kong* (London: Palgrave Macmillan, 1997), 60 fn. 10).

13. Constitutional amendments that made no relevant changes are excluded from Table 2.1. The table displays the *maximum* number of Members permitted by the constitution, which is not necessarily the same as the *actual* number of Members.

Table 2.1 (continued)

Governor	Amendment	Official Members (including the Governor)	Unofficial Members
	1971	The five Official Members identified by the offices they held (i.e. Governor, Colonial Secretary, Attorney-General, Secretary for Home Affairs, and Financial Secretary) and those who are not 'others' to be referred to as *ex officio* Members	No change
MacLehose	1972	15: 'others' increased to up to 10	15
	1976	23: 'others' increased to up to 18; 'Colonial Secretary' renamed 'Chief Secretary'	23
	1977	25: 'others' increased to up to 20	25
	1980	27: 'others' increased to up to 22	27
Youde	1983	29: Secretary for Home Affairs removed (decreasing the number of *ex officio* Members to four) and 'others' increased to up to 25	29
	1984	No change	32: a greater number than Official Members for the first time

Table 2.2 reflects changes that resulted from the 1985 amendment to the Royal Instructions brought in under Governor Youde. This amendment required elections for certain Legislative Council seats and replaced clause XIII, which had previously dictated the maximum number of Official and Unofficial Members, with new wording that did not state maximums. Instead, membership was to be determined by law rather than by the constitution. In Table 2.2, ex officio *Members included the Chief Secretary, Financial Secretary, Attorney General, and the Governor who was also President of the Council. In February 1993 – which was not an election year – Governor Patten gave up his seat on the Council, bringing the number of* ex officio *members down from four to three. The Electoral College included ten District Board seats (one for each constituency), one Urban Council seat, and one Regional Council seat. The composition of the Election Committee is detailed in Section 6.*

Table 2.2: Changes to the Legislative Council, 1985–1995, compiled by the author based on various sources

<table>
<tr><th></th><th></th><th colspan="5">Unofficial Members</th><th colspan="2">Official Members</th><th></th></tr>
<tr><th>Governor</th><th>Election year</th><th>Geographical constituencies</th><th>Functional constituencies</th><th>Electoral College</th><th>Election Committee</th><th>Appointed</th><th>Officials</th><th>Ex officio (including the Governor until 1993)</th><th>Total</th></tr>
<tr><td>Youde</td><td>1985</td><td></td><td>12</td><td>12</td><td></td><td>22</td><td>7</td><td>4</td><td>57</td></tr>
<tr><td rowspan="2">Wilson</td><td>1988</td><td></td><td>14</td><td>12</td><td></td><td>20</td><td>7</td><td>4</td><td>57</td></tr>
<tr><td>1991</td><td rowspan="2">18</td><td rowspan="2">21</td><td rowspan="2"></td><td rowspan="2"></td><td rowspan="2">18</td><td rowspan="2"></td><td>4</td><td>61</td></tr>
<tr><td rowspan="2">Patten</td><td>1993 (no election)</td><td>3</td><td>60</td></tr>
<tr><td>1995</td><td>20</td><td>30</td><td></td><td>10</td><td></td><td></td><td></td><td>60</td></tr>
</table>

Section 4. The Joint Declaration and the Basic Law, 1980s–1990s

Hong Kong had become a British colony in three steps: two leases ceded portions of land in perpetuity during the nineteenth century, and in 1898 a ninety-nine-year lease, which would expire in 1997, expanded the colony northwards. Governor MacLehose and China's Deng Xiaoping first discussed the issue of the 1997 lease expiry in a March 1979 meeting. Sino-British negotiations followed in 1983–1984 and resulted in the 1984 Joint Declaration, which determined that Hong Kong would pass from Britain to Beijing. Although the Joint Declaration did not replace the colonial constitution, it did require the creation of a new constitution: the Basic Law. Chen and Ng have calculated that around half of the Basic Law's provisions find their origin in the Joint Declaration.[14] *Thus, the Joint Declaration can be considered a defining document in Hong Kong's constitutional history.*[15]

Document 2.6: Annex I of the Joint Declaration of the Government of the United Kingdom of Greater Britain and Northern Ireland and the Government of the People's Republic of China on the Question of Hong Kong.

The National People's Congress of the People's Republic of China shall enact and promulgate a Basic Law of the Hong Kong Special Administrative Region of the People's Republic of China (hereinafter referred to as the Basic Law) in accordance with the Constitution of the People's Republic of China, stipulating that after the establishment of the Hong Kong Special Administrative Region the socialist system and socialist policies shall not be practised in the Hong Kong Special Administrative Region and that Hong Kong's previous capitalist system and life-style shall remain unchanged for 50 years.

To write this new constitution, in July 1985 China established the Basic Law Drafting Committee. The Basic Law was eventually adopted by the National People's Congress in April 1990 and would replace the Letters Patent and the Royal Instructions on 1 July 1997.

14. Albert H. Y. Chen and Michael Ng, 'The Making of the Constitutional Order of the Hong Kong SAR: The Role of Sino-British Diplomacy (1982–90)', in *Constitutional Foundings in Northeast Asia*, ed. Kevin Y. L. Tan and Michael Ng (Oxford: Hart Publishing, 2022), 42.
15. Miners, *Government and Politics*, 63.

Document 2.7: The Basic Law of the Hong Kong Special Administrative Region of the People's Republic of China.

2. The National People's Congress authorizes the Hong Kong Special Administrative Region to exercise a high degree of autonomy and enjoy executive, legislative and independent judicial power, including that of final adjudication, in accordance with the provisions of this Law. . . .

5. The socialist system and policies shall not be practised in the Hong Kong Special Administrative Region, and the previous capitalist system and way of life shall remain unchanged for 50 years. . . .

17. The Hong Kong Special Administrative Region shall be vested with legislative power. . . .

If the Standing Committee of the National People's Congress, after consulting the Committee for the Basic Law of the Hong Kong Special Administrative Region under it, considers that any law enacted by the legislature of the Region is not in conformity with the provisions of this Law . . . the Standing Committee may return the law in question but shall not amend it. Any law returned by the Standing Committee of the National People's Congress shall immediately be invalidated. . . .

18. . . . National laws shall not be applied in the Hong Kong Special Administrative Region except for those listed in Annex III to this Law. . . .

The Standing Committee of the National People's Congress may add to or delete from the list of laws in Annex III after consulting its Committee for the Basic Law . . . Laws listed in Annex III to this Law shall be confined to those relating to defence and foreign affairs as well as other matters outside the limits of the autonomy of the Region as specified by this Law.

In the event that the Standing Committee of the National People's Congress decides to declare a state of war or, by reason of turmoil within the Hong Kong Special Administrative Region which endangers national unity or security and is beyond the control of the government of the Region, decides that the Region is in a state of emergency, the Central People's Government may issue an order applying the relevant national laws in the Region. . . .

26. Permanent residents of the Hong Kong Special Administrative Region shall have the right to vote and the right to stand for election in accordance with law. . . .

45. The Chief Executive of the Hong Kong Special Administrative Region shall be selected by election or through consultations held locally and be appointed by the Central People's Government.

The method for selecting the Chief Executive shall be specified in the light of the actual situation in the Hong Kong Special Administrative Region and in accordance with the principle of gradual and orderly progress. The ultimate aim is the selection of the Chief Executive by universal suffrage upon nomination by a broadly representative nominating committee in accordance with democratic procedures. . . .

55. Members of the Executive Council of the Hong Kong Special Administrative Region shall be appointed by the Chief Executive from among the principal officials of the executive authorities, members of the Legislative Council and public figures. Their appointment or removal shall be decided by the Chief Executive. . . .

Members of the Executive Council of the Hong Kong Special Administrative Region shall be Chinese citizens who are permanent residents of the Region with no right of abode in any foreign country. . . .

68. The Legislative Council of the Hong Kong Special Administrative Region shall be constituted by election.

The method for forming the Legislative Council shall be specified in the light of the actual situation in the Hong Kong Special Administrative Region and in accordance with the principle of gradual and orderly progress. The ultimate aim is the election of all the members of the Legislative Council by universal suffrage. . . .

158. The power of interpretation of this Law shall be vested in the Standing Committee of the National People's Congress. . . .

159. The power of amendment of this Law shall be vested in the National People's Congress.

By the 1990s, Hong Kong's civil society featured dozens of established, professional political parties and pressure groups. One group, the Hong Kong Journalists Association, joined forces with Article 19, a London-based human rights organisation. In a jointly authored report, they criticised several discrepancies between the Joint Declaration and the Basic Law. On the constitution in particular, they argued that Article 158 gave Beijing too much power of interpretation.

Document 2.8: Article 19 and the Hong Kong Journalists Association, *Urgent Business: Hong Kong, Freedom of Expression and 1997* (1993): 8–9.

One of the Basic Law's most controversial provisions concerns the power of interpreting the constitution itself . . .

Article 158 provides that the power of interpreting the SAR [Special Administrative Region] constitution "shall be vested in the Standing Committee of the National People's Congress". . . .

The power of interpretation under Article 158 is widely regarded as being inconsistent with the stipulation in the Joint Declaration that the SAR courts are to have "independent judicial power, including the power of final adjudication" [misquoting 3(3)].

In the early 1980s, Hong Kong had been presented with the Joint Declaration and told there was no alternative, gaining tacit approval. But by the 1990s and within the context of a growing civil society and political consciousness, the Basic Law came under much greater scrutiny, as Document 2.8 shows.

Section 5. Electoral Reform, 1982–1987

As Hong Kong's post-1997 future was defined during the 1980s, the Hong Kong government dabbled with ways of enhancing representation. A White Paper published in November 1984 proposed that in the following year, twenty-four Unofficial Members of the Legislative Council should be elected. There would be two methods of election: half would be voted in by electoral colleges while the other half would come from nine functional constituencies, wherein members of major professional organisations and associations representing particular sectors ('commercial, industrial, financial, labour, social services, education, legal, medical, and engineers and associated professions')[16] could vote for a candidate for their industry. In addition to twenty-four elected Unofficial Members, the Governor would appoint twenty-two Unofficial Members and there would be eleven Official Members including the Governor. The White Paper also committed the government to a formal review of representative government in 1987, made it policy to expand direct elections by 1988, and created an expectation that direct elections would increase significantly by 1997. As the White Paper itself commented, implementing these recommendations would entail 'amendments to the two main constitutional instruments'.[17]

Having gained greater leverage over Hong Kong affairs since signing the Joint Declaration, Beijing protested against the White Paper. Beijing bullishly demanded that the Hong Kong government refrain from introducing significant political changes during the transition period, warning that the city's stability might otherwise be threatened. Further, it demanded that the Hong Kong government ensure 'convergence' with the Basic Law, which Beijing alone was empowered to draft. However, recently declassified files show that behind closed doors, Beijing adopted a more pragmatic, discursive attitude while the British sought common ground.[18] In a meeting between British and Chinese representatives, the latter conceded it would be best for the Hong Kong government to proceed with

16. Hong Kong Government, *White Paper: The Further Development of Representative Government in Hong Kong* (Hong Kong: Hong Kong Government Printer, 1984), 6.
17. Hong Kong Government, *White Paper*, 13.
18. Chen and Ng, 'Making of the Constitutional Order', 54.

its plans, albeit to the most limited extent possible. Remarkably, the two sides concurred that public opinion about direct elections in Hong Kong was mixed. Although Beijing claimed to hold all the cards in public, in private Chinese officials remained in negotiation with the British throughout this period.

Document 2.9: TNA, PREM 19/1796, confidential telegram 'Secretary of State's [Sir Geoffrey Howe] Meeting with [Director of the Hong Kong and Macao Affairs Office] Ji Pengfei: 13 October', British Ambassador to Beijing Sir Richard Evans to the British Foreign and Commonwealth Office, 14 October 1986.

10. Ji continued that he wished to raise the representative system in Hong Kong. This involved the question of direct elections. The review would take place next year [1987]. The Chinese side considered that it would be best for the review not to take place or to be delayed. However, as HKG [Hong Kong Government] had already undertaken to hold a 1987 review the Chinese agreed that this could be carried out. They thought that it would be best if the review did not refer to direct elections: if however direct elections were mentioned in the review it would be best if no decisions were taken. In the . . . work of drafting the BL [Basic Law], China attached great importance to this issue, on which Hong Kong opinion was divided. In particular some from the upper and middle classes opposed direct elections. A cautious attitude must be adopted. . . .

11. The Secretary of State agreed that . . . confidence must be maintained. . . . But HKG must not be seen to renege on commitments because of criticism or pressure from the Chinese side. This is why it was so important that the 1987 review should proceed as promised. Neither HKG nor HMG [Her Majesty's Government] had any preconceived views about direct elections. The review would not be slanted in any particular direction. . . . Opinion in Hong Kong on the subject was divided.

The 1985 elections proceeded but the 1987 review shows that this short-lived attempt at reform stalled by the late 1980s under pressure from Beijing. The first page of the 1987 Review of Developments in Representative Government *stated that any further developments must be 'conducted within the framework of Hong Kong's existing constitutional arrangements'.*[19] *Thus, the Hong Kong government 'decelerated the pace and narrowed the scope'*[20] *of democratisation by the late 1980s, during which time the British*

19. Hong Kong Government, *Green Paper: The 1987 Review of Developments in Representative Government* (Hong Kong: Hong Kong Government Printer, 1987), 5.
20. Lo, *Politics of Democratization*, 90.

believed that an emollient approach was critical to maintaining Hong Kong's stability. This attitude would change under Governor Patten's governorship.

Section 6. Patten's Plans, 1992–1997

When Patten arrived in 1992, only eighteen of the Legislative Council's sixty-one seats were directly elected via the geographical constituencies (Table 2.2). The scope for Patten to implement changes to the composition of the Legislative Council was hampered by plans already in place for 1995, when direct elections in geographical constituencies would return twenty seats, functional constituencies thirty, and the Election Committee ten.[21] *Patten instead sought to exploit the remaining grey areas to install democracy to the greatest extent possible without coming into direct conflict with existing plans, the Joint Declaration, or the Basic Law.*

In plans publicised in October 1992, Patten proposed that the Election Committee be formed of District Board and Municipal Council members, themselves elected at the local level. The Governor also sought to extend eligibility to vote as broadly as possible by reducing the voting age from twenty-one to eighteen, changing the functional constituency system from corporate to individual votes, and creating nine new functional constituencies. This would give 2.7 million more people a vote.[22]

Beijing criticised Patten for abandoning the principle of convergence. Beijing pointed to a secret exchange of notes in 1990. Accusing the British of reneging on agreements reached via these missives, Lu Ping famously described Patten as 'a sinner for a thousand years'[23] *while Patten claimed to have no prior knowledge of the correspondence.*

Document 2.10: Extracts from an exchange of seven notes between British and Chinese officials enclosed within TNA, PREM 19/3800, confidential letter, Hong Kong Government to British Embassy (Peking), 26 October 1992.

[Note 1: British Foreign Secretary Douglas Hurd to Chinese Minister of Foreign Affairs Qian Qichen, 18 January 1990]

2. I have considered carefully your suggestion that we should restrict the number of directly elected seats in 1991 to 15, in return for which you would allow for 20 directly elected seats (one-third) in a legislature of 60 in 1997, which would thereafter increase to 40 per cent in 1999 and 50 per cent in 2003. . . .

---

21. Michael Sheridan, *The Gate to China: A New History of the People's Republic & Hong Kong* (London: William Collins, 2021), 217–19.
22. Chris Patten, *The Hong Kong Diaries* (London: Allen Lane, 2022), 54–55.
23. Lu Ping, Head of the Hong Kong and Macao Affairs Office, at a press conference on 17 March 1993.

4. If we were to decide, despite the clearly expressed desire of large sections of the community, that we were to introduce a lower number in 1991, I believe this could only be done if there were a sufficient number of directly elected seats for 1997 and development thereafter . . .

5. . . . But I fear that your suggestion for 20 seats in 1997 would not be sufficient to command support. If, however, the Chinese side were prepared to increase the figure for 1997 to 24 seats (40 per cent) I believe that there is a good chance that the provisions for political development in the Basic Law would receive support within Hong Kong.

[Note 2: Qian to Hurd, 20 January 1990]

[T]he Chinese side cannot bring itself to agree to the Right Honourable Foreign Secretary's proposal that in 1997 the proportion of the directly elected seats in the first Legislature of the Hong Kong Special Administrative Region be set at 40%. However, if the British side agrees to the percentages of the directly elected seats in the Legislature in 1997 and thereafter . . . a Legislature of 60, 33.3% of the seats will be directly elected in 1997, 40% in 1999 and 50% in 2003 . . . the Chinese side is ready to consider the British suggestion that the number of directly elected seats of the Legislature in 1991 be increased from 15 to 18.

[Note 7: Hurd to Qian, 12 February 1990]

I am now prepared to confirm an understanding with the Chinese government on the following lines. If the final version of the BL provides for 20 directly elected seats in the SAR legislature in 1997, 24 in 1999, and 30 in 2003, the British government will be prepared to limit to 18 the number of directly elected seats to be introduced in 1991.

You will, however, be aware from my previous messages that this rate of progress in introducing directly elected seats would not be as rapid as many people in Hong Kong or we ourselves would have liked.

Once this secret correspondence was published, it was clear that Patten's 1992 plans did not contradict any of the agreements reached between Hurd and Qian in 1990. Nonetheless, the incident was acutely embarrassing for the new Governor. It also exacerbated distrust within Hong Kong society because the letters showed that Britain and Beijing had been bartering over the city's future while keeping such discussions from Hong Kong itself.

In April 1993, the two sides entered into talks to try to find a compromise. However, by November, negotiations had collapsed. A blow-by-blow account remains unavailable to researchers but a report presented to Parliament in 1994 gives us glimpses into the negotiation room and spells out why, from the British perspective, the talks failed.

Document 2.11: Foreign and Commonwealth Office, *Representative Government in Hong Kong* (Command Paper 2432), 1994.

41. In informal discussion during Round 17, the Chinese side put forward two texts for an oral understanding . . . The formula they put forward was as follows:

"The British side propose to abolish appointed seats in the District Boards and Municipal Councils . . . The Chinese side propose to retain an appropriate proportion of appointed seats in the District Boards and Municipal Councils . . . The Chinese side state that, from 1 July 1997, the Hong Kong Special Administrative Region Government will determine the number of appointed seats of the District Boards and Municipal Councils in accordance with . . . the Basic Law".

42. This formula was different from that put forward in Round 15, notably in the omission of the words "on its own" after the reference to the Hong Kong Special Administrative Region Government. . . . It did not mean that the Special Administrative Region Government would in the future determine on their own whether to retain or abolish appointed seats; that decision would be for "the Chinese side".

43. . . . The Chinese proposal represented an erosion of the autonomy promised to the Hong Kong Special Administrative Region under the Joint Declaration and the Basic Law. It should be for the Special Administrative Region authorities on their own to determine by law the composition for the "district organisations", inducing the question of what (if any) should be the number of appointed District Board and Municipal Council members. This should be a matter within the high degree of autonomy that Hong Kong is guaranteed under both the Joint Declaration and the Basic Law. . . .

44. . . . it became apparent during Round 17 that it would not be possible to reach agreement on the issues covering the British draft Memorandum of Understanding . . .

Patten's plans were implemented nonetheless and the Letters Patent and the Royal Instructions amended – despite the 1987 Review's commitment to keep any future changes within the bounds of the existing constitution. In September 1995, fewer than 650 days before Beijing would take control of Hong Kong, elections for the first fully elected Legislative Council were held. It would prove to be the last fully elected Legislative Council to date.

On 30 June 1997, the eve of Hong Kong's transfer to China, British officials delivered farewell speeches. Prince Charles eulogised 'the British values and institutions that have been the framework for Hong Kong's success' and said Britain could be 'proud of the rights and freedoms that Hong Kong people enjoy'. Governor Patten's speech similarly emphasised the role of British administration in Hong Kong.

Document 2.12: Speech, Governor Chris Patten at the sunset farewell ceremony in Hong Kong, 30 June 1997.

As British administration ends, we are, I believe, entitled to say that our own nation's contribution here was to provide the scaffolding that enabled the people of Hong Kong to ascend: the rule of law, clean and light-handed government, the values of a free society, the beginnings of representative government and democratic accountability. . . . I have no doubt that, with people here holding on to these values which they cherish, Hong Kong's star will continue to climb. Hong Kong's values are decent values. They are universal values. They are the values of the future in Asia as elsewhere. A future in which the happiest and the richest communities, and the most confident and most stable, too, will be those that best combine political liberty and economic freedom as we do here today. . . . Now, Hong Kong people are to run Hong Kong. That is the promise and that is the unshakeable destiny.

This chapter began by reviewing Governor Young's 1946 plans for constitutional reforms, which were shelved in 1952. For almost forty years, the constitution was seldom debated and was not subject to significant changes until the 1985 amendment under Youde and Patten's interventions around the edges of the constitution in the 1990s. Patten undeniably launched 'the beginnings of representative government and democratic accountability'. But this belated and relatively modest step towards representative government was, to borrow from the Article 19 and Hong Kong Journalists Association joint report, 'too little and too late'.[24] *The departing British colonial administration hurriedly installed democratic reforms partially as an attempt to improve its colonial legacy, as exemplified in Patten's speech (Document 2.12). However, when seen against the backdrop of decades upon decades of failing to institute meaningful reforms, there appears little of which to be proud.*

* My thanks to David Clayton for his feedback on an earlier draft of this chapter.

24. Article 19 and Hong Kong Journalists Association, *Urgent Business*, 4.

Suggested Readings

Chen, Albert H. Y., and Michael Ng. 'The Making of the Constitutional Order of the Hong Kong SAR: The Role of Sino-British Diplomacy (1982–90)'. In *Constitutional Foundings in Northeast Asia*, edited by Kevin Y. L. Tan and Michael Ng, 47–71. Oxford: Hart Publishing, 2022.

Cheng, Joseph Y. S. 'Sino-British Negotiations on Hong Kong During Chris Patten's Governorship'. *Australian Journal of International Affairs* 48, no. 2 (1994): 229–45.

Ghai, Yash. 'The Past and the Future of Hong Kong's Constitution'. *The China Quarterly* 128 (1991): 794–813.

Goodstadt, Leo F. 'The Rise and Fall of Social, Economic and Political Reforms in Hong Kong, 1930–1955'. *Journal of the Royal Asiatic Society Hong Kong Branch* 44 (2004): 57–81.

Hook, Brian. 'The Government of Hong Kong: Change within Tradition'. *The China Quarterly* 95 (1983): 491–511.

Tsang, Steve Yui-Sang. *Democracy Shelved: Great Britain, China, and Attempts at Constitutional Reform in Hong Kong, 1945–1952*. Hong Kong: Oxford University Press, 1988.

3

Political Culture

Florence Mok

The older Hong Kong literature portrayed the colony's political situation as relatively stable compared with other societies that were undergoing decolonisation. The level of political participation of Hong Kong Chinese in formal politics also remained extremely low. According to the older generation of political and social scientists, the colony's political stability was attributable to a general lack of interest in political participation.[1] They described the political culture in Hong Kong using the term 'political apathy'.[2] This apathetic attitude was formed for a number of reasons. Firstly, political upheavals led to the formation of a 'refugee mentality' among the Hong Kong Chinese in the post-war period. Many believed they were only sojourners and considered Hong Kong to be 'a lifeboat' in the sea of China. Coming to the colony to seek security and stability, many avoided getting involved in politics and conflicts and were primarily driven by instrumentalism.[3]

Secondly, Confucian values also constituted political conservatism among Hong Kong Chinese. According to the schooling in Confucian classics, the ideal relationship between government and people was 'analogous to that which should exist between parents and children, or between a shepherd and his flock'.[4] Under this ethos, ordinary people were not involved in policy formation. The harmony of society was stressed and social conflicts were condemned. Thirdly, despite the

1. Norman Miners, *The Government and Politics of Hong Kong* (Hong Kong: Oxford University Press, 1975); Ambrose Y. King, 'Administrative Absorption of Politics in Hong Kong: Emphasis on the Grass Roots Level', *Asian Survey* 15, no. 5 (1975): 422–39; J. S. Hoadley, 'Hong Kong Is the Lifeboat: Notes on Political Culture and Socialization', *Journal of Oriental Studies* 8 (1970): 206–18.
2. King, 'Administrative Absorption of Politics', 427; Miners, *The Government and Politics*, 32.
3. Miners, *The Government and Politics*, 34; Hoadley, 'Hong Kong Is the Lifeboat', 210–11.
4. J. S. Hoadley, 'Hong Kong Is the Lifeboat: Notes on Political Culture and Socialization', *Journal of Oriental Studies* 8 (1970):613.

absence of democracy, the colonial state had gained public recognition through its practice of administrative co-option in the Legislative and Executive Councils and through pressure groups.[5] The City District Officer Scheme, introduced under the supervision of the Secretary for Home Affairs in 1968, further represented the colonial government's attempt to incorporate grassroots opinions into the administrative system.[6] This 'administrative absorption of politics' provided channels for ordinary Hong Kong Chinese to express their opinions despite the absence of democracy.

In the 1980s, sociologist Lau Siu-kai described a laissez-faire state and a politically apathetic Chinese society in Hong Kong. According to Lau, social conflicts were rare in the colony. Under typical circumstances, it was difficult to mobilise Hong Kong Chinese to engage in 'a sustained, high-cost political movement'. Although social conflicts and violence occurred in 1956, 1966, and 1967, their scale was relatively small to moderate.[7] Lau believed the underlying social ethos was 'utilitarianistic familism': even in a hyper urban-industrial setting, familial interests remained the primary consideration among most Hong Kong Chinese, placed above communal interests. This resulted in the absence of public spirit and low public morale, and subsequently a low level of political participation in Hong Kong – what he called 'political aloofness'.[8] Within these familial groups, economic interdependence and mutual assistance were emphasised. In other words, Chinese households in the colony relied on familial networks and were capable of self-regulating; they did not require the state to intervene and deliver equity.[9]

Since the 1990s, revisionists have refuted this claim of political stability and passivity. For example, Lau's assertion about class was challenged by Tai-lok Lui and Thomas Wong, who argued that the society of Hong Kong should not be treated as 'some amorphous entity'.[10] As Lui and Wong have suggested, 'instead of having a uniform, across-the-board accommodative mechanism, familistic-network in character, depoliticising in effect, there are in fact different class based mechanisms at work'.[11] Lam Wai-man's seminal work further expanded the formerly narrow definition of political participation to include unlawful and informal activities, such as protests, signature campaigns, petitions, and discursive discussions. She pointed

5. Endacott, *Government and People in Hong Kong, 1841–1962* (Hong Kong: Hong Kong University Press,1964), 188–89; 229–31; King, 'Administrative Absorption of Politics', 425.
6. King, 'Administrative Absorption of Politics'.
7. Lau Siu-kai, *Society and Politics in Hong Kong* (Hong Kong: Chinese University of Hong Kong Press, 1982), 68–85.
8. Lau, *Society and Politics in Hong Kong*, 102; Lau Siu-kai, 'Chinese Familism in an Urban-Industrial Setting: The Case of Hong Kong', *Journal of Marriage and Family* 43, no. 4 (1981): 978–86.
9. Lau, 'Chinese Familism', 988.
10. Thomas Wong and Tai-lok Lui, *From One Brand of Politics to One Brand of Political Culture* (Hong Kong: Occasional Paper 10, Hong Kong Institute of Asia-Pacific Studies, 1992), 2.
11. Wong and Lui, *From One Brand of Politics to One Brand of Political Culture*, 40.

out that political mobilisations were never absent in Hong Kong; the extent of civil society and advocacy for reforms had been grossly underestimated.[12] Although the culture of de-politicisation continued to exist due to people's previous experience as refugees and the influence of the Cold War, it did not stop political activism; it only constricted the movements in terms of their scale and level of radicalness. The tensions between political activism and the culture of de-politicisation gave rise to the middle ground: 'gradualism and reformism within a framework of stability and prosperity', which in turn benefited the colonial government.[13]

Recently, Florence Mok's work has also examined how civil society and various groups of activists utilised different strategies to pressurise the colonial government to introduce institutional, legislative, and administrative changes from the 1960s. She also shows that political cultures in Hong Kong varied in accordance with class and age, and that they changed in significant ways over the late colonial era. For example, students and elites engaged vigorously in social movements. They were critical of the colonial administration and perceived informal political engagement as their right. The upper class believed that political activism was undignified and undermined political stability. The working class, driven by instrumentalism, distanced themselves from social movements espousing liberal values and addressing the agenda about the rights of colonial subjects. However, in general, from the 1970s, all Chinese communities demonstrated an increased readiness to engage in political movements and discourses.[14] Using archival records, this chapter provides useful insights into how political cultures and civil society changed from 1945 to 1997, primarily focusing on the political attitudes and orientations of the general public.

Section 1. From Sojourners to Settled Population, 1945–1965

After the Second World War, Hong Kong's political system remained largely unreformed. However, in the immediate period, the legitimacy of the colonial rule was rarely challenged; the general public primarily expressed their opinions and grievances through informal channels, such as Chinese leaders and Kaifong associations. However, Hong Kong's demographic composition soon changed with former migrants and refugees becoming a settled population in the colony. By the late 1950s, the sojourner mentality held by recent migrants faded, and more people perceived themselves as permanent residents of Hong Kong– this led to a change in the political culture. The government soon defined the influx of migrants from China as 'a problem of people', which had major implications

12. Lam Wai-man, *Understanding the Political Culture of Hong Kong: The Paradox of Activism and Depoliticization* (New York: M.E. Sharpe, 2004), 47–52 and 181.
13. Lam, *Understanding the Political Culture of Hong Kong*, 184–85, 211–30.
14. Florence Mok, *Covert Colonialism: Governance, Surveillance and Policymaking in British Hong Kong, c. 1966–97* (Manchester: Manchester University Press, 2023).

for the development of a local sense of community. It first adopted the 'local integration' approach, which could absorb the migrants and transform troublemakers into responsible citizens, and that benefited Hong Kong's industrialisation, even it might have strained the originally already underdeveloped local welfare system and housing stock.

Document 3.1: 'Chapter 1: Review – A Problem of People', *Hong Kong Annual Report, 1956* (Hong Kong: Hong Kong Government Printer, 1957).

. . . Looking back over this period, one can say that there is little that has been done that would not have been done differently in some way if one problem had never existed. Finance, education, medical and health services, social welfare, prisons, police, industry, commerce, labour relations, land policy, housing, agriculture and fisheries, political relations — even the law itself — all bear the unmistakable surcharge (in a few cases an almost obliterating surcharge) of this single problem. It is the problem of a vast immigrant population; vast because for every resident of the Colony at the British reoccupation in 1945 there are now *four* residents.

A few figures will explain the position more precisely . . . At the outbreak of the Japanese war the population had increased to 1,600,000. On the British reoccupation in 1945 the wholesale expulsions enforced by the Japanese had reduced that number to 600,000. By the end of 1946 the population was 1,600,000; by 1950 it was 2,360,000 and by the end of 1956 something over 2,500,000. Not all of the increase between 1945 and 1956 (nearly two million) was immigrant population. Perhaps a figure of 400,000 represents the natural increase in the population and a further 400,000 the people who were residents of the Colony before the war and returned to it after the Japanese surrender. The increase between 1945 and 1956 due to immigration was, therefore, somewhere about one million, and of this number Dr. Hambro, who conducted a survey on behalf of the United Nations High Commissioner for Refugees in 1954, has estimated that about 700,000 were refugees . . .

The reader may well ask why this was *allowed* to happen. A small integrated community with resources appropriate to its size surely has a right to protection against an inundation of strangers. This is an internationally accepted principle, and Hong Kong's own pre-war and more recent history has shown that it can and must be applied when the situation becomes threatening — or (the cynical reader may add) when the Government wakes up to its responsibilities to its established citizens. Why was the situation ever allowed to develop into the vast problem that now faces the Government? Was it assumed that up to one million immigrants could be assimilated to an acceptable degree and in reasonable time?

The answer to these questions may fall oddly on modern ears. The immigrants were admitted on humanitarian grounds alone and the problems to which they would give rise if they did not return or emigrate elsewhere were deliberately accepted. The first influx fled from the shattered economy and threat of famine which followed the Pacific War. The people who followed in the second influx voted with their feet against the new régime which was established when the Nationalists withdrew to Formosa. In either case the immigrants sought in Hong Kong something sufficiently important to themselves to necessitate the abandonment of their homes, the severance of family ties and the renunciation of traditional allegiances. No one will ever know what it cost them to abandon the land on which their ancestors had made their living. They were not denied what they sought, and Hong Kong accepted the burden which they brought with them in the name of humanity rather than because it had any special standing in the matter other than the accident of contiguity.

There were, of course, no homes at all for the great majority of the refugees. There were two reasons for this. In the first place, the serious overcrowding, which had necessitated both immigration control and rent control immediately before the Pacific War, began to build up again very shortly after the Japanese surrender, and by 1950 the pressure of population was worse than it had ever been in the Colony's history. In the second place, although conventional war damage was comparatively slight, neglect and decay had made serious inroads into the quality and quantity of domestic buildings. There had been no building at all during the occupation, and world-wide shortage of supplies and shipping in 1946 and 1947 delayed even the rehabilitation of such buildings as could have been quickly repaired.

If accommodation was desperately short, so was land. Even ten years ago there were few vacant levelled sites. Building land in Hong Kong is not found, it is made; either hacked out of the hills or created by reclamation. And there are clear limits to either process. Most of the refugees were farmers, a true cross-section of the population of China which is overwhelmingly agricultural . . . . The rural land already had more farmers than it could support.

. . . It has been said of these people that nothing but land for them to farm would make them happy and contented members of society. There was no land, and if they were to remain and become good citizens they had to be weaned away from their discontent and transformed by some social alchemy from the mentality of the farmer to that of the industrial worker. Until that transformation was achieved, the seeds of discontent would remain. Around them they saw a flourishing community, well established and battening on the post-war boom. The majority were far enough removed from that community in the economic and social sense, but they were still further removed in their political views. The Communist Government of China was rapidly establishing itself and it lost no time in trying to win over the whole-hearted allegiance of overseas Chinese. It was the traditional policy of the Government to hold itself firmly aloof from the internal politics of China and to prevent China's battles being fought out in the streets of Hong Kong. The application of this policy had always required considerable dexterity but the situation which now presented itself called for a subtle combination of firmness, perspicacity, patience and understanding . . .

Hong Kong's economic survival was due to the expansion of, and a revolution in, its industry; and this was made possible in some measure by the three gifts which some of the political refugees brought with them from China: the first a surplus of labour, the second new techniques from the North coupled with a commercial shrewdness and determination superior even to that of the native Cantonese, and the third new capital seeking employment and security . . . There are now 3,319 factories and workshops employing 146,877 persons, and the number of persons directly or indirectly dependent on industry is probably at least 50% of the population. More important, however, has been the revolution in techniques and the improvement of quality. Although in general the emphasis is still on consumer goods, there has been a great diversification of products . . . Since 1949, therefore, industry has been Hong Kong's economic salvation. It has also meant salvation for the refugees though it could provide for many of them little more than a bare subsistence.

How is one to hope to integrate these new communities, which Government is creating as fast as its resources will allow, into the existing social system unless a special and equally comprehensive effort is made throughout the whole range of social welfare? . . . It is perhaps not too much to say that the people of Hong Kong have pledged a portion of their own future for the benefit of strangers who took refuge here; and – sometimes it almost looks as if they are also required to pay interest on the pledge at compound rates.

Document 3.2: HKPRO, HKRS 934/17/47, 'Increase of Staff 1958/59: Community Development Office', enclosed in Colonial Secretary to Secretary for Chinese Affairs, 16 September 1957.

1. Since the Pacific War, Chinese communities in the Colony have shown a very keen interest in the field of social welfare work. The bitter experience of the war years enabled people to realise the utmost significance of mutual help. Within a short period of ten years, hundreds of voluntary organisations of all kinds but under different names have been formed, and there is a tendency that more of these organisations are being planned to meet the immediate demand of the community. The prominent ones among this group are the Kaifong Welfare Associations, Clansmen

and District Associations, Women's Welfare Clubs, Benevolent Societies, Tenants & Residents Associations and the charitable religious bodies . . .

2. The rapid growth of this civic spirit is partly due to the encouragement of government and partly due to the changing political and social environments. The large proportion of the Chinese communities, including local born and refugees, will no longer treat Hong Kong as a transit camp, temporary shelter or adventurer's paradise, but as their permanent and real home where they can settle down peacefully to bring up their young generation with determination and confidence. Moreover, the average men nowadays are not only interested in making their own living or improving their skill and profession, but are proud to have a share in contributing to the wealth and prosperity of the community, in which he may be promised a fair place in the complicated social and political organisation of to-day. Therefore, it is my opinion that civic spirit is not made but it grows in itself, and in Hong Kong this spirit will continue to flourish. Its lasting success depends largely on the government to support and encourage the determination of the creative bodies as discovered in the Kaifong movement whose leaders believe nothing but their own ideal in building a better community under difficult circumstances. It is just as dangerous for government to ignore or overlook as to discourage or whip up their immature enthusiasm. The time has come that it is utmost important to cultivate good leadership among these voluntary organisations.

3. The membership of Kaifong Welfare Associations is steadily increasing. To date, there are over 300,000 members, equivalent to one-tenth of the population in the Colony. Besides operating varied welfare activities in their neighbourhood, both urban and village, they act as a 'bridge' between government departments and citizens. They interest themselves in everything which may be of concern or benefit to their districts, and make strong representations to government on such matters as hawkers, street lighting, road repairs, public latrines and markets, and have cooperated with the government in such other matters as registration of persons, vaccination and diphtheria immunisation campaigns, and spreading propaganda on water saving, fire precautions and blood donation. Moreover, these Kaifong Welfare Associations have done much in the fields of education and public health for underprivileged citizens . . .

5. The history of the Clansmen and District Associations in this Colony is not very long. The sudden prosperity of these associations is due to the influx of refugees from China since 1949. As they came from various provinces in China, speak different dialects, and often feel strangers in a new place, the yearning to meet people of common interests is increasing day by day. These associations had a period of prosperity at their early stage, chiefly due to an outburst of enthusiasm and generous

contributions from the start. It is surprising to note that most of them are gradually withering. The main reason, according to careful investigation and keen observation, may be either due to lack of a staying power, or genuine enthusiasm. But the most important factor is the lack of proper advice and guidance. It is amazing to find out that many of these associations have no system and even no responsible office-bearers.

In this period, the ethos of conservatism and familism could still be observed among most of the Hong Kong Chinese, as the Colonial Secretariat had pointed out in the extract below. People were largely reluctant to engage in politics and interact with officials. Many were instrumental and their everyday lives were occupied by economic concerns. Familial interests were also placed above those of society.

Document 3.3: HKPRO, HKRS 894/1/9, 'Some Characteristics of Chinese Society in Hong Kong: A Brief Note Prepared by the Hong Kong Government', by Colonial Secretariat, Holmes, March 1962.

Hong Kong could not exist on its present form were it not for the special habits, attributes and virtues of the Chinese people who form 98 per cent of the population. The government's policies and methods must at all times be framed in the light of these factors if they are to be realistic, enlightened and effective. What are these characteristics? . . .

Conservatism:

Western influence has made itself felt for centuries in China, but its effect on the social habits of the Chinese people has been comparatively small, even in the coastal areas which have been most exposed to it. The Chinese have been subjected to much bad government in their own country in the past and the traditional attitude of the average Chinese man or woman towards the Hong Kong or any other government is the hope that it will leave him alone as much as possible. The Chinese people, unlike the Indians, are not litigious, and in normal circumstances they are averse from becoming involved with the law or the Police Force or officialdom. We have to avoid regimentation and regulation for their own sakes and we have to proceed cautiously with the introduction even of measures which would be taken for granted in any Western city of this size and density. It may sometimes seem that we concede too much to the traditional habits of the Chinese people, but by comparison with other Asian cities Hong Kong has gone far on the road towards providing a foundation of Western administration and law for this basically Chinese society. But we have gone slowly, for these things cannot be done quickly . . .

Independence:

This does not mean individualism exactly, for in Chinese society the unit is not the individual but the family, which in turn falls into place in an elaborate clan structure where the clan members recognise obligations to kinsmen so distant that in the West they would scarcely be acknowledged at all. The average Chinese think first of his primary duty of supporting, protecting and strengthening his family; he is not accustomed to outside help in this, except from his own clan, and he expects and demands that he should be free to devote all his native ingenuity, resource and industry to this primary task. He does not expect an easy environment, nor does he find one, for the only limit to population in Asia is the number which its agriculture, commerce and industry can support, so that the weak go to the wall. He likes to run his own business and he likes to have his own home. In a fundamentally hostile economic environment he carried on an endless struggle to maintain and improve his family's circumstances. What is more, he enjoys it, and he takes a lot of beating. He will change his job as the economic wind veers and he will constantly strive to provide goods and services at a cheaper rate than his competitors. He will invent new methods, and indeed new trades are invented almost daily in Hong Kong . . . If we regiment or circumscribe it more than is absolutely necessary in the general public interest we shall be throwing away one of our most precious assets.

However, the prevalence of political conservatism does not necessarily mean that there were no complaints against the colonial government, which was asked to intervene in emergencies such as the water shortage in 1963–64. Complaining to newspapers and petitioning officials in Hong Kong and London were the most common ways for people to express their grievances from the 1940s to the 1960s. Reservation in politics could be observed when people reported cases of complaints and shared their views with newspapers anonymously.

Document 3.4: HKPRO, HKRS 70/3/798, 'Water Situation', *South China Morning Post*, 10 December 1963.

In spite of this fact may I nevertheless beg of you the privilege of a portion thereof in which to print a layman's views of Hong Kong's current critical water situation? It is freely admitted by the authorities that we are consuming (and probably wasting) water at a far greater rate than is wise, or safe. With the greatest humility, may I therefore venture to disagree with our authorities, especially the Water Authority, and of course with the Director, Public Works Department, and government, because their present 'laissez-faire' attitude could lead us all (close to four million) straight into economic collapse . . . .Our greatly respected government in all its glory cannot at this moment state categorically that the 'rainy season' will commence on May 15 or June 1, or any other date, and that we shall have a normal, or a greater than normal rainfall in 1964 . . . With this possibility in mind it is therefore suggested, with the utmost respect, that government cannot and should not gamble. The right policy, it is suggested, is for government to prepare us all for yet another 'below normal' rainfall this summer for safety's sake . . . But most important of all is to start at once on the laying of pipelines (four or five 42-inch pipes, or say two or three 104-inch pipe lines from the East river to Shumchun). To delay this most important matter, and mess about with Plover Cove and tunnels which come into operation five to ten years hence is unpardonable.

. . . We need action now to ensure that there is a next generation 'to be cared for'. Let us be realistic. The government to the North proved to be practical and cooperative by the Shumchun Reservoir agreement to supply water-which has saved us a very great deal of inconvenience the past several years– at a fair price– far lower indeed than the sea-water distillation dreams can ever attain.

Section 2. Watershed, 1966–1967

However, Hong Kong's changing demographic composition and the development of the Cold War in the post-war period soon led to changing political culture in the society. Living in an undemocratic colonial political system began to frustrate the post-war baby boomers, who started to 'reflect their life and their role in the local society, and voice their views in a significant way', leading to changes in Hong Kong's political culture in the 1960s.[15] *This shift could be observed in the 1966 riots, which took place in April. In 1965, the Star Ferry Company applied for a fare increase of between 50 and 100 per cent, which was approved by the Transport Advisory Committee in March 1966. So Sau-chung and Lo Kei initiated a protest in early April 1966 which eventually developed into a violent riot that is commonly known as the 1966 Star Ferry riots in Hong Kong history. One person died and many were injured. More than 1,800 people were arrested as a result. The incident led the government to set up a Commission of Inquiry to investigate the root causes of the riots. According to the investigation report, there was evidently a communication gap between the governmemt and the Chinese society.*

15. Steve Tsang, *A Documentary History of Hong Kong Government and Politics* (Hong Kong: Hong Kong University Press, 1995), 248.

Document 3.5: Hong Kong Government Printer, 'VI. The Immediate Cause of the Disturbances and Alleged Cause of Underlying Unrest or Discontent', *Kowloon Disturbance 1966: Report of Commission of Inquiry* (Hong Kong, 1967), 113–15.

415. Discontent at social or economic conditions is seldom sufficient by itself to make people riot. Moreover, conditions in Hong Kong have been improving for the bulk of the population, although there has been some increase in the expression of dissatisfaction in recent years. This is by no means an uncommon companion to improving conditions, when some relaxation in the struggle for existence makes more time and energy available for voicing protest against what has not yet markedly improved or has not improved rapidly enough.

416. The main ground, however, for discounting discontent as the direct cause of the riots lies in the evidence of the participants themselves, which emphasised curiosity and excitement as the principal motives for their participation rather than any strong 'cause'. Moreover, the disturbances were restricted to a comparatively few participants, to a comparatively small area of the Colony and to a comparatively short period of time, which would not, we think, have been the case if discontent had been as widespread and serious as alleged . . .

417. The absence of older persons from the disturbances suggests that the degree of discontent of the population at large has been exaggerated in certain quarters, as also has been the part played by such discontent in the causation of the riots. The fact that the participants were virtually confined to the younger age groups would seem to point in the same direction.

418. Nevertheless, we agree with the view that the demonstrations would have attracted less support from the general public if there had not been some underlying social and economic dissatisfaction in the community . . .

445. . . . If a similar problem arises again, how are the man in the street and the man at the council table to be brought close together, so that the divergence of their views does not become so menacing and so ready an opportunity for conflict as on this occasion? How can this gap be bridged? To put the uniformed or inadequately informed at the council table, so that the advice tendered will reflect these qualities, would not appear to be a very satisfactory solution. It would seem that the solution towards which we must strive is to give the man in the street the measure of information and understanding, that capacity to form a sound judgement which will bring him close to the council table . . .

The 1967 riots inspired by the Cultural Revolution across the border were another turning point affecting Hong Kong's political culture. After the riots, the post-war baby boomers rethought their relations with colonialism. Along with rapid economic development and increased economic and cultural exchanges between Hong Kong and China, a distinctly local political culture emerged. The extract below from the student newsletters of the Hong Kong University Students' Union shows how the younger generation increasingly paid attention to local affairs and the future of Hong Kong.

Document 3.6: 'Editorial: The Big Question Mark', *Undergrad*, Special Issue, 17 May 1967.

Before the recent riots, few people wanted to question the future of Hong Kong. During the riots, there seemed to be no future to many, and now that things are quieting down, this touchy question is again left alone . . . Indeed, everything seems to be going back to normal. There is no serious threat from China at the moment. Left-winged newspapers are certainly making a lot of noise, but the almost empty Communist department stores show how Hong Kong people have turned against the source of our agitation . . . In a time of crisis, everybody is rallying round the Government, we have the support of the Government in Britain, and there is still certainly much confidence in Hong Kong, and this confidence, we believe, should continue.

But the question remains: What is the future like, and what can be done about it? It is very doubtful that there is any way at the moment to find out. But the riots should teach us a lesson, for the cause of the panic is largely that the people in Hong Kong are caught unprepared. While one still hears of attempts to teach people of self-government, one may wonder if it is too much to ask that the problems concerning the future of Hong Kong be brought before the general public. We can raise just one question to start with: What is the attitude of the Foreign Office towards Hong Kong? We do not want a reply from the Foreign Office, but the question should be pondered on.

Or, is independence for Hong Kong really impossible? There are advocates for independence, but we need a critical study on the issue. The point which can be raised here is just that no study has actually been made, or if made, has been widely publicised, about the possibilities of our future. Without this, can we safely talk of reforms, self-government? This is perhaps not a job for a Government Commission, but it is the sort of work local political organisations can carry out. The findings of such studies may turn many faces red, but at least we will know more of our chances and start preparing for it.

Section 3. Reduced Fear towards Officialdom, 1968–1982

This period witnessed a changing political culture in Hong Kong. The sojourner mentality had faded and people started considering Hong Kong to be their home despite continued connections with China. With increased education, there was increased attention paid to local affairs; political discourse became localised. Fear towards officialdom had been greatly reduced and political communications had been improved due to administrative reforms, in particular the introduction of the Independent Commission Against Corruption (ICAC) and the City District Officer Scheme. The public could be mobilised, especially if their economic interests were at stake, although there remained few constitutional demands and little understanding of governance.

Document 3.7: HKPRO, HKRS 488/3/11, 'Speech by D.C. Bray, Deputy Secretary for Home Affairs to Seminar of C.D.O. Staff in Kowloon, Sunday', 25 May 1969.

The People of Hong Kong

7. The people of Hong Kong all have sentimental links with China because they are Chinese. I think you will find that practically everybody will describe as his native place a village or district in China the only exception being those who describe their native place as being in the New Territories and a small number of people not of Chinese origin. While people retain their sentimental links with China they do not on the whole seem to have much liking for the form of government either on the mainland or Taiwan. Most people, I think, are not frightfully interested in the activities of any government anyway and I think one of the most surprising features of the 1967 confrontation was the way in which people demonstrated that they did not want to change the government set up in Hong Kong. One obviously should not conclude from the massive support that the government was given at that time that all government policies command equal support. At the same time I think it was clearly demonstrated that people do not want to give up the basic nature of the government that they have in exchange for becoming a part of Kwang Tung province.

8. China derives advantages from Hong Kong but would also face serious administrative problems if Hong Kong were to absorbed into China. We have here four million people- 10 per cent of the population of Kwang Tung province- all thriving on private enterprise. The absorption of such awkward people into a communist society would be a monstrous task.

9. I believe people here are very conscious of the economic benefits derived from living in Hong Kong. People know what conditions are like in China because a good

many of them visit China at New Year and at other times. They are not like overseas Chinese or other people who lived in Malaysia, American or England. They know what things are like. They do not have to rely on printed material issuing from the country.

10. While people in Hong Kong do not want change in the basic nature of government, I think we must also recognise that the population is becoming increasingly sophisticated and that as time goes on more men and women are becoming concerned about public affairs. This is mainly due to the increasing standard of education that has been brought about in Hong Kong over the last twenty years and we must expect [this] trend to go on in the future.

By developing a clean government, the ICAC generated political dividends for colonial rule and enhanced the credibility of the colonial government. It also created an impression that Hong Kong was more civilised than other Asian countries, including China, where corruption remained entrenched. However, the ICAC was formed in 1974 partly because of the changing local political culture, where people increasingly became more vocal about anti-corruption and less tolerant towards official misdeeds. The following three unofficial abstracts show how newspapers and activists tried to press the government to strengthen anti-corruption measures. China Mail *set up a hotline and an opinion poll to gauge popular views towards corruption and encourage people to share their experiences of bureaucratic corruption. Both were received positively by the public. Elsie Tu (later known as Elsie Elliot), an Urban Councillor, continued her anti-corruption campaign through mass media, even after the formation of the ICAC.*

Document 3.8: 'Rich Get Richer . . . Poor Get Poorer', *China Mail,* 3 April 1973.

The *Mail* has received more than 1,000 replies to our opinion poll. And letters are still coming in.

'I want to submit to you an alarming figure on Government corruption. There is a regulation at the licence unit of the Transport Department. The regulation stipulates a taxi licensee must have a garage where he can park his vehicle. How can there be enough garages or parking places for all the taxis in HK today, especially when the rent is so high? An ordinary taxi licensee has to pay more than $10,000 to Government or other licensees for a taxi. This burden is heavy enough. Where can he find a garage where he can park his car? This is a regulation set up by Government to make the civil servants to get rich quick. Only the small taxi owners suffer. I changed a new car last month and the car seller wanted me to produce a garage paper. But where could I get one? A sales representative of the car firm told me he could do it without a garage paper but had to pay $200 to the license unit of the Transportation Department. I did as he said and gave him the money. Later he came back and asked for another $20 which he said was the commission for an "elder brother", who brought tea during the process of getting my license. Please count it out for me, how many taxi owners have to change their cars in a month? Last month, the Government issued 350 new taxi licenses, another 1,000 are on their way. It would make an alarming corruption figure.'

'Corruption in Hong Kong has become unofficially legalised'. I feel that corruption is inseparable from the social structure and its judiciary system. For example: in Mongkok, a European police officer recently paid a visit to a gambling den with a Chinese inspector. The officers also had a hearty chat with the gamblers there. What's more, I wonder if you have heard of the Rent Collectors. They make more money than the Governor. What are the Rent Collectors, you may ask. They are those people who go around to illegal set-ups to collect protection money for the people in power. They are the collectors of these senior officers.'

Document 3.9: 'A Letter to the Governor', *China Mail*, 20 September 1973.

It must have seemed at times that every day you picked up a newspaper or turned on the TV that there were reports about Hong Kong. And these reports could hardly have made entertaining holiday fare. For Hong Kong, so recently viewed throughout the world as a shining example of a young and industrious community grown rich through its own efforts, has suddenly been transformed into something else. The way they are writing about us today, Hong Kong is some sort of sleazy Sodom and Gomorrah, vicious, cruel and corrupt, living out its final days in an orgy of decadence. I know this is not true. You know it is not true. But I hope you would agree with me that Hong Kong today is living through its greatest crisis of confidence since the bloody days and nights of 1967 . . . This atmosphere of cynicism and distrust, if allowed to continue, will destroy the confidence of Hong Kong to tackle the very real problems that face the colony in an increasingly competitive world . . . Today, because of Peter Godber, the standing and reputation of Hong Kong police – unjustly perhaps – has never been lower in public esteem. The one bad apple, it is argued, must have polluted half the barrel. The only organisation empowered to separate truth from rumour in these allegations is the Anti-Corruption Branch. And that, because it if controlled by the police, is seen by the public– again unjustly perhaps– as a prejudiced court. So it is essential in the interests of justice and the wellbeing of Hong Kong that the Anti-Corruption Branch should be re-established in a way that will inspire total confidence in its work. The first move must be the appointment at its head of a man of unimpeachable integrity and wide experience of life in Hong Kong. A man who is known and trusted by the public and who is impervious to intimidation. Does such a man exist in Hong Kong today? It is now being widely suggested that there does. He is Mr Jack Carter [*sic*], the 51 year-old Secretary for Home Affairs who is due to leave the Government next month to take up a post in private business.

Document 3.10: Elsie Elliott, 'I Want the Whole System Cracked', *Star*, 28 August 1974.

. . . I have one or two questions to ask of the police and the Independent Commission Against Corruption. Recently some students demanded to know what is happening about the Sergeant Khan case; he reported corruption in an area where it is now admitted there was corruption for promotion. Though no action has been taken to look into the charges and set things right, there has been plenty of activity to charge him with petty offences, I suspect to ruin his record and get him out of the force. What is the ICAC doing about this? Then there is the case of two policemen who carried out a vice raid and did a bit of sex business for themselves in the process. We are told they will be not sacked (apparently their crime is not as bad as the crime of reporting corruption). We are assured there will be departmental action. As a taxpayer, I demand to know what that departmental action is. I also insist that they should both be sacked. How can we teach young boys not to indulge in vice, if they are being shown this kind of example by police who take advantage of their position to get sex on the cheap? It is an outrage to the Chinese and I demand their dismissal, though I would prefer punishment too, since they have damaged our society by their examples. Finally, now that charges have been laid for corruption in promotion, in traffic affairs and many other fields, what is being done to reward and safeguard Mr Mak Pui-yuen, who was persecuted in 1970 for reporting extortion from minibus drivers, and has been unable to earn his living as a driver since then? Should he not be rewarded for his courage, instead of going down on record as an 'unreliable informer' as the police involved in such rackets gazetted him? I am sure that many members of the public like myself, want to see, not just a few scapegoats to prove that something is being done, but cracking of the whole system.

In general, most activists employed collaborative strategies to mobilise the public in the 1970s. They often resorted to petitions, signature campaigns, and setting up ad hoc organisations to pool resources, rally support from external parties, and pressurise the colonial government to introduce changes. Direct confrontation was rare and largely confined to the 'radicals'. Both ideological and instrumental reasonings were deployed, as demonstrated by the campaign against telephone rate increases. In 1975, the Hong Kong Telephone Company, the only provider of telephone service in Hong Kong, a monopoly endorsed by the colonial state, was applying for a 70 per cent increase in charges, less than a year since the last increase. This news soon sparked colony-wide protests of unprecedented scale, in which activists adopted both collaborative and confrontational strategies. The various strategies employed by activists showed that there were different political cultures in Hong Kong.

Document 3.11: HKPRO, HKRS 394/27/11, 'Telephone Charges increases', Memo from City District Commissioner (Kowloon), A. F. Neoh to Deputy Direction of Home Affairs, 20 January 1975.

Public temperament continues to heat up during the week. Apart from comments from the press and the escalation of the political lobbying, public temperament has found expression in the hoisting of banners at the Tai Hang Tung Estate and the paintings of large red characters at conspicuous public places in various part of Kowloon. These characters were: 'Hang Haddon Cave' (Financial Secretary of Hong Kong), 'Hang P.C. Woo' (chairman of the Telephone Committee). While these red characters may have been the work of lunatic fringe, public temperament, being as emotional as it has been, thus tend to resonate with the feelings conveyed by these characters.

. . . The momentum of community pressures described last week, have with continuing silence from government, increased . . . This development has followed the wake of the politicising of the three main lobbies represented by the Christian Industrial Committee, the Vici Association and the Reform Club. These three lobbies have been trying to solicit the support of the same group of organisations which comprise kaifong associations, district and clansmen associations, area committees, and even Mutual Aid Committees. As a result, these associations have now either been allied to one of the three lobbies just mentioned or they are taking or are contemplating to take own initiatives.

. . . The main political lobbies have now increased and have in general, tended to fall into two distinct categories-which forms the bulk of the movement, and which still believes in collaborative strategy (i.e. meetings, petitions etc.) and the other which believe that the issue can now only be solved by conflict (i.e. demonstrations, sit-ins and other methods of direction action).

By the mid-1970s, it is evident that political cultures differed in accordance with social class. The upper class enjoyed a relatively flexible lifestyle; they acquired multiple citizenships and only returned to the colony after the 1967 riots died down. The middle class tended to be pro-establishment and politically conservative, advocating caution in the changing state–society relations. The working class were mainly driven by instrumentalism, leading them to keep themselves distant from political activism. They were unaware of the implications of an increasingly responsive reformist colonial state and were not interested in how Hong Kong was governed as long as their livelihoods were unaffected.

Document 3.12: HKPRO, HKRS 394/26/12, 'Public Attitude towards Living in Hong Kong', MOOD, 25 September 1975.

5. In 1967, a significant number of bourgeois families left Hong Kong to settle in the United States and Canada, after selling out their Hong Kong businesses, practices and other property, at very cheap prices. When the confrontation was over, many of them returned to Hong Kong, regretting bitterly their decision to migrate on what turned out to be [a] false alarm, because they discovered to their cost that life in these overseas countries was so taxing and trying.

6. Nevertheless, there has still been in recent years, a tendency for wealthy Hong Kong families to invest in overseas countries. As 'the shrewd hare should have three different holes to hide in when he is being chased', so circumspect and calculating men of substance should establish a foothold in some overseas country to which they can quickly and safely retreat should the status quo in Hong Kong change drastically or suddenly. Some of them went as far as to take out American or Canadian citizenship to gain a guaranteed right of entry into these countries at short notice . . . This social group will certainly continue to live in Hong Kong unless circumstances force them to leave, but they are taking precautions to have a safe place to go in that event.

10. Another group in support of the status quo and social order- and becoming more important politically in the broad sense– are those with established careers and sufficiently substantial vested interests in Hong Kong. They are by no means as wealthy or influential as the magnate entrepreneurs mentioned above, but they have by and large succeeded in going some way up the social ladder, often through hard work and persevering effort, and do not wish to lose that position. Middle-scale proprietors of good going concerns (whether it be a small factory, a prosperous cooked food stall, a team of public light buses, or a successful noodle and wun tun shop), have been doing well and try to do even better . . . .The future may well be uncertain, but since it is determined by factors completely beyond their control, they see no point in worrying about it and thus concentrate their attention and effort on their business and problems.

11. Lower income groups, particularly blue collar workers, are mainly concerned with their workaday livelihood and problems affecting their family. They do not worry or care about much else. Subjects like the future of Hong Kong are too

remote, and too much above them, to be of much interest. Over the years their wage levels rose steadily with the growth of Hong Kong's economy. As their families grew up, their adolescent and adult children reinforced the families' earning power and enlarged the total income.

During the reign of Murray MacLehose (1971–82), a number of administrative, legislative, and institutional reforms were implemented to instil a sense of belonging among the Hong Kong Chinese, which he believed was key to the enhancement of the colonial government's legitimacy. The development of civic pride in particular was important, as the state could not aim at national loyalty; only by convincing the public that their interests were genuinely the object of the government could the legitimacy of the colonial government be retained without the introduction of a democratic electoral system. One major reform was the formation of the ICAC in 1974, after a series of anti-corruption campaigns which took place before and after the escape of Peter Godber, the Deputy District Police Commander of Kowloon in 1973. The ICAC further altered political culture in Hong Kong. People were less reluctant to report corruption and their fear towards officialdom was greatly reduced despite continued misunderstanding about the operation of the ICAC.

Document 3.13: HKPRO, HKRS 471/3/2, 'Public Impressions of the Independent Commission Against Corruption', MOOD, 4 March 1980.

Publicity and community reactions:

Respondents generally felt that ICAC publicity has been extensive and effective. The anti-corruption message was clearly brought home to the community at large. The ICAC hot line - 266366 was also well-known amongst respondents. However, some pointed out that there should be clearer explanation on what constituted corruption or corruption offences. There should also be improvement on the publicity APIs [Announcements in the Public Interests], some of which were dull and monotonous and inclined to be didactic. Respondents regarded the ICAC drama series as making the most impact.

On community relations, respondents felt that the ICAC has done a good job in building up a respectable community image and so far successful efforts had been made towards the long-term aim of inculcating, amongst the general public, a healthy attitude towards corruption. However, some considered that there was the need to step up the good-will visits to MACs [Mutual Aid Committees], kaifongs etc. as much still needs to be done if the intention of the Commission was to correct the wrong attitude prevalent especially amongst the grassroot sectors of not having anything to do with the Commission.

Effectiveness of ICAC:

Respondents felt that the ICAC had been effective in tackling syndicated corruption and that corruption today consisted mainly of cases of individual corruption rather than organised crimes. The Commission has at least made it less necessary for the average man-in-the-street to have to pay his way in order to secure services or facilities . . . The amnesty was still regarded to have dealt a severe blow to the morale and efficiency of the ICAC, the impression of respondents being that the Commission has become less active ever since as indicated in the reduction in the number of prosecutions and then only on small-scale corruption . . .

However, whereas the message of anti-corruption seemed to have been brought home to the community, there was still a certain social stigma which discouraged direct involvement with or working in the ICAC. Less-educated housewives, for example, had said that they would not like their children to work in the Commission. Some young people were also hesitant partly because they believed that their friends might keep them at arms' length or at least with some suspicion. For those young people who had indicated a readiness to join the ICAC, they maintained that they were attracted by the handsome salary and gratuities apart from its being a challenging job.

Despite the shifting political culture, most people were indifferent towards Hong Kong's governance methods and constitutional reforms. As the extract below shows, many did not fully understand the functions of Green and White Papers. Very few people would spend time in reading policy papers, partly due to difficult translations and limited political knowledge. This reveals the persistence of political conservatism and misinformation.

Document 3.14: HKPRO, HKRS 163/13/68, 'Green Papers: Post-Mortem on an Interesting Consultation Exercise', MOOD, 3 May 1978.

A. The Purpose of Green Papers not well understood

a) The majority of respondents did not know what a green paper was, and could not tell the difference between a green paper and a white paper.

b) Some interested observers including those with a good education background, thought that the proposals published in the Green Papers were firm government policies announced prior to implementation.

c) After the correct position had been explained by Home Affairs Department staff, some critics suggested that, instead of calling them green and white papers, terms alien to the Hong Kong community, they should be called by some appropriate Chinese name to reflect their correct status.

d) Although the overall response was initially uninformed with many misconceptions, the consultation exercise was, in retrospect, worthwhile in educating the public on a new process of policy formation. The exchange of ideas between officials and unofficials generally facilitated better communication and understanding.

e) Some radical groups thought that attacking the Green Papers was attacking the government, and worked themselves up to a high pitch of emotional reaction.

B. Some critical after thoughts

a) Issuing and publishing several Green Papers in rapid succession added considerable problems to the endeavour of achieving effective consultation. Some Home Affairs Department contacts did not have sufficient time to digest the contents and comments and suggestions received from them tended to be intuitive and superficial. A certain amount of confusion was created by overlapping areas of interest covered by related Green Papers, e.g. the Green Papers Services for Elderly and Development of Social Security.

b) The Chinese translation, in attempting to adhere as faithfully as possible to the English text, was inevitably somewhat stiff in language style, and was not conducive to easy comprehension, particularly in paragraphs dealing with conceptual argumentation or discussion of policy. One way of overcoming this problem for the future might be to rewrite the paper in Chinese instead of translating the contents sentence by sentence, but this would require the author to be highly proficient in both languages and sufficiently knowledgeable about the subject matter. There might be some risk of misrepresentation, or inadvertent change of emphasis when a Chinese version, for the sake of fluency, had to be rewritten outside the rigid framework of the English text, especially in paragraphs where the expressions had to be chosen with the greatest care to convey accurately sensitive or complicated points.

c) Even well-educated respondents found some parts of the Green Papers difficult to understand, unless they happened to have a good knowledge or background of subject through profession or community services rendered in relevant sectors. It was suggested that the technical jargon and specialised terms should be either omitted or carefully annotated . . .

D. Opinion of the community

a) Except for affected sectors and groups with vested interests, the community at large remained somewhat passive and indifferent to the publications of Green Papers. Only a very limited number took the trouble of reading any green paper in full.

Apart from social class, age also played an important role in one's political attitudes. The younger generation tended to be more critical of the colonial administration and advocated increased political participation as a citizen's obligation. Compared with their older counterparts who adhered to collaborative strategies to pressurise the colonial government, they tended to adopt confrontational strategies to pursue their goals, as the Precious Blood Golden Jubilee Secondary School dispute from February 1977 to July 1978 has demonstrated. In early 1977, teachers found evidence of financial mismanagement at the Precious Blood Golden Jubilee Secondary School. This led to a student campaign that captured the attention of the press and the public. The Education Department subsequently ordered the school's closure. The campaign involved sit-ins, signature campaigns, demonstrations, and petitions, which were generally considered by the public to be 'radical' tactics in the 1970s.

Document 3.15: HKPRO, HKRS 471/3/1/1, 'The Golden Jubilee Controversy', MOOD, Home Affairs Department, 24 May 1978.

3. There was widespread criticism (particularly from parents, headmasters and middle-class community leaders) against the Chan group for staging sit-ins, which these critics deplored as an undesirable and dangerous method of airing grievances by junior secondary students. This view was clearly reflected in editorial comments during this phase, many of which advocated that, regardless of whether the Chan group had a valid complaint, they should seek redress through normal channels. The insistence of the sit-in groups on the dismissal of the principal for apparently no cogent or convincing reason, failed to win public support, and tended to show their case in a bad light.

4. Even during this phase, the Chan group succeeded in lobbying a certain amount of support from some post-secondary student leaders, who because of their own bias and inclinations, were more disposed to believe the radicals' version given by the Chan group. The student leaders suspected Principal Kwan of being reactionary and disciplinarian, and deliberately vindictive and suppressive against the Chan group for having exposed the irregularities of the school management last year. They advocated that the Education Department should have carried out a detailed and impartial investigation before declaring its unequivocal support for Principal Kwan.

In contrast, the general public were inclined to view the Chan group as troublemakers and rabble-rousers exploiting the gullibility of teenage students.

In this period, advocacy groups continued to play an important role in Hong Kong's society. Not only did they and individual activists engage in campaigns that concerned Chinese language, corruption, and utilities, some continued to pressurise the government to introduce changes to improve people's livelihoods and make the colonial polity more representative. The extract below shows that the Reform Club urged the colonial government to introduce more democratic changes in the Urban Council.

Document 3.16: 'More Democracy or We'll Quit, Vows Reform Club', *South China Morning Post*, 19 December 1979.

Reform Club members have decided to withdraw from the Urban Council unless it is made a more democratic body. They have decided not to stand for any more council elections unless elected members are given a majority within it. Every 'true' citizen of Hong Kong– aged over 19 and with either five or seven years' residence– should be allowed to vote at the elections. The ultimatum was issued by the chairman, Mr Brook Bernacchi, at the club's annual general meeting last night . . . The club has been clamouring for a more democratic Hong Kong through reforms to both the Legislative and Urban Councils for many years and has seen several senior Chinese and United Kingdom Government officials in the process. Mr Bernacchi reported that council has been 'going down-hill from the date it was made so-called financially independent in 1973'.

. . . In September, the club approached three Members of Parliament here on a visit . . . In February, the club urged the Government to curb the influx of Chinese immigrants . . . During the year, the welfare section of the club handled over 1,000 cases on housing, legal assistance, employment and family disputes. About 70 per cent of the cases were dealt with successfully and many of the rest were given help of some kind, Mr Bernacchi said.

Section 4. Changing and Diverging Views towards Political Communication and Democratisation, 1982–1988

At the beginning of the Sino-British negotiations, the general public had little desire for major constitutional reforms, meaning that the government had no clear mandate for change. By 1984, opinions were obviously different. Although not everyone supported major constitutional reforms/democratisation, appointing Legislative Councillors was no longer considered appropriate and officials anticipated that public support for democratisation would continue to rise. Many also considered existing political communication channels to be inadequate.

Document 3.17: HKPRO, HKRS 1443/4/38, 'Report on a Poll on What People Think about the Government Generally (1984)' (Second Benchmark Survey on Public Attitudes), by Home Affairs Branch Government Secretariat, June 1984.

Representative Government

7. Two years ago, people expressed no strong feelings about the system of appointment of Legislative Councillors by the Governor. There was no clear mandate for change. The mood is now obviously different. The system is no longer considered appropriate although the number of people who really want to see changes is still less than half. This trend is likely to continue and public support for changes will increase.

Communication with the People

8. There has been no change in the percentage of people being aware of channels of communication with the government and in the proportion of people regarding the channels as inadequate; i.e. slightly over half of the people are aware of the channels and six out of ten of those who know the channels exist consider them inadequate.

9. The government's efforts in disseminating information are also thought to be inadequate. Six in ten of those who believe the government keeps the public informed considered the information disseminated inadequate.

After the agreement of the Sino-British Declarations, there were renewed demands for the introduction of direct elections in the Legislative Council although opinions differed on the pace and extent of democratisation. By 1986, the colonial government felt there was a general understanding that democratisation could not go further, as bound by the Basic Law. However, the issue of constitutional reforms continued to attract the greatest public interest, with diverging views, as the following two extracts reveal.

Document 3.18: HKPRO, HKRS 394/29/53, 'Situation and Mood in Hong Kong', telegram from Hong Kong to E. Youde, 1 September 1986.

Constitutional Government and the Basic Law

4. General understanding that the 1987 review cannot go further in changing the structure than the Basic Law is likely to go. Importance of convergence well understood, but Chinese must understand that they should take into account Hong Kong opinion. Increasing dialogue with Chinese officials at various level is important and fully supported by the Executive Council.

5. Public interest for the 1987 review focuses principally on:

a) possibility of some directly elected members to the Legislative Council– it seems that a small step in this direction would be generally acceptable, but this is not by any means a certainty, and there are indications that opinion is swinging against it;

b) whether the Governor should be replaced as the President of Legislative Council;

c) whether there should be some change in the way in which Executive Council members are appointed/selected;

d) anumber of less important issues such as the voting age and the relationships of Urban Council/Regional Council and the District Boards.

Document 3.19: TNA, FCO 40/1927, 'Representation Government: Memorandum by the Foreign and Commonwealth Office', Cabinet Defence and Overseas Policy Committee Sub-Committee on Hong Kong, October 1986.

The state of opinion in Hong Kong on the 1987 Review

13. The issue of direct elections continued to attract the greatest public interest. Views are divided. Those strongly in support of direct elections maintain they are the only way of ensuring the evolution of a genuinely representative government, capable of sustaining the 'high degree of autonomy' provided for in the Joint Declaration. Those against argue that the Hong Kong community is not ready for such a development, which could be destabilising. The debate is now focusing increasingly on the timing of the introduction of direct elections and the proportion of Legislative Council members to be selected by this method. There seems to have been an acceptance, even among the more conversative business and professional groupings, that the direct election of up to 25 per cent of the Legislative Council would be tolerable: and might neutralise demands for even more radical change. However, business groups are in private becoming increasingly doubtful about the wisdom of introducing them in 1988.

14. Despite recent controversy surrounding the role of appointed members there is still a wide measure of public supported for retention of a substantial appointed element in the Legislative Council. The system of indirect elections based on functional constituencies is also generally supported, and there are calls for its further expansion.

15. There is less unanimity of view on the electoral college. Members of the District boards and two regional councils will probably support its retention, because

it provides them with district access to membership of the Legislative Council. However, there is concern that membership of the electoral college is too narrowly-based. If the concept is to be retained there is a widespread feeling that the system of election should be changed to avoid the unpleasant factional rivalries within District Boards which developed in 1985.

The period witnessed the opening up of the colonial polity and the emergence of political parties. These political parties had different views towards democratisation. For example, those that were comprised of grassroots groups, business, and industrial sectors were largely against rapid democratisation as they believed it would jeopardise Hong Kong's political stability, while intellectuals within the middle class, such as the Joint Committee for the Promotion of Democratic Government, largely advocated and supported direct elections to safeguard Hong Kong's future autonomy.

Document 3.20: 'Group Appeals for More Democracy', *South China Morning Post*, 5 September 1988.

A delegation from the Joint Committee on the Promotion of Democratic Government will go to Beijing at the end of this month to lobby Chinese officials for greater democracy in Hong Kong after 1997.

A member of the committee's secretariat, Mr. Wai Hing-cheung, said they would leave on September 27 for a three-day visit.

While in Beijing, they hope to see the secretary-general of the Basic Law Drafting Committee, Mr. Li Hou, to present their views.

The committee which consists of more than 100 local social and political groups, calls for the future chief executive to be chosen by a 'one man, one vote' system.

It also says that future legislature should comprise no fewer than 50 per cent of directly elected seats.

Meanwhile, a total of 26,220 signatures were collected at all MTR [Mass Transit Railway] and KCR [Kowloon–Canton Railway] stations between 10 am and 6 pm yesterday in a campaign aimed at rallying public support for the committee's recommendations.

Section 5. Expanding Political Parties and Political Resilience, 1989–1997

The Tiananmen incident in 1989 changed Hong Kong's political culture, especially among students and the younger generation, who had become even more anti-establishment and spontaneous. And for conservatives and democrats, despite political differences, the incident encouraged them to strengthen the case for protection rooted in a strong, locally based political authority with existing legal and institutional frameworks. Political parties were moreover expanding, including the formation of the pro-Beijing Democratic Alliance for the Betterment of Hong Kong and the merger between the United Democrats and the Meeting Point, which further stimulated public discourse. Political resilience had also been strengthened, as the three extracts below show.

Document 3.21: 'China's Favoured Hong Kong Son', *South China Morning Post*, 21 May 1992.

The territory's first pro-China political party, the Democratic Alliance for the Betterment of Hong Kong, was launched on Tuesday . . .

Where the Democratic Alliance and its trade union backers most clearly differ from United Democrats, although not necessarily from other liberal groups, such as Meeting Point or the Association for Democracy and People's Livelihood, is on the need for better and more cooperative relations with China.

He [Legislative Councillor Tam Yiu-chung] claims his organisation can represent all the Hong Kong people. But he leaves the impression that his understanding of 'representation' would sit better with an appointed legislator or one of China's new Hong Kong advisers, several of whom are founder members of the Democratic Alliance than with the founder of a fledgeling party aiming for direct election.

Not only has he not yet decided to stand for election, but he does not seem to see any urgency in acceleration in democratic development. On the contrary, he argues that democracy was introduced by the British to present China with a changed society. It would not have happened so quickly without the Joint Declaration . . . He side-steps several questions as to whether this was an act of British hypocrisy or a deliberate provocation of China, and refuses to say why Britain should behave in such way. He explains China's opposition is based on a desire to maintain stability and prosperity and on a fear more rapid change may not be accepted by society as a whole.

Document 3.22: TNA, FCO 40/3575, 'Sino-British Dispute over Hong Kong's Constitutional Development', Talking Points, 6 November 1992.

1. Respondents continued to be concerned over the prevailing dispute over Hong Kong's constitutional development. Views remained divided as to whether any 'deal' existed as reflected from the seven documents released by the British and Chinese governments. While most did not consider that there had been a legally binding

agreement, many felt that some form of tacit understanding had been reached. Some believed that there had been a general consensus on the direction of the 1995 electoral arrangements and that both sides had acknowledged the need for further consultation on details. These felt that the proposals had offended the spirit, if not the letter, of the Basic Law. Some suggested that the different views expressed by the two sides were a result of different interpretations and different cultural backgrounds. Some respondents commented that the disclosure of the documents only added fuel to the dispute, while some other respondents felt that the documents reflected that both sides did not represent to the full the interest of the Hong Kong people. Respondents however held that they had the right to know and urged that future negotiations on Hong Kong should be made more transparent to the public.

2. Many respondents expressed their wish that the dispute would end soon and that the matter could be resolved rationally. Some noticed that there were signs that talks might be able to resume and that officials in the Hong Kong and Macau Office had ceased to hurl criticisms at the Governor's proposals during the past week. They urged that the Joint Liaison Group should be convened to discuss ways to break the ice.

3. A number of respondents indicated their preference to see the prevailing freedoms and stability continue rather than some democracy. Some other respondents felt that the Legislative Council debate should focus on the various welfare services proposals, the implementation of which should not be held up by the argument over political reforms.

Document 3.23: TNA, FCO 40/3932, 'The Mood of the Community', telegram from Hong Kong to Foreign and Commonwealth Office, 31 December 1993.

1. The Minister will find that since his September visit, the territory has become more robustly self-confident than before despite the breakdown of constitutional talks with the CPG. The business community is very upbeat about economic prospects for 1994. Support for the administration remains steady and solid . . .

'Political resilience' of the territory

3. The community displayed little anxiety about the Chinese People's Government's (CPG) indignation. The public at large seemed somewhat relieved that, at least, the constitutional impasse was to be resolved one way or another after so many months of fruitless diplomatic wangling.

4. The current level of optimism is in marked contrast to the anxiety so much in evidence, particularly among the business community, almost exactly a year ago. In part, Hong Kong has benefited from a shift in CPG tactics. Peking has learnt from its mistakes when it attempted to intimidate the territory in the winter of 1992. Instead, the CPG has gone out of its way in recent weeks to reassure the community of a continuing commitment to its economic well-being.

6. The opinion polls indicate that by now, the community has developed a considerable capacity to reach its own assessment of Hong Kong's political needs even in the face of strident Peking propaganda.

Suggested Readings

Hoadley, J. S. 'Hong Kong Is the Lifeboat: Notes on Political Culture and Socialization'. *Journal of Oriental Studies* 8 (1970): 206–18.

King, Ambrose Y. 'Administrative Absorption of Politics in Hong Kong: Emphasis on the Grass Roots Level'. *Asian Survey* 15, no. 5 (1975): 422–39.

King, Ambrose Y. 'The Political Culture of Kwun Tong: A Chinese Community in Hong Kong'. *Asian Journal of Social Science* 5, no. 1 (1977): 123–41.

Lam, Wai-man. *Understanding the Political Culture of Hong Kong: The Paradox of Activism and Depoliticization*. New York: M.E. Sharpe, 2004.

Lau, Siu-kai. 'Chinese Familism in an Urban-Industrial Setting: The Case of Hong Kong'. *Journal of Marriage and Family* 43, no. 4 (1981): 978–86.

Lau, Siu-kai. *Society and Politics in Hong Kong*. Hong Kong: Chinese University of Hong Kong Press, 1982.

Mok, Florence. *Covert Colonialism: Governance, Surveillance and Policymaking in British Hong Kong, c. 1966–97*. Manchester: Manchester University Press, 2023.

Mok, Florence. 'Public Opinion Polls and Covert Colonialism in British Hong Kong'. *China Information* 33, no. 1 (2023): 66–87.

Wong, Thomas, and Tai-lok Lui. *From One Brand of Politics to One Brand of Political Culture*. Hong Kong: Hong Kong Institute of Asia-Pacific Studies, 1992.

4
Economy and Trade

James Fellows[1]

The history of Hong Kong's post-war economic trajectory has been narrativised and mythologised in both contemporary and subsequent accounts. Internal and external champions of the Hong Kong 'success story' – Hong Kong experienced double-digit economic growth for much of the post-war period – often attributed it to the colony's combination of economic liberalism and Chinese industriousness. Academic historical accounts have taken a more nuanced approach, focusing instead on unpicking the combination of local, regional, and global conditions which underpinned the various shifts and trends in Hong Kong's post-war economy, and identifying its continuities as well as its transformations.

Scholars have shown that it was Hong Kong's position in relation to the Chinese mainland that most shaped its economic trajectory – the territory's relative geographical isolation and political separation provided an outlet for Chinese people and capital during moments of turmoil and isolation on the mainland.[2] When China was at its most isolated from the 1950s to the 1970s, Hong Kong experienced rapid industrial growth, becoming one of the world's leading textile and clothing exporters in the 1960s and 1970s – a phenomenon which has been the attention of much academic enquiry.[3] Scholarship has likewise shown how in the late 1970s and into the 1980s, when China began to re-engage with the global capitalist economy, Hong

1. I am grateful to the Hong Kong General Chamber of Commerce, the Modern Records Centre (University of Warwick), and the Hong Kong Heritage Project for their permission to reproduce excerpts from their holdings. Thanks also go to Catherine Schenk for advice on finding material, and to K. Y. Lau for help with translation.
2. Ho-Fung Hung, *City on the Edge: Hong Kong under Chinese Rule* (Cambridge: Cambridge University Press, 2022); John M. Carroll, *Edge of Empires: Chinese Elites and British Colonials in Hong Kong* (Cambridge, MA: Harvard University Press, 2005).
3. For example, Yin-Ping Ho, *Trade, Industrial Restructuring and Development in Hong Kong* (Honolulu: University of Hawai'i Press, 1992).

Kong was best placed to reap the benefits, becoming China's largest source of external investment. China's market reforms therefore facilitated a new level of regional economic integration in the Pearl River Delta region.[4]

Works have also explored how Hong Kong's international links – in terms of financial and monetary systems, but also networks of people – shaped the colony's economy during this period.[5] This includes the implications of Hong Kong's colonial status, in areas such as trade rights, monetary system, and financial policy, with much focus on the colonial administration's attempts to obtain autonomy in these areas in order to advance Hong Kong's distinct economic interests (as they perceived them).[6] At the same time, Hong Kong elites with overseas ties in places other than Britain, in particular the United States, reoriented Hong Kong's economic interests away from the metropole, further reducing the importance of the colonial connection.[7]

Furthermore, in much work focused on the local level, and aided by the availability of government records, the focus is on industrial and commercial policy and state–business relations. Such work interrogates the supposed exceptionalism of the political economic model in the colony – one of an ideological commitment to laissez-faire or 'positive non-interventionism' – and takes a more nuanced approach to exploring how the state managed competing interest groups, such as the traditional European merchant class, local industrialists, and emigres from Shanghai.[8] Finally, as employment conditions in Hong Kong faced much scrutiny during the colony's industrial peak, studies have explored labour relations in the colony, and how these were shaped by local and metropolitan pressures and interests.[9]

---

4. For example, Wang Daonan, 'The Economic Relations between China and Hong Kong: Prospects and Principles', in *Industrial and Trade Development in Hong Kong*, ed. Edward K. Y. Chen, Mee-Kau Nyaw, and Teresa Y. C. Wong (Hong Kong: Centre of Asian Studies, University of Hong Kong, 1991), 447–63.
5. Catherine R. Schenk, *Hong Kong as an International Finance Centre: Emergence and Development 1945–65* (London and New York: Routledge, 2001).
6. Ray Yep, ed., *Negotiating Autonomy in Greater China: Hong Kong and Its Sovereign Before and After 1997* (Copenhagen: Nordic Institute of Asian Studies, 2013); James Fellows, 'Britain, European Economic Community Enlargement, and "Decolonisation" in Hong Kong, 1967–1973', *The International History Review* 41, no. 4 (2019): 753–74.
7. Peter E. Hamilton, *Made in Hong Kong: Transpacific Networks and a New History of Globalization* (New York: Columbia University Press, 2021).
8. Tak-Wing Ngo, 'Industrial History and the Artifice of Laissez-Faire Colonialism', in *Hong Kong's History: State and Society under Colonial Rule*, ed. Tak-Wing Ngo (London: Routledge, 1999), 119–40; Leo F. Goodstadt, *Uneasy Partners: The Conflict Between Public Interest and Private Profit in Hong Kong* (Hong Kong: Hong Kong University Press, 2005); Wong, Siu-Lun, *Emigrant Entrepreneurs: Shanghai Industrialists in Hong Kong* (Hong Kong: Oxford University Press, 1988).
9. For example, David Clayton, 'From "Free" to "Fair" Trade: The Evolution of Labour Laws in Colonial Hong Kong, 1958–62', *Journal of Imperial and Commonwealth History* 25, no. 2 (2007): 263–82.

Given the breadth of historical work on Hong Kong's post-war economy, the sources that follow touch on some (but by no means all) of these aspects and aim to give an indication of the diversity of material available. This includes declassified government records in Britain and Hong Kong, proceedings of Hong Kong's Legislative Council, records and speeches by commercial organisations representing Hong Kong businesses, oral histories by workers and entrepreneurs, government-published statistics, and other miscellaneous material such as promotional material and a report by a mainland Chinese official.

Section 1. Post-war Economic Reconstruction and Restructuring

Hong Kong entered an eight-month period of military administration following liberation from Japanese occupation in 1945, followed by the restoration of civil rule on 1 May 1946. In order to rehabilitate Hong Kong's economy and overcome resource shortages, during the latter half of the 1940s and into the early 1950s the colonial government monopolised the import and distribution of not only foodstuffs, but also raw materials – an episode often downplayed in accounts emphasising Hong Kong's 'laissez-faire' ethos.[10] *As the account of this period by the Hong Kong General Chamber of Commerce (HKGCC) below indicates, this was a radical departure from the colony's usual commitment to free trade. The HKGCC, established in 1861, was originally dominated by European merchant firms and had close links with the colonial government and with chambers of commerce in Britain, and it was therefore instrumental in representing expatriate business interests in the colony.*[11]

Document 4.1: Hong Kong General Chamber of Commerce, *Report for the Year 1941–1946*, 10–13.[12]

The Liberation.

When the Colony was liberated at the end of August, 1945, a short interregnum occurred during which Colonial Government officials from the Internment Camp, under the leadership of Mr. F. C. Gimson, C.M.G. (now Sir Franklin Gimson) took charge of affairs. To this the Japanese consented. The Military Administration, which was set up on September 1, 1945, therefore found the rudiments of government already begun and the principal public services in partial operation, the

10. Schenk, *Hong Kong as an International Finance Centre*, 6–7.
11. David W. Clayton, 'Industrialization and Institutional Change in Hong Kong 1842–1960', in *Asia Pacific Dynamism*, ed. A. J. H. Latham and Heita Kawakatsu (London: Routledge, 2000), 152.
12. This source is available online at https://www.chamber.org.hk/en/about/annual.aspx.

Japanese officials and soldiery taking orders from the interim administration and helping to maintain order. Rear-Admiral C. J. H. Harcourt, C.B., (now Vice-Admiral Sir Cecil Harcourt, K.C.B.), was in command of the Military Administration which re-established the public office, and set up new ones manned by Naval, Military and Air Force officers, some of them former public officials temporarily in uniform. Brigadier D. M. MacDougall, C.M.G. (Hong Kong Cadet Service) was in charge of Civil Affairs with Col. W. M. Thomson (of the same Service) second-in-command.

It had been announced that for six months there would be no commercial trading but that the Military Administration would be responsible for necessary supplies of foodstuffs and everything else necessary for the maintenance of the life of the people. This came as a surprise to a community which lives by world-trade and gave rise to many and varied problems. Business men who had been in prisoner-of-war or internment camps were advised to "Go, Get Fit and Come Back" (as a newspaper headline summarised the official advice). Large firms were in a position to find substitute staffs: those who owned one-man businesses were naturally loth to withdraw lest business connections should be lost forever. . . .

. . . Stimulating Trade.

The Department of Supplies, Trade and Industry was at this time functioning as the principal trading organisation in the Colony. It despatched special missions to all neighbouring countries to obtain necessary supplies; e.g. Borneo for firewood; Shanghai and Hongay for coal and Kwongchowan for peanut oil. In December a representative mission, including some business men, went to Australia to explore the possibilities of obtaining building materials, furniture and household supplies. Endeavours were made in January to get cotton yarn from India in order to set local factories in operation. Cotton yarn, however, was found to be one of the world's most acute shortages. India could not spare any, having the needs of her own hand loom weavers to consider. The Department of Supplies, Trade and Industry therefore requisitioned such cotton yarn as the Japanese had left in the Colony and turned it over to certain suitable weaving factories for conversion into canvas so that the rubber shoe industry could manufacture footwear to supply local demand at controlled prices. Their costs of operation were too high to permit them to enter their pre-war markets, principally the United Kingdom and the British West Indies: furthermore the quantities it was possible for them to manufacture barely met local needs. They received further assistance from the Department in obtaining supplies of rubber from Malaya.

The change-over from worthless yen to the Hong Kong dollar (linked with sterling at the former rate of 1s 3d. to the dollar), was a painful but necessary operation and brought its own problems for the Military Administration. To ease the shock, various emergency measures were adopted, including the allocation of $150,000 to provide free food for the destitute (never less than 20,000 a day); and the employment of tens of thousands of labourers to clear the streets of refuse. Scavenging was an activity which the Japanese had allowed to get into arrear to a dangerous degree.

Section 2. Industrial Take-off

Hong Kong was traditionally a commercial entrepôt for China's regional and global trade, but often overlooked is the early emergence of industry in the nineteenth century, in sectors such as shipbuilding, rope-making, sugar refining, and cotton spinning and weaving. As the official account below outlines, preferential trade relations with Britain and the Commonwealth also provided a spur to export-oriented manufacturing in the colony before the war. The colony's industrial development accelerated in the post-war decades, aided by an influx of labour and capital from mainland China. Such official accounts also identified embargoes against China as effectively ending Hong Kong's traditional economic lifeblood – the re-export trade to China. Such trade continued via smuggling, however, and Hong Kong continued to be the most important avenue of re-exports from (rather than to) China.[13] *Nevertheless, manufacturing grew to become the most important source of employment in the colony.*

Document 4.2: *Hong Kong: Annual Report 1955* (Hong Kong: Government Printer), 49–51.

In the last ten years the pattern of Hong Kong's economy has changed profoundly, and industry which, prior to the Second World War, was only of minor importance, has now assumed the major role.

The Colony's first industries were in the nature of services allied to the development of the port. The earliest was, of course, shipbuilding and repairing. The first locally built vessel, the *Celestial*, 80 tons, was launched in 1943. Two sugar refineries were established, the first in 1878, the second in 1882, not so much to satisfy the needs of the then small population, but the requirements of ships' victualling officers. In 1885 a rope factory was started, again primarily to cater for the seafaring trade. A cement factory was transferred to Hong Kong from Macau in 1899.

At times there were tentative efforts to set up new modern industries, but these faded out, like the spinning mill which was started in 1899 and closed down a few

13. Ho, *Trade, Industrial Restructuring and Development*, 55–57.

years later. However, some industries obtained a firm foothold, such as the manufacture of rattan ware, which started in 1902, and of cotton knitted singlets and vests, which started in 1910. These however flourished more or less unnoticed amid the Colony's growing entrepôt activities.

The first real stirrings in industry occurred during the First World War, and in the years following there was some expansion. A weaving factory, operating 20 hand looms, was established in 1922, and in 1927 the first flashlight factory came into being.

It was the Ottawa Agreement of 1932, under which Hong Kong products became entitled to Imperial Preference, which provided the first major encouragement to local industry, assisting existing manufacturers to seek wider markets for their goods and attracting new investors. Additional stimulus was provided in the first years of the Second World War, when locally-manufactured military and civilian supplies aided the Allied cause. It is estimated that in 1940 there were about 800 factories.

Factory rehabilitation after almost four years of enemy occupation was rapid, urged on by an acute shortage of goods throughout the whole of war-scarred South-East Asia. A vital year for local industry was 1948, when the influx of refugees from China reached its peak. While most arrived destitute, many brought capital and technical skill which found ready employment in Hong Kong.

When the Korean War and the resultant embargo on trade in strategic materials with China drastically reduced the volume of Hong Kong's commerce, only industrial expansion could ward off the dangers threatening economic stability and provide employment for a greatly swollen and still increasing population. Local manufacturers reacted quickly to the new situation, and, in spite of difficulties in obtaining certain raw materials, a growing volume and range of Hong Kong goods from many new industries, and from re-invigorated older ones, began to flow out to the world.

Today Hong Kong possesses 2,925 registered and recorded factories, employing a labour force of 129,465 workers. In addition to these registered undertakings, there is a very large number of smaller concerns, many of which pursue handicraft activities of a traditionally Chinese character, some of which have been set up by refugees. It is estimated that just under 200,000 people find employment in these smaller industrial undertakings.

The variety of goods turned out by local industry is considerable, but, in general, while heavier industries, such as shipbuilding, continue to be important, the Colony has become noted for the price, quality and range of the products of its light industries. Among the most important of these products are cotton piece-goods, cotton yarns, towelling, ready-made garments of all kinds, enamelware, aluminium ware, torches, torch batteries and bulbs, vacuum flasks, plasticware, paints and varnishes, rubber and leather footwear, and rattan ware. Among the traditional Chinese goods produced, brocade piece-goods, embroideries and drawnwork, crocheted gloves and paper novelties are the best-known.

In 1954 exports of local products were valued at £42,617,436. In 1955 this figure rose to £45,644,910, representing 29% of the total value of the Colony's exports. The United Kingdom was the best customer. Although South-East Asian countries are naturally important buyers of Hong Kong goods, economic restrictions in some parts of the region and industrialization in others have forced the Colony's merchants and manufacturers to look further afield for new markets.

There is without doubt scope for further industrial development in the Colony, but certain difficulties have to be faced. The first of these is the severe shortage of water. This will be ameliorated to some extent when Tai Lam Chung Reservoir is completed. The second difficulty is a shortage of suitable industrial land in Hong Kong's hilly terrain. In the past much of the Colony's residential and commercial development has been achieved by the simple expedient of excavating hillsides and using the spoil to reclaim land from the sea. This method is being used to make the reclamation at Kun Tong referred to in the Review of the Year, and which will provide within the next few years about 140 acres of land for industrial sites.

Hong Kong's early industrial growth was primarily in labour-intensive, light manufactures such as clothing, textiles, electronics, toys, and other plastic goods. Hong Kong's rapid population growth provided an abundance of cheap labour, making the colony's goods highly price-competitive in global markets. In the account below, Yeung Bo Yee, born in 1946, recalls her experience of living and working in To Kwa Wan in Kowloon in the 1960s. Her varied experience in the manufacturing industry sheds light on the diverse nature of such employment, from standard factory jobs to more casual work in the form of subcontracting and homework, a form of employment particularly common among women.[14] *In this excerpt Yeung begins by describing the plastic factory on the ground floor of her residence on Hung Wan Street before describing the practice of outsourcing in various industries.*

14. Tai-lok Lui, *Waged Work at Home: The Social Organization of Industrial Outwork in Hong Kong* (Aldershot: Avebury, 1994).

Document 4.3: 'Types of sub-contracting jobs casual workers like Yeung Bo Yee received from factory buildings surrounding Thirteen Streets', Yeung Bo Yee, 03/04/2013 (translated).[15]

Interviewer: May I ask if there were any factories located between the residential buildings at that time?

Yeung: There was a plastic factory located on the ground floor of my residence. In the early days, most of Hong Kong's factories were plastic factories, and the shops located on the ground floor of my residence were also plastic factories.

Interviewer: Are there any ground floor shops in the buildings on the nearby streets?

Yeung: Yes, each building has multiple shops on the ground floor. In the past, most of them were plastic factories whose main task was to put plastic raw materials into machines and press out plastic moulds.

Interviewer: What street are the plastic factories located on?

Yeung: They are located on the ground floor of my residence.

Interviewer: Is it on Hung Wan Street?

Yeung: It's Hung Wan Street. Shim Luen Street sells liquor and grains such as rice. Shim Luen Street is near Mok Cheong Street. Why do I know? My father asked me to buy liquor and gave me gifts. I remember those shops also sold rice. The plastic factory was also located nearby. The ground floor of my residence later became a place for manufacturing velvet flowers. I remember that velvet flowers were considered high-end products at that time.

Interviewer: So do you remember what was inside the plastic factory at that time?

Yeung: There were machines inside the factory.

Interviewer: How many machines were there approximately?

Yeung: There were at least six machines. When the central part of each mould was removed, all the moulds could be connected together.

Interviewer: Were the workers male at that time?

15. From *Hong Kong Voices Oral History Archives*, Hong Kong Memory website: https://www.hkmemory.hk.

Yeung: All of the workers were male. This job was very profitable at that time. Garment factories also outsourced the sewing and cutting of threads for jeans, as well as the stitching of buttons on clothes for children's dolls.

Interviewer: Have you ever seen people bringing work back home?

Yeung: Yes. At that time, plastic factories often outsourced the threading process to workers like me, who then brought the moulds home to connect them.

Interviewer: Where did you get the work?

Yeung: At the factory downstairs from my residence. Many factories could be found there. Later, the work changed and I began making velvet flowers. In fact, having factories downstairs from our residence was very dangerous.

Interviewer: Were all of the factories the same one?

Yeung: No, there were many different ones. All the factories offered a lot of outsourcing jobs for casual workers. Plant owners often posted street bills to recruit manpower, and some even sent trucks to designated places to collect finished goods. Job opportunities were plentiful back then, but now they're scarce. At the time, store rents were also cheap.

Interviewer: So did you notice that these factories were all located downstairs from residential buildings?

Yeung: Most of them were located downstairs from residential buildings.

Interviewer: On Hung Wan Street, there were many factories, such as plastic factories and velvet flower factories. Do you know which other streets had factories?

Yeung: I didn't pay attention to other streets because I rarely went into them. I only knew that there were jobs in the factory buildings on Mok Cheong Street when I went to school. I often did work such as sewing baby pants and diapers, trimming threads, and doing embroidery. I really enjoyed doing embroidery back then. Nowadays, all of these are gone.

Interviewer: Did all of these occur prior to marriage?

Yeung: Yes, I was not yet married.

Interviewer: Did you continue your studies at that time?

Yeung: Yes, I was concurrently studying and working.

Interviewer: How did you become aware of job opportunities at the factory?

Yeung: The factory advertised job openings and occasionally dispatched job vehicles to collect goods, with employees able to inquire about positions and prepare accordingly. Nowadays, such practices are less common, but it was still possible to earn an income from home provided one was willing to work. However, the present circumstances make it much more challenging.

Interviewer: Did you ever collect job assignments from the job vehicles?

Yeung: No, I did not. I seldom sewed jeans as bolts of denim fabric were too heavy to handle.

Hong Kong's successful penetration into foreign markets was met with a protectionist backlash, particularly in the clothing and textile industries in the UK, Europe, and the United States: industry representatives, politicians, and trade unionists argued that cheap imports from Hong Kong were an unfair source of competition. They argued that Hong Kong manufacturers used 'sweated labour' and re-exported falsely labelled goods from Japan and China to take advantage of preferential duties. Politicians, journalists, and academics also criticised the use of child labour in the colony. In response to such allegations, the colonial state and groups representing industrial interests began an information counter-offensive.[16] *The 1959 pamphlet 'Hong Kong and Its Textile Industry', printed by the local English-language newspaper* South China Morning Post *and circulated in Britain, was one such example. The pamphlet directly responds to various 'allegations' made against Hong Kong, such as workers being underpaid, but in doing so focuses on the conditions inside larger spinning mills. Other restrictions, such as on working hours, are dismissed as unwanted by the workers themselves.*

Document 4.4: HKPRO, Government Records Service, 382.45677 HON., Hong Kong General Chamber of Commerce, *Hong Kong and Its Textile Industry* (Hong Kong: South China Morning Post, *c.* 1959).

Cost of Labour.

This is the main basis of the claim for protection and one on which it is virtually impossible to draw a true comparison. The cash take home of the Hong Kong worker is substantially lower than that of his counterpart in Lancashire and his standard of living is also lower. This standard is however high when viewed against the general pattern of life in the Far East. It must be remembered that food, clothing, and most other essentials are considerably cheaper in Hong Kong than in the U.K., and that in

16. David Clayton, 'Constructing Colonial Capitalism: The Public Relations Campaigns of Hong Kong Business Groups, 1959–1966', in *Imagining Britain's Economic Future, c.1800–1975: Trade, Consumerism, and Global Markets,* ed. David Thackeray, Andrew Thompson, and Richard Toye (London: Palgrave Macmillan, 2018), 231–51.

addition to this, the 19 principal mills in Hong Kong provide many social benefits including free housing with water, light and heat, free medical treatment, and free or subsidised meals. In terms of real worth to the individual, the disparity is much smaller than would be indicated by a comparison of figures . . . The only valid yardstick is as to whether the wages paid, taking all circumstances into account, represent a fair return to the Hong Kong worker. This we believe they do.

A precisely similar comparison could be drawn between wage levels in Lancashire and those in the United States, Canada and Australia. To ask for protection on grounds of comparative wage costs, as Lancashire is doing against India, Pakistan and Hong Kong, is clearly a most dangerous precedent.

Hong Kong has been accused of employing "sweated" labour. At least three quarters of all cloth shipped to the U.K. from Hong Kong is spun and woven in the 19 mills referred to above. Nine of these work three eight hour shifts and the rest two twelve-hour shifts, including overtime. Conditions in the remainder of the industry are admittedly less satisfactory and it is hoped that they can be improved. The nature of many of them is such that it will be far from easy to devise appropriate legislation which will be practically enforceable but as shown above their output represents a relatively small proportion of the whole and does not materially affect the present issue.

The Chinese worker is industrious and thrifty. He hopes to become independent—to get into business for himself. He is ever anxious to earn more, and prefers to work overtime rather than to have more time off for recreation. He would object to limitation that might deprive him of opportunity to add to his pay.

Section 3. Banking and Currency

In addition to abundant labour supplies, Hong Kong's rapid industrial growth depended on an extensive and sophisticated financial infrastructure. While HSBC was the largest and most well-known bank, locally owned banks, Chinese state banks, and foreign banks were all active in the colony. Yet despite the stellar performance of the Hong Kong economy during this period, Hong Kong's banks experienced frequent crises and failures, which the colonial government proved unwilling or incapable of preventing – in part due to a deep aversion to the collection of financial data.[17] *In 1962 a Bank of England expert was appointed in Hong Kong to advise on new regulation, which is referred to in an excerpt*

17. Leo F. Goodstadt, *Profits, Politics and Panics: Hong Kong's Banks and the Making of a Miracle Economy, 1935–1985* (Hong Kong: Hong Kong University Press, 2007), 24–27.

from the Legislative Council proceeding below. The subsequent 1964 banking ordinance eventually provided tighter regulations for the issuing of bank licences.

Document 4.5: Hong Kong Legislative Council, Official Report of Proceedings, Meeting of 19th June 1963, Banking Bill 1963, 210–11.[18]

BANKING BILL, 1963

THE FINANCIAL SECRETARY moved the First reading of a Bill intitled "An Ordinance to repeal and replace the Banking Ordinance, Chapter 155, and to make better provision for the licensing and control of banks, banking business and matters connected therewith".

He said: Sir, Honourable members are, I think, aware of the events which gave rise to this Bill—a run in 1961 on a bank with very large deposits and negligible liquid assets led to the appointment last year of Mr H. J. TOMKINS of the Bank of England to advise on new legislation.

The need to impose a degree of control on the growing banking system, and more particularly on banks dealing with personal savings, was under consideration in 1940 but nothing was done before the outbreak of war. The Banking Ordinance of 1948 now in force did little more than provide for the licensing of banks, as its purpose was not so much control of banking as control of the growth of small exchange shops which were then assisting speculation against the Chinese currency. The Ordinance is of little practical use for the protection either of depositors or of the general financial security of the Colony.

Our banking system has expanded very rapidly in recent years. It has become a more vital and integral part of the economy of the Colony than in earlier days when its main function was exchange banking; and a special feature has been the growth of the banking habit among the general public as evidenced by the rapid rise in savings deposits. This is a sign of economic maturity and plays a substantial part in our economic growth but it brings problems and dangers. The whole banking system on which our economy now depends so largely has become more vulnerable to any loss of confidence in banks on the part of the general public; and protection of the savings of the individual, who relies on the fiduciary status implied by the title "bank", has become a matter of greater public concern.

A recent editorial in the Financial Times began with the remark "Banking, in its nature, tends to be a conservative occupation". Most of our bankers are indeed

18. This source is available online at https://www.legco.gov.hk/yr97-98/english/former/lc_sitg.htm.

conservative men, in the good sense; and I must pay a tribute here to the imagination and foresight with which they have nurtured the growth of our commerce and industry and of all the other elements in our economic and social development. But there are a number of bankers who have conducted and are still conducting their affairs in a manner completely foreign to the traditions of sound banking. The truth is that they are not really bankers, either by experience or in practice. They regard their banks as convenient channels for securing control of the public's funds for their own speculations in land, in shares and in similar ventures, without regard to banking principles. It is against this kind of abuse of banking and of the name "bank" that this Bill is aimed. Sound banks will hardly be affected by it as it embodies the principles they already follow.

The Bill is very largely a re-arrangement of the Bill drafted by Mr TOMKINS. As the Bill is fully commented on in Mr TOMKINS' report I will not go into its detailed provisions or their purpose. In general terms it is designed to provide a minimum paid up capital and published reserves, to ensure adequate liquidity, to prevent speculation with depositors' funds and, by a system of bank inspection, to ensure the maintenance of sound banking practices.

Being a colonial dependency conferred some economic advantages, such as being part of the colonial monetary system. The Hong Kong dollar was re-pegged to British sterling following the Second World War and was backed by large pound sterling reserves in London. This bestowed important advantages: membership of the Sterling Area conferred stability and freedom from exchange controls between members. In reality, the colony had the best of both worlds, as the free exchange of US dollars in Hong Kong was also tolerated by London due to the colony's status as a trade hub. At the same time, the devolution of the pound sterling by 14 per cent in 1967, in response to balance-of-payments crises in Britain, reduced the value of Hong Kong's sterling assets by £56 million.[19] *The decision was met with a major backlash in the colony, and the colonial administration was able to leverage Hong Kong's substantial sterling reserves to obtain important monetary freedoms – the right to set its own exchange rate and a guarantee on its reserves in the event of further devaluation.*

Document 4.6: Hong Kong Legislative Council, Official Report of Proceedings, Meeting of 29th November 1967, Adjournment, 502.[20]

THE FINANCIAL SECRETARY replied as follows:–

19. Catherine R. Schenk, 'The Empire Strikes Back: Hong Kong and the Decline of Sterling in the 1960s', *The Economic History Review* 57, no. 3 (2004): 568.
20. This source (and other meeting records) is available online at https://www.legco.gov.hk/yr97-98/english/former/lc_sitg.htm.

I sometimes wonder if it is fully appreciated what a momentous and indeed revolutionary decision we finally made on Wednesday night, with all its incalculable ramifications, to abandon a parity with sterling that had stood for 30 years, and to set at such short notice and with only a minimum of consultation possible, a permanent new relationship with the pound. How successful and rapid a readjustment we make to the new parity remains to be seen. While I am sure that we have kept fully adequate reserves of strength in our currency and our banking system and that the cost of living will not be seriously affected, I remain a little concerned about the possible effects of sterling devaluation on those industries and exporters with sterling contracts. I have heard rather more cheerful news during the last few days about this but I would all the same appeal to those unauthorized exchange banks to whom we have afforded uncovenanted protection, not for their own sakes but for the sake of the whole community, to play their part by seeing their constituents through any difficulties they are facing, even if this means assuming rather greater risks than usual.

I should like to finish by saying that we shall be having a very close look at our future monetary arrangements. But I am afraid that it is not easy for a currency in an economy like ours to function as it should without a strong link with an established reserve currency or with gold. Over our whole history the Hong Kong dollar has been tied either to sterling or to silver. Dollars, sterling, gold or a mix all have their problems; and there are political aspects, too. It is not going to be easy to choose between flexibility and stability. But I think I can make one claim—that the Hong Kong dollar came of age last week.

In 1972, Hong Kong took advantage of its monetary freedom to switch from sterling to the US dollar as a peg, before moving to a floating rate regime in 1974. In 1983, the Hong Kong authorities decided to link the Hong Kong dollar to the US dollar at a fixed exchange rate. The decision has often been regarded as a move to restore public confidence in the context of the stalling Sino-British negotiations over Hong Kong, the falling Hong Kong dollar, slowdown in the property sector, and rumours of capital flight. A more recent study has revealed this to be an oversimplification and uncovers how the measure followed a year of discussion and debate between different parties – departments of the British and Hong Kong governments, the Bank of England, and banks in Hong Kong – over how best to manage Hong Kong's currency crisis, with not all parties agreeing to a currency peg as the right solution.[21] *As the extract from a Bank of England paper at the time reveals, the US dollar was also not the only fix considered.*

21. Asa Malmstrom Rognes and Catherine R. Schenk, 'One Country, Two Currencies: The Adoption of the Hong Kong Currency Board, 1983', *The Economic History Review* 76, no. 2 (2023): 477–97.

Document 4.7: Bank of England, 'Hong Kong monetary crisis papers 1' (Freedom of Information), C. D. Elston to the Governor's Private Secretary, 30 September 1983, attached report 'The Crisis in Hong Kong'.[22]

Three main variants of a solution have been proposed — the Greenwood scheme [named for John Greenwood, a Hong Kong economist] (Annex 1) , the Walters' scheme [named for Prof. Alan Walters, economist and advisor to the British government] (see manuscript comments on Annex 1) and the Hong Kong Government scheme, called for ease of reference the Youde scheme [named for Hong Kong Governor Edward Youde] (Annex 2).

It is the primary intention of each scheme to prevent any further collapse of the Hong Kong dollar exchange rate. While this objective is clearly desirable, all the schemes suffer from the disadvantage that the rate chosen for pegging the Hong Kong dollar to an outside currency (whether sterling, the US dollar or possibly a basket of currencies) would be arbitrary and therefore possibly inappropriate. The Youde scheme suggests the possibility of an adjustable peg, but knowledge of the possibility of adjustment would increase its likelihood and the scheme would not achieve its objective.

Greenwood and the Youde scheme are similar in that both involve pegging the Hong Kong dollar through the use of the existing foreign currency holdings of the Exchange Fund.

The Youde scheme suggests pegging in terms of US dollars, and the Greenwood scheme in terms of sterling. Since Hong Kong naturally uses the US dollar more than sterling, and far more of its trade and financial dealings are with the USA than the UK, the Youde scheme is economically preferable in this respect, but political factors might tell in favour of the Greenwood scheme. In both schemes Hong Kong dollar notes are effectively made convertible into US dollars/sterling at the pegged exchange rate. Both schemes also imply that Hong Kong banks would retain complete normal convertibility between Hong Kong currency and Hong Kong dollar deposits. This means, in effect, that all Hong Kong money holdings, ie bank deposits and currency, would be made convertible at the pegged rate into either dollars or sterling. The immediate question then arises whether the Exchange Fund's foreign currency reserves are sufficient to finance the potential massive, and continued, demand for diversifying out of Hong Kong currency and into foreign assets that is quite likely to persist and increase at times of political doubt up to 1997.

22. This source is available online at https://www.bankofengland.co.uk/freedom-of-information/2019/hong-kong-monetary-crisis-1983.

Section 4. Hong Kong–UK Economic Relations

As the 1967 devolution of sterling episode had shown, Hong Kong business and government elites did not rely solely on Britain to safeguard the colony's economic interests, but instead pursued financial and monetary autonomy where possible. A major indicator that Hong Kong's and Britain's economic interests were not always aligned was in the textile trade: Hong Kong was subject to successive export restrictions by Britain and other nations for most of the post-war period, beginning in 1959. In 1969 Britain also imposed a tariff on such goods, and although this came with the assurance that quotas would therefore be dropped, the Conservative British government made the decision in late 1971 to continue with a policy of quotas on textile goods. As the record below of discussions between Hong Kong and British officials reveals, this was a source of much resentment in Hong Kong and cast doubt on whether Britain had Hong Kong's best interests at heart when it came to other commercial decisions, especially the decision to join the European Economic Community (EEC) – a move which threatened the end of imperial preference.

Document 4.8: TNA, FCO 40/381, 'Record of Discussions Held with Representatives of the Hong Kong Government 10–14 January 1972', first session, 10 January 1972.[23]

Mr Haddon-Cave [Philip Haddon-Cave, Hong Kong's Financial Secretary] opened for Hong Kong. He recalled that in the first arrangement between Hong Kong and UK in January 1959, HMG [Her Majesty's Government] had recognised that Hong Kong was acting in a spirit of Commonwealth economic co-operation by temporarily limiting the rate of growth of her exports of cotton textiles to a level suited to Lancashire's needs. This arrangement had survived for thirteen years, and its coverage had broadened during that period. Its effect was to limit the expansion of Hong Kong's trade to a modest 11m. sq. yds. (from 185m. sq. yds. in 1962 to 196m. sq. yds. in 1972) or 10% over ten years, compared with a growth rate of 5% per annum to which signatories are normally entitled. These points were particularly important to the Hong Kong industry at the present time; exporters felt that HMG had certain obligations towards them given that the restraint arrangements were to be maintained for the foreseeable future.

23. The consultations were chaired by P. W. Ridley from the Chemical and Textiles Division of Britain's Department of Trade and Industry. The British side also featured members of the Commercial Relations and Exports division of the same department, and officials from the FCO. In addition to Financial Secretary Haddon-Cave, the Hong Kong side included Assistant Director of Commerce and Industry L. W. R. Mills, Trade Officers from DC&I, and D. M. Sellers from the Hong Kong Government Office.

2. The recent history of the UK's cotton textile policy since 1969 and Hong Kong's own doubts as to its efficacy and practicability had been discussed at length during the December talks. Mr Haddon—Cave had explained then the suspicions aroused in Hong Kong about HMG's motives in announcing one policy in July 1969, with many assurances as to its immutability, and changing to another at very short notice in December 1971; the situation now was that Hong Kong officials were accused of being insufficiently alert in not foreseeing the change . . . Hong Kong attached importance to re-formalising trading relations between the two countries after this incident and to agreeing a joint intention to follow in the future at least some of the guidelines on procedure laid in GATT [the General Agreement on Tariffs and Trade].

3. Finally Mr Haddon—Cave said he did not wish to dwell at length on the embarrassment caused to the Hong Kong Government by HMG's volte—face, but he wanted to put on record the ill—feeling and uneasiness it had caused in Hong Kong's industrial community. It had been interpreted (perhaps wrongly) as a precursor of worse things to come, and as setting a pattern for the future, particularly when conflicts of interest arose out of the forthcoming alignment of EEC/UK commercial policy. There was apprehension that Hong Kong's interests would be sacrificed when the UK became a member of the enlarged Community, and a suspicion that HMG would find it difficult to continue to offer support to the Hong Kong textile industry. The change in policy had occurred at a time when the industry was already complaining bitterly about the US "ultimatum" technique, and about Canadian and Australian unilateral action on shirts and knitted outer garments. The industry expected better treatment from the UK, but any attempt by the Hong Kong Government to bring a more balanced view to bear inevitably gave rise to accusations that they were taking a soft line with HMG.

Section 5. Support for Industry and Diversification

Unlike the Hong Kong General Chamber of Commerce, which was dominated by European merchants, the Chinese General Chamber of Commerce and the Chinese Manufacturers' Association of Hong Kong (CMA) had a more contentious relationship with the colonial state: their open support for the Chinese Communist Party alienated them from the colonial establishment, and the CMA—the first association dedicated to representing the Chinese-dominated industrial sector—frequently demanded more government support for industry in the form of industrial finance, cheaper land, protective tariffs/quotas, and support for industrial diversification to escape protectionism against the colony's dominant industries. The speech below by the CMA chairman Ngai Shiu-kit also reveals a number of economic challenges facing the colony during the 1970s, as well as the opportunities presented by China's normalisation of relations with Western powers.

Document 4.9: HKPRO, HKRS 1462/1/118, Speech at CMA Annual General Meeting, 22 March 1979, 2–7.

The viability of Hong Kong's economy depends heavily on its export industries. The establishment of diplomatic relations between the USA and the People's Republic of China has positive implications on Hong Kong. The current harmonious Anglo—Chinese relationship coupled with China's modernization programmes will enlarge supplies of raw materials needed by our industry, enhance Hong Kong's importance as an entrepot port and boost the tourist industry. In the long run, however, Hong Kong will still depend primarily on industrial development. In his recent budget speech, the Financial Secretary proposed to take steps to cool down the overheated economy including cutbacks in government spending and, as a move to encourage industrial investment, increase the rates of depreciation allowance for the manufacturing industry. We are glad that the government has become aware of its responsibilities towards the growth and pattern of the economy. This is a very welcomed change from the past. On the other hand, the measures in the Budget to curb supply and reduce credit aimed to contract internal demand and suppress inflation will lead to high interest rates, and I should like to call the government's attention that this will adversely affect the cash flow and business development of manufacturers and traders. Since the government has recognized the importance of industry to Hong Kong's economy, it should seek ways and means to assist and promote industrial development for strengthening our economic base. We trust the Advisory Committee on Diversification has already reviewed Hong Kong's economic growth in the past and will no doubt make recommendations on the strategy for further development in the years to come...

Hong Kong's economy is experiencing a number of negative factors, notably the acute shortage of labour, rocketing labour costs, rising inflation, the weakening Hong Kong dollar and growing protectionist measures overseas. The increase in OPEC oil prices early this year has led to higher materials cost, disrupting production and marketing in many cases. In the light of these difficulties, the future prospects of Hong Kong industry seems uncertain and worrying. I should like to call on all manufacturers to do their utmost, make use of the favourable conditions and the unique geographical situation of Hong Kong and work together for the further advancement of industry. Given this spirit of determination and cooperation, I am confident that industry will ride over its problems and Hong Kong will continue to grow. We are very pleased that His Excellency the Governor, will be visiting Beijing on March 24. We feel certain that his visit will further strengthen the ties between China and Hong Kong. In particular, I hope the Governor will have discussions with the Chinese authorities to ensure greater supplies of raw materials which are essential to our manufacturing industry on the one hand, and to develop and expand trade between China and Hong Kong to satisfy mutual needs and to bring mutual benefit on the other.

Despite the pressures mentioned in the previous document, there was no top-down effort to restructure the Hong Kong economy. The advisory committee on diversification mentioned by the CMA chairman released its report in December 1979, but it largely reaffirmed existing government policy with regard to directly managing the economy.[24] *The narrative promulgated by the colonial government was that Hong Kong's economic achievements were underpinned by a commitment to free enterprise, and that their role was to provide the right environment for enterprise to flourish: through enforcing rule of law including property rights; by implementing necessary regulations to ensure Hong Kong goods met international labelling standards; and by providing adequate land, infrastructure, and essential services. This was the subject of much promotional material circulated overseas by government departments concerned with attracting investment to Hong Kong, namely the Commerce and Industry Department, the Information Services Department, and the Trade Development Council. The excerpt below is from a glossy pamphlet filled with colour images of Hong Kong's industries and infrastructure, along with rhetoric extolling the colony's advantages to overseas investors and buyers.*

Document 4.10: *Hong Kong: Your Manufacturing Base* (Hong Kong: Commerce and Industry Department, 1976), 3–4, Confederation of British Industry Archive, Modern Records Centre, University of Warwick, MSS.200/C/3/INT/9/14.

HONG KONG – A GROWTH ECONOMY

Hong Kong is among the twenty largest trading communities in the world. Its economy depends heavily upon the export of locally manufactured goods, but it has also upheld its position as a regional centre for commerce, banking and trade.

The Hong Kong Government seeks to promote continued industrial, commercial and economic development by means of a policy which is unusual and probably unique in the world today. Whatever can be done by private enterprise is left to private enterprise to do. This applies to such matters as deciding which industries

24. Norman Miners, *The Government and Politics of Hong Kong* (Hong Kong: Oxford University Press, 1984), 58.

should be established, by whom they should be owned, and how they should be financed and run.

The Government believes in the profit motive; it considers that only profitable business will benefit the economy and that businessmen with their own capital at risk will take decisions leading to the greatest profitability if untrammelled by Government direction or interference. On the other hand – and this clearly follows as a concomitant of this policy – there are no tax concessions or other special incentives to any particular sector of industry or the community.

There is no need to emphasise Hong Kong's success for the facts speak for themselves. Of the 4½ million population, 630,000 work in the manufacturing industries. Over the past twenty years exports of Hong Kong manufactured goods have increased by ten times and Government revenue has increased by fifteen times. In 1975, total domestic exports amounted to US$4,535 million. Hong Kong is now the world's largest exporter of garments and toys; the second largest exporter of watches and a very significant exporter of sophisticated electronic products. The precision engineering industry is developing strongly and several individual companies in this field are already the world's largest in their own specialities. Of equal importance, these industries are all becoming sophisticated and are achieving high technological standards.

At the end of 1975 there were over 270 factories in Hong Kong either fully or partly owned by overseas interests. They employed some 10 per cent of all workers in Hong Kong's manufacturing industries. The total direct investment by overseas companies in manufacturing was about US$340 million.

The attractions of Hong Kong as a manufacturing centre for both local and overseas industrialists stem from the fact that Hong Kong has:

(1) a stable political and economic situation;

(2) attractively low rates of taxation (profits tax for corporations is 17%);

(3) a stable Government which offers full cooperation to all business and industry;

(4) a low rate of inflation (wages rose by 3% and consumer prices by in 1% in 1975);

(5) well developed banking services able to offer loans at attractively low rates of interest;

(6) an efficient commercial infrastructure;

(7) well developed supporting industries;

(8) modern industrial sites and buildings;

(9) excellent labour relations;

(10) a well trained and industrious labour force.

Section 6. Reintegration with China – Challenges and Opportunities

By the 1980s, the most important influence on Hong Kong's economy was China's emergence into the global capitalist economy. While China began experimenting with market reforms from the early 1970s, especially in the south, they accelerated at the end of the decade under Deng Xiaoping's leadership and a policy of reform and opening from 1978. China's modernisation programmes and opening to trade and investment provided an opportunity to overcome the challenges facing the Hong Kong economy in the 1970s. The prospect of the expiry of the New Territories lease in 1997, however, was a source of uncertainty. The Hong Kong business community had different views on the issue. To some, the economic reforms in China offered reassurances that Hong Kong's capitalist model would not be compromised, while at the same time, Special Economic Zones provided clues to how Hong Kong might operate as part of China politically. Others thought that Hong Kong's economy depended on the continuity and stability conferred by British rule. After visiting Beijing in September 1982 to discuss the issue of the lease, UK Prime Minister Thatcher met with prominent figures in Hong Kong, including businesspeople. Topics included whether the progress of the Sino-British negotiations should be made public, and the need to preserve the free enterprise system of Hong Kong.

Document 4.11: TNA, PREM 19/788, 'Record of the Prime Minister's Meeting with Businessmen at 1445 on 27 September', 28 September 1982.

(The Prime Minister was accompanied by the Governor, the Financial Secretary, Mr. Gray, Mr Butler and Mr. Ingham. A list of the businessmen attending is attached.)

The Prime Minister said that she wished to take the opportunity to hear the views of those present on the future of Hong Kong; on what was needed to retain business confidence; and on the outcome which they would wish to seek. She also wished to discuss how the Chinese might be brought to understand what made Hong Kong successful, and the nature of confidence in Hong Kong. The Government in Peking was isolated and did not understand things which were second nature to all present. They had no idea of the subtleties of administration in a free society or of the structure of liberty.

Mr. Duncan Bl[u]ck [Swire Group] said that business confidence was fragile, and keeping the talks confidential would be a real problem. News would leak out; the important thing would be to ensure that what became known was fact. The Prime Minister said that negotiation in a mass meeting and through the media was impossible. She accepted that it would be necessary to say something about the negotiations from time to time; the press abhorred a vacuum. But it would be impossible to give full details. Dr. Andrew Chuang [Chuang's Holdings] said that the problem was that the Chinese might not maintain confidentiality. The Prime Minister remarked that Premier Zhao had spoken to the press before her meeting with him about Hong Kong.

Mr. Victor Fung [Li & Fung, a supply chain management company] said that his personal opinion was that the ideal solution would be the continuation of the status quo indefinitely, with 25 or 50 years notice of termination. He realised that might be hard to achieve. A key element in Hong Kong's success was a system which allowed full scope to business enterprise. He hoped that could be preserved even if there should be joint administration. Without the free market system, Hong Kong would not work. As for what Hong Kong businessmen might do to help, most of those present had business contacts with China. They could use those contacts to get across the message of how much Hong Kong depended on the free enterprise system. He added that he was not sure that China and Britain meant the same thing when they talked about maintaining the stability and prosperity of Hong Kong. The Prime Minister said that the Chinese would say that they wished to preserve the capitalist system in Hong Kong but they did not know what it meant. As for the second point, she hoped that those speaking to the Chinese would not stop at the need to preserve the free enterprise system. Other things, including the law, were equally important. Dr. Fung had mentioned joint administration. Britain had had experience of that with the French in the New Hebrides. It had been far from satisfactory. Mr. Philip Kwok [Wing On Bank] asked how the Chinese could be brought to understand what made Hong Kong tick. The Prime Minister said that the Chinese would look to Singapore and see that there a successful community had been built on a combination of Chinese people and the free enterprise system. They would think that they could do the same with Hong Kong, forgetting that Singapore was a sovereign and independent state. They would not be able to achieve their objective if they sought to substitute Chinese for British rule.

While Hong Kong's political future was still being decided, the colony's economic integration with Guangdong was already underway. Special Economic Zones permitted duty-free imports of goods involved in the production of exports and encouraged investment through low taxation and minimised bureaucracy. Hong Kong's entrepreneurs, particularly in the clothing industry, took advantage of lower labour costs across the border to open factories and transport goods back to Hong Kong to be finished and exported, or sold locally where permitted. It was not always plain sailing, however, as challenges could include transport costs and finding skilled and reliable workers, as Francis Chin-pang Chan, owner of clothing company Kam Ah Fashion, recalls.

Document 4.12: Excerpt from Transcript of Interview with CHAN, Chin-pang Francis (Reference code I317), Interviewer: Edward Kwong, 28/08/2009, Oral History Collection, The Hong Kong Heritage Project (translated).

KWONG: In Hong Kong, was the garment industry booming in the 70s and 80s?

CHAN: It was actually in the 80s that it was the most prosperous, you could say.

KWONG: Then how did you cope with the competition with many large factories at that time?

CHAN: Actually, the strategies were different. If you're talking about large factories, as far as we know, companies like today's Lai Sun, started developing near us in the early days. I know about them, but gradually, as they shifted towards exports, they moved to areas like the Castle Peak Road. Also, in terms of their target audience, for those making things like shirts, they focused more on exports, whereas we mainly focused on domestic sales, selling within Hong Kong. Our customer bases were somewhat different.

KWONG: The customer base was different. So, did they have to obtain quotas back then?

CHAN: Yes, yes.

KWONG: Were you mainly focused on domestic sales then?

CHAN: Yes, because there is a bit of history to it. In fact, I remember my maternal uncle was quite close with Lai Sun. From what I heard from my mom, they used to work for Mr. Lam of Lai Sun before.

KWONG: Oh really? So, during this first stage for your family and your dad [CHAN: Yes], did you manage to make money at that time?

CHAN: You can say so. It was quite good, [KWONG: quite good], not bad, okay. In comparison to an average household, we were considered a comfortable or well-off family.

KWONG: And how was the second phase?

CHAN: In the beginning, around the 1980s when Hong Kong's economy was booming, for all industries, it was challenging to hire people because the demand for labour was high. Additionally, property prices started going up. For businesses like ours that relied heavily on manual labour, the most difficult thing was to find and hire workers. If you managed to hire workers, the cost of labour increased, and even if you managed to pay higher, you still might not find workers, so you need to consider relocation. So in the 1980s, as you may remember China's economy began to open up. In the early 80s, many towns and villages in China offered favourable conditions to attract businesses, encouraging them to set up factories or facilities. Taking advantage of such opportunities, we also tried establishing a factory in mainland China, in Guangdong Province.

KWONG: Set up a factory there directly?

CHAN: Yes.

KWONG: Also manufacturing children's clothing?

CHAN: Yes, we still are. At that time, our main customer base was children's clothing. It was before the significant changes occurred.

KWONG: So, did you hire people there and then transport the products back to Hong Kong to sell?

CHAN: Yes, because that's how it worked at the time. We imported raw materials, but the finished products had to be exported back to Hong Kong; we were not allowed to sell them domestically [in mainland China].

KWONG: So, was the cost lower than in Hong Kong?

CHAN: Certainly, because labour costs were lower. The transportation costs were a bit high, but at that time, wages in mainland China were lower, which made it cost-effective. However, a challenge was quality control, as many workers might have been farmers or had different backgrounds. Training them to reach the same skill level as workers in Hong Kong was not straightforward, so the scrap rate might be high.

KWONG: So, does that mean the skills in Hong Kong, especially the skills of female workers or those who specialize in tailoring, was superior to theirs at that time?

CHAN: You can say so. To put it this way, because Hong Kong was already quite developed at that time. However, in the mainland, if you were given a farmer, it's not easy to take the time to train them to the required level. Moreover, the quality of manpower there was not as good. According to what I heard back then (I wasn't involved at that time), during the manufacturing process, some might have taken some of the materials for themselves. In reality, when you calculate the losses, it's even greater. For example, if you were making a hundred pieces of clothing, you might need to actually order two hundred zippers, buttons, and so on.

KWONG: And you wouldn't know where they [the extra ones] went?

CHAN: No, you wouldn't.

KWONG: But you still kept this going for quite a while, the factory in mainland China.

CHAN: Actually, it wasn't for a very long time, and it wasn't very successful. So, we only did it for a relatively short period, around one or two years.

Hong Kong quickly emerged as the largest source of external investment in China – 75 per cent in value terms from 1979 to 1987.[25] *While this started primarily in manufacturing, it later expanded to include retail, tourism, and financial services. Investment was not unidirectional: Chinese investment in Hong Kong became the second largest source after that from Britain, and Chinese firms including state-owned enterprises raised funds by listing on Hong Kong's Stock Exchange. China's reforms, particularly in Guangdong, also provided opportunities for joint ventures involving both private and state capital. One such example was Guangdong's Daya Bay Nuclear Power Plant – a joint venture between the Hong Kong-based CLP Holdings Limited (25 per cent) and the Guangdong Nuclear Investment Company (75 per cent). The report below to China's State Department by Guangdong's Party Secretary Wang Quanguo outlines the advantages of the project to both Hong Kong and Guangdong in meeting energy needs, but also in financing – selling electricity to Hong Kong provided China with an opportunity to repay the borrowing costs of the project.*

Document 4.13: Wang Quanguo, *Guangdong Nuclear Power Selected Manuscripts, 1979–1994* (Beijing: Atomic Energy Publishing House, 2002), A report concerning the 'Guangdong Nuclear Power Plant Joint Venture Project Plan' (10 March 1981), 5–6.[26]

Guangdong Electric Power Company (GEPC) and Hong Kong and China Electric Power Co., Ltd. (CLP) conducted a one-year joint study on the feasibility of building a nuclear power plant in Guangdong Province. In December 1980, the "Guangdong

25. Daonan, 'The Economic Relations between China and Hong Kong', 451.
26. Document originally in Chinese: 王全國，《廣東核電文稿選編, 1979–1994》（北京：原子能出版社，2002），關於上報《合營廣東核電站工程計劃任務書》的報告（1981年3月10日），5–6.

Nuclear Power Plant Joint Venture Joint Feasibility Report" was signed by both parties. A meeting of experts was held from 7–13 January 1981, and a meeting of the Guangdong Nuclear Power Plant Leading Group was held from 27–30 January. The feasibility study report was reviewed, and the necessity of constructing the Nuclear Power Plant and the feasibility of the joint venture were studied.

Since the founding of the People's Republic of China, the power industry in Guangdong has developed a lot. However, the power industry still lags behind the development of the national economy. In particular, Guangdong's implementation of special policies and flexible measures, the four modernizations goals, and the people's daily needs have led to increased power supply needs. Judging from the current situation of primary energy resources in Guangdong Province, it is difficult to solve the problem of insufficient electricity in Guangdong Province. It is necessary to develop new energy sources and build nuclear power plants, while developing coal and oil shale power plants and small and medium-sized hydropower plants.

The power supply in Hong Kong has grown rapidly in the past 10 years. However, the world energy crisis, the political situation of some Gulf states, and the skyrocketing price of oil in the international market has had a greater impact on Hong Kong's power industry. Therefore, in the long run, it is economically and politically beneficial for Hong Kong to build nuclear power plants while building new coal-fired power plants. Therefore, CLP has shown a positive attitude towards joint venture construction of nuclear power plants.

Guangdong is adjacent to Hong Kong and Macau, and has favourable conditions for attracting foreign investment, selling electricity to Hong Kong and Macau, and earning foreign exchange to repay loans: Guangdong should make full use of these conditions to build a joint venture with CLP to build nuclear power plants and take a step ahead in the use of nuclear energy.

The consensus of the meeting of experts and the leading group meeting is that the construction of a Guangdong nuclear power plant is reliable in safety, technically feasible, and economically significant. It not only opens a new energy outlet for Guangdong, but also a nationwide one. A good start can promote the development of China's nuclear power industry. Relevant departments across the country are working together to help Guangdong build and manage the first large-scale commercial nuclear power plant in mainland China.

The Guangdong nuclear power plant is a project with advanced technology, a large engineering investment undertaking, and a Sino-foreign joint venture project, involving a wide range of areas, and is the first large-scale commercial nuclear power plant in mainland China. It must be run well. In order to strengthen leadership and coordinate all aspects of work, the expert meeting and the leading group meeting unanimously requested the State Council to designate a deputy prime minister to be responsible for the construction of the Guangdong nuclear power plant and proposed the establishment of a leading group to be fully responsible for the construction and organizational leadership of the Guangdong nuclear power plant.

The "Guangdong Nuclear Power Plant Joint Venture Project Plan" is now submitted. In view of the fact that Guangdong Nuclear Power Plant is a joint venture with foreign businessmen, which involves major political and economic issues at home and abroad and requires a lot of work, the State Council is requested to organize the approval as soon as possible and include it in the national Sino-foreign joint venture construction plan.

While Hong Kong had always been an important link between China and the global economy during even its more isolated periods, the market reforms solidified Hong Kong's status as China's offshore financial and services hub. The tables below provide an insight into the changing structure of the Hong Kong economy during this period. By shifting manufacturing production across the border, Hong Kong experienced drastic deindustrialisation, while the importance of the service and financial sectors in employment and in share of the Hong Kong economy grew rapidly. Manufacturing peaked in importance to the economy in 1992 before declining in real terms, while services more than quadrupled in value terms from 1986 to 1995. Meanwhile, employment in manufacturing nearly halved despite growing in all other sectors of the economy.

Document 4.14: Census & Statistics Department, *Hong Kong Annual Digest of Statistics* (Hong Kong: Census and Statistics Department, 1997), Table 2.5 'Employed Persons by Industry', 16.[27]

2.5 按行業劃分的就業人數
Employed Persons by Industry

千人
Thousands

行業	Industry	1987	1990	1992	1993	1994	1995	1996
製造業	Manufacturing	916.0	751.0	650.5	594.0	562.6	534.6	482.1
建造業	Construction	215.5	226.0	231.2	221.1	220.5	229.3	269.6
批發、零售、進出口貿易、飲食及酒店業	Wholesale, retail and import/export trades, restaurants and hotels	626.1	703.2	747.9	795.8	827.6	824.9	887.4
運輸、倉庫及通訊業	Transport, storage and communications	228.0	268.4	294.7	314.9	340.0	327.7	331.8
金融、保險、地產及商用服務業	Financing, insurance, real estate and business services	170.3	208.6	231.9	289.2	326.2	341.7	353.6
社區、社會及個人服務業	Community, social and personal services	464.5	511.8	542.1	547.7	558.8	609.8	649.5
其他	Others	60.5	42.7	39.3	37.3	37.1	37.1	33.8
總計	Total	2 680.8	2 711.5	2 737.6	2 800.1	2 872.8	2 905.1	3 007.7

註釋： 數字是該年四季綜合住戶統計調查得到的估計數字的平均數。

由一九九三年開始，綜合住戶統計調查採用的行業分類，基本上遵照「香港標準行業分類（一九九一年）」劃分，香港標準行業分類(一九九一年)所採用的分類方法，修訂了在以前進行的統計調查中採用的分類方法，因此一九九三年或以後的統計數字不能與一九九三年以前的相應數字作嚴格比較。

資料來源： 政府統計處綜合住戶統計調查組(二)
（查詢電話：2887 5508）

Notes : Figures are averages of the estimates obtained from the quarterly General Household Surveys of the year.

From 1993 onwards, the industrial classification used in the General Household Survey basically follows the 'Hong Kong Standard Industrial Classification (1991)' which is an updated version of the classification used in previous rounds of the survey. Figures from 1993 onwards are thus not strictly comparable with the corresponding figures prior to 1993.

Source : General Household Survey Section(2),
Census and Statistics Department
(Enquiry Telephone No.: 2887 5508)

27. This source (and digests for other years) is available on the C&SD website at https://www.censtatd.gov.hk/en/EIndexbySubject.html?pcode=B1010003&scode=460#section3.

Document 4.15: Census & Statistics Department, *Hong Kong Annual Digest of Statistics* (Hong Kong: Census and Statistics Department, 1997), Table 17.8 'Gross Domestic Product (GDP) Estimates at Current Prices by Economic Activity', 314.[28]

17.8 按經濟活動劃分的本地生產總值(以當時價格計算)
Gross Domestic Product (GDP) Estimates at Current Prices by Economic Activity

百萬元
$ million

經濟活動	Economic activity	1986	1989	1991	1992	1993	1994	1995
農業及漁業	Agriculture and fishing	1,308	1,386	1,441	1,468	1,612	1,596	1,453
工業	Industry	89,820	132,992	145,625	152,943	153,459	156,103	163,426
採礦及採石業	Mining and quarrying	346	224	222	205	197	249	317
製造業	Manufacturing	66,836	96,170	97,223	99,764	92,582	87,354	84,770
電力、燃氣及水務業	Electricity, gas and water	8,385	10,860	13,521	15,637	17,591	22,175	23,578
建造業	Construction	14,253	25,738	34,659	37,337	43,089	46,325	54,761
服務業	Services	204,880	364,557	484,448	577,709	675,098	792,472	851,231
批發、零售、進出口貿易、飲食及酒店業	Wholesale, retail and import/export trades, restaurants and hotels	66,020	124,749	163,284	190,760	224,462	249,167	270,521
運輸、倉庫及通訊業	Transport, storage and communications	24,192	44,654	60,604	71,227	78,993	92,109	101,357
金融、保險、地產及商用服務業	Financing, insurance, real estate and business services	50,306	97,297	143,296	178,923	214,550	254,346	249,391
社區、社會及個人服務業	Community, social and personal services	47,406	70,124	94,293	110,703	130,408	151,293	176,808
樓宇業權	Ownership of premises	30,034	51,534	68,873	80,941	89,862	115,659	134,416
非直接計算的金融中介服務調整	Adjustment for financial intermediation services indirectly measured	-13,079	-23,800	-45,902	-54,846	-63,177	-70,101	-81,262
以要素成本計算的本地生產總值(生產估計)	Gross domestic product at factor cost (production-based estimates)	296,008	498,935	631,514	732,120	830,169	950,172	1,016,111
生產及入口稅	Taxes on production and imports	15,212	25,390	36,323	48,777	53,278	56,286	52,971
以市價計算的本地生產總值(生產估計)	Gross domestic product at market prices (production-based estimates)	311,220	524,326	667,837	780,897	883,447	1,006,458	1,069,082
以市價計算的本地生產總值(開支估計)	Gross domestic product at market prices (expenditure-based estimates)	312,561	523,861	668,512	779,335	897,463	1,010,885	1,084,192
統計差額	Statistical discrepancy	-0.4%	0.1%	-0.1%	0.2%	-1.6%	-0.4%	-1.4%

資料來源： 政府統計處國民收入統計科(一)
(查詢電話：2582 5077)

Source : National Income Branch (1), Census and Statistics Department (Enquiry Telephone No.: 2582 5077)

28. This source (and digests for other years) is available on the C&SD website at https://www.censtatd.gov.hk/en/EIndexbySubject.html?pcode=B1010003&scode=460#section3.s.

Suggested Readings

Goodstadt, Leo F. *Uneasy Partners: The Conflict between Public and Private Profit in Hong Kong*. Hong Kong: Hong Kong University Press, 2005.

Goodstadt, Leo F. *Profits, Politics and Panics: Hong Kong's Banks and the Making of a Miracle Economy, 1935–1985*. Hong Kong: Hong Kong University Press, 2007.

Hamilton, Peter E. *Made in Hong Kong: Transpacific Networks and a New History of Globalization*. New York: Columbia University Press, 2021.

Ho, Yin-Ping. *Trade, Industrial Restructuring and Development in Hong Kong*. Honolulu: University of Hawai'i Press, 1992.

Hung, Ho-Fung. *City on the Edge: Hong Kong under Chinese Rule*. Cambridge: Cambridge University Press, 2022.

Ngo, Tak-Wing, ed. *Hong Kong's History: State and Society under Colonial Rule*. London: Routledge, 1999.

Schenk, Catherine R. *Hong Kong as an International Finance Centre: Emergence and Development 1945–65*. London: Routledge, 2001.

Yep, Ray, ed. *Negotiating Autonomy in Greater China: Hong Kong and Its Sovereign Before and After 1997*. Copenhagen: Nordic Institute of Asian Studies, 2013.

5

Fiscal and Budgetary Policy

Fung Chi Keung Charles

Fiscal policy and budgeting shed important light on how state and society interact. A state cannot function properly unless it establishes institutions that generate sufficient resources – in monetary form or otherwise – to support the administrative apparatus for maintaining socio-political control.[1] Fiscal policy thus reflects how state survived by illuminating how it tapped into societal resources, especially by taxing resources generated from economic activities. With these resources, the state can decide what to spend, and this turns into public goods and government services. The way in which the state raises and spends its resources constituted the budgets, which tell us how the state survived and how the state governs.

This chapter builds on revisionist studies of the history of fiscal policy and budgeting to illustrate one key insight: these processes were inherently political. Unlike previous economic narratives that underscore the economic functions of the fiscal system and budgetary guidelines in serving developmental goals,[2] revisionist studies illustrate that the making of the fiscal institution (i.e., income taxation, also known as the 'light and simple tax system') and processes of budgeting were outcomes of

1. Charles Tilly, 'Extraction and Democracy', in *The New Fiscal Sociology: Taxation in Comparative and Historical Perspective*, ed. Isaac William Martin, Ajay K. Mehrotra, and Monica Prasad (Cambridge: Cambridge University Press, 2009), 173–82, at 178.
2. See, for example, Alvin Rabushka, *Value for Money: The Hong Kong Budgetary Process* (Stanford, CA: Hoover Institution Press, 1976); Shu-hung Tang, 'Hong Kong: Revenue Policy under the British Administration', *Asia-Pacific Journal of Taxation* 1, no. 3 (1997): 81–113; Shu-hung Tang, 'Budgetary Guidelines and Fiscal Performance in Hong Kong', *International Journal of Public Sector Management* 10, no. 7 (1997): 547–71; Ho Henry Chun Yuen, *The Fiscal System of Hong Kong* (London: Croom Helm, 1979).

negotiation.[3] This insight is seen in Littlewood's study of the making of a peculiar form of income taxation that was schedular, Ure's study of public policymaking, and Goodstadt's studies of state–business relations and how they conditioned the colonial state in deciding how to spend its resources.[4] The upshot of these negotiations between colonial bureaucrats and business elites was the creation of the 'schedular income tax system' where individual income is taxed separately according to the type of source (e.g., property, salaries, business profits) rather than a unified whole that characterised income tax systems elsewhere.

These historical studies traced the behind-the-scenes processes to reveal that the colonial state often had to juggle between two nexuses: one was between the colonial state and its alliances, who were mostly commercial and banking elites; another was between the colonial state and London. By showing how the colonial state juggled these two nexuses, this chapter also demonstrates how colonial bureaucrats – notably the Governors and the Financial Secretary – made decisions, such as preserving the peculiar tax structure, maintaining low tax rates, and spending less on social services. The reader can thus understand how these choices shaped the social development of contemporary Hong Kong.

Nonetheless, the reader must beware of two caveats when going through the documents included in this chapter. Firstly, given the limited space, it is impossible to include all documents that are crucial for understanding the history of fiscal policy and budgeting. For instance, the chapter does not include documents such as 'The War Revenue Ordinance 1940' and the three 'Inland Revenue Review Committees' inaugurated between the 1950s and that 1970s on which Littlewood focused on.[5] Nor does it include statistical sources such as revenue and expenditure

---

3. See, for example, Stephen W. K. Chiu, 'Unraveling Hong Kong's Exceptionalism: The Politics of Laissez-Faire in the Industrial Takeoff', *Political Power and Social Theory* 10 (1996): 229–56; Brain C. H. Fong, *Hong Kong Public Budgeting: Historical and Comparative Analyses* (Singapore: Palgrave Macmillan, 2022); Ray Yep and Tai-lok Lui, 'Revisiting the Golden Era of MacLehose and the Dynamics of Social Reforms', *China Information* 24, no. 3 (2010): 249–72; Leo F. Goodstadt, 'Fiscal Freedom and the Making of Hong Kong's Capitalist Society', *China Information* 24, no. 3 (2010): 273–94; Gavin Ure, *Governors, Politics, and the Colonial Office: Public Policy in Hong Kong, 1918–58* (Hong Kong: Hong Kong University Press, 2012); Michael Littlewood, *Taxation without Representation: The History of Hong Kong's Troublingly Successful Tax System* (Hong Kong: Hong Kong University Press, 2010); Ian Scott, *The Public Sector in Hong Kong*, 2nd ed. (Hong Kong: Hong Kong University Press, 2022). For a general review of the colonial state's role, see David W. Clayton, 'From Laissez-Faire to "Positive Non-interventionism": The Colonial State in Hong Kong Studies', *Social Transformations in Chinese Societies* 9, no. 1 (2013): 1–19.
4. Littlewood, *Taxation without Representation*; Ure, *Governors, Politics, and the Colonial Office*; Goodstadt, 'Fiscal Freedom and the Making of Hong Kong's Capitalist Society'; Leo F. Goodstadt, *Uneasy Partners: The Conflict between Public and Private Profit in Hong Kong* (Hong Kong: Hong Kong University Press, 2005).
5. For a summary, see Littlewood, *Taxation without Representation*, 4–10.

that are digitally available elsewhere.[6] Doing so would consume much of the space for other documents that are equally important. The selection of documents thus entails a trade-off. A list of suggested readings is available at the end of the chapter so that interested readers can follow up. Secondly, although this chapter is organised chronologically, readers must remember that the decisions made in one period had a cumulative effect on possible choices. That is to say, earlier choices might foreclose subsequent opportunities to change the trajectories of fiscal policy and budgeting practices. This shows *how* history matters.

Section 1. Re-instituting Income Taxation, 1945–1947

In May 1946, Mark Young resumed the colonial governorship. During the Second World War, the British had set up a Planning Unit in London and instructed that the fiscal and tax laws of Hong Kong established before the war would be reintroduced. Unlike the 1922 Model Ordinance that directed the colonial government to levy tax on total personal income, what was enacted in Hong Kong was a schedular income tax system, levying taxes separately on profits and earnings. It was also different from the 1922 Model Ordinance in that it did not levy tax on income received in Hong Kong. In early 1947, the Secretary of State for the Colonies instructed Governor Young to 'introduce a normal income tax system' and set the tax rates 'as high as possible'. The colonial government appointed a Taxation Committee to consider the measure. Still, its decision to introduce income taxation attracted widespread opposition, notably the Anti-Direct Tax Introduction Commission organised by the Chinese merchants in the colony. The following long despatch written by Governor Young recounted the process and explained why several temporary concessions, such as retaining the schedular framework and setting the tax rate at 10 per cent, were made. The main rationale was to enact the Ordinance and establish 'the machinery for direction taxation' so that they could adjust the tax rates later when oppositional forces died down. Given the presence of 'the very strong opposition' in the colony, the Colonial Office in London considered these various modifications reasonable.

Document 5.1: TNA, CO 129/615/2, Letter from Governor Mark Young to Arthur Creech Jones, 16 May 1947.

2. As enacted, the Ordinance [i.e., An Ordinance to Impose a Tax on Earnings and Profits] differs in a number of respects from the Bill . . . In its original form, the Bill was published for general information on the 7th March and thereafter it

6. Statistical sources of revenue and expenditure (e.g., Hong Kong Statistics 1947–1967) are available online through the Census and Statistics Department website: https://www.censtatd.gov.hk/en/EIndexbySubject.html?scode=460&pcode=B1010003.

was referred to the Taxation Committee for an expression of their views. For this purpose, the Committee was augmented by the inclusion in its number of all the Unofficial Members of Legislative Council.

3. The Unofficial Members of the Committee agreed in principle that direct taxation should be imposed but expressed themselves as being in favour of postponement of the operation of the tax to a future date. The view was also expressed by all except three of the Unofficial Members of the Committee that, in their opinion, it was imperative that the standard rate should be low and that it should not exceed 10%. They also considered that the Bill required more detailed examination than had hitherto been possible and that it should be referred to a Committee for further examination . . .

4. The Committee's view that the introduction of the tax should be postponed for at least one year commanded widespread public support. It was known that the enactment of a similar measure in Singapore and Malaya had been deferred and it was argued that, if these colonies had been given this breathing space in order that business firms might have a longer period in which to recover from their war losses and in order that private individuals might not be called upon to pay the tax until conditions had become more normal, it was only reasonable that a similar concession should be given in Hong Kong. I did not feel able to accept this recommendation of the Committee and decided that the Bill must be proceeded with.

5. I considered that, in view of the very strong opposition to the measure from all sections of the community which had taken the form both of a press campaign and the presentation of a number of petitions, it would be desirable, if possible, to accept the Committee's recommendations on the other two points, namely, the standard rate of tax and the question of examination of the Bill by a further Committee. I was naturally reluctant to force the Bill through with the official majority in the face of a unanimous unofficial veto and there were indications that the opposition of some Unofficial Members, and indeed of a large section of the public, was not directed against the Bill as a whole but arose from the fear that it would be forced through with a high standard rate.

6. . . . there can be no doubt that the ordinary individual in Hong Kong is finding extreme difficulty in meeting essential commitments even though on paper he may enjoy what appears to be a high salary . . . it seemed to me that the argument was well founded that a higher rate than 10% would, in present circumstances, result in a good deal of hardship. I therefore agreed to the inclusion of a 10% rate in the Bill. I felt that the main consideration was to establish the machinery for direct taxation, for once that was accomplished any adjustment in rate which might become

necessary to meet a change in conditions would not present the same difficulty. I hoped, too, that this decision might result in one or two Unofficial Members voting with the Government. In this, my hopes were more realised for four Unofficial Members finally supported the measure . . .

9. Although not provided for in the London draft, it was later proposed to tax income arising in, derived from or received in the Colony, and such a provision was included in the draft published for general information on the 7th March. The Committee recommended that tax should be restricted to income arising in or derived from the Colony. This was the same basis of taxation as in 1941 and, on further consideration, the amendment proposed by the committee appeared to me to be justifiable. This Colony differs from the majority of Colonial dependencies in that a number of head offices of important businesses are established here. Profits resulting from businesses activities in other countries must pass through the books of the head offices and if such profits were taxable here all sorts of complicated claims in respect of double taxation would arise. The committee felt that this might tend to discourage firms from establishing their head offices here and that Hong Kong's position as a financial and commercial centre might be adversely affected . . .

14. In order to impose such a measure of higher taxation on higher incomes as is possible under the present system of taxation, the scale of incidence under salaries tax and personal assessment had been increased in the Bill as originally published . . . But a member of a business firm who is paid partly in the form of salary but principally by participating in the profits, would naturally not elect to be personally assessed. In order not to penalise a salaried individual as compared with such a person, the committee recommended the insertion of a proviso to the effect that in no case should the total amount of tax chargeable on any individual exceed the standard rate on the whole of his income before deducting any allowances . . .

18. The Bill passed its first reading on the 24th April without a division, but up to a few days before the second reading which was fixed for the 1st May, it seemed very probable that it would be necessary to use the official majority. There were, however, last minute indications that the fact that a 10% standard rate had been agreed to and that the recommendations of the Morse Committee had been accepted by Government had swayed certain sections of the public in favour or the Bill. This appreciation of the position proved to be correct and several Unofficial Members spoke in favour of the Bill during the debate on the second reading. On a division being called, the motion was carried by thirteen votes to three which meant that four Unofficial Members, including one Chinese member, had voted with the Government . . .

Document 5.2: TNA, CO 129/615/2, Letter from H. Palmer (Colonial Office) to David R. Serpell (Treasury Office, London), 26 June 1947.

I think the Hong Kong administration are to be congratulated on the fact that, in spite of very considerable earlier opposition the Bill was finally passed without the use of the Official majority . . .

2. In accepting the various modifications . . .The fact is of course that the potential revenue to be derived from the direct taxation will be nothing like fully tapped in the current year. Our telegram of 26th January emphasised the importance we attached to putting the standard rate at as high a level as the Governor considered practicable. The standard rate of tax originally contemplated was 25% but this was subsequently reduced to 10%. I think we must accept the advice that the measures embodied in the Ordinance represent the most it is feasible to achieve in present circumstances, and that to have attempted more at the present stage would only have resulted in harder and more widespread opposition. I suggest we must judge the measure essentially on a long-term view.

Section 2. Defending the Fiscal Status Quo and Achieving Fiscal Autonomy, 1948–1958

After Young's departure, Alexander Grantham assumed the governorship in mid-1947. During his governorship (1947–57), he sided with the commercial elites in the colony and made several attempts to defend the schedular income tax system. One measure was to demand the relaxation of treasury control once the schedular income tax system generated sufficient resources for the colonial government to balance the budget. A second type of tactical measure was to minimise expenditure unless programmes and projects were considered necessary, such as the civil defence programme and infrastructural projects. A third type of measure entailed the establishment of 'fiscal cushions' such that these fiscal instruments could provide cushions against economic shock that could undermine the budgetary position of the colonial government. The list is not exhaustive, but the main ramification was that the colonial government was able to accumulate fiscal surplus. With a robust fiscal position and as long as Hong Kong was not financially reliant on London, the colonial government was enabled to argue against reforming the income tax system and substantially raising the tax rates. It also enabled Governor Grantham to fend off London's proposal to increase the tax rates. Upon the request of Governor Grantham in 1956, and in view of the sound financial and administrative records, London eventually granted fiscal autonomy to Hong Kong in 1958, as seen in Document 5.8. This is an important landmark in the fiscal history of Hong Kong. While the standard tax rates were increased from 10 per cent to 12.5 per cent in 1950, the schedular framework remained intact.

Document 5.3: TNA, CO 1030/392, Letter from Arthur Creech Jones to Governor Alexander Grantham, 24 September 1948.

2. At recent discussions in which Mr. Follows participated the general financial policy of Hong Kong was reviewed. Observations arising from these discussions have been conveyed to you in my despatches Nos. 209 of the 13th July, 1948, and 303 of 24th September, 1948. As a result of these discussions it has been agreed, subject to any comments you may wish to make, that the former Treasury control of Hong Kong finances should cease and that arrangements as indicated below should be considered as in operation from the 1st April, 1948. These arrangements should be subject to review at the 1st April, 1949 . . .

4. The key-note of the proposed arrangements is intended to be consultation rather than control, and in order that this end may be achieved you will, I am sure, appreciate that I shall need to be kept as fully as possible informed of financial trends in the Colony and be consulted at an early stage regarding proposals for expenditure which require my approval . . . or under specific Colonial Regulations such as Colonial Regulation 267.

Document 5.4: HKPRO, HKRS 163/1/1367, Despatch from Governor Alexander Grantham to the Secretary of State, 22 February 1951.

I hope to present the estimates for 1951/2 to Legislative Council on the 7th March, Revenue is expected to total $247,280,850 as against an estimated expenditure figure of $233,465,137 thus providing for a surplus of $13,815,713 . . .

3. The total expenditure figure represents an increase of some $32.5 million on the approved estimate for the current year and this occurs almost entirely under Other Charges and Special Expenditure, particularly under the latter . . . This is only a tentative figure as the amount of the contribution in respect of the coming year is of course a matter for negotiation, but it is felt that it should be related to local expenditure on defence and security generally and in particular to re-votes amounting to over $7.5 million which it has been necessary to include to cover the completion of the present civil defence programme . . .

5. So far revenue which was estimated very conservatively has been coming in extremely well, and it is expected to exceed the original estimate by $70 million, half of which excess is derived from duties, tobacco again being responsible for a

large share. Expenditure has been closely controlled and heads of departments were urged to exercise every possible economy. The result has been that even after charging off $50 million of loan advances to expenditure a surplus of some $23.5 million is expected on the current year's working. The revenue estimate for 1951/52 allows for a drop of $27 million as compared with the revised estimate for the current year and is considered reasonable on the information available, as it seems clear that there will be a considerable time lag before the full effects of the American embargo are felt even if efforts to secure some degree of relaxation fail. Moreover the revenue total includes a final payment of $6 million due on a large estate and also $4 million in respect of the Business Registration Tax which was approved in your telegram No. 482 of 4th April 1950.

6. Serious difficulties were encountered both over plans for the practical administration of the proposed tax and drafting of the necessary legislation, particularly in regard to the question of premises as the tax had to apply equally to ordinary business premises and to a substantial business conducted from a hotel room. It was only recently that these difficulties were fully resolved and it is proposed to introduce the necessary legislation early in the financial year . . .

9. In view of the fact that in addition to budgeting for a modest surplus we proposed to set up a Development Fund and have charged off $50 million loan advances to expenditure, you will I am sure appreciate that it would be politically quite impossible to suggest further taxation at the moment though a warning will be given that the American embargo and other control measures may have a very serious effect on revenue for 1952/53 even though they may be modified long before that date. Any proposals for additional taxation now would inevitably raise the constitutional question which would be most undesirable. We should be accused of deliberately shelving constitutional reform in order to be able to force through this fresh taxation.

Document 5.5: HKPRO, HKRS 163/3/37, Letter from Governor Alexander Grantham to Oliver Lyttelton (Secretary of State for the Colonies), 22 December 1951.

[1.] I have the honour to inform you that I have for some time been considering the establishment in this Colony of some form of Reserve Fund, which would have the effect of cushioning the shock which might be occasioned to the financial position of the Colony by a sudden depression such as that which occurred in the thirties. You will recollect that the position at that time was such that in 1936 it was necessary drastically to curtail public services and even to impose a levy on the salaries of civil servants in order to balance expenditure against revenue.

2. Any such course of action must now, I feel, be regarded as highly undesirable, but any sudden crisis would still under present circumstances have to be met by reduction in establishment, and in expenditure on items other than personal emoluments; and by increased taxation. Such measures might on the one hand prove in the event to have been quite unnecessary, as the duration of the crisis might have been over-estimated; and on the other hand might prove inadequate, or too late, to forestall a deficit on the year's working, with consequent injury to the Colony's credit despite the existence of a substantial General Revenue Balance . . .

6. The general effect of these proposals thus would be that in general the Colony's accounts would continue to be maintained on a cash basis, with all expenditure whether recurrent or non-recurrent being met from revenue so far as is practicable. The Development Fund would continue to be used to finance large scale and long term schemes which on completion would contribute to revenue, or at the very least would not constitute a recurrent charge on revenue, and the Revenue Equalization Fund would provide the necessary cushion to tide over the difficult adjustment period which must necessarily follow any sudden economic crisis.

Document 5.6: TNA, CO 1023/93, Letter from Governor Alexander Grantham to Oliver Lyttelton (Secretary of State for the Colonies), 9 February 1952.

7. I cannot find that on this Colony's record since the war there has been any real shortage of funds for social development or for building up adequate reserves. The fact appears to be that His Majesty's Government takes the view that its funds are excessive and has hence requested, and received, annual contributions to the defence burden of the United Kingdom. Economically, I am inclined to the view that the Colony is over-developed. Socially, Hong Kong, with a remarkable lack of help from outside, has shouldered the burden of caring for the health and welfare of hundreds of thousands of refugees from Communist China at very heavy cost. Nevertheless the Colony's financial reserves continue to grow, and in such case I feel that the first reason [the need for increased revenue to finance schemes of social and economic development and to establish adequate reserves] can hardly be considered valid . . . I am convinced that increased taxation will be accepted only if it can be shown that the necessity for it is imperative. For example, the necessity for the large-scale and expensive squatter resettlement scheme has been accepted, but it still remains to be seen whether additional taxation to pay for it will be accepted, if it proves necessary . . .

10. There is one aspect of this matter of increasing direct taxation on which the despatch merely touches but which is nevertheless of paramount importance. I refer to

the serious shortage of assessing staff. The situation has now come to the point that in the Inland Revenue Department there is only one assessor adequately qualified and competent to conduct company assessments. You have recently authorised an increase in the number of posts of Assessors . . . and have succeeded in obtaining two candidates, and I have just sent the Commissioner of Inland Revenue to Australia to endeavour to recruit some qualified assessors there. It seems to me somewhat unrealistic to consider increasing rates of tax when it is not possible at the moment to assess tax at existing rates, much less endeavour to ascertain whether evasion is being attempted on any considerable scale . . .

Document 5.7: TNA, CO 1023/93, Minute Written by J. B. Sidebotham (Colonial Office), 19 June 1952.

. . . I am bound to say that there is a good deal in this despatch which arouses my strong disagreement. I do not think there is much point in discussing with the Governor the taxation issue as such, since I agree that we cannot press our point further at the present time. I do feel, however, that we might perhaps discuss with him, in a more general context, some of the underlying implications of all this. I think he has forgotten that at least one of the origins of the whole correspondence about Hong Kong taxation was the proposal by the Hong Kong Government to raise large sums externally for the Tai Lam Chung Reservoir. In this context it was obviously pertinent for us to point out that Hong Kong could not expect to raise external funds until it had taxed itself properly – and incidentally the implication of the Governor's paragraph 7 is that the Colony does not now and will not in the future require finance from external sources. If he is really ready to maintain that position, then perhaps he can also maintain that we have no right to poke our noses into Hong Kong's fiscal policy.

Document 5.8: HKPRO, HKRS 229/2/1, Colonial Secretary Alan Lennox-Boyd to the Officer Administering the Government of Hong Kong, 14 January 1958.

I have the honour to refer to Mr. Creech Jones's despatch No. 302 of the 24th September, 1948, on the subject of the control exercised by Her Majesty's Government over the finances of Hong Kong.

2. In reviewing the operation of those arrangements, I have come to the conclusion that they no longer allow adequate recognition of the good standing, financial and administrative, of Hong Kong and its Government and that the principle of consultation rather than control, enunciated in paragraph 4 of the despatch under reference, ought now to be further developed. I consider that in future I may be

best equipped to discharge my ultimate responsibility to Parliament for the financial affairs of Hong Kong by making the maximum use of the process of informal consultation with you before decisions are taken and by reducing routine formalities to a minimum.

Section 3. Accumulating Reserves and Hong Kong's Dilemma, 1959–1971

Between 1959 and 1971, the colonial government continued to accumulate fiscal reserves. This was accomplished by spending less than it could have done, despite the Chinese refugee influx, which put pressure on the colonial government, particularly on the task of providing social services. In 1966, the colonial government further adjusted the tax rate from 12.5 per cent to 15 per cent. It is interesting that, as the Financial Secretary admitted in his correspondence with the Colonial Office, in case there was a deficit, the colonial government could increase indirect taxation through extending the geographical coverage of rating and increasing duties. Cowperthwaite also disclosed that the colonial government was stuck with a dilemma where local opinion preferred external borrowing over direct taxation to raise resources but, to raise funds externally, foreign lenders preferred the government to resort to internal measures such as internal borrowing and taxation first. Although the colonial government appointed an Inland Revenue Ordinance Review Committee in 1964, the Financial Secretary revealed in 1963 that the Review was for curbing tax evasion rather than introducing a full income tax. This explains why the Review's terms of reference, as the excerpt from the Report below shows, was so restrictive that members were not capable of proposing a change of the schedular framework of the income tax system, which was seen as inherently inequitable. While accumulating fiscal reserves by under-spending was possible in the 1960s, a downside was that there would be an insufficient provision of social services. The colonial government recognised this. After the 1966 disturbance and 1967 leftist riots, the colonial government decided to rectify the situation in order to prevent the communists from exploiting social problems while undermining public confidence in the colonial administration.

Document 5.9: HKPRO, HKRS 163/1/2210, Letter from John J. Cowperthwaite to J. D. Higham (Colonial Office), 17 January 1962.

8. This leads me to taxation for next year. Let me say at once that after much heart – (and head) searching on the subject of direct taxation, I cannot bring myself to any conclusion other than that there are no grounds for an increase at present in the standard rate. I am aware that you will view this conclusion with disapprobation but I feel that I cannot avoid it. The fact is that the increase in revenue from current taxes has once again kept pace with our capacity for useful expansion of public services

– and that although we expanded expenditure by about 19% in 1961/62. With this and our existing reserves in mind I cannot argue that we need extra direct taxation next year. It is not possible to justify raising the rate on the grounds that we will need the money one day and should take it while it is there. For one thing there is our past inability to realise deficits; I cannot prove that this will not continue to happen. For another, investment by the private sector is of very great importance to our development and prosperity and our profit-earners have a very good record of productive re-investment; Government investment, unlike that of many other Colonial governments, has a comparatively small productive element. We have built up substantial reserves in the past but by under-spending rather than by raising tax rates. It is important that the community's savings should "fructify in the pockets of the taxpayers" instead of being held in our reserves. Money for private development is tight at present, although bank deposits continue to increase, and I should not like to be accused of making it tighter. Money we do not take now will come back to us, I believe, with interest when we need it unless external forces combine to depress our industry and trade. We also do not wish to encourage civil service pay claims which would arise on the combined grounds that the increase in tax has lowered net emoluments and that Government has plenty of cash from which to afford increases . . .

10. There is one further point about direct taxation which I should mention although it does not have any immediate bearing on a decision about rates of taxation. I have made no progress with the proposal to bring in a full income tax system . . . I propose to get down to it after the Budget but it is important not to under-estimate the difficulty I shall have in getting it through against unofficial opinion. The defects of the present system are that it does not provide really adequate safeguards against evasion and makes it impossible to levy progressive rates on high individual "unearned" incomes. A change would of itself, however, not produce much extra revenue.

11. If I do find that the final deficit in the budget is greater than I think it will be at present, I may of course yet be forced to change my view. If the deficit is not so high as to have that effect, but is yet substantial, I may feel it advisable to raise a small additional amount of $3-4 million by raising the duty on alcohol. Tobacco revenue has been disappointing this year and I do not think that it will stand a further increase yet . . . It is also proposed to introduce rating over the whole of the New Territories. This will not produce much revenue next year and may cause a political row but we are spending so much on services and development there now that we cannot justify exemption much longer, particularly for the rich new-comer. There is also the Lottery arrangements for which are well in hand and which is estimated to produce $2 million; we have had, however, to undertake to spend this only on social services . . .

15. What I do recognise is, not a circular argument, but a dilemma. The dilemma is that local opinion is against taxation, particularly direct taxation, for capital expenditure until we have raised all we can by borrowing (and in this context they mean external borrowing); while potential foreign lenders are unlikely to lend until we have increased taxation (and attempted to borrow internally). I do not think that planning a capital programme will in any way help in "breaking out of the maze" because the size of the programme does not affect this issue; and in any case, particularly in the light of past experience of estimated deficits turning into surpluses, the "requisite financial measures" some years ahead will not be at all obvious to the man in the street. But I think I will in the event be able to "break out" by other means, largely persuasion and attempts to borrow locally . . .

Document 5.10: HKPRO, HKRS 163/1/2210, Letter from John J. Cowperthwaite to D. J. Kirkness (Colonial Office), 20 March 1963.

I am afraid that the radical amendment of our income tax structure by introducing a full income tax has slipped a bit into the background. While the standard rate of tax is low, the present system is not so inequitable as to provide strong grounds for a full income tax; and until we manage a deficit or two I could never get an agreement to an increase in the standard rate. So far as opportunities for evasion are concerned (as opposed to inequitable incidence) I am considering ways and means of tightening things up. But it won't be popular.

As regards a development plan I fear it is not in our philosophy. But it is a little hard, I think, to describe our present policy as "incoherent" or as "merely paying for as much of current departmental forecasts as the money ran to". It is little more than that; indeed local criticism is that we have not spent the money available. Development plan may look good politically, and may be necessary to secure political loans, or to induce growth into a sleepy economy (and into a sleepy Government); but we prefer the flexibility we consider as very persuaded when the "advanced" countries adopt development planning rather than a series of spending programmes, only loosely related.

Document 5.11: HKPRO, HKRS 163/1/2210, Extract from *Review of Political and Economic Developments*, 27 May 1964.

17. There are, however, two possible dangers on the horizon. First, economic expansion has taken up most of the readily available slack in the economy, both in the form of labour and of suitable land. There have been signs of stress and strain throughout the economy, aggravated by the massive efforts undertaken in certain social fields such as housing. Both wages and industrial land values are under particular upward

pressure. The latter pressure can be relieved in time by an intensification of the effort of land development, but it may impose a temporary brake . . . Hong Kong cannot adjust demand to meet costs; it must always adjust costs to meet demand.

Document 5.12: HKPRO, HKRS 163/9/245, a Revised Draft of Part II of the Inland Revenue Ordinance Review Committee's Report, attached in Letter from Secretary of the Inland Revenue Ordinance Review Committee E. S. Thomas to All Members of the Inland Revenue Ordinance Review Committee, 19 January 1968.

The general tax structure of the Inland Revenue Ordinance

1. We considered, Sir, that a report from a Committee specially appointed to consider and advise on certain matters connected with the Inland Revenue Ordinance should include some general examination of the tax structure of the Ordinance. We propose therefore to record our observations on the operations of the Colony's system of tax on earnings and profits which imposes separate taxes on particular classes of income as compared with the orthodox system which imposes one tax on the total income of the person. Before doing this, it would seem useful to take a look at the evolution in Hong Kong of taxation on earnings and profits . . .

8. We found ourselves in much the same position as the 1952 Committee since we too considered that we were not authorised by our terms of appointment to propose a change in the present system of taxation of earnings and profits which the previous Committee were unanimous in declaring as inherently inequitable. Indeed, whilst comments on this aspect might be considered to be equally beyond our terms of reference, we feel obliged at least to record our observations, which now follow, on the operations of the present system.

9. The schedular type of tax system as contained in the Colony's Inland Revenue Ordinance followed that which was introduced first in the United Kingdom by Addison's Act of 1803 . . . This system had its attractions for Hong Kong particularly as a measure for collecting revenue during wartime as it was directed at the source of the income rather than the person deriving the income . . . In short, the system worked well and though it followed, only in a very general way, the principle of imposing tax according to the ability of the individual to pay, the low tax rate and the comparatively generous personal allowances tended to obscure the inequities of incidence of taxation as between persons chargeable under the Ordinance. However, the tax system commended to lose its simplicity and its attraction, as a medium of collecting taxes easily, with the introduction of Personal Assessment.

Document 5.13: HKPRO, HKRS 742/13/1, Despatch from Governor David Trench to Secretary of State for Foreign and Commonwealth Affairs Michael Stewart, 23 April 1970.

30. To sum up, it has been a good year. The people of Hong Kong have responded to the favourable economic climate with their usual high degree of enterprise and hard work, and most are enjoying a well-earned improvement in living standards. With all this inevitably comes increased expectations and a growing, but not as yet very widespread, concern for the less privileged who for one reason or another cannot share in this prosperity. For its part, the Government is pressing on with a wide range of programmes in the social service areas, as well as in the more concrete field of improvements in the general environment. We are aiming at a steady improvement in the Government's performance at the level at which it has direct impact upon ordinary people, and as close a correlation between public policy and public opinion as sound administration permits . . . Indeed, while 1967 was a year in which many plans had to be dusted off and momentum regained, 1969 has seen many of them brought to fruition or far along the road towards it. I believe that our efforts to improve the quality of life in the Colony for people of all social classes are generally and quietly appreciated, and that we can look forward to a continuation of the satisfactory relationship between the Government and the people that has brought us through so many difficult periods in the past.

31. Nevertheless Hong Kong socially, politically and economically is pre-eminently a community that depends on confidence. On all three points we are vulnerable and it is essential that . . . the Government of Hong Kong should continue, albeit with the minimum of provocation, to be firm in resisting any encroachment on the interests of the people. A loss of confidence could only too easily be generated by the successful exploitation of social and administrative problems by the Communists, or an erosion of our export markets by overseas interests.

Section 4. Social Reforms and Fiscal Conservatism, 1972–1980

During the 1970s, the colonial government's social reforms and policies improved the living standards of Hong Kong residents. It is inaccurate to describe Murray MacLehose as the initiator, but his role was crucial in terms of injecting momentum to sustain the reformist trend. In doing so, Governor MacLehose hoped that the British would have a better bargaining position in Sino-British diplomatic negotiations in the early 1980s. The geopolitical calculation of making Hong Kong a model city is crucial in understanding how the Governor understood the importance of social reforms, as seen in his 'Hong Kong Objectives' despatch. Although Governor MacLehose recognised the need for social reforms, he hoped that these reforms could be implemented without changing the tax rates or substantially drawing on the colony's reserves. In the same period, London became proactive in pressuring the colonial government to undertake a more comprehensive reform package, as seen in the Planning Paper drafted in mid-1976. Tensions between Hong Kong and London became acute and disputes arose around the colonial government's fiscal philosophy and budgeting approach, which London deemed too conservative and regressive. Governor MacLehose sided with Financial Secretary Haddon-Cave, who wanted to slow down the pace of development to achieve a balanced budget. Haddon-Cave also worried that the members of LegCo [Legislative Council] and ExCo [Executive Council] would not agree with having substantially higher taxes. By 1976, it was clear to London that the colonial government aimed to preserve the schedular framework of the income tax system and low tax rates while modernising Hong Kong. This in turn explains why, even though the colonial government appointed the third – and the last – Inland Revenue Review Committee in 1976, it refused to alter the basic feature of the tax structure. In 1975, the tax rates were modestly adjusted from 15 per cent to 16.5 per cent. The social reforms eventually implemented in Hong Kong were less drastic when compared with the original Planning Paper, and the fiscal limitations could be regarded as a reason for that. Still, the new social reforms impressed the residents of Hong Kong. The fiscal approach established in this decade had a lasting impact on public finance even after 1997.

Document 5.14: TNA, FCO 40/547, Despatch from Governor Murray MacLehose to the Secretary of State for Foreign and Commonwealth Affairs, 27 May 1974.

10. I think we should do everything we can to make Hong Kong a model city, of international standing, with high standards of education, technology and culture, as well as industrial, commercial and financial facilities, from which China can gain great benefit, but which China might be reluctant to try to absorb while she still has some need of the material benefits it offers and while her own conditions remain so different . . .

11. I think we should also get a move on. Firstly because there is much that needs doing, secondly because to retain the interest and loyalty of the population progress must be visible, and thirdly because we do not know how long the present state of good relations with China will last, and some of the conditions of life that exist at present are easy to exploit for political purposes. Yet another and conclusive reason for a spurt is that the shadow of the end of the lease in 1997 will start to make itself

felt in the '80s. This will be the time to do everything possible to increase confidence and profitability and thus promote employment and living standards in the Colony. It will be a time to decrease rather increase taxes and charges. So problems should be faced and solved now, within the next decades, at whatever cost is necessary compatible with the continued expansion of the economy and its attractiveness to investors, in the hope of being able to ease up in the '80s. This at least is how I myself and my advisers see it. Hong Kong's exposure and vulnerability in the '80s and '90s will be very great in any case, for obvious reasons outside the control of the Hong Kong Government, but it will be that much worse unless many of her traditional social problems are solved in the 70's . . .

13. However we have concluded that a major effort must now be made to put a term to the deficiencies that exist and have therefore drawn up major programmes to be completed within the next decade in the fields of Housing, Education, Medical and Health Services and Social Welfare . . . The programmes have caught the imagination of the public, and generally improved its confidence in the Government and in the Government's concern for public welfare . . .

19. When formulating these policies and operations we have hoped to cover the expenditure at constant tax rates . . . In the light of all this we concluded that if our programmes were to be achieved sufficiently fast, and if we were to avoid overstraining our capacity in their first three years both some rephrasing was necessary and that additional resources were required. With regard to the latter we have raised the overall level of revenue from taxation of all sorts this year by 2.8 per cent and have put the public on notice that from 1975/76 new money of the order of $650 million a year will have to be found, of which hopefully $150 million a year might come from loans (from the Asian Development Bank) and the balance from additional taxation . . .

21. The Government did consider drawing on its reserves . . . or alternatively of attempting to borrow on a much greater scale than that . . . However both alternatives were rejected . . . in any case with such large spending programmes drawn up for the next 10 years, and liable as the Colony is to chronic uncertainty about its trade and thus its revenue, we thought it prudent to harbour these resources until a real need arises . . .

Document 5.15: TNA, FCO 40/522, Internal Minute from A. C. Stuart of the Hong Kong and Indian Ocean Department to Mr Male and Sir D. Watson, 22 July 1974.

2. On the financial situation Mr. Haddon-Cave explained to me at length that a slowing down of the pace of development might be necessary . . . recurrent expenditure was already rising so fast that, even without additional capital commitments, it would be very difficult to balance the budget. The three ways of raising new money were by loans, by increased taxation, or by the use of Hong Kong's reserves. For loans, as the Governor had told us, Mr Haddon-Cave hoped to raise about HK$150 million a year for three years from the Asian Development Bank and other sources. He also intended to propose some increases in taxation. But, although the members of LegCo and ExCo had told the Governor they would support this, Mr. Haddon-Cave was not hopeful that they would actually agree to substantially higher taxes when I come to the crunch. Lastly, he himself did not consider that it would be prudent to run down Hong Kong's reserves any further . . . a large proportion of the reserves had to be held against contingencies such as debt servicing . . . a new development . . . was that the Exchange Fund was not sufficient to cover 100% of the Hong Kong note issue. This meant that part of the Fiscal Reserve had to be tacitly earmarked against the shortfall in the Exchange Fund . . .

3. When I discussed all this with the Governor he agreed that Mr. Haddon-Cave might well be making too cautious a view . . . Nevertheless Sir Murray could not afford to take Mr. Haddon-Cave's advice lightly. He would be responsible if things went wrong and the results would be very serious. While he remained convinced that there was no alternative to pressing ahead with his development plans . . . he felt concerned at his own lack of financial expertise and weight . . .

13. The personal pressures of all this are quite strong . . . The most immediate problem is the Financial Secretary . . .

Document 5.16: TNA, FCO 40/701, Despatch entitled 'Hong Kong – Domestic Policies up to the 80s' from Governor Murray MacLehose to James Callaghan, 6 March 1976.

This despatch describes the objectives and content of the social, economic and political plans of the Hong Kong Government up to the 80s. It is very long because of the size of the subject . . .

<u>The Problem</u>

2. H.M.G.'s policy is to administer Hong Kong in the interests of the people of Hong Kong. The circumstances of the Colony impose both priorities and limitations on policy options:-

a) the special position of China, and the absence of any possibility of normal progress to either an elected government or independence.

b) The deficiencies in social and economic infrastructure resulting from the quadrupling of the population in the last 25 years.

c) Total dependence of the economy on exports.

d) The need to maintain a comparatively low tax structure to retain, attract and encourage a high rate of investment to maintain growth and employ the population despite lack of assurance about the Colony's long-term future.

e) The ultimate responsibility of Parliament coupled with absence of representation of Hong Kong in it, and the formal devolution of financial autonomy to, and practical exercise of commercial autonomy by the Hong Kong Government . . .

5. The policies being followed to resolve this complex of problems have frequently been discussed with the Department and are recapitulated in this despatch. It is rather long because of the breadth of the subject. But in simplest terms they are . . .

a) to make good the material and social deficiencies, which are the principal concern of the population, by the early or mid-'80s through selective crash programmes.

b) To safeguard the position of lower income groups by schemes of heavily subsidised housing and heavily subsidised or free education and health services, financed from general revenue; and in addition to maintain the incomes of vulnerable groups such as the handicapped, aged or unfortunate by cash payments, supplemented where appropriate by special services, also all financed from general revenue.

c) To maintain a high rate of economic growth to maintain employment and a rising standard of living and obtain the revenue to pay for (a) and (b); and for this latter purpose also to reform the tax system to make it yield the necessary revenue at rates that will still retain, attract and encourage at a high rate the investment on which competitiveness and revenue depend . . .

The limitations on a faster rate of progress

10. While the budgetary and other limitations on a faster speed or more extended field of advance are not absolute, they are real and must be clearly understood:

a) Taxes on earnings and profits must be comparatively low, partly to retain and attract investment in spite of long term political uncertainty to ensure employment, and partly to stimulate reinvestment and growth with the same objective . . .

b) There are technical problems connected with the four separate levies on profits and earnings that make them extremely inflexible and inequities and loop-holes have also developed in them. I have appointed an Inland Revenue Ordinance Review Committee under the chairmanship of an ex-Commissioner of Inland Revenue in the United Kingdom, to examine the whole problem and report by the end of this year. I hope that its recommendations will assist both to make the system more productive at constant rates, and also indicate ways in which, if otherwise desirable, these taxes may be raised or made progressive . . .

Document 5.17: TNA, FCO 40/756, Telegram no. 820 from Governor MacLehose to Foreign and Commonwealth Office, 12 August 1977.

1. The proposals have been prepared following wide informal consultations, and are designed to produce the maximum support from the people of Hong Kong. To this end, we have concentrated on providing additional aid for those incapable of self support . . . and for those with low incomes. The unemployed have not been singled out for special treatment but will benefit from the various improvements in public assistance.

2. The proposed contributory scheme breaks entirely new ground in Hong Kong. We have not therefore attempted to make it comprehensive at this stage. If it is successful, however, and there is public support for its extension, there is no administrative reason why it might not be extended to cover unemployment. To start with unemployment, however, would in our judgement jeopardise public acceptance of the scheme . . .

6. The estimated costs (Dollars Million) of the additional expenditure on cash payments and services recommended in the whole review are substantial, as the table below makes clear –

Fiscal Year	Social Security (cash payment)	Elderly (excluding medical costs)	Services for youth (including family life education)	Rehabilitation	Total
1978/79 Recurrent capital	53.00 (-)	7.00 (0.10)	20.00 (1.60)	19.00 (19.00)	99.00 (20.70)
1979/80 Recurrent capital	102.00 (-)	13.00 (0.33)	25.00 (-)	37.00 (25.00)	177.00 (25.33)
1980/81 Recurrent capital	134.00 (-)	19.00 (0.38)	33.00 (0.20)	51.00 (18.00)	237.00 (18.58)
1981/82 Recurrent capital	158.00 (-)	28.00 (0.77)	34.00 (0.20)	63.00 (14.00)	283.00 (14.97)
1982/83 Recurrent capital	177.00 (-)	34.00 (0.49)	36.00 (0.20)	76.00 (11.00)	323.00 (11.69)
Total	624.00	103.07	150.20	333.00	1210.27

7. It should be emphasised that these estimates (which are subject to amendment) are all for extra expenditure on new programmes not provided for in current forecasts, nor do they include any provision for additional expenditure arising from demand by the community for expansion of current programmes. The expenditure on services will build up more slowly than that on cash payments because of the need to train specialist staff.

Document 5.18: Official Report of Proceedings, Hong Kong Legislative Council, 25 February 1976.

(7) Economic Implications of the Budget

207. Public expenditure tends to be determined by political and social, as well as economic, considerations and so it is important that the size of the public sector does not exceed a certain limit. Otherwise, there is a risk that public sector activities will damage the growth rate of the economy. It is a matter of opinion when this limit is reached, but it is clearly lower in an open economy such as ours, necessarily dependent on a relatively narrow range of industries manufacturing for export, than

in a closed economy. But, in my opinion, if one measures the size of the public sector in terms of the ratio of total public expenditure to the GDP, the outside limit should be set at 20%; and, when the economy is enjoying strong growth, the ratio should fall. Inevitably, the ratio rose in the two years of economic recession 1974 and 1975, to just over 19%, after being just over 16% in 1972 and 1973 and just under 14% in the first two years of the decade. In the coming year, the ratio will rise a little further to just over 20%, assuming total public expenditure is as high as budgeted for (at $8,225 million) and the GDP at current prices is of the order of $41,000 million.

208. If the ratio were to be as high as this in a year in which the economy grows at an above average rate, then we shall have to ask ourselves whether there is any likelihood of it ever falling for it would be dangerous for it to be 20% or even higher on the next downturn leaving no room for the public sector to expand temporarily as it has been able to do so recently . . .

216. The first two Review Committees appointed in 1954 and 1966 did not consider that the basic structure of the ordinance fell within their purview and so their recommendations were largely of a technical and administrative nature only. By contrast, the intention is that the third Review Committee will examine the basic structure of the ordinance. By "basic structure" I mean such matters as the existence of separate schedular taxes, the territorial ambit of the charge and the lack of progression in the rates. The committee will also be asked to consider the treatment of dividends and, in particular, the proposals formulated in 1975 for a dividend withholding tax and associated measures. The committee will not be required to concern itself with administrative matters, nor with questions of fiscal policy, that is to say, actual rates of tax. Administrative matters have been thrashed out in detail in recent years; and fiscal policy questions must be left to the Government. In addition, the Committee will not deal with the level and extent of personal allowances, except insofar as they are related to any particular term of reference, such as the taxation of husbands and wives.

217. In case the appointment of this committee generates a degree of despondency, let me hasten to add that there is no intention on the part of the Government to pursue change for the sake of change, particularly where it can be claimed that the present system works. But the fact is that the underlying principles on which the present ordinance is structured were formulated in war-time haste 35 years ago and it is time we considered whether or not they still meet the needs of modern Hong Kong. Quite apart from the fact that there are certain inherent inequities in the present system I am doubtful whether, at given tax rates, it is as productive of revenue as it could be. This is not just a matter of rates, let alone efficiency of administration, but of the provisions of the ordinance itself. In our circumstances, characterised as

they are by a unique dependence on external trading transactions, our direct tax system must be low so as to ensure, *inter alia* a high rate of capital investment and a high growth rate of the economy. It must also be simple and inexpensive to administer. But if we are to maintain our low tax system—as I firmly believe we must — and yet, at the same time, meet our obligations as a Government—as obviously we must—then the ordinance must be more productive of revenue.

Conclusion

218. Sir, the budget I have just presented to honourable Members seeks to provide appropriately for what I described earlier as measurable advances in certain high priority areas of concern now that improved economic conditions are in prospect. At the same time, it is consistent with that traditional mix of fiscal conservatism and economic liberalism which I firmly believe is the mainspring of progress in our circumstances and, like you, Sir, I take it as a good omen that we enter the second half of this decade in the Year of the Dragon.

Document 5.19: TNA, FCO 40/761, Minute from J. A. B Stewart of the Hong Kong and General Department to Mr Cortazzi and Lord Goronwy-Roberts, 22 November 1977.

(a) Social Progress

A Planning Paper drawn up in mid-1976, and agreed with the Hong Kong Government, set out a programme of social and economic development for the next 5 years. I attach a summary of its main recommendations . . .

(i) Social Security: We should like to see faster progress towards an effective, non means-tested scheme for unemployment benefits and old age pensions;

(ii) Budget and Taxation: Taxes remain very low in Hong Kong, with a maximum rate of income tax at only 15% and few indirect taxes. The Government maintain that, with adequate revenue to meet current public expenditure, there is no need to change this state of affairs (which is one of the main causes of the Colony's success in attracting foreign investment). But a recent World Bank report criticizes the low proportion of GDP being devoted to public expenditure (17% compared with 54% in the UK). The present policy in Hong Kong is to estimate revenue then tailor policies to the funds available. We should like to see a more positive approach. This may well lead to an increase in public expenditure, which should be partly financed by introducing an element of progressivity into the tax system thus increasing its redistributive effect.

Document 5.20: TNA, FCO 40/965, Minute from Michael Stewart to J. Stewart (Hong Kong and General Department), 24 February 1978.

2. In general, I agree with your minute . . . to Mr Murray, and with the draft letter to the Governor. In particular, I would certainly support your proposal that the section on expenditure should come first, to be followed by the passages dealing with the raising of revenue. As you say, this would help to focus attention on the economically rational way of determining the balance between public and private expenditure, rather than treating public expenditure as a kind of residual, dependent on the revenue which a particular tax structure happens to yield . . .

4. This brings me to a more fundamental point, which it would probably not be appropriate to raise in your letter to the Governor, but which seems to me to need thinking about. Every time I look at anything to do with the Hong Kong budget, I am struck by the prevalence of concepts which seem quite inappropriate when managing an economy, as opposed perhaps to a domestic household. This applies to the idea that there should be free reserves at the beginning of a financial year equivalent to 15% of estimated expenditure in the ensuing year; to the idea that there should be certain percentage relationships between particular revenue and expenditure flows; and indeed to the idea that there is a hard and fast distinction between capital and current expenditures, and capital and current revenues. These concepts may be of some validity if one is concerned with the rational allocation of a particular fixed quantity of resources, such as the spending by a household of a weekly income which is fixed by circumstances outside its control. But the concept is much less relevant to the management of an economy, since both the total resources available can be varied by policy which determines the level of output and employment in the economy, and the resources available to the Government, whether or not the economy is at full employment, can be varied by decisions on the nature and level of taxation. Thus the sort of guide-lines and requirements with which budget speeches in Hong Kong tend to be obsessed are likely to make it difficult or impossible to manage the economy in an optimal way. In short, the improvements one can make in the Hong Kong budget are rather limited . . . as long as the budget is constructed within the present framework. What is needed is the building of a new framework which sees the budget as a crucial instrument of macro-economic policy for the economy as a whole, and not just a matter of balancing Government expenditure and Government revenue.

Section 5. Consolidation of Prudent Fiscal and Budgetary Policy, 1981–1997

The 1984 Sino-British Joint Declaration concluded that Hong Kong would cease to be a British colony in 1997 and become a Special Administrative Region (SAR) within the sovereign control of China. No more review committees have been appointed since the 1980s. This marked the beginning of the transition period (see Chapter 3), in which maintaining Hong Kong's stability and prosperity were considered a common agenda between Britain and China. Fiscal policy and budgeting became an issue during the Sino-British negotiations when Deng Xiaoping expressed his hope to Governor Edward Youde to maintain the value of the Hong Kong dollar and stabilise the land market. To do so, the colonial government would have to retain fiscal reserves for stabilising the value of the Hong Kong dollar. A Capital Works Reserve Fund was also established to finance public works projects. This drew further fiscal resources away from the general revenue account that the colonial government could otherwise use for alternative purposes such as social welfare and housing provisions.[7] Most importantly, the British promised that Hong Kong would 'continue to finance itself on the same prudent and skilful basis'. This shaped the subsequent development of the fiscal policy and budgeting. The colonial government introduced several reforms to ensure that prudent management of fiscal policy and resources could be achieved. This included implementing financial management reform, reformulating budgetary strategy that stipulated 'growth rate of public expenditure should be based on the trend growth rate of the economy', and developing a rational resource allocation system.

Document 5.21: TNA, FCO 40/1777, 'Record of a Meeting between the Secretary of State for Foreign and Commonwealth Affairs and Chairman Deng Xiaoping at the Great Hall of the People, Peking', 31 July 1984.

8. The Secretary of State assured Chairman Deng that HMG was determined to do everything necessary and possible to ensure a smooth transition in 1997. HMG had this as much at heart as did Chairman Deng . . . HMG were determined to do everything to cherish and preserve the vase [i.e., Hong Kong] and to ensure that they handed it over in good condition to maintain the stability and prosperity of something in which both countries had the highest interest. But if this were to be an example to other countries to settle similar problems, they must continue to cooperate to make it the desired success. He hoped that until 1997 cooperation would continue as at present and that China would listen to the UK's advice about the best way to ensure success . . .

7. See, for example, Alan Smart and Fung Chi Keung Charles, *Hong Kong Public and Squatter Housing: Geopolitics and Informality, 1963–1985* (Hong Kong: Hong Kong University Press, 2023), chapter 11.

10. Chairman Deng said that there should be good cooperation between the two sides. He considered the important question to be the kind of people to fill such posts in Hong Kong. This would be tackled in the latter half of the transitional period. The two sides should cooperate very closely and consult one another throughout that period...

11. Chairman Deng then turned to Sir Edward Youde. He said the Governor's responsibility was heavy. He hoped that:

(a) The value of the Hong Kong dollar would not be shaken. Its credibility was based on the Exchange Fund. He understood that the Exchange Fund was greater than the amount of Hong Kong dollars issued. There should be no change in the monetary situation.

(b) The land market would not be shaken. The Chinese side had agreed that land leases could be granted by the British Hong Kong authorities whose terms would run 50 years after 1997. They had also agreed that the British Hong Kong authorities could use the income from the grants corresponding to the period after 1997 on condition that such grants would be used for land development and capital construction in Hong Kong and not as government expenditure.

(c) The British Hong Kong authorities would not increase the number of public servants and substantially increase their salaries and pensions in the transitional period. This would be a heavy burden for the SAR...

12. The Secretary of State said it was very important that they should understand one another on this point. They shared a common objective. Hong Kong had achieved its present prosperity and stability because of the extent to which the UK had cared for all these things...

14. The Secretary of State continued that he had described some of the appointments of Hong Kong people to senior posts. Continuity was important . . . This would be achieved because of HMG's interest in maintaining stability and prosperity, and their desire to hand over a stable and prosperous Hong Kong, taking account of all the things mentioned by Chairman Deng. The Secretary of State referred to his experience of four years as Chancellor of the Exchequer. He could assure Chairman Deng that no finances were more prudently managed than those of Hong Kong. That would continue. The size and salaries of the public service would continue to be prudently managed. Chairman Deng had said China would impose no taxes on Hong Kong. Hong Kong would continue to finance itself on the same prudent and skilful basis. The Chinese side should be in no doubt about that. Nobody realised

better the importance of the Hong Kong dollar. The UK would continue to do its utmost to sustain it. The Exchange Fund would continue to be used for the good of the Hong Kong economy. As an ex-Finance Minister and as Foreign Secretary and on behalf of HMG, he could give his absolute assurance that China need have no worries on this score. It was as much in the UK's interest as China's for Hong Kong's finances to remain sound. Chairman Deng had been right to emphasise the importance of land. Here too the Chinese Government should have no fear. He gave his personal assurance, and that of HMG that the Hong Kong Government would continue to manage land in the best interests of the Hong Kong SAR.

Document 5.22: HKPRO, HKRS 394/29/202, 'Chief Secretary's Committee – Financial Management Reform', by Finance Branch on 26 October 1987.

Key Principles of Sound Financial Management

2. In considering the way forward for improving financial management, Finance Branch has assumed the following key principles:

(i) financial management is: the planning, application, monitoring and control of financial resources to achieve results. It goes in this sense much wider and deeper than traditional public sector concepts of provision and control. It is fundamentally concerned with the value obtained for the taxpayer's money;

(ii) the Hong Kong government is now too large, too complex and too diffuse for financial controls to be exercised solely from the centre. Financial management, and the responsibility for maximising value for money, needs to be made much more clearly the business of every manager in government;

(iii) the concept of responsibility for financial management is meaningless unless managers are given the freedom to manage. At the same time, they must be held clearly accountable for the exercise of such freedoms;

(iv) some constraints on the freedom of managers to manage are inevitable. Such constraints derive, for example, from the fundamental responsibility of the government to plan and maintain a realistic and sensible budget strategy. But the constraints on managers should be kept to the minimum consistent with sound financial management practices . . .

3. Much has been achieved in recent years to bring the practices of the government closer to the principles of best practice set out above. For example:

(i) the introduction of LAFIS [Ledger Accounting and Financial Information System] into departments has significantly improved their ability to monitor expenditure against provision and to take corrective action where necessary;

(ii) financial delegations from Finance Committee to Finance Branch and from Finance Branch to departments have been progressively increased so as to allow Controlling Officers greater authority in financial matters;

(iii) the development of the Medium Range Forecast has given government a more objective means of assessing future trends in income and expenditure. This, in turn, has enabled the government to identify the 'room for manoeuvre, particularly in terms of the scope for funding new and improved services;

(iv) the development of the resource allocation system over the last two years has given CSC [Chief Secretary's Committee] as a whole, and policy secretaries individually, greater say in the overall strategy of the government and in the priorities that should be attached to new developments within the funds available;

(v) value for money studies are playing an increasingly important part in helping Controlling Officers to get better value for the resources under their control; and

(vi) the initial work done by policy branches and departments on the development of programme definitions has already begun to focus the attention of Secretaries and Controlling Officers on the results they achieve with the resources under their control. This has been helped by the decision that Controlling Officers' reports in the 1988-89 Estimates should, wherever possible, report performance and targets on the basis of their objectives rather than their activities.

Document 5.23: HKPRO, HKRS 394/29/204, 'CSC Paper – 1989 Resource Allocation System (1989/90–1993/94)', by Finance Branch, 25 May 1989.

General Preface – Budgetary Strategy

A key element of budgetary strategy is that the growth rate of public expenditure should be based on the trend growth rate of the economy. This is designed to ensure that steady growth is maintained (which is necessary for the orderly development of public services) and that this growth can be sustained without the public sector claiming too great a share of the territory's resources. The level of public spending is therefore governed, not by the revenue available or the size of the reserves, but by what the economy can support. The reserves assist in supporting this strategy by enabling steady growth to be maintained during cyclical changes in revenue levels. They also cover the Government's contingent liabilities. In last year's RAS [Resource Allocation System], a figure of 6% per annum was assumed for GDP growth over the forecast period. This figure is maintained in this year's exercise.

2. In this context, the rate of growth in the size of the civil service is particularly relevant. In recent years, the rate of growth in terms of establishments has been consistently greater than the budgetary guideline of 2.5% per annum. The rate of growth in strength however is considerably less; in 1988-89 it was 1.6%. As a result, the vacancy rate has steadily increased and now stands at over 5%. It is particularly important to bear this in mind in this year's RAS as the allocation of resources to staff intensive activities may achieve little more than to increase the vacancy rate. Considerable scope therefore exists for the redeployment of existing posts to take on new tasks.

Document 5.24: HKPRO, HKRS 394/29/204, 'Public Sector Reform', by Finance Branch, 25 May 1989.

This paper sets out for CSC's discussion a possible way forward for the implementation of public sector reform. In preparing the paper regard has been had to comments received on the public sector reform booklet prepared by Finance Branch and also to the discussions at the recent seminars on the subject.

<u>The need for reform</u>

2. Why is a reform programme needed? Although the consultants drew on experience overseas as well as in Hong Kong, it is worth underlining that the booklet also drew together a number of separate strands of thought which predated this study. A number of problems were perceived to exist, in particular –

(a) a need to continue to develop the resource allocation system so that the Administration was better able to shift priorities, and to review the whole of public expenditure not just the money available for new items;

(b) given that demands for resources were likely to increasingly outstrip the supply, a need also to emphasise "value for money" and "savings from the baseline";

(c) a feeling that to varying degrees the relationship between Secretaries and Heads of Departments, and other bodies, needed to be clarified. And perhaps also that Branches were in danger of being overwhelmed by "fire-fighting", dealing with LegCo etc., and not being able to spend enough time on strategic, policy type work (perhaps partly because of dealing with issues over which under the present division of responsibility they have little or no influence);

(d) perhaps coupled with (c), a feeling that some non-policy work had become over-centralized, and that the move by Finance Branch to delegate more should be continued and spread to other branches . . .

Document 5.25: HKPRO, HKRS 394/29/205, 'Paper for the Chief Secretary's Committee Resource Allocation System: Capital Works Reserve Fund Public Work Programme (1989–90 to 1993–94)', by Finance Branch on 4 September 1989.

[1.] On 12 June 1989, CSC discussed Paper No. 9/89 and endorsed the approach and procedures, as set out below, for this year's resource allocation exercise on the Capital Works Reserve Fund (CWRF):

(a) the allocation of a basic figure to each Policy Secretary to meet the balance of the 1988 agreed non-new town and new town RAS programmes, with the remainder to be allocated by CSC against bids;

(b) the submission by each Policy Secretary of a list of non-new town projects (in order of priority) to be funded from the basic figure, and the requirements beyond that level;

(c) the submission of three programmes on new town projects by SLW [Secretary for Planning, Environment and Lands] (a basic programme which is a roll-on from the 1988 RAS programme, a reduced basic programme, and a supplementary programme of major developments proposed by SLW); and

(d) the pooling together of resources for capital subvention projects with those for government capital projects.

2. The meeting noted that public sector expenditure must not exceed what the economy could afford. Given the likelihood of bids exceeding the available resources, the meeting also noted that a critical assessment of the relative priority for different programme areas would be needed.

3. Policy Secretaries have now made their submissions on non-new town projects. SLW has also submitted the three programmes on new town projects which took into account the views expressed by concerned policy branches at the Development Co-ordinating Committee (DCC) . . .

4. In addition, concerned Policy Secretaries have been requested by Finance Branch to put up bids for capital resources required to proceed with Strategy a (i.e. with a replacement airport at Chek Lap Kok) under the Port and Airport Development Study.

Suggested Readings

Chiu, Stephen W. K. 'Unraveling Hong Kong's Exceptionalism: The Politics of Laissez-Faire in the Industrial Takeoff'. *Political Power and Social Theory* 10 (1996): 229–56.

Clayton, David W. 'From Laissez-Faire to "Positive Non-Interventionism": The Colonial State in Hong Kong Studies'. *Social Transformations in Chinese Societies* 9, no. 1 (2013): 1–19.

Fong, Brian C. H. *Hong Kong Public Budgeting: Historical and Comparative Analyses.* Singapore: Palgrave Macmillan, 2022.

Goodstadt, Leo F. *Uneasy Partners: The Conflict between Public and Private Profit in Hong Kong*. Hong Kong: Hong Kong University Press, 2005.

Goodstadt, Leo F. 'Fiscal Freedom and the Making of Hong Kong's Capitalist Society'. *China Information* 24, no. 3 (2010): 273–94.

Ho, Henry Chun Yuen. *The Fiscal System of Hong Kong*. London: Croom Helm, 1979.

Littlewood, Michael. *Taxation without Representation: The History of Hong Kong's Troublingly Successful Tax System*. Hong Kong: Hong Kong University Press, 2010.

Rabushka, Alvin. *Value for Money: The Hong Kong Budgetary Process*. Stanford, CA: Hoover Institution Press, 1976.

Scott, Ian. *The Public Sector in Hong Kong*. 2nd ed. Hong Kong: Hong Kong University Press, 2022.

Tang, Shu-hung. 'Budgetary Guidelines and Fiscal Performance in Hong Kong'. *International Journal of Public Sector Management* 10, no. 7 (1997): 547–71.

Tang, Shu-hung. 'Hong Kong: Revenue Policy under the British Administration'. *Asia-Pacific Journal of Taxation* 1, no. 3 (1997): 81–113.

Ure, Gavin. *Governors, Politics, and the Colonial Office: Public Policy in Hong Kong, 1918–58*. Hong Kong: Hong Kong University Press, 2012.

Yep, Ray, and Lui Tai-lok. 'Revisiting the Golden Era of MacLehose and the Dynamics of Social Reforms'. *China Information* 24, no. 3 (2010): 249–72.

6
Transport and Communications

Adonis M. Y. Li

Hong Kong sees itself, and is seen by others, as a city constantly on the move. For those looking from outside, it is a window or gateway into China, especially after the Communist takeover in 1949. Academics, businesspeople, and athletes alike transit through Hong Kong on trips to China. Hong Kong's international airport is a key node in global aviation networks; its Mass Transit Railway (MTR) Corporation is renowned internationally for its clean and punctual service and its financially impressive model, attained by acting as a real estate developer first and a transport service second. Hong Kong's trams and ferries are tourist attractions in the region, providing a historical, colonial feel to an otherwise modern city.

Hong Kong's intra-city mobility is just as important to its people's self-identity. At a concert welcoming Queen Elizabeth II at the Hong Kong Coliseum in 1986, pop stars from the colony sang 'The underground rail flies to Kwun Tong / The Tram reaches the Peak / The iron tube traverses the seabed / Fast cars swarm on the Island Eastern Corridor / Coming to and fro hastily / Hong Kong loves to hurry.'[1] In more recent times, transport enthusiasts descending onto a railway station platform to say their farewells to rolling stock being retired from service made front-page news.[2]

It is striking, then, that few academic histories of the city's transport have been written. Hong Kong is often 'presumed to be a regional hub with diverse transnational networks and worldwide exchanges', but this is rarely fully explained and

1. Penned by legendary Hong Kong lyricist James Wong, 'This Is Our Home' would later be released on an album by Radio Television Hong Kong in 1990. Joanna Ching-Yun Lee, 'Cantopop Songs on Emigration from Hong Kong', *Yearbook for Traditional Music* 24 (1992): 19. See also Chapter 9, 'Cultural Policies'.
2. 'Farewell at End of Line', *South China Morning Post*, 7 May 2022, A1.

problematised.[3] Hong Kong's pre-war transport development has been appraised by Ma Koon-yiu,[4] but the nearest we have to an academic reappraisal of the post-war period approaches transport development widely but not in depth.[5] For depth, one must delve into works by enthusiasts and non-professional historians, which can range from detailed but dry compendia of rolling stock and fleet information, to qualitative works complete with oral histories conducted with former and current transport workers.[6] Recently, academic historians have begun to study Hong Kong's transport history from perspectives such as business history and international relations.[7] This chapter acts as a brief introduction to Hong Kong's post-war transport development and also points researchers towards possible avenues of further research. It is roughly chronological and brings together different modes of transport, but due to space constraints, not every single mode of transport or service provider will be discussed. The field of transport history has progressed in recent years. Multi-modal, holistic histories of mobility have developed out of earlier single-modal histories.[8] Hong Kong's dense population and mobility channelled through various road, rail, and water corridors mean that discussions of mobility in Hong Kong are necessarily multi-modal.[9]

Section 1. The Kowloon–Canton Railway

The Kowloon–Canton Railway (KCR) was one of the first modes of transport to be rehabilitated after the Japanese surrender. The line was originally built to make Hong Kong the terminus of a Beijing–Hankou–Guangzhou trunk line, but the China-spanning line was

3. Siu-Keung Cheung, 'Hong Kong: Geopolitics and Intellectual Practice', *Inter-Asia Cultural Studies* 13, no. 3 (2012): 337.
4. Ma Koon-yiu 馬冠堯, *Cheshuimalong: Xianggang zhanqian lushang jiaotong* 車水馬龍：香港戰前陸上交通 [Streams of horses and carriages: Hong Kong's pre-war land transport] (Hong Kong: Joint Publishing, 2016).
5. Peter F. Leeds, 'Evolution of Urban Transport', in *Land-Use/Transport Planning in Hong Kong: The End of an Era*, ed. Harry T. Dimitriou and Alison H. S. Cook (London: Routledge, 1998), 13–33.
6. Some outstanding examples can be found in the Suggested Readings section of this chapter.
7. John D. Wong, 'Flexible Corporate Nationality: Transforming Cathay Pacific for the Shifting Geopolitics of Hong Kong in the Closing Decades of British Colonial Rule', *Enterprise & Society* 23, no. 2 (2022): 445–77; Adonis M. Y. Li, 'Hindrance or Helping Hand? Hong Kong and Sino-British Railway Commercial Diplomacy, 1974–84', *The International History Review* 45, no. 3 (2023): 590–605.
8. Tim Cresswell, 'Towards a Politics of Mobility', *Environment and Planning D: Society and Space* 28, no. 1 (2010): 17–31; Gijs Mom, 'The Crisis of Transport History: A Critique, and a Vista', *Mobility in History* 6 (2015): 7–19; George Revill, 'Histories', in *The Routledge Handbook of Mobilities*, ed. Peter Adey et al. (London: Routledge, 2014), 506–16; Mimi Sheller and John Urry, 'The New Mobilities Paradigm', *Environment and Planning A: Economy and Space* 38, no. 2 (2006): 207–26.
9. For a broader discussion of Hong Kong and mobility history, see Adonis M. Y. Li, 'Visions of Public and Private Mobility: The Kowloon Railway Terminus in Hong Kong", *Urban History* (2023).

not completed until the mid-1930s, and the KCR was not connected with the Guangzhou–Hankou line until 1937.[10] *It provided the majority of China's munitions supply between July 1937 and the fall of Guangzhou in October 1938.*[11] *After the war, re-establishing the connection to Guangzhou was paramount. Reconnection with China was not only practical, but also symbolic. The railway symbolised Hong Kong's link to China, perceived as the colony's most important external linkage. The KCR ran cross-border passenger services to Guangzhou until October 1949, after which travellers to China had to cross the border bridge on foot. Cross-border freight services resumed shortly thereafter. This mostly comprised materials and foodstuffs from China to Hong Kong, earning valuable foreign exchange for the Beijing regime.*[12] *Document 6.1 is an excerpt of the first monthly report by General Manager Ivan B. Trevor after British re-occupation.*

Document 6.1: HKPRO, HKRS 170/1/568/1, Manager of Railways to D. D. Works, Hongkong, 'Kowloon Canton Railways [*sic*] Progress Report – 12th Sept. to 15th Oct.', 19 October 1945.

Administration: the administration is at the moment being carried out by myself assisted by a F/O R.A.F. [Field Officer, Royal Air Force] and a warrant officer who is a master fitter R.A.F. There is no Mechanical Engineer nor a Civil Engineer. The services of a Chinese Locomotive Engineer have been asked for from the Ministry of Communications. . . .

The native staff have returned in some numbers and if the desired senior supervisory staff are found the line can be operated satisfactorily and at a cost which will compare favourably when compared with that of a railway operating company.

Buildings: Buildings were found to be leaking, and had been badly looted. Station buildings at outstations were for the most part standing but are in need of essential repairs. Gangers' huts along the [permanent way] had had their roofs removed for firewood. . . .

---

10. Norman Miners, 'Building The Kowloon–Canton–Hankow Railway', *Journal of the Royal Asiatic Society Hong Kong Branch* 46 (2006): 5–24; Thomas Spain and Oliver Betts, 'Developing China's "International" Railway: The Canton–Hankow Line, 1898–1937', *Journal of Transport History* 40, no. 3 (2019): 322–40.
11. Chan Lau Kit-ching, *China, Britain and Hong Kong, 1895–1945* (Hong Kong: Chinese University Press, 1990), 268–92; Zhang Jia'ao 張嘉璈 [Chang Kia-ngau], *Zhanshi jiaotong wenti* 戰時交通問題 [Issues of wartime transportation] (n.p. [Chongqing]: Zhongyang hunlian tuan dang zheng hunlian ban, 1940).
12. For two officially sanctioned accounts of the KCR's history, see Robert J. Phillips, *Kowloon–Canton Railway (British Section): A History* (Hong Kong: Urban Council, 1990), and Peter Moss, *A Century of Commitment: The KCRC Story* (Hong Kong: Kowloon–Canton Railway Corporation, 2007).

Track: The track is in reasonably good condition and concrete sleepers have helped considerably in keeping it to gauge at many points. The rails in the main line are worn, but the whole length of 22½ miles was overdue for renewal when hostilities commenced, and renewal is not a military commitment except when failures occur. Actual track removal should, however, be replaced as they are likely to prove operationally necessary, except some 5,280 ft. for a cemetery siding at Fanling. The total length amounts to approximately 8,100 yards. . . .

Machine tools: Practically all machine tools have disappeared. Such as remain so badly rusted as to affect their standard gauge or size. Work on cleaning, oiling, and listing is in hand. . . .

Tonnages carried: Tonnage carried during the period 20th Sept. to 15 Oct. is approximately as follows:-

UP tons	DOWN Tons
135	3,760

In the up direction rice was conveyed for relief purpose and rations to troops, and in the down direction the traffic has consisted of firewood, to maintain the power station in the absence of coal and to provide a reserve, captured ammunitions, rice and wheat and baggage of Chinese troops passing into the colony. . . .

Relations with Canton: This line must necessarily work as an integral part of the Chinese National Railways System, and its influence extended beyond the borders of the Colony, as far as Canton at present, and further north to the YANGTSE at no distan[t] date if supplies for China enter through the Port of Hongkong. A visit was paid to Canton on 7th Oct., and Chinese Government and Railway Officials visited the Colony by train on the 13th Oct., and were entertained. Good relations were established and arrangements are in hand for a daily through train each way with Canton using coal allotted by the H.K. Government. The track is considered good enough to warrant a schedule of 7 hours for the 111 miles. It is intended the train should be a mixed one conveying what supplies Hongkong can offer and passengers on the up journey and vegetables, peanut oil, etc., and passengers on the downward trip. . . .

Capability of Railway to meet military needs: Immediate military needs are being fulfilled. The Economic needs of the Colony as a whole can be extended with additional supplies of coal enabling trains to work through to PINGWU on the Chinese Section for firewood, cattle, pigs and some vegetables, and also to Canton.

Section 2. Hong Kong Tramways

Besides the aforementioned suspension of cross-border railway services, the 1949 founding of the People's Republic had other ramifications for Hong Kong transport. This was perhaps most keenly felt in the field of labour relations. Pro-Beijing trade unions dominated certain trades, including transport. The 'ding-dings', as the trams are affectionately nicknamed after the bells, began service in 1904. From late 1949 to 1955, there were continual waves of industrial action and targeted redundancies in the Tramways company.[13] *The Beijing-backed Tramway Workers' Union resented General Manager C. S. Johnston and termed his measures 'Johnston-style crazed firings'. Document 6.2 is an extract from a pamphlet distributed by the union. Document 6.3 is part of a dossier compiled by Johnston, explaining his actions during labour disputes. The row eventually ended with the laid-off workers returning their uniforms and other company property and receiving a severance package higher than what was first offered.*

Document 6.2: Tramway Workers' Union, 'The Truth Behind Johnston's Unjust Removals: Tram Labour Dispute Special Issue', 8 October 1954, Chinese University of Hong Kong Library Special Collections, 7–11.

The Truth Behind Johnston's Unjust Removals[14]

1. Many removals despite huge profits, intentionally increasing unemployment . . .

How does Johnston treat toiling tramway workers? He gets rid of a large number unjustly. According to records, he removed thirteen batches of workers from September 1952 to July 1954. On 15 March of the present year, 32 tramway workers were removed as part of the twelfth batch. On 31 July, the thirteenth batch of 31 workers was removed. In total, 184 workers were unjustly removed. Whilst earning large profits, Johnston removes large amounts of workers, producing unnecessary unemployment. If the average worker has a wife, a son, and a daughter, then in the past two years Johnston has made over 700 people suffer the pain of hunger.

In 1952, Hong Kong suffered economically under the American trade embargo. The embargo deepened the pain of workers in Hong Kong and Kowloon and furthered unemployment, yet it was in this year that Johnston removed nine batches of workers, increasing anxiety in society, whilst the Tramway Company's net income reached $4,617,000. Johnston's evil intentions are on display here.

13. An account very sympathetic to the union can be found in Lu Yan, *Crossed Paths: Labor Activism and Colonial Governance in Hong Kong, 1938–1958* (Ithaca, NY: Cornell University Press, 2019), 233–59.

14. The term used by the Tramway Workers' Union (in Chinese, 除人) lies somewhere between being made redundant and being fired. I have used 'removal' to capture the sense suggested by the union.

2. Removals lead to a lack of manpower, adding to workers' burdens

In a letter to the *Kung Sheung Daily News* published on 14 August, Johnston admitted that years ago, the Tramways Company hired 1,850 workers, but now it only hires 1,500. At the same time, the Company's fleet increased from 103 trams in 1948 to 131 trams currently. More trams, less workers: why?

Johnston claims that on the newly purchased trams, doors are no longer hand-operated, removing the need for gate boys. But if we do some calculations, we can see that after Johnston's removals, the workforce is shorthanded. . . .

Many workers fall ill from being overworked, yet management refuses to give them sick leave, so workers have to work through their illnesses, which often adds to their pain. Some workers suffer injuries, have no choice but to work without treatment, and die as a result. We cannot forget the pain of seeing the tragic deaths of Wong Kam-kau from the traffic department, and mechanic Chui Chung. . . .

3. Citizens demand an increase in service due to cramped trams, yet Johnston removes workers and reduces service frequency, disregarding public welfare

Everyone can see the cramped conditions currently on the trams. In 1948, the trams carried 87.5 million passengers, but by 1953 this number rose to 136.8 million passengers; in 1948 the fleet numbered 103 trams, but right now that number has only risen to 131, and only 120 trams are actually in use. Cries to increase service frequency are widespread and desperate, so it should follow that Johnston would hire more workers, yet instead he has chosen to remove workers. . . .

4. Workers were fired despite their lack of wrongdoing; Trade union's rights harmed . . .

If not for bad business, inability to continue services, or worker wrongdoing, workers should not be fired. Besides, many of those who Johnston removed are skilled workers who have worked on the trams for over 20 years and served passengers for a long time – this is totally unreasonable.

Johnston completely disrespects the union's legal rights and arbitrarily fired union officials, especially union chairman Chan Yiu-choi, a loyal old servant and skilled worker who has worked for the company for 29 years. He is also an official of the Hong Kong and Kowloon Federation of Trade Unions, putting in sizeable effort for workers' welfare.

Document 6.3: C. S. Johnston, 'Extract from Manager's Report for 1955 Dealing with Labour Relations', October 1956, in 'Labour Relations', Hong Kong University Library Special Collections Hong Kong Collection.

Some have asked why the Company left it so late before commencing to get rid of the more active Communists amongst its employees. The answer is that until 1952 the political climate was not suitable and the Communists had not been sufficiently discredited in the eyes of our employees. It must be appreciated that such a step as the dismissal of selected groups of employees is completely impractical unless it has at least the tacit approval of a majority of the workers - and they must know for certain what is being done, and why, before they will give that approval. Therefore it could not have been done earlier.

In July 1950 the Company withdrew recognition from the Hongkong Tramway Workers' Union. This step was taken because it was found that the reports that the Union gave to mass meetings of talks between the Union and the management were lying misrepresentations devised solely to create as much discontent as possible amongst employees. The Union Chairman, Chan [Yiu-choi], admitted to the Manager that he had on at least one occasion threatened the property and families in China of employees unless they obeyed the Union's instructions. On this occasion a 20-paged letter was sent to the Union giving examples illustrating the Company's case. The Union was bringing false charges against men who refused to join the Union or refused to pay their dues and demanding their dismissal from the Company, it was attempting to force men by violence and threats to boycott the Welfare Centre recently built by the Company at a cost of $750,000 and was causing lying reports against the Company and its supervisory staff to be published in the local Communist press. The Union has never replied to this letter.

In 1950 also the Company took the biggest step to date to improve Conditions of Service. This was the consolidation of about $3 per day into basic pay. The cost to the Company of this step in the first year for all employees amounted to about $1,000,000 and involved a further annual addition to labour costs in future years of about $300,000. The Communist Union at once saw the danger to their cause of this generous act. They re-acted with vigour, ingenuity and, of course, the usual brutal intimidation but, in spite of all their efforts, by the end of the year all employees had voluntarily asked for and been given the new improved conditions offered by the Company. It was during this year that the Company learnt the wisdom of the principle of never, under any circumstances negotiating with Communists.

Section 3. Crossing the Harbour

Crossing Victoria Harbour has long been one of Hong Kong's most pertinent transport issues. The city's economic activity was centred on the built-up areas on either side of the harbour. Before the advent of road tunnels, passengers, light freight, and vehicles alike depended on ferry services. Documents 6.4 and 6.5 are related to the vehicular ferries, once ubiquitous but soon eclipsed by the advent of road, and later, rail crossings. Both documents speak to Hong Kong as an importer of mobility technologies, and how the long influence of colonial regulations affected such technologies' proliferation in the colony.

Document 6.4: H. Behrends, Volkswagenwerk GmbH. to Messrs. Jebsen & Co., 25 June 1958, vol. 5: Ring binder notes, Hongkong and Yaumati Ferry Collection, University of Hong Kong Libraries Special Collection.[15]

We refer to your later dated 17th June 1958, and regret that the Volkswagen is being classified as a big car on the ferry between Hongkong and Kowloon, whereas vehicles as, for instance, Hillman, Vauxhall and Ford are being registered as small cars. We have contacted our technical department and were informed that the figure of 14.8 HP is correct. This figure has been worked out to the English RAC formula, which is as follows:[16]

$$\frac{(D^2 \times n)}{2.5}$$

This formula, however, is very old and according to information received by us is not being used any longer by Great Britain. The Volkswagen has got a square shaped engine that means the cylinder radius is bigger compared to the cubic capacity. Since this formula refers to the cylinder radius only, the Volkswagen is being classified rather unfortunately.

We hope that in future the fares on the ferry will be charged according to the measurements, respectively [length] of the car, which is in our opinion the only justified classification.

15. Original was in German; letter was translated by Jebsen in Hong Kong.
16. *D* is the diameter of the automobile's engine in inches; *n* is the number of cylinders. This 'tax horsepower' or 'RAC (Royal Automobile Club)' horsepower was abandoned by the UK soon after the Second World War.

Document 6.5: Lau Chan Kwok, Managing Director, Hongkong and Yaumati Ferry Co., to Hon. Colonial Secretary, 14 August 1965, vol. 4: Ferry vessels; Ferry services; Miscellaneous, Hongkong and Yaumati Ferry Collection, University of Hong Kong Libraries Special Collection.

<u>Basis for Vehicular Ferry Charges</u>

1. We have the honour to address you on the subject of the basis for charging vehicular ferry fares.

2. Under the terms of our franchise, cars of 12 h.p. and under are classified as small cars and pay a fare of $2.00 per crossing. Cars of over 12 h.p. are considered as large cars and pay a fare of $3.00 per crossing.

3. A few years ago Government changed their licensing system of cars by substituting cylinder capacity for horsepower in calculating different license fees.

4. In recent years car makers often keep the same appearance of a car model, but change the engine power making it difficult for our pier staff to assess fares. This has also led to friction between passengers and ferry staff.

5. In view of paragraphs 3 and 4 above, we wish to enquire whether Government would consider a suggestion that vehicular ferry fares be changed according to cylinder capacity i.e. cars of 1200 cc. and under, be charged as small cars and cars of over 1200 cc. be charged as large cars.

   The advantage of this method of charging is that the license disc which is required to be affixed to each vehicle, gives its cylinder capacity and would swiftly remove any argument as to what fares are chargeable.

Following British re-occupation, the government commissioned British town planner Sir Patrick Abercrombie to undertake a wide-ranging study into the future of town planning in Hong Kong.[17] *These were his recommendations for a cross-harbour tunnel 'from the centre of Hong Kong to the tip of Kowloon'.*

17. For more on this report and its influence on town planning in Hong Kong, see Lawrence Wai-Chung Lai, 'Reflections on the Abercrombie Report 1948: A Strategic Plan for Colonial Hong Kong', *Town Planning Review* 70, no. 1 (1999): 61–87.

Document 6.6: Hong Kong Government Printer, Patrick Abercrombie, *Hong Kong Preliminary Planning Report* (Hong Kong, 1948), 14.

61. The engineering problems require to be further investigated and the cost brought into relation to the economic position of the Colony: but sooner or later the Tunnel must be constructed.

62. The following are some of the planning considerations. There must be facilities for pedestrians as well as motor cars (these are not provided in the Liverpool Tunnel). There should also be electric trains, either on a narrow gauge, like the London Tubes, giving direct access to the general station at Kowloon in its new location; or, if the main line were electrified, it might be possible to run trains direct from the New Territories into Hong Kong, with great advantage for (a) farm and fishing produce, (b) for recreation from the crowded urban centres.

63. The exits will require most careful planning, with escalators as well as a sloping ramp for cars: this will form the real gateway to Hong Kong. On the Kowloon side it will be desirable to plan a triple entrance (a) for passengers at Tsim Sha Tsui (b) for the Kowloon Docks (c) for the underground connection to the new railway station at Yau Ma Ti.

64. The Tunnel will be something much more than an underground traffic link. It will be a symbol of the unity of interests of the Colony: it is impossible to predict all the effects which it may have, but provided strong planning control both in use of land and in direction of traffic is exercised, it is difficult to see in what way it can be other than beneficial.

The planning and financing of the cross-harbour road link proved difficult. There were initial ideas for a bridge in the early 1960s, but the government was wary of potential opposition from aviation and marine interests. In fact, the scheme was pushed largely by private interests, while the government was made to follow along. The Legislative Council agreed to grant a franchise to build a four-lane tunnel in August 1965, to the trepidation of councillors.[18] *By 1967, the Cross-Harbour Tunnel Company had received bids from various firms and consortia, and although its chairman Douglas Clague favoured the British bid, the riots of 1967 meant Britain's Export Credit Guarantee Department (ECGD) sought stringent guarantee arrangements for a potential loan.*[19] *This situation dragged on until 1969, when the threat of American, French, or Swiss finance meant*

---

18. *Hong Kong Hansard*, 11 August 1965, 490–520.
19. Clague was later credited as the 'visionary behind Hong Kong's first Cross-Harbour Tunnel' who 'almost single-handedly' found the financing required. Jason Wordie, 'Clague, Sir John Douglas', in *Dictionary of Hong Kong Biography*, ed. May Holdsworth and Christopher Munn (Hong Kong: Hong Kong University Press, 2012), 100–101.

ECGD loosened its requirements. The tunnel finally opened on the evening of 2 August 1972. The following are excerpts from correspondence between Hong Kong and London on this issue.

Document 6.7: TNA, CO 1030/1697, 'XCR(63)109: Cross Harbour Road Link: Memorandum for Executive Council', 1 April 1963.

[F]ull implications of a large scheme like this are capable of almost indefinite study and analysis, but further delay in reaching a decision will cause increasing difficulties in land utilization and planning. There is no certainty that a cross harbour road link would bring any major benefit to the Colony's economy or effect any worthwhile improvement in its public transport systems, although transit time across the harbour would undoubtedly be reduced. It can be said that there are strong, if not conclusive, objections to a bridge, but no conclusive objections to a tunnel. On the other hand there is no ground for believing that the real benefits of a cross harbour road link to the community are likely to be more than marginal. In view of other claims on public resources, it is therefore clearly undesirable that there should be investment of public funds in such a scheme. On the other hand, if private enterprise wished to proceed with a tunnel scheme, there might be ways in which Government should consider facilitating the development, and negotiation would be necessary on the almost certain claims from the ferry companies. It should, however, be a necessary feature of any commitment of this nature which government undertook that the costs, or at least most of them, would be recoverable by way of royalties or otherwise.

Document 6.8: TNA, FCO 40/133, Ken W. Cotterill, ECGD, 'Hong Kong Tunnel: Richard Costain Limited', 22 March 1967.

It may be argued that there are strong political reasons why this contract should come to the U.K. It is not for E.C.G.D. to comment on this although the somewhat lukewarm attitude of the Hong Kong Government in committing itself to the project would hardly seem to support this view. If, however, the Departments concerned consider that it is in H.M.G.'s wider interest to support the winning of this contract for a British company they may wish to consider the possibility of H.M.G. financing the balance of the funds required as an expression of H.M.G. colonial lending or aid policy.

Document 6.9: TNA, FCO 40/133, B. Thorne, Acting Principal Trade Commissioner to M. Morris, CRED, Board of Trade, 8 August 1967.

I fear that the continued delay in taking a decision on the tunnel is doing nothing but harm to our commercial prospects in Hong Kong.

For better or for worse, the tunnel has become a symbol. From the start of what is now locally called "confrontation" (inaccurately and probably unwisely in my view) people have talked of the starting of the tunnel as something that will indisputably prove two things: Hong Kong's faith in itself because of all the local investment involved, and Britain's steadfastness because of our involvement in financing the contract. It has been further elevated in significance because in "pre-confrontation" days the Hong Kong Government never had the courage publicly to spell out the importance they really attached to it as a social and communications project. So, when trouble struck they were driven to support the project to a far greater degree, financially, than they had planned; and to give it an importance that was not in accord with their original scale of priorities.

We have therefore reached a point where nearly everyone who matters commercially in this Colony, plus a sizeable part of ordinary public opinion, believes that the tunnel is crucial to Hong Kong and that failure to reach the decision is the fault of a cowardly, ventilating Britain which is waiting to see which way the wind blows. In well-informed circles the villain of the piece is more specifically ECGD – thanks largely to the conversation of certain Tunnel Company directors. Hong Kong Government officials are themselves quite bitter about the complete absence of any official indication from London of what the delay is about or when it will end.

The resultant fears that, despite Governmental protestations, London is quite cynical about the future of Hong Kong make my job very difficult. A simple illustration is that I depend on Col. Clague, a principal shareholder in the Tunnel Company, for his goodwill as Chairman of the Working Party dealing with the Yorkshire textiles problem.

Document 6.10: TNA, FCO 40/242, David Trench, Governor of Hong Kong, to FCO, 8 January 1969.

The object of my approach is to emphasize the adverse political consequences here if it is publicly demonstrated that a French state-owned bank and an official French credit institution should appear to have more confidence in the future, both political and economic, of Hong Kong than has an agency of the British government. It is, of course, public knowledge that negotiations with E.C.G.D. broke down largely because of their insistence, by reason of their assessment of the political risk, on what was effectively a guarantee from this government; I am aware that there was a secondary consideration relating to the commercial risks involved and the low ratio of equity to loan capital proposed but this naturally plays no part in the construction put on the requirement by public opinion.

Section 4. Minibuses

Bus services began in Hong Kong in the interwar years, and in 1933 various firms were consolidated into Kowloon Motor Bus in Kowloon and New Territories, and China Motor Bus on the Island.[20] *Service coverage extended with the expanding road network. During the 1967 riots, bus drivers led by the pro-Beijing unions went on strike. The demand for road journeys was filled by minibuses, illegal but condoned by the government. After the riots, they were formally codified into law. The following extracts from the proceedings of the Legislative Council give an insight into how the government and councillors saw this issue.*

Document 6.11: *Hong Kong Hansard*, 13 March 1968, 105–8.

Mr K. A. Watson:[21] There is no need to stress the growing traffic congestion in our streets. The persistent use by the public of illegal forms of transport, *paak pais*,[22] dual purpose vans and lorries, underlines its need for a more convenient or a more comfortable service. Partly because of this competition, partly because of the increasing labour costs and a reluctance to raise the fares, our franchised companies are finding it increasingly difficult to operate profitably. A time may rapidly be approaching when they will have to be run as non-profit public service corporations. Some hard thinking is needed about how they can continue to operate until the end of their franchises and what to do with them afterwards.

Document 6.12: *Hong Kong Hansard*, 18 June 1969, 371–75.

Road Traffic (Amendment) Bill 1969

The Attorney General moved the second reading of: — "A bill to amend further the Road Traffic Ordinance."

20. C. K. Leung, 'The Growth of Public Passenger Transport', in *Asian Urbanization: A Hong Kong Casebook*, ed. D. J. Dwyer (Hong Kong: Hong Kong University Press, 1971), 139–40.
21. Kenneth Albert Watson, businessman and appointed unofficial member of the Legislative Council, 1964–70.
22. *Paak pai* is the literal translation of 白牌.

He said: - Sir, the object of this bill is to provide the necessary legislative power to regularize and control the operation of minibuses.

I have used the word regularize, although the publication of this bill has been described, very understandably, in the press and elsewhere as part of a process designed to legalize the minibus.

The present Road Traffic (Registration and Licensing of Vehicles) Regulations make provision for the charging of licence fees in respect of dual purpose vehicles of three classes of user: firstly, as a private car and goods vehicle; secondly as a taxi and goods vehicle; and thirdly as a public car and goods vehicle. There is, however, no corresponding subdivision for the purpose of the registration of Dual Purpose Vehicles.

In a recent decision of the Full Court it was ruled that because the Road Traffic Regulations only makes it an offence to use a dual purpose vehicle for the carriage of the passengers for hire or reward if it is registered as a private car and goods vehicle (a subdivision of the class of dual purpose vehicle which as I have just said was not effectively created) it is not an offence merely to use a dual purpose vehicle for the carriage of fare-paying passengers, though of course many minibuses are operated in contravention of other provisions of the law, particularly with regard to insurance and stopping near bus stops. It is, therefore, in view of this decision, more accurate to describe the present proposal as designed to regularize rather than to legalize minibuses, though it was until very recently believed that their operation for the carriage of fare-paying passengers was illegal and this was certainly the intention behind the legislation.

At present, vehicles which are registered as goods vehicles, private cars, dual purpose vehicles and New Territories taxis are operating as minibuses. In future, any vehicle of the minibus type which wants to ply for hire and to carry fare-paying passengers will have to be licensed as a Public Light Bus. Other vehicles of the minibus type will be registered as Private Light Buses, but these will not be allowed to take fare-paying passengers, except that students and staff, carried in private light buses to and from educational establishments at which they study or work, may be charged fares. . . .

Public Light Buses will generally be able to operate anywhere in the Colony, but power will be conferred on the Commissioner for Transport to prohibit them from plying for hire in specified areas where their operation would cause unreasonable congestion. However, they will not be able to stop close to bus or tram stops, since this would constitute a naked poaching in the Bus Companies' preserves, or near pedestrian crossings, for safety reasons. . . .

The bill follows closely, with a few modifications, the recommendations of the Transport Advisory Committee, for whose valuable work on a most difficult subject the Government is duly grateful. It is the Government's hope that this bill, and the regulations to be made under it, will enable the operation of minibuses, in the future, to be conducted in a manner which will ensure a proper protection for the interests of the public and of competing forms of transport and give the minibus operator the opportunity to earn legally a fair return for his enterprise.

Section 5. Modernizing and Electrifying the KCR

The KCR ran without significant upgrades from the end of the Japanese occupation until the 1970s. This drew criticism from the public, as seen in Document 6.13. Long-standing issues with punctuality, safety, and passengers' comfort could not be resolved without the line's modernization, and capacity was hampered by old carriages and the single-track line. The government's New Towns project also promised to increase demand on the KCR. The 1970s and 1980s saw gradual, then transformative, development of the KCR. This started with moving the terminus from Tsim Sha Tsui to Hung Hom, completed in 1975, followed by double-tracking the line.[23] Finally, the entire line was electrified in 1983.[24] Document 6.13 shows Acting Governor Roberts's views and hopes for the modernising railway; Document 6.14 reflects the public response to the new station.

Document 6.13: 'Public Hits at Railway: Unchanged since 1910', *Sunday Star*, 4 April 1971, 3.

The Kowloon-Canton Railway was one of the surprises of the *Star*'s Government "popularity poll" – it received almost no praise at all and finished only 16th. As one commuter put it: "Established 1910 – system unchanged . . . only the carriages are a little dirtier."

It is this apparent complete lack of improvement in service, cleanliness and general approach to the problems which have given the impression that the department "couldn't care less". It was suggested that what was required was some direct competition or the appointment of a non-Government manager of high calibre charged with tackling the problems with vigour. His efforts would, of course, be wasted if he did not receive financial support to carry out reforms where they can be justified. . . .

23. For more on moving the terminus from Tsim Sha Tsui to Hung Hom, see Li, 'Visions of Public and Private Mobility', and Catherine S. Chan, 'Belonging to the City: Representations of a Colonial Clock Tower in British Hong Kong', *Journal of Urban History* 45, no. 2 (2019): 321–32.
24. For more on the procurement of trains for the electrified line, see Li, 'Hindrance or Helping Hand?'.

Document 6.14: HKPRO, HKRS 461/1/15, Speech by His Excellency the Acting Governor on the Occasion of the Opening of the Hung Hom Railway Station on Monday, 24 November 1975.

General Manager, Ladies and Gentlemen,

I am delighted to have been given the opportunity to declare open this fine new Railway Terminus building. It will provide not only first class facilities for railway passengers, but also a major bus station, a multi-storey car park and a concrete podium over which we hope to build an indoor stadium. . . .

Those who were responsible for its planning realized that it would, like its predecessor, have to be more than a railway station. If it was to be of maximum benefit to the community, it would have to be a focal point for both public transport services in Kowloon and for the service of China's export trade to Hong Kong. Consequently, provision has been made for the transhipment of goods arriving by rail to road transport or to the nearby wharves and extensive warehousing for both government departments and commercial concerns is available.

Railway passengers will be able to continue their journeys in a variety of ways. By a ferry service from the nearby pier to the Island, by buses which will run from the adjoining bus station to the Island and to all parts of Kowloon; and in due course, from an underground station within close reach.

All these linked facilities will be necessary to deal with the growth in goods and passenger traffic which we believe will be generated by future improvements to the KCR and by the expansion of our economy. In particular, I hope that it will not be long before the pattern of our trade with China will make it essential for the KCR to be double tracked all the way to Lo Wu. When this happens, what may at this stage look like an unnecessarily generous provision at Hung Hom will be seen to have been prudent and far-sighted. . . .

The building is a fine example of the ability of Hong Kong's builders to derive the maximum effectiveness from a limited site and to construct in a way which gives pleasure to the eye and yet serves a severely practical end. It is a handsome addition to our skyline and a reminder of the importance which the Government attaches to the development of the KCR, which has a vital role to play in the communications of this complex and fascinating territory.

Document 6.15: Inconvenienced Traveller, 'Was This Move Well Advised?', *South China Morning Post*, 10 April 1976, 9.

. . . In order to build an expensive Cultural Centre, for the benefit of relatively few people, Kowloon Canton Railway, which carried a large number of passengers to Tsimshatsui had to move its terminus to a less accessible location in Hunghom at a cost of millions of dollars. Many of its former passengers must now use other means of transport to reach Tsimshatsui creating the need for the expansion of bus services and terminal facilities in that area.

Would it not have been wiser and saved money all around if the Railway Terminus had remained at Tsimshatsui?

The corporate structure of the KCR also changed drastically. In 1984, the Railway Department was 'corporatized' into the Kowloon–Canton Railway Corporation, a statutory corporation owned by the government but autonomous in operations.[25] *Documents 6.16 and 6.17 show two KCR general managers' dissatisfaction with the KCR's operations falling under the umbrella of the government. Document 6.18 provides the government's reasoning for 'hiving-off' the Railway Department.*

Document 6.16: HKPRO, HKRS 163/1/366, I. B. Trevor, minute to Hon C S [Honourable Colonial Secretary], 5 February 1948.

I enclose a cutting from the *China Mail* of the 3rd. February, 1948 and shall be grateful for information as to what "bright light" in the Government firmament has committed Government to an acceptance of 10 [cents] per square foot per month in view of the advertising rentals ruling in the Colony to-day.

My own Department charges as high as $1.00 per square foot per month for advertising hoardings on Railway premises, and this is considered a reasonable but possibly conservative figure.

I suggest that before officers commit Government to a loss of revenue that they should make proper enquiries as to the ruling rentals rather than take advice from vested interests at cocktail parties and other social occasions. A certain local character in this field has already asked us if we intend to continue our "exorbitant rates".

On numerous occasions this Department has pleaded to be allowed to function as commercially as possible although the Railway is a Government Department, but this latest instance affords the best example so far of my contention that unless it be

25. Rikkie Yeung, *Moving Millions: The Commercial Success and Political Controversies of Hong Kong's Railways* (Hong Kong: Hong Kong University Press, 2008), 74–77.

independent it will be frustrated from obtaining the full amount of revenue to which Government is entitled. . . .

I intend to press with great insistence at the Colonial Office during my leave in the United Kingdom the desirability of this Department functioning independently, and will draw attention to this case as a typical example of a quite unnecessary loss in revenue.

Document 6.17: HKPRO, HKRS 597/4/87, R. E. Gregory, General Manager, Railway to New Territories Development Branch, Public Works Department, 'Tai Po Market Station: Study of Development Possibilities', 9 September 1975.

8. It would be useful to elaborate in the implementation section on the organization for the development. I have in mind that based upon your outline proposals developers would be invited to bid for the project and, in view of the necessity to maintain the railway service and the necessary momentum of railway investment the K.C.R. and successful developer should form a joint company to exploit the site. K.C.R. would be the recipient of the lease payments and co-ordinator of the interests of other Government departments.

Document 6.18: HKPRO, HKRS 934/10/51, 'XCC(81)102: The Future Organization of the Kowloon–Canton Railway: Memorandum for Executive Council', 3 September 1981.

2. The Government is undertaking a major construction programme at a cost of some $3,500 million to modernize and electrify the KCR. Work is progressing satisfactorily. The inner suburban electrified service from Kowloon to Sha Tin is scheduled to commence in the spring of 1982, and total electrified services to Lo Wu are to follow at the end of that year.

3. From then onwards, to meet the needs of the new towns and developing northern New Territories, fast and frequent services will increase the passenger capacity of the railway tenfold, while freight capacity should go up at least three times.

4. All this has obviously involved a concentration of effort on the construction programme over the last few years. But this now has to be complemented by the development in parallel of an effective management organization to make sure that the new railway is operated efficiently so as to meet its commercial targets. The organizational structure of the KCR has, however, changed very little since the War, and it will not be able to cope with the challenge of operating much expanded and

more sophisticated electrified services without substantial strengthening and a major overhaul of structure and functions.

Future Management Objectives

5. The objectives of the Management of the new KCR must be :-

(a) to ensure safety at all times;

(b) to run efficient and reliable passenger and freight services of a frequency commensurate with emerging demand;

(c) to operate its services on a commercial basis, i.e. to compete with other carriers and to maximize net revenue consistent with objective (b) above: in other words to earn a fair return on investment;

(d) to respond quickly to market influences;

(e) to recruit, train and employ staff to provide these services;

(f) to develop railway land on a commercial basis (including air space above stations);

(g) to develop ancillary revenue sources such as from advertising.

6. The question is whether these objectives could be met by a strengthened organization which nevertheless retains the KCR as a Government department; and the answer appears to be no, because Government systems and procedures are not designed to meet this range of challenges.

The Advantages of Hiving-off

7. The alternative would be to move towards some form of corporation separate from the Government to run the railway. The advantages of this would seem to be:-

(a) it would result in a more flexible organization which could operation on a fully commercial basis;

(b) proper weight could be given to commercial development, to matters such as land use, marketing, advertising and other similar functions; the railway must be sold to the users;

(c) an independent organization would have more flexibility with regard to fares and freight charges (taking into account transport policy considerations) and to take whatever decisions were necessary to meet its budgets, which Government will need to establish;

(d) it would be easier to recruit senior staff in both the management and professional streams if it was not necessary to follow civil service procedures and to maintain parity of renumeration and conditions with the rest of the civil service;

(e) the same argument would apply to other levels of staff where competition with the private sector will otherwise pose problems;

(f) the need to adhere to Government's financial and management procedures would be obviated, and the funding of any future development would no longer need to be via the Public Works Programme, thus facilitating timing and economies;

(g) an independent body would probably reduce the risk of conflict between the public and the Government on railway matters including the fixing of fares.

Section 6. Mass Transit Railway

The MTR is almost synonymous with Hong Kong public transport. The huge initial capital needed to start the project and the disruption caused to residents was not without controversy. The MTR Corporation is now hugely successful with its pioneering Rail-plus-Property model, and it operates railways in mainland China and across the world, with perhaps the most symbolically significant one being the Elizabeth Line in the former imperial metropole, London. Document 6.19 is part of the initial report on the feasibility of an underground mass transport system in Hong Kong, based on a design year of 1986. A Japanese consortium had agreed to build the entire system under a turnkey contract but later withdrew, as outlined in Document 6.20.[26] *Though Hong Kong was something of a pioneer in contactless payment technologies with the Octopus card in 1997, the travelling public had to be taught to use the MTR's Automatic Fare Collection (AFC) system in 1979, as shown in Document 6.21.*

Document 6.19: Hong Kong Government Printer, Freeman, Fox, Wilbur Smith and Associates, *Hong Kong Mass Transport Study* (Hong Kong, 1967).

The object of this Study has been to develop the best solution to Hong Kong's long-term mass transport problems consistent with planning goals, development plans

26. For more on the Japanese turnkey contract and the fallout from its collapse, see Fujio Mizuoka, *Contrived Laissez-Faireism: The Politico-Economic Structure of British Colonialism in Hong Kong* (Cham: Springer, 2018), 163–210, and Li, 'Hindrance or Helping Hand?'.

and a level of mobility that will allow the Colony to continue to prosper. The long-term needs were established by an analysis and projection of information gathered in various planning and travel surveys. . . .

The people of Hong Kong are using their public transport system more each day. Ten years ago the average person made 244 public transport trips per year; now he makes 335. This reflects a rising standard of living among the lower income groups. Many people who had to walk in the past now ride. There are also indications that trips are getting longer as new residential, commercial and industrial developments spring up in formerly vacant areas. . . .

Although the number of motor vehicles in Hong Kong compared to the population is small it is growing rapidly. In 1956 there were 11 motor vehicles for every 1,000 people, and now there are 25. There are 10 times as many private cars in the Colony as there were in 1948. The number of vehicles per mile of road is extremely high by world standards. Only Monaco and Gibraltar have more.

Consideration of these and many other factors has led to the conclusion that the travel needs of Hong Kong cannot continue to be wholly served by surface transport. Increasing congestion is already evident at many places and it is likely to get much worse. As it does, public transport vehicles will have to operate on slower and slower schedules which will require many more vehicles just in the attempt to maintain a constant level of service. The additional vehicles will, of course, increase the cost of providing service and cause more road congestion. On the other hand, these very factors will ensure the success of a grade-separated rapid-transit system. . . .

Recommended System

The recommended system is the outcome of penetrating studies conducted over the past two years. It combines the most advantageous features of several alternative plans tested against the forecast pattern and volumes of traffic loads. It has been designed to match capacity with these loads and provide a balanced plan for the movement of over seven million public transport passengers per day mostly by bus and rail.

The principal recommendation is that a 40-mile rail rapid-transit system be built to improve transport service and to relieve the burden on the surface street system. Projections of travel show that vast improvements to the surface street system would be needed by 1986 just to serve the needs of public transport if such a grade-separated system is not constructed. The capacity of many existing and proposed major roads could be exceeded by bus traffic alone, leaving no room for cars, taxis and lorries.

The rapid-transit system has been designed to operate as four separate lines, namely:

The *Kwun Tong* line, from Western Market to Ma Yau Tong

The *Tsuen Wan* line, from the Naval Dockyard to Tsuen Wan

The *Island* line, from Kennedy Town to Chai Wan

The *Sha Tin* line, from Tsim Sha Tsui to Sha Tin

with convenient passenger interchange facilities at several stations. Most of the system will be underground but about eight miles will be on overhead structure. The lines have been routed so as to penetrate the most densely developed areas, and the stations have been located to serve the maximum number of people commensurate with rapid operation.

There are 50 stations on the system, 8 of which are common to 2 or more lines. The average station spacing is 0.72 miles but is about 0.5 miles in the more intensively developed areas. This spacing will allow average speeds *including* station stops of 20 miles per hour or more – nearly double present public transport speeds.

It is envisaged that a complex system of bus routes will connect with the rapid-transit system to serve passengers who do not have origins or destinations within walking distance of stations. A hovercraft ferry service between Hong Kong Island and Castle Peak is also planned. The Peak Tramway, the Kowloon-Canton Railway, the outlying ferry services, and at least one cross-harbour ferry are expected to be operating in the design year as they do now. The volume of bus travel will continue to grow throughout the next 20 years even though the rapid transit is expected to be carrying 33 per cent of the total public transport load by 1986.

Construction of the system is planned in six stages. Although in each stage work on two, and sometimes three, stages would be going on simultaneously, most of the Kwun Tong Line would be built in Stage 1, most of the Tsuen Wan line in Stage 2, most of the Island Line in Stage 3 and all of the Sha Tin Line in Stages 5 and 6. With the aim of having the entire system in operation by 1985, detailed design is scheduled to start in 1968 and construction in 1970. The first line should then be ready for operation in 1974; additional lines coming into service about every two years thereafter.

After considering all the various alternatives it was concluded that the best service consistent with low cost and dependability can be provided with electrically-powered, steel-wheel cars operating on steel rail. The system has therefore been designed to accommodate trains of large, powerful, high-capacity cars. Stations, platforms, car doors and seating arrangements have all been laid out for quick loading and unloading under heavy traffic conditions. Automatic train control and possibly automatic fare collection will assure maximum efficiency with minimum manpower.

Cost and Revenue

The total cost to build and equip the system is estimated to be $3,404 million – an average of about $200 million a year throughout the 17-year period of design and construction. Of this amount, 58 per cent is for line and station construction, 36 per cent for equipment and furnishings and 6 per cent for land. The total annual operating expenses, including depreciation, range from $21.9 million in 1974 to $104.8 million in 1986. . . .

The estimated annual gross revenue from the rapid-transit system based on the recommended fare schedule ranges from $36 million in 1974, the first year of operation, to $342 million in 1985 when the entire system will be in use. The total net revenue available for debt service from start of operation to the year 2004, 20 years after completion of construction, is $6,286 million. Discounted cash flow calculations ignoring the residual value of the system after 2004 show that this amount is sufficient to pay for the system at an interest rate of 4.2 per cent.

Finance at this low interest rate is unlikely in practice to be obtainable and some assistance from public funds in the early years is likely to be necessary. This can be justified in light of practices in other cities, but still more important it can be justified in consideration of the many benefits to all the people of Hong Kong. The benefits will not be limited to those who use the system but will be spread among all who travel. The routes, stations, trains and fare structure have all been designed to attract the maximum number of people away from the streets and thus to leave them as uncongested as possible for the free movement of the Colony's commerce.

While all travellers will receive some benefits, public transport passengers and more particularly rapid-transit users will receive the most. It has been estimated that over 270,000 hours will be saved each day in the design year by public transport users. If time is valued at only $1.20 per hour, the direct time savings alone will amount to $11 million in 1986 which exceeds the whole cost of operating the rapid transit for that year, and is more than half the average annual capital outlay during the building period, 1968-1984.

Document 6.20: 'Image of Japan Firms Tarnished', *South China Morning Post*, 15 January 1975, 1.

The reputation of major Japanese industrial concerns has plummeted to rock bottom in the estimation of Hongkong officials with the announcement yesterday that the Mitsubishi consortium had withdrawn from the mass transit railway project.

The feeling in the top echelons of government is that the Japanese have acted "ineptly and in bad faith" and there was a strong desire to use these words in the official communique.

In any case, Hongkong will be "conveying its disappointment" to the Japanese Government in no uncertain terms - the wounded feelings of Government officials have not been soothed by the gesture the Japanese consortium made of an ex-gratia offer of $5 million.

The offer was rejected with barely concealed contempt. It now remains to be seen what attitude the Government will adopt towards any Japanese tenders that are submitted either for the mass transit system or indeed for any Government public works projects.

Hints were dropped yesterday that Japanese firms in future could find themselves pushed to the end of the queue and preference given to firms from other countries though officially, the Government is unlikely to depart from the principle of competitive tendering for the majority of its projects. . . .

In accepting the Japanese letter of intent, the Hongkong negotiators had taken into account factors such as the "national discipline" of Japanese businessmen, the fact that the Tokyo Government was behind the venture, and the some of the most prestigious names of Japanese industry were involved.

The belief is that while the former Tanaka government was behind the venture, the change-over that took place in the administration late in November was an adverse development for Hongkong.

Hopes that the new administration would continue to lend its support and its financial backing for the MTR dwindled.

The Financial Secretary, Mr Philip Haddon-Cave, did not pull any punches when he told a news conference of the latest developments.

He charged that the Japanese consortium had made "a serious error in judgement" which had led to their inability to fulfil the letter of intent in building the tube according to specifications laid down by Hongkong and within a ceiling of $5,000 million.

Stressing that Hongkong should not pay the price of the error, Mr Haddon-Cave went on to rap the consortium for making what he described as a "derisory offer" of $5 million as a ex-gratia payment for withdrawing from the negotiations.

Both the consortium's counter proposals for the modification of the tube's design and an escalation of prices above the stipulated ceiling as well as its ex-gratia offer of $5 million had been rejected by the Executive Council, he said.

Asked whether the Mass Transit Provisional Authority should not shoulder part of the blame because it had chosen to negotiate with the Japanese in the first place, Mr Haddon-Cave said the decision to accept the Japanese bid was taken for two reasons:

- It was the only bid which came within the price ceiling of $5,000 million.
- It held out the opportunity of an early start and an early finish for the project, namely 1979. . . .

Document 6.21: *Official Souvenir Book to Commemorate the 1st Day of Running MTRC Trains* (Hong Kong: MTR Corporation, 1979).

How to use A.F.C. Equipment

→ The ticket you hold enables you to enter any entrance serving the nine stations outlined on the previous pages.[27]

→ As you have already purchased a ticket, proceed directly to the entry gates, and insert your ticket into the slot on the front of the gate.

→ Collect the ticket back as you proceed through the barriers.

→ Take an escalator to the platform to board a train. Stand behind the yellow line on the platform, when a train arrives, wait for passengers to disembark before getting on. Stand back from the doors when told to do so on the public address system.

→ The ticket enables you to ride anywhere between the stations listed on the previous pages. To change direction, get off the train, cross the platform and board another train.

→ Trains only stop for 30 sec. at each station. Get off the train promptly and take an escalator to the concourse if you wish to leave the station.

27. Shek Kip Mei, Kowloon Tong, Lok Fu, Wong Tai Sin, Diamond Hill, Choi Hung, Kowloon Bay, Ngau Tau Kok, and Kwun Tong.

- → Place your ticket into the slot on the front of the exit gate, and proceed through the barrier. Normally the ticket would be taken away from you, but so as you can keep the commemorative ticket as a memento, it has been encoded so that the exit gate will return it to you.
- → Leave the station of your choice.

Section 7. Containerization

Less frequently discussed, but a key part of Hong Kong's transport history, is the process of containerization. Hong Kong's container port at Kwai Chung, which opened in 1972, is notable for that period (though not unique) in that its construction was privately funded.[28] *Documents 6.22 and 6.23 reflect how the business community in Hong Kong foresaw and saw the port of Hong Kong's containerization. Note how Hong Kong's development was consistently couched in terms comparing the colony with its perennial competitor Singapore. Document 6.23 outlines certain measures the government had to take to enable private finance to succeed in building a massive infrastructure project.*

Document 6.22: Elizabeth Yung, 'Hongkong: On to a New Record', *Far Eastern Economic Review*, 229–30.

It may not be long before Hongkong's overall port activity surpasses the record established in 1966. In the financial year 1968-69 cargo movements were 13% over the previous year's total – and the swing is continuing upward. Part of the boom is explained by a doubling of the China trade, with a steady monthly influx of some 100,000 tons of meat, vegetables, textile fabrics, paper, chinaware, cement, etc. But there is significant increase in other trade as well. Glen Line, running express services between Far East and Europe thrice a month, reports a 20% increase in the volume of cargo from Europe to Hongkong since last year. Jardines reports similar increases in the US-Hongkong and South Africa-Hongkong as well as Europe-Hongkong cargo traffic.

However, Hongkong's attitude to the new trend of containerization has been somewhat lukewarm. A Container Committee was set up in 1966 to study the feasibility of setting up a container terminal. After a great deal of debate, it now seems certain that a terminal will be built at Kwai Chung in Kowloon. The port will have four

28. The other exception was Felixstowe, UK; all other major container terminals in the world were publicly funded: Marc Levinson, *The Box: How the Shipping Container Made the World Smaller and the World Economy Bigger* (Princeton, NJ: Princeton University Press, 2016), 319.

berths and the first stage consisting of two berths will take two and a half years to complete. The bulk of the finance is likely to come from private interests.

Perhaps one reason why Hongkong manufacturers are not terribly keen about containerization is that shipments of five freight tons and below constitute as much as 52% of the main individual shipments from Hongkong. An average shipper's consignment therefore is grossly inadequate for the giant 20-foot containers with a capacity of 15 to 20 tons. It will be some time before local exporters work up a situation where the advantages of containerization outweigh the shortcomings implied in their present practices. It is by now clear that, should Hongkong lag behind in the switch to containerization, bulk carriers will treat the Colony as a secondary port to be fed by a leader like Singapore. . . .

Document 6.23: Bruce Maxwell, 'Start of a New Era of Cargo Handling in HK', *South China Morning Post*, Business News Supplement, 6 September 1972, I.

Inauspiciously Hongkong's new container terminal received its first ship yesterday – the 58,000 ton Tokyo Bay. No beating of drums, breasts, or anything else. No spruced up and gleaming terminal. And the Tokyo Bay's owners, due to address a press conference on board, had some difficulty getting to the berth.

Yet against the odds, the whole operation looked startlingly efficient.

It was known, of course, that the first berth, run by Modern Terminals Limited, would not be finally completed until November, bringing it up to the spick-and-span condition of Singapore's facilities at their recent grand opening.

Despite this, the crane operator at Kwai Chung yesterday could have taken three-quarters of the day off and still run rings around his Singapore counterparts.

He was almost blatantly nonchalant about it all – and handling a giant container crane is by no means easy. The straddle-carrier drive[r]s (these stilt-like vehicles pick up the landed containers and stack them) also looked as though they had been doing some serious practice. By far the most impressive part, however, were the load-discharge figures for the ship.

Fifty containers were offloaded yesterday – and no less than 600 are being picked up when Tokyo Bay returns from Japan next week. Compared with Singapore, where it was a fight to find 100 containers for the first ship, or else with the Trio group's break-even figure of 750-1,000 containers per vessel, this is an impressive start indeed. . . .

A Government statement last night said that "to enable the large containers ships to reach berths at Kwai Chung the Government has dredged more than three million cubic yards of seabed material from the Rambler Channel.

"The approach channel was dredged to a depth of 40 feet below chart datum – the minimum depth required for large container ships.

"One-and-a-half miles of roads and a flyover is being built to provide easy access to the container terminal. The Kowloon Foothills Road corridor, due for completion in 1975, will greatly improve traffic flow between Kwai Chung and industrial towns in Kowloon.

"Two other container lots at Kwai Chung are being held in reserve by the Government and can be made available for future development when a clear need develops."

Section 8. Light Rail

The now-corporatized KCRC built and operated the Light Rail network in the new northwestern New Territories towns of Tuen Mun, Yuen Long, and Tin Shui Wai. The government had originally asked Hong Kong Tramways to build and operate this network, but it declined. Around this time, tramways and light rails saw something of a 'renaissance' in Western Europe and elsewhere.[29] *The area was already served by bus services before the construction of the light rail system. Bus services in the area were restricted to secure the KCRC's revenue stream. Documents 6.24 and 6.25 reflect local residents' dissatisfaction with the imposition of the new mobility regime over pre-existing everyday practices. They also illustrate the nascent local democracy in the new towns and the growing recognition of local stakeholders taking part in debates over local and regional mobilities.*

Document 6.24: HKPRO, HKRS 461/1/134, Judy Li for District Officer (Yuen Long) to Secretary for Transport, 'Tuen Mun/Yuen Long Transport Services: Light Rail System', 25 October 1988.

At the YLDB T&TC [Yuen Long District Board Traffic and Transport Committee] meeting held on 20.10.88, most members criticized Government for failing to properly supervise the LRT [Light Rail Transit] service in the areas of (i) safety (ii) fare levels and (iii) service. It was raised that under the existing legislation, only the Board of Directors of the KCRC is empowered to direct and supervise the LRT service and that only the Governor-in-Council has the power to overrule decision made by the Board on public interests grounds. But if the latter's decision is in contrast to the

29. Dejan Petkov, *Tramway Renaissance in Western Europe: A Socio-technical Analysis* (Wiesbaden: Springer, 2020).

Corporation's commercial interest, Government has to make appropriate compensation to the Corporation. The other two task groups, namely, the Govt.-KCRC LRT Liaison Committee and the YL-TM JMG [Yuen Long–Tuen Mun Joint Monitoring Group] on LRT service, simply play the monitoring and consultative roles and their views are not always accepted/respected by the Corporation.

2. After protracted discussions, the T&TC deliberated to tend the following proposals to Government/KCRC for consideration:-

(i) in order to strengthen the supervision of the LRT service, two DB [District Board] members, one from YLDB and another one from TMDB, should be allowed to join the KCRC Board of Directors. The two representatives should be nominated by the respective DB and not appointed by Govt. The YLDB T&TC decided to request for a representative from the YLDB and would support the TMDB to make a similar request.

(ii) to relax the existing boarding and alighting restriction imposed upon KMB [Kowloon Motor Bus] within the LRT service area. In the interim, passengers on Kowloon-bound KMB buses should be allowed to get off the vehicles within the Transit Service Area and KMB drivers should be instructed to allow for alighting upon request. In the long run, amendment to the present legislation governing the boarding and alighting restrictions should be amended because the latter is considered as a breach of human right.

(iii) that Government, KCRC or any concerned groups should organize public hearing sessions on a frequent basis to obtain views from the YL/TM residents regarding the LRT service.

Document 6.25: HKPRO, HKRS 461/1/134, Christopher K. B. Wong for Secretary of Transport to Simon Cheung for Commissioner for Transport, 'Yuen Long District Board Traffic & Transport Committee', 13 December 1988.

At the coming meeting on 16 December 1988, please respond to the suggestions raised, along the following lines –

(a) the suggestion for one member each from the Tuen Mun and Yuen Long District Boards to be appointed to the KCRC's Managing Board has been noted but given the Board's existing membership and the three-tier monitoring system already in place, the Administration is of the view that the public interest is more than adequately safeguarded. The power to appoint members to the KCRC Board rests with the Governor who would no doubt take into account the need to provide adequate representation of the interest of Tuen Mun and Yuen Long residents as well as the importance of having a balanced and objective composition on the Board;

(b) the KCRC is keenly aware of the complaints that have been raised and adjustments are being made on a continuing basis to improve the level and quality of service provided. Examples include improved frequencies for both LRV [Light Rail Vehicles] and feeder buses, deployment of additional LRVs and the introduction of auxiliary bus routes. So far, the Corporation has responded positively to the demands for improvements and the Administration is confident that it will continue to do so in the future.

It should also be pointed out that the boarding and alighting restrictions form an integral part of the Transit Service Area (TSA) concept based on which the Corporation has agreed to construct and operate the LRT system. To relax the restrictions would erode the TSA concept specifically provided for in the KCRC ordinance, altering the basis of the Corporation's evaluation when it first took on the project. It is therefore neither appropriate nor fair for the Government to relax the restrictions unilaterally without KCRC's consent; and both the Administration and the KCRC have formal contacts with the District Boards through representation on their Traffic and Transport Committees and the Joint Monitoring Group on LRT Service. Consultation with DB Members and residents' groups is done on an ongoing basis for the purpose of further improving LRT service. Opinions expressed by the general public in the media are also closely monitored.

Section 9. Civil Aviation

Hong Kong had long harboured dreams of becoming an aviation hub, and this status was borne out of networks which existed long before flying technology became popularised.[30] *The city's first international airport at Kai Tak was infamous globally for being dangerously close to urban, residential high-rises in Kowloon. Soon after the Japanese surrender, colonial authorities pondered moving the airport to a more suitable, less precarious location. They first considered Ping Shan in the north-western New Territories, but as the following documents show, this too was unsuitable, not because of geography but because of geopolitics. The government then considered Deep Bay, further north-west from Ping Shan. This time, the change in regime in China meant a massive infrastructure project*

30. John D. Wong, *Hong Kong Takes Flight: Commercial Aviation and the Making of a Global Hub, 1930s–1998* (Cambridge, MA: Harvard University Asia Center, 2022), 21–26.

on the Hong Kong–China border was untenable.[31] *Hong Kong settled for Kai Tak until 1998, when the new international airport at Chek Lap Kok opened.*

Document 6.26: TNA, FCO 371/53629, F 455/113/10, C-in-C. Hong Kong to Cabinet Offices, 3 January 1946.

[1.] Mr. T.W. Kwok who is representative Chinese Government in Hong Kong requested an interview with me today and stated he had been instructed by his Government to protest against construction of Ping Shan airfield, and to request pending settlement of status of Kowloon the work on airfield should be stopped. He handed me text of a telegram Chinese Minister for Foreign Affairs giving reasons for this protest. The text is contained in my immediately following signal.

2. I told him that I noted his request which would be passed to H. M. Government as this was a matter for discussion between our two Governments, but said that I could not stop work on airfield without instructions from H. M. Government. I added a first class airfield was required at Hong Kong if Hong Kong was to perform the full services to China of which it was capable. I also explained to him the measures which were in hand for dealing justly with displaced Chinese Nationals.

3. I asked him unofficially what really was the objection to our construction of this airfield and he said he thought that if we had asked the consent of Chinese Government before starting it he doubted if there would have been any objection. I did not comment on this attitude.

Document 6.27: TNA, FO 371/53629, F 456/113/10, C-in-C. Hong Kong to Cabinet Offices, 3 January 1946.

Following is text of protest begins.

1. Kowloon though under lease to British, is Chinese territory and such large scale constructive project should not be undertaken without consent of Chinese Government.

2. Airfields construction causes displacement of large number of Chinese nationals resident in that area whose interests are of concern to Chinese government. At the time of conclusion of new treaty with British, Chinese government reserved question of Kowloon for negotiation after war.

3. Pending settlement of status of Kowloon Hong Kong government is requested to discontinue the projected construction.

31. Wong, *Hong Kong Takes Flight*, 48–54.

Document 6.28: TNA, FO 371/53630, F 900/113/10, Air Ministry to C-in-C Hong Kong, 10 January 1946.

. . . Air Ministry and Ministry of Civil Aviation have now examined further the possibility of developing Ping Shan airfield to civil international standard. It seems doubtful whether from engineering aspect development of airfield to full international standard is possible without very considerable expenditure.

Ministry of Civil Aviation also fear that the meteorological and topographical features of the site may not be acceptable to civil operators.

2. We propose therefore to despatch as soon as possible an expert Mission representing Air Ministry and Ministry of Civil Aviation to report on suitability of Ping Shan and if necessary to examine any other possible site in Hong Kong or New Territories. Details of composition and date of despatch of Mission will follow.

3. In the meantime, construction of airfield to minimum military requirements should continue.

Percy Cradock was British Ambassador to the PRC (1978–1983) and headed the British negotiating team during the early Sino-British talks over the transfer of Hong Kong's sovereignty. British Prime Minister Margaret Thatcher saw Cradock as a trusted Sinologist, as did her successor John Major, at least at the start of his premiership. Cradock's memoirs, an excerpt of which follows, were written to exonerate his actions, including those related to the new Hong Kong airport.

Document 6.29: Percy Cradock, Experiences of China (London: John Murray, 1999), 237–43.

Though the Governor's decision to build a new airport, announced in October 1989, was part of the confidence-building operation, the project had its own compelling rationale. Anyone making the hair-raising descent into the existing airport at Kai Tak, surrounded by high-rise blocks, could appreciate the requirement for a better site. There were also strong economic grounds. The existing airport was near saturation point and would soon constrict Hong Kong's growth. Something of a different order was urgently needed to match the territory's position as a major international financial, commercial and communications centre. There had been the usual history of abortive planning for another location, interrupted by political or financial crises. It was time for a bold move. A site on Lantau Island with associated plans for extensive port facilities was chosen. It was naturally a big project, worth around £8 billion and extending well beyond 1997. But the Hong Kong budget could readily carry its share, and 40 per cent of the money would come from the private sector.

The plan had ample publicity and was spoken of to Zhou Nan. At first the Chinese government expressed no particular interest or objection. They had other preoccupations at the time. By the end of 1989, however, there were ominous mutterings from Peking. They related to cost, fears that the plan might be over-ambitious and, more precisely, that it could leave the Special Administrative Region in a weaker financial position in 1997. We were encountering a more refined version of Deng Xiaoping's worries in 1984 that we would deliberately impoverish the territory before leaving; the airport was seen as a means by which British companies would be enriched and Hong Kong's treasury emptied. . . .

This was the situation in the summer of 1991. A breakdown looked likely. The Chinese were threatening to publish their account of the negotiations in order to demonstrate British 'insincerity'. There was a point fast approaching when the Governor could no longer postpone a public decision: the calls for tenders on two of the main contracts were overdue. . . .

At this point I became involved as an actor rather than simply an adviser and observer. The Prime Minister, now John Major, asked me to go to Peking as his representative on a make-or break visit. . . .

There was no Hong Kong representative present. This was unfortunate but, in the circumstances, unavoidable. The Governor, whom I had seen in London the day before leaving, was very understanding; and he and his Executive Council were kept throughout in the closest touch. . . .

A major factor, which became apparent on the afternoon of 28 June, when I saw him, was Li Peng's interest in an early visit by John Major to sign any agreement we reached. In Peking's planning the airport was therefore to become an instrument in China's full rehabilitation after Tiananmen. This greatly assisted our leverage. Nor was it so extravagant a wish as some of the commentators made it seem: the international 'quarantine consensus' of June 1989 had already crumbled; the Japanese Prime Minister was coming to Peking in August, the Italian Prime Minister probably in September. But there were problems in Li Peng's wish to delay any announcement on the airport until full signature: that could mean months of delay, with leaks and uncertainties in the interval. We wanted work to begin at once, at least on the most urgent of the core projects.

There would undoubtedly be domestic sensitivity about a visit by Mr Major to Peking. But there were powerful arguments in its favour, relating to the airport, Hong Kong's confidence and prosperity, and the recovery of Sino-British cooperation, both over the territory and generally. I put them as cogently as I could in my telegram home, adding that there would be advantage in the Prime Minister raising the issue of human rights on the visit and letting it be known that he had done so. . . .

The final stages of our negotiations turned on the likely timing of the Prime Minister's visit, the timing of the publication of the agreement and the scope of the construction works that could begin on initialling only. The Chinese fought for a complete embargo until the two leaders had met; and for a time on the last day the whole agreement seemed in jeopardy. But it was eventually initialled on 30 June and published four days later.

It was brief and to the point. In return for certain financial assurances and strictly limited undertakings on consultation, the Chinese expressed their support for the airport, their willingness to take part in its construction and their undertaking to recognize after 1997 obligations entered into by investors.

Issues continued to plague the airport, from diplomatic and political disagreements to what one British newspaper termed 'Communist mismanagement' at the beginning of operations.

Document 6.30: James Pringle, 'Hong Kong Defies China with Cash for Airport', *Times*, 28 November 1992, 13.

Hong Kong's legislative council last night narrowly agreed to provide the government with funds to continue preparations for the building of its new airport at Chek Lap Kok.

By 27 votes to 25, the council's finance committee voted to permit £567 million to be injected into the Provisional Airport Authority to enable it to award contracts for site preparations — preliminary runway and terminal construction. China says the project, which is tied up with the row over democratic reform in Hong Kong, is too expensive, and has urged members of the council to reject it. Peking says if Britain goes ahead without its consent it will be breaking an agreement signed by John Major, the prime minister, last year. During almost six hours of debate, punctuated by procedural wrangles, members questioned the future status of the project if agreement with China is not forthcoming. But Hamish Macleod, the financial secretary, said the government had not received any formal approach from China not to proceed.

"We are taking a step-by-step approach," said Mr Macleod. "I have been trying to keep avenues open for talks. For me to start discussing possible scenarios beyond this next step will achieve precisely the opposite of what I believe most members want, which is to carry out constructive talks with China and reach a sensible agreement." . . .

Document 6.31: James Pringle, 'Hong Kong's Pride Hit by Airport Chaos', *Times*, 10 July 1998, 18.

James Pringle on Communist mismanagement at territory's £12bn showpiece.

Operations at Hong Kong's state-of-the-art airport at Chek Lap Kok, opened with fanfare by President Jiang Zemin of China just a week ago, continued to be in a state of near-bedlam yesterday.

The publicity hype lavished on the £12 billion airport has evolved into a public relations nightmare. The fourth day of operations yesterday saw more angry and famished passengers. Meanwhile, cargoes worth millions of pounds — wilting flowers, stinking seafood, rotting vegetables and fruit and out-of-date newspapers — have been dumped, with freight companies suffering huge losses. . . .

As tempers frayed at the airport, one passenger called police on his cellular phone after he and a planeload of arriving passengers had waited in their seats for two hours for buses to ferry them to the terminal. . . .

Over the past few days, passengers have had a litany of complaints regarding long delays for flights; long periods of waiting inside aircraft to disembark; lost and delayed baggage; overcrowded restaurants in the terminal; inadequate toilet facilities; malfunctioning air-conditioning in stifling heat; phone booths without phones; and stalled escalators. As I flew out of the airport this week, I received an embossed certificate lauding me "as one of our first travellers", but once on board the aircraft, the Dragon Air captain told passengers as the loaded plane sat for an hour on the runway: "Welcome to the chaos of the new airport." . . .

Suggested Readings

Atkinson, R. L. P., and A. K. Williams. *Hongkong Tramways: A History of Hongkong Tramways Limited, and Predecessor Companies*. Rustington, UK: Light Railway Transport League, 1970.

Chen Zhihua 陳志華, and Li Jianxin 李健信. *Xianggang bashi bainian tuibian* 香港巴士百年蛻變 [A hundred years of metamorphosis on Hong Kong's buses]. Hong Kong: Chung Hwa, 2021.

Chiu, T. N. *The Port of Hong Kong: A Survey of Its Development*. Hong Kong: Hong Kong University Press, 1973.

Fung, Chi Ming. *Reluctant Heroes: Rickshaw Pullers in Hong Kong and Canton, 1874–1954*. Hong Kong: Hong Kong University Press, 2005.

Ho, Pui-yin. *Ways to Urbanization: Post-War Road Development in Hong Kong*. Hong Kong: Hong Kong University Press, 2008.

Ho, Pui-yin. *Making Hong Kong: A History of Its Urban Development*. Cheltenham, UK: Edward Elgar, 2018.

Leeds, Peter F. 'Evolution of Urban Transport'. In *Land-Use/Transport Planning in Hong Kong: The End of an Era*, edited by Harry T. Dimitriou and Alison H. S. Cook, 13–33. London: Routledge, 1998.

Leung, C. K. 'The Growth of Public Passenger Transport'. In *Asian Urbanization: A Hong Kong Casebook*, edited by D. J. Dwyer, 137–54. Hong Kong: Hong Kong University Press, 1971.

Leung, C. K. 'Mass Transport in Hong Kong'. In *Asian Urbanization: A Hong Kong Casebook*, edited by D. J. Dwyer, 155–66. Hong Kong: Hong Kong University Press, 1971.

Li, Adonis M. Y. 'Hindrance or Helping Hand: Hong Kong and Sino-British Railway Commercial Diplomacy, 1974–84'. *The International History Review* 45, no. 3 (2023): 590–605.

Li, Adonis M. Y. 'Visions of Public and Private Mobility: The Kowloon Railway Terminus in Hong Kong'. *Urban History* (2023).

Li Junlong 李俊龍. *Xianggang dianche: dingzhu yi yi ling nian* 香港電車——叮囑一一〇年 [Hong Kong tramways: A glimpse of its century]. Hong Kong: Chung Hwa, 2014.

Ma Guanyao 馬冠堯. *Cheshuimalong: Xianggang zhanqian lushang jiaotong* 車水馬龍：香港戰前陸上交通 [Streams of horses and carriages: Hong Kong's pre-war land transportation]. Hong Kong: Joint Publishing, 2016.

Miners, Norman. 'Building The Kowloon–Canton–Hankow Railway'. *Journal of the Royal Asiatic Society Hong Kong Branch* 46 (2006): 5–24.

Moss, Peter. *A Century of Commitment: The KCRC Story*. Hong Kong: Kowloon–Canton Railway Corporation, 2007.

O'Young, Anneliese. *Moving Experience: The MTR's First 36 Years*. Hong Kong: South China Morning Post, 2011.

Phillips, Robert J. *Kowloon–Canton Railway (British Section): A History*. Hong Kong: Urban Council, 1990.

Wong, John D. *Hong Kong Takes Flight: Commercial Aviation and the Making of a Global Hub, 1930s–1998*. Cambridge, MA: Harvard University Asia Center, 2022.

Yeung, Rikkie. *Moving Millions: The Commercial Success and Political Controversies of Hong Kong's Railways*. Hong Kong: Hong Kong University Press, 2008.

7
Education

Allan T. F. Pang[1]

Like the topics explored in previous chapters, the history of education has allowed historians to investigate a great variety of primary sources. This abundance of materials has attracted scholars across disciplines to study education development in Hong Kong. Historians, educationalists, sociologists, and others have made great contributions to the field. Among them, two general histories of education in Hong Kong by Anthony Sweeting have been the most significant.[2] Approaches in other works vary. Some focus on the changes and continuities of education policies, while others investigate how the broader political context shaped education in Hong Kong.[3] Scholars have also focused specifically on certain institutions and schools.[4] Readers may refer to the Suggested Readings at the end of the chapter for more examples of these works. This chapter builds on previous chapters of this volume and illustrates how education was part of late colonial governance in Hong Kong. It focuses on the linkages between education policies and the wider historical context,

---

1. I thank the Bodleian Libraries at the University of Oxford, University Archives at the University of Hong Kong, and History Society, Arts Association, Hong Kong University for their permission to reprint some of the documents.
2. Anthony Sweeting, *Education in Hong Kong, Pre-1841 to 1941: Materials for a History of Education in Hong Kong* (Hong Kong: Hong Kong University Press, 1990); Anthony Sweeting, *Education in Hong Kong, 1941 to 2001: Visions and Revisions* (Hong Kong: Hong Kong University Press, 2004).
3. See, for example, Lachlan Crawford, 'The Development of Secondary Education in Hong Kong', *History of Education* 24, no. 1 (1995): 105–21; Edward Vickers, *In Search of an Identity: The Politics of History as a School Subject in Hong Kong, 1960s–2002* (New York: Routledge, 2003).
4. For instance, see Peter Cunich, *A History of the University of Hong Kong*, vol. 1 (Hong Kong: Hong Kong University Press, 2012); Patricia P. K. Chiu, *Promoting All-Round Education for Girls: A History of Heep Yunn School, Hong Kong* (Hong Kong: Hong Kong University Press, 2020); Moira M. W. Chan-Yeung and contributors, *Daily Giving Service: A History of the Diocesan Girls' School, Hong Kong* (Hong Kong: Hong Kong University Press, 2022).

the significance of education policies in the history of Hong Kong, and the interaction between those policies and the people's voices. This chapter does not aim to be comprehensive. Instead, it is selective to illustrate how the government 'politicised' and 'depoliticised' education in different historical contexts.

The chapter divides Hong Kong's education development from 1945 to 1997 into three eras. The first focuses on the period 1945–1960s. Documents 7.1–7.3 reveal how the colonial government gradually increased its control over curricula and textbooks due to the Cold War and the confrontation between the Kuomintang (KMT) and the Chinese Communist Party (CCP). Officials depoliticised curricula and textbooks to prevent students from being exposed to political ideologies from either Chinese regime. The second section focuses on the 1970s and the early 1980s. 'Reforms' and 'welfare' have been two common keywords in describing education policies of this era. As this section shows, it was also a period of activism and resistance. Document 7.4 showcases the official perspective in describing this development. Documents 7.5 and 7.6 reveal students' and teachers' activism and the government's passive response. The final section focuses on the era from the 1980s to 1997. Preparing for the retrocession became a major task. Documents 7.8–7.11 demonstrate how the government explicitly politicised education in the final days of colonial rule. Document 7.10 also illustrates the social and economic changes that contributed to the policy shifts. This chapter selects primary sources commonly used in studies of education history, including curriculum documents, student writings, and oral recollections. These documents showcase the changes and continuities of how various historical actors interacted with the politics of education. By comparing the documents, readers can understand the government's contrasting attitudes towards political education in Hong Kong.

Two other themes deserve attention. The first one is the agency of the historical actors. The chosen documents emphasise not only policymaking but also the activities of students and teachers, who were the receivers and practitioners of education, respectively. This chapter thus aims to bridge top-down and bottom-up approaches to studying education. The transregional nature of Hong Kong's education development is the second theme. Teachers, students, and textbooks in Hong Kong were part of the transregional flow of people and ideas. Examples in this chapter include the networks of colonial control across East and Southeast Asia (Document 7.2), student movements (Document 7.5), and economy and trade (Document 7.10).

Section 1. Censorship and the Cold War

The local confrontation between the KMT and the CCP heightened the politically sensitive nature of education in Hong Kong. Before the Japanese occupation, Chinese middle schools in Hong Kong adopted textbooks from China. After 1949, the Hong Kong government hoped to stop the import of textbooks that contained political ideologies from both mainland China and Taiwan. In 1952, the colonial government established the Syllabus and Textbook Committee to regulate education in Hong Kong. It also formed a Chinese Studies Committee to review Chinese subjects in schools. The committee's report in 1953 emphasised the need to adopt locally published textbooks and to focus on the social and cultural aspects (instead of the political dimension) of Chinese studies. Back in May 1949, the Colonial Office had enquired about textbook policies in Hong Kong. Below is an excerpt of the reply from Governor Alexander Grantham.

Document 7.1: HKPRO, HKRS 41/1/5032, Colonial Censorship of Textbooks, 28 June 1949.

(a) A standing Textbook Committee, constituted before the war, was revived in 1948. It consists of a chairman, members and two joint secretaries, all of whom are nominated by the Director of Education. Each member of the Textbook Committee is in turn the convenor and chairman of a standing sub-committee dealing with a specific subject. Each sub-committee is composed of, in addition to the Convenor, two or more members nominated by the Director of Education, and two or more members nominated by the Council of the Hong Kong Teachers' Association.

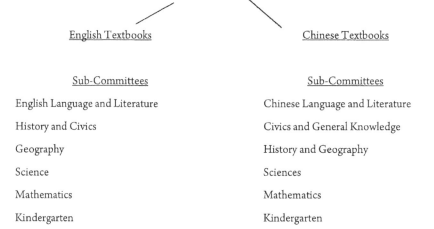

General Textbook Committee

English Textbooks	Chinese Textbooks
Sub-Committees	Sub-Committees
English Language and Literature	Chinese Language and Literature
History and Civics	Civics and General Knowledge
Geography	History and Geography
Science	Sciences
Mathematics	Mathematics
Kindergarten	Kindergarten
Music	

Joint Secretaries

Women Inspector of Schools (English)

Inspector of Vernacular Schools (Chinese)

The Committees' term of reference are: - "To report to the Director of Education, in accordance with the Grant Code, and the Regulations under the Education Ordinance, on the school textbooks which he should (a) recommend, and (b) approve or permit for use in all registered schools".

The Committee meets when consideration of textbook problems of a general nature is required. The sub-committees meet more frequently: as new textbooks appear on the market they are considered and appropriate recommendations made to the Director of Education through the Chairman of the General Committee.

(b) In Government and non-Government schools, the procedure for selecting and buying textbooks is the same,

(i) Selection. Heads of Schools make their own selection from the lists of recommended and approved books issued by the Director of Education. If they desire to choose books not appearing on these lists, they are required to forward copies of such books for the consideration of the appropriate sub-committees. The Director's approval of these books is determined by the recommendations of the sub-committee concerned.

(ii) Purchase. Books are purchased by the pupils, on the orders of the schools, from commercial firms in the Colony.

(c) The supply of textbooks is not governed by a capitation grant. In Government and Grant-in-aided Schools, however, a government grant of approximately $1 per pupil is provided for the purchase of teacher's textbooks and reference books. Small library grants are made to government schools . . .

Re your paragraph 6 there is a great need for textbooks (both English and Chinese) written by local teachers to meet specific local needs, particularly in such subjects as Civics, Geography, History, Hygiene and English. Suitably qualified teachers might be encouraged to undertake this work either by financial assistance or by the grant of special study leave.

Colonial officials often viewed Hong Kong as part of the transregional control across territories. In 1959, Regional Education Adviser in South East Asia David McLellan, who was the Deputy Director of Education in Singapore in the early 1950s, assessed the Cold War position of Hong Kong in Southeast Asia's Chinese education. McLellan described not only the Hong Kong government's efforts but also the transregional networks (both existing and potential ones) resisting communist education.

Document 7.2: TNA, CO 1030/900, Notes by David McLellan, 26 June 1959.

The following are general impressions gathered during a brief stay in Hong Kong. No records or statistics were available at the time of writing, but it is hoped that the paper may indicate some ways in which Hong Kong could help other countries in the region . . .

8. The Government has had several clashes with the Communist schools during the past year or so. In some cases it has tried to enforce regulations recently introduced into the Education Ordinance to strengthen its powers; e.g. it forbade the flying of the 5 star flag and closed down the Chung Hwa school on the grounds that it was structurally unsafe. In each case it was forced to withdraw from its stand, the moral being that action should not be started on uncertain grounds. On the other hand, it was able to deport the Principal of Pui Kiu Middle School and withdraw the subsidy from the Workers' Children's Society of Plantation, so far with less opposition than was expected. The timing of these actions is important; clearly it helps if the C.P.G. [Central People's Government of the People's Republic of China] is preoccupied elsewhere, e.g. with Tibet and the Committee. The more experience one has of action against Communist schools, however, the more one realizes how difficult it is to draft an Education Ordinance which can be effectively enforced, and how useful it is to have the Public Security Ordinance to fall back on.

9. The news from the publishing field is depressing. The Communists have enormous initial advantages of which they have made full use. Even the United Publishing House which was set up with Government support to supply textbooks for Chinese schools in Singapore and Malaya is now largely under Communist control. The Americans are subsidizing publishers, e.g. the Union Press through the Asia Foundation, but they are very dissatisfied with the meagre results so far achieved. The Hong Kong Education Department has its own Syllabuses and Textbooks Committee, but this seems to have done little since I left in 1953. Most of the needs of the primary schools had then been met and a start had been made on the following textbooks for Middle Schools:-

(i) a Social and Cultural History of China;

(ii) a Junior Middle Geography;

(iii) a General World History.

The first two (in Chinese) are now in use; the third, which is to be published in English first and the adapted/translated into Chinese, is, I believe, almost ready for printing. With some modification these books could be used in other territories, though the value of (i) is less than it otherwise would be because it stops short at 1911.

10. There is in Hong Kong a reservoir of experienced Chinese teachers and scholars who could do more than they are now doing to meet the textbook needs of the region. Many are in Government service, though, and the Government discourages their efforts by restricting their earnings from textbooks written even in their spare time.

11. I suppose it is now too late to revive the idea of a Regional Literature Agency? You will remember that it was proposed nearly ten years ago to establish such an agency to meet the needs of Malaya, Singapore and the Borneo territories for textbooks and general reading matter in the various local languages – mainly Chinese and Malay. . .

12. Briefly then, Hong Kong might be able to help other countries in the region:

(a) by its special knowledge of Communist methods of indoctrination and infiltration;

(b) by admitting students to post-secondary courses;

(c) by helping with the writing of Chinese textbooks with a regional rather than a Chinese (C.P.G. or K.M.T.) outlook.

On the one hand, the colonial government strove to shift the focus of humanities subjects to society and culture. On the other hand, it deliberately depoliticised official curricula to prevent radical political sentiments from arising. History was one of the affected subjects. The following extract illustrates this further 'depoliticisation' process.

Document 7.3: HKPRO, HKRS 1225/1/86, Suggested History Syllabus for Anglo-Chinese Secondary Schools, 1964 Revised Edition.

AIMS AND METHODS

Teachers of history should aim not merely at examination successes but also should encourage their pupils to develop a 'sense of curiosity' and the 'habit of logical reasoning'. Pupils, instead of being supplied with ready-made facts and dictated notes, should be trained as far as possible to seek for such information themselves; the role of the teacher should be that of 'organizer of the lesson'. . .

FORM 1

In Form 1 it is advisable to try to give pupils an insight into history as a whole. This can be done by a study of the lives of people who have affected the world in some noticeable way – explorers, inventors, philosophers, religious teachers, artists, conquerors and rulers.

Studies of lines of development may also be undertaken – suggested topics are farming, building, transport, science, industry and education. . .

FORMS 2 AND 3

In these forms it is desirable that the topics for study should be selected after deciding which sections of the School Certificate Syllabus are to be taken in Forms 4 and 5. . . In general it is desirable that pupils, by the time they reach Form 4, should be aware of the major epochs in history, as well as the achievements of some of the great people of the past. They should have some knowledge of how men have lived in the past and how important institutions and activities have developed. It should be remembered, however, that interest in purely political affairs develops relatively late. 'Man, the adventurer' rather than 'Man, the politician' is the proper study of pupils in the early years of secondary school. . .

Section 2. Adjustment and Activism

Murray MacLehose, the colony's governor from 1971 to 1982, recalled his memory of education policies during his governorship in an interview by historian Steve Tsang. The following excerpt of the interview transcript describes education development from MacLehose's official perspective. It reveals his judgement of the education scene in Hong Kong. Compared with other historical actors who wrote other documents in this section, MacLehose may have emphasised different aspects of local education.

Document 7.4: Oxford, Bodleian Libraries, MSS. Ind. Ocn. s. 377, Transcript of Interviews with Murray MacLehose, 1989 and 1991, 277–86.

DR TSANG: What are your recollections of the development of education in Hong Kong during your Governorship?

LORD MACLEHOSE: Well, this was an on-going interest. There was a Board of Education with very expert and dedicated chairmanship and membership and the subject's very well covered in the various policy statements I made about education in annual speeches to Legislative Council. I really haven't got much to add now. Obviously the change was from compulsory primary education for all to compulsory secondary education for all - free - and a very large expansion of opportunities in post-secondary. This was as a result of the increased national product which made it possible to fund this. In view of the importance of the subject – because this was what parents wanted, it was obviously vital for the future of Hong Kong that the people had good education - it made it very important that the teaching profession should be represented on the Legislative Council. This was done. As well as a Vice Chancellor we had school teachers who played a very prominent part in these changes. It's quite interesting to record that while they supported these changes to some extent on detail and on their pace and they were proved right. They said it was all going far too fast and that quality would be affected, and also that to introduce compulsory secondary education would result in an entirely new phenomenon in Hong Kong, which was a reluctant student. If we were going to introduce this, and they understood why we were going to introduce it, it would be very important to have increased staff with counsellors and people who would have a look at the problems of reluctant students and see that they weren't disruptive to the work of the school. It sounded to us as if they were using the changes as an excuse for getting more staff, and overdoing things. In fact they were absolutely right and it was eventually done as they wished a year or two later. It shows how important it was to have professional representation. My feeling was that we were always balancing the numbers against quality and that numbers tended to win. You can see why, and I don't say that this was wrong, but it posed a problem for the teachers, who were right. I think the problem's still there...

DR TSANG: In the '70s were you and your advisers still worried that some of Hong Kong's schools were strongly influenced by either the Kuomintang or the Chinese Communist supporters?

LORD MACLEHOSE: No, not really. It's quite true that a decade or so earlier this was a problem but really, by the '70s, what interested parents and really children too, was having a school that produced an education that would allow them to pass their exams and consequently have good opportunities in later life. That was the first priority. Obviously ideology didn't come into this. It might have done once but it certainly didn't much then.

DR TSANG: But there still [*sic*] some of the schools which were identifiable as being pro-Communist schools or pro-KMT schools. Did Government take any special notice of them?

LORD MACLEHOSE: If any school didn't accept Government inspection, it wasn't eligible for grant obviously, and this applied to some Communist schools I think. Eventually I think they did accept it. I can't remember. But that was the point – they had to be inspected and they had to have a curriculum that was suitable for the examinations – a basic curriculum that was suitable – and certainly at the beginning of my time this made it impossible for Communist schools. I'm not sure the extent to which it changed towards the end of my time there, but the fact was that there were very few parents who wanted their children to go there because the academic results, certainly in the early '70s, were so poor.

DR TSANG: Apparently most of the graduates of the Communist schools and the Workers' Children's Schools were not recruited to the Civil Service. Was that just because of their poor academic performance, or was that a conscious policy on the part of Government?

LORD MACLEHOSE: No, well, as far as I know I think it was just poor academic performance.

DR TSANG: What about the question of instilling in Hong Kong's youngsters a sense of citizenship - civic education?

LORD MACLEHOSE: I don't think this was an element in the curriculum that I can think of. Certainly the sense of being proud of Hong Kong I thought was something important – it applies to any city, anywhere in the world – and some sense of participation... [A]s for schools being asked to teach citizenship, I don't think so, I don't think it was defined as such...

DR TSANG: There is also one rather interesting omission in Hong Kong's education curriculum which is that there is hardly anything which teaches pupils or students about Commonwealth history. That seems to be a major omission.

LORD MACLEHOSE: I didn't know that but I don't see why it's a major omission. There was no policy of building up... to tell you the truth I've never thought about it which perhaps answers your question. Hong Kong was British and there were certain benefits in being British; there were equally certain historical reserves [*sic*] which <u>any</u> ethnic Chinese has about Hong Kong being British. . . But no attempt was made to buttress this by inculcating flag-waving loyalty to Britain or the Commonwealth... I suppose the major attraction of Hong Kong to most of the population was simply that it was so obviously preferable to life in China, and there was no need to complicate this understandable attitude with any political veneer.

DR TSANG: Indeed, and the curriculum seems, in a way, to reflect this.

LORD MACLEHOSE: Yes.

DR TSANG: European history, American history, Chinese history, and even Japanese and Southeast Asian history appear far more prominent than Commonwealth history or British history in Hong Kong school curricula.

LORD MACLEHOSE: Oh, yes. I think this probably sounds right to me. Let's take another question...

Many university students participated in the Chinese Language Movement that began in the late 1960s. They demanded that the colonial government grant equal and official status to both the Chinese and English languages. The Hong Kong Federation of Students (HKFS), an organisation jointly formed by local university student unions, spread the protest to other parts of the world. In 1971, the National Union of Students (NUS) of the Universities and Colleges of the United Kingdom wrote to the Foreign and Commonwealth Office (FCO) to support the movement in Hong Kong. The following letter demonstrates the interconnectedness of student movements after the late 1960s, when waves of youth protests swept the world.

Document 7.5: TNA, FCO 40/341, Letter from the National Union of Students of the Universities and Colleges of the United Kingdom, 29 September 1971.

We are writing in relations [*sic*] to the work of our colleagues in the Hong Kong Federation of Students (HKFS) concerning the use of Chinese as an official language in the Colony.

We would like to inform you that, in line with a resolution adopted by the Second Commonwealth Students Conference in Kumasi, Ghana, in January 1971, the NUS has fully supported the efforts of the HKFS Language Action Committee and of its Chairman, James Chui, in seeking an exact parity of treatment of Chinese and English as official languages in Hong Kong.

We have read the reports of the Chinese Language Committee, produced between February and July, 1971, and read with interest the "Position Paper of the HKFS on the Matter of Legislative Declaration of Chinese as an Official Language of Hong Kong."

We would express our strong support for the points made in that Position Paper (a copy of which we enclose) and wish to add our own voice to the recommendation made in Section A(2) of the Paper: "that both the Chinese and English languages be made official through formal legislation by the Legislative Council of Hong Kong, and be incorporated into the laws of Hong Kong. . .".

We would welcome your views on this matter, and trust that they might accord with the recommendations of our Hong Kong colleagues.

In 1974, the Legislative Council passed the Official Languages Ordinance, declaring the official status of both the Chinese and English languages. Movement participants perceived this as a victory. Nevertheless, students and activists later recognised how official policies disrespected the Chinese language in government operation. English continued to dominate official communications and documents. Its superior status also persisted in the education system. In 1978, the 'Second Chinese Language Movement' began. The following newspaper excerpt describes an exhibition by the HKFS. This exhibition in 1979 featured the students' discontent towards official language policies in education and employment. The excerpt documents the pro-Chinese elements of student activism in 1970s Hong Kong. President of the Hong Kong Baptist College Tse Chi-wai, who spoke at the exhibition's opening ceremony, became a member of the Legislative and Executive Councils in the mid-1980s.

Document 7.6: Public Criticism of Official Language Policies, *Wah Kiu Yat Po*, 23 November 1979, 6.4 (translated).

To promote the Chinese Language Movement, the HKFS organized an exhibition named 'Reality and Illusion – Equal Attention on the Chinese and English Languages?' from yesterday until the 25th in the Exhibition Hall, Low Hall of the Hong Kong City Hall...

Tse Chi-wai Chairs the Opening

When chairing the exhibition's opening ceremony, the President of the Hong Kong Baptist College, Dr Tse Chi-wai, pointed out that 'People always regard the Chinese Language Movement as an action based on a narrow sense of nationalism. This is an unnecessary illusion. This is because the value of the Chinese language is an achievement of human beings. This is an objective and commonly recognized fact.'

Dr Tse said at the end that the Chinese language was a precious heritage of human beings and a language used by a quarter of the world's population; he therefore hoped that, through this exhibition, people from various sectors could deeply reflect [on the value of the language] and have greater determination and efforts in learning and using the language...

Chinese Glorious Traditions

Based on the various reports, the exhibition aims to convey to the government that it should no longer use English as the only criterion for hiring. It should support actual actions. The investigation also shows that students have better abilities in using Chinese than English. However, their Chinese levels are also worsening nowadays, leading to the equally bad quality of their Chinese and English. This is a disastrous consequence of 'emphasizing English over Chinese'.

The exhibition hopes that various sectors should actively demand the Hong Kong government implement the policy of having Chinese as an official language. Most importantly, the public should learn and respect Chinese to carry forward the glorious Chinese culture and tradition.

Teachers also voiced their discontent towards official policies. The Report of the Special Commission on the Certificated Masters of 1973 (known as the 'T.K. Ann Report', published in 1976) proposed switching government primary schools to aided schools, which would be managed by unofficial sectors. In the following letter, Leung Yim-tong, president of the Government School Non-Graduate Teachers' Union, condemned the government for this proposal. Considering documents in Chapter 3 on Political Culture, especially the one on the Precious Blood Golden Jubilee Secondary School, student and teacher activism was a major theme that characterised education in 1970s Hong Kong. The government did not implement this recommendation.

Document 7.7: TNA, FCO 40/807, Petition by Leung Yim-tong, President of the Government School Non-Graduate Teachers' Union, 11 June 1977.

The whole of the Government School Non-Graduate Teachers denounce and firmly oppose to the Government's captioned policy, of which we trust that you have been aware. In fact, right after the T.K. Ann Report, we have accordingly expressed our opposition to the captioned, claiming that the detachment of Government Primary Schools from the Education Department is inappropriate. In addition, we demand that matters regarding or affecting the Government school non-graduate teaching staff should be first consulted to our Union, and should be negotiated between both parties for full agreement.

On 19th October 1976, Government School Non-Graduate Teachers' Union submitted our letter to the Chief Secretary, protesting the captioned subject matter and ignorance attitude of Government. We proposed Consultative Meetings to be held and stressed that the Government should cease the trading of Government Primary Schools until full agreement can be reached. In our letter dated 11th November 1976, we urged for immediate reply from the Chief Secretary and in return, we were instructed to refer to aforesaid to the Education Department Consultative Council. It is unfortunate we have confronted with the delaying tactics while the negotiation power and representation of the Education Department Consultative Council were in doubt. We regret that the status of our Union in particular relevant benefits of our members have not been properly recognized and respected by the Government. Owing to the aforesaid, the 2,000 members of the Government School Non-Graduate Teachers' Union are under the impression that all of our previous efforts have been totally ignored. We hereby demand for proper solutions and stipulated reasons for our opposition to the captioned as follows:-

1. THE GOVERNMENT IS LIABLE TO FURNISH SOUND EDUCATION AND SHOULD NOT EVADE ITS DIRECT RESPONSIBILITY OF RUNNING GOVERNMENT SCHOOLS

Education in Hong Kong – A Direct Responsibility to the Government

"To serve and to construct" is the role of the Government to whom we regard as civil servants. . . The running of Education in Hong Kong certainly reveals the following discrepancies:

(a) The Government overrides its freewheel in running Government schools. It is irrational and objectionable to see that Government schools, which have been run by the Education Department all these years, to be turned over to the Aided Sectors.

(b) The pretext of "let citizens of Hong Kong participate in running schools" is totally misleading and inexcusable; instead, it is the sole responsibility of the Government to carry out its full range in Education, in its best possibility. To evade the mentioned duties will, of course, contradict to the principle of Government.

(c) There are only 70 in number of Government Primary Schools out of 1,000. The aforementioned figure reveals an extremely poor proportion. Moreover, the Government is still trading the remainings [*sic*] and letting off its duties in this connection. This retreating movement is again contradicted to its policy as the Government claimed that "there will be a full scale development in secondary schools by Government from now on" . . .

2. THE TRADING OF THE EXISTING GOVERNMENT PRIMARY SCHOOL TO THE AIDED SECTORS

1965 Education White Paper

"The expansion and development of primary and secondary schools should be carried out mostly, if possible, by aided sectors" claimed 12 years' age in the 1965 Education White Paper, in respect to the Ten Years' Primary School Expansion scheme. It is noticeable that what is defined 12 years age would not be applicable nowadays. We quote other relative contents from the same documents to verify our statements:

(a) Every ten classes should be staffed by 13 teachers – in fact, 11 teachers is the true figure at present.

(b) Each classroom should accommodate 35 students/the correct number of students as per each classroom is 45 and not 35. The aforementioned reveals what the Government override its freewheel in adopting policies which they consider favourable and totally ignore applicability and accuracy. We are of the opinion that -

(i) By trading of Government Primary Schools to the Aided Sectors, the Government evade its responsibility in developing and supporting education. A movement quite contradicted to the principle of Government and the public's will, as free education is being emphasized. Placing the Government Primary Schools to Aided Sectors is indeed a cutting of education fund and not an encouragement.

(ii) The redevelopment of Government Primary Schools, if any, should be expanded to Government Secondary Schools instead of turning-over to Aided Sectors. Bargaining the property and facilities of Government Primary Schools to the Aided Sectors is improper. . .

Section 3. Politicisation and Retrocession

In the mid-1980s, the colonial government shifted its aim to preparing for Hong Kong's return to China. Political education became a new feature in local curricula only in the final years of British rule. The following excerpt recorded the internal discussion on how the Education Department should implement civic education and embedded political knowledge at schools.

Document 7.8: Excerpt of Minutes of the Board of Education, 25 June 1984, Box 9, Anthony Sweeting Papers, University Archives, HKU.

To note for information/discussion a paper on Civic Education and Political Knowledge and Awareness in Schools

4. The Chairman said that civic education and political knowledge and awareness had recently been raised in the Legislative Council on a number of occasions and that there was growing public concern and interest on the subject. He considered it timely that the Department should review the situation as a whole to determine whether existing opportunities in schools for promoting civic knowledge and political awareness should be further improved. The present strategy paper had therefore been prepared and Members were invited to give their comments on it and to endorse in particular the general principles outlined in paragraph 9 and the suggested strategy outlined in paragraphs 10-23 of the paper.

5. Mr. Chan asked the Chairman how far the Department intended to go in terms of promoting political knowledge and awareness in schools, noting that students in the universities were very vocal on this subject.

6. The Chairman replied that the paper was intended to give a clear indication of what the Department intended to do to promote political knowledge and awareness

in schools. He stressed that the Department was advocating a line of enquiry in schools designed to deepen pupils' understanding and appreciation of the open and free society in which they lived and providing an education to prepare them for their role as well-informed and responsible adults.

7. Mr. Tisdall whilst agreeing that the promotion of political awareness and the democratization of the existing system should be handled with care, cautioned that it would be wrong for the Government to take the view that democratization could proceed only very slowly in Hong Kong. He was also of the view that there should be plenty of room in the curriculum for schools to facilitate political discussion.

8. The Chairman said that the paper had already made it quite clear that there were at present ample opportunities both within the curriculum and through extra-curricular and related activities for students to develop a basic knowledge and understanding of Hong Kong's existing political system and structure.

9. Professor Brimer pointed out that to allow democratization to grow was a right and proper thing and stressed that one could not do this by means of persuasion alone but that there should be a will and intent among those who wished to become politically aware. He was in favour of strengthening civic education and political knowledge in the school curriculum. He also agreed with the intention behind the statement that 'schools should teach student how to think but not what to think' but pointed out that it was subject to interpretation. Students should be educated in such a way as to enable them to become prepared for 1997. They should be made aware of the change that was due to come and should be helped to adapt themselves to the change, for better or for worse.

10. On the point of the guidelines, Dr. Legg stressed that there should be a broad scope for the development of political knowledge and awareness. The Department should avoid adopting a kind of 'forbidden subject' approach but should provide sufficient knowledge and information on the subject to enable students to form their own views. He considered it essential that there should be clearly defined objectives.

11. Professor To regarded the paper not only timely but basically progressive [*sic*]. He said that the paper and the attached syllabuses provided sufficient and accurate knowledge for the education of youth in political awareness. Students, he thought, should be taught democratic thinking and good leadership and should be prepared to cope with the political change that was due to come. He also pointed out that the Department should pay particular attention to the problem of teacher preparation.

12. Mr. Lim raised two points. First, he said, for over twenty years, teachers and pupils had been told not to be involved in politics and they were happy to refrain

from doing so. Many of the teachers did not know what politics actually was and how it should be taught. If they were required to teach the subject, they must do the job well or else the situation would be chaotic. In his view, the problem faced by the Department was how to train teachers to teach the subject properly and usefully. Second, there was the age factor. He said that people in Hong Kong were very reserved. They seldom talked about politics. Forms 1-3 students could not talk sensibly about politics. Forms 4-5 could be taught civics perhaps, but not really politics. At what level therefore should politics be introduced?

13. To this, the Chairman replied that politics like sex education was not to be introduced as a set subject. Political awareness should be inculcated in students through integration in various subjects and outside the curriculum by a variety of means but not as a single subject taught to a particular age group.

A year later, the colonial government issued the following guidelines for implementing civic education. The following excerpt illustrates the political education that the government hoped to implement in preparation for the people of Hong Kong to rule Hong Kong.

Document 7.9: HKPRO, Excerpt of Guidelines on Civic Education in Schools, 1985.

Junior secondary (extract)

Knowledge	Attitudes	Skills
3. The individual and society (Hong Kong)		
a. Introduction to Hong Kong with basic knowledge of its history, its geographical setting, its people, its industrial, commercial, financial, social, and cultural development	Sense of belonging to Hong Kong Appreciate the cultural heritage of Hong Kong An awareness of the importance of cultural exchange Appreciate the factors which are responsible for Hong Kong's earlier success and future stability and prosperity Sense of duty to Hong Kong	To identify one's relationship with Hong Kong To describe Hong Kong with a certain degree of accuracy about its history, geography and economic development To present a good image of Hong Kong To participate in community service

b. How Hong Kong is governed: a brief description of the administration of Hong Kong; the importance of law and order to a community; the government and the people	Appreciate the functions of the government Co-operate with the government Respect for law and order Support for common good An awareness of Hong Kong Government affairs	To think logically and rationally To evaluate the performance of government objectively Group interaction skills, e.g. discussions, debates Social and political participation skills To participate in activities in support of common good particularly government sponsored campaigns

Senior secondary (extract)

Knowledge	Attitudes	Skills
3. <u>The individual and society (Hong Kong)</u>		
a. The Hong Kong Government: functions and policy making – Need for rules and regulations – Types of rules in society	Greater awareness of the functions of government Appreciate the importance of rules and regulations in a stable society Appreciate the influence of rules on individual behaviour	Analyse and interpret information objectively Exercise self-control for the common good Relate one's behaviour to the needs of the community
b. The government and the people – Representative system under liberal democracies – Consultation with people – Major official channels for the redress of grievances – Informal influences on policy making	Respect for equality, liberty and rationality Readiness to give constructive criticism Appreciate the importance of these channels of communication Appreciate the value of informal influence on government policy	Express personal feelings and convictions regarding liberal democracies Give constructive criticism Present a case objectively Identify channels for redress of grievances

The Education Department kept reviewing Hong Kong's curricula in the years before the retrocession. It established a committee to review the Secondary School Curriculum. The following document reveals their concerns. Apart from upcoming political changes, economic and social phenomena also led to new features in the curriculum. New technological and vocational subjects, such as Computer Studies, Travel and Tourism, and Accommodation and Catering Services, became new choices for students.

Document 7.10: HKPRO, HKRS 2131/2/8, Review of the Secondary Curriculum, 17 December 1987.

Recent Changes in Hong Kong and their Implications on Curriculum Development

Changes in H.K. in recent years	Implications on Curriculum Development
Economic & technological changes	
1. H.K. has become the world's leading commercial and financial centre	– importance of science, technical and practical subjects grows. These subjects become more attractive to students
2. H.K. has developed into a major manufacturing centre	– increased demand for training in technical and practical skill [sic]
3. The development of automation in the industrial world	– continued importance of English as a medium of communication in trade, commerce, industry and tourism
4. H.K. as gateway to China	
5. Tripartite economic power in HK	– increased importance of Putonghua and the Chinese Language
6. The society becomes more and more automated	– increased knowledge of China
	– new demand for vocational training such as training programmes for translators and interpreters
	– training programmes for services personnel, e.g. hotel management, tourism, public relations
	– increased demand for computer literacy
Social changes	
1. Improved welfare for working class	– education for leisure
2. The Society is becoming more urbanized and industrialized	– more emphasis on creative activities and cultural subjects required
	– demand for environmental protection
Political changes	
Sino-British Agreement on the future of H.K.	– increased demand for civic awareness

One of the final changes in local curricula was the inclusion of Hong Kong history. This topic became a highly contentious issue in the early 1990s. One debate was whether to include local history in the 'Chinese History' subject or the '(World) History' subject. The Education Department decided to include Hong Kong history in the History syllabus. It saw this new addition as part of its civic education efforts. Any terminologies and events that might be sensitive to either the British or Chinese perspective did not appear in this syllabus.

Document 7.11: HKPRO, HKRS 1225/15/29, Extract of the New Junior Secondary Syllabus on Hong Kong History, 1996.

S2	*Transition to Modern Times*				
	Topic		*Teaching points*	*Key concepts*	*Explanatory notes*
Topic 5	Growth and development of Hong Kong up to the early twentieth century	1. British administration since 1842	• the government structure, including the Legislative Council, Executive Council, Heung Yee Kuk, Sanitary Board (Urban Council) • role played by the Chinese • social conditions, e.g. diseases and natural disasters, education, law and order, population growth		The focus should be on the political, social and economic changes in Hong Kong since 1842 up to the early twentieth century. An understanding of our heritage should be developed and an awareness of protection of historical buildings should be cultivated.
		2. Growth of Hong Kong into an entrepot	• early trade and industries • reclamation and urban development • development of transport • new industries and entrepot trade	• entrepot	
		3. The study of local history through buildings, organizations and streets	• buildings, e.g. Main Building of Hong Kong University, French Mission Building, Old Stanley Police Station, Government House, Old Tai Po Market Railway Station, Bishop's House, Old Kowloon-Canton Railway Terminus, Old Wanchai Post Office • social organizations, e.g. Tung Wah Group of Hospitals, Po Leung Kuk, religious organizations • streets, e.g. Boundary Street, Pottinger Street, Possession Point and Possession Street, Queen's Road, Dex Voeux Road	• heritage • preservation • declared monuments	

S3	The Twentieth Century				
	Topic		*Teaching points*	*Key concepts*	*Explanatory notes*
Topic 2	The growth and development of Hong Kong in the twentieth century	1. The Japanese occupation	• the fall of Hong Kong • life under the Japanese occupation		Students should develop an awareness of the growth and development of Hong Kong in the twentieth century. The focus should be on life under the Japanese occupation, post-war development from an entrepot to an international financial centre, and relations with China.
		2. From an entrepot to an international financial centre	• reasons for the development • development of social services (education, housing, social welfare) • impact on the livelihood of people of Hong Kong	• manufacturing industries • community building • infrastructure	
		3. Popular culture	• songs • movies and TV	• popular culture	
		4. Relations with China	• Hong Kong and the 1911 Revolution • China's contribution to the development of Hong Kong • transition to a Special Administrative Region	• Joint Declaration • Basic Law	

The transition towards 1997 was not a smooth process. Many students, teachers, and publishers worried that the CCP would intervene in local education policies. In the mid-1990s, textbook publishers avoided sensitive topics and followed politically correct terminologies in mainland China to ensure their books could be used in Hong Kong's classrooms after 1997. This sense of uncertainty also existed among university students, who worried that the CCP would intrude on Hong Kong's higher education. In 1996, the executive committee of the History Society (HISO), a student body representing history undergraduates at HKU, interviewed three faculty members of HKU's History Department. The following article, published in the society's bulletin in March 1996, reveals both students' uncertainty and the historians' temporary optimism for Hong Kong's future. All three historians researched and taught Chinese history at HKU. Ming K. Chan also specialised in China–Hong Kong relations. Elizabeth Sinn is a specialist in Hong Kong history and has published widely in the field. She later became the Deputy Director of the Centre of Asian Studies at HKU.

Document 7.12: Views by University Students and Teaching Staff Regarding 1997 [HISO Bulletin, 1996] (Translated).

All professors expressed that the History Department would not change its teaching principles greatly due to political issues after 1997. Nevertheless, both Dr Adam Lui and Dr Ming K. Chan expressed that they might change to teach Chinese history in the Chinese language...

Regarding their views towards changes in the History Department after 1997, they tend to think that, unless the university introduced any administrative guidance, the department will maintain its status quo and emphasize academic freedom and autonomy. It will not suppress any opinion and will allow the existence of various interpretations. Moreover, the department will still emphasize both Chinese and Western history, but it will undoubtedly care more about Chinese history education.

When asked whether they were worried that the CCP would intervene in Hong Kong's academic freedom, all three professors had a cautious and optimistic attitude. Dr Elizabeth Sinn thought we should not lose hope towards everything and give up from the beginning. Instead, we should be confident and face 1997 with a positive attitude. Dr Lui held a similar view. He pointed out that Hong Kong people feared 1997 because we had too little contact with and understanding of the mainland. We, therefore, think that our present way of life is the best and cannot accept anything from the mainland. All these conceptions are biased.

They used the mainland's contemporary academic and economic development to support the above views. Dr Sinn mentioned that people in mainland China were very interested in researching Hong Kong history. This commercial market supported this research and published *Nineteenth-Century Hong Kong* and *Twentieth-Century Hong Kong*. They no longer understood Hong Kong purely from the ideological perspective and perceived Hong Kong as "a colony under the suppression of imperialism." Instead, they researched Hong Kong's development empirically. . .

Dr Ming K. Chan also believed that, in the short term, the mainland would not greatly intervene in Hong Kong after 1997. Even if changes occur, they may not come from official and direct pressure from the mainland. They may simply be influenced by the social atmosphere, self-evaluation and self-regulation by certain individuals. These changes are not concrete. This made the writer remember that when Dr Lui described the current situation in the mainland, he said that the government allowed universities and professors to enjoy autonomy. However, after 4th June 1989 [The Tiananmen Square Massacre], many professors felt they were in danger and thus restrained themselves [from expressing their opinion]. When we apply these two professors' words into some Hong Kong people's actions during the transitional period, is there a sense of 'seeing the bloom of willow trees before the coming of spring'? Does this reveal Hong Kong's future political situation?

Suggested Readings

Burns, John P. 'The State and Higher Education in Hong Kong'. *China Quarterly* 244 (2020): 1031–55.

Chiu, Patricia P. K. *Promoting All-Round Education for Girls: A History of Heep Yunn School, Hong Kong*. Hong Kong: Hong Kong University Press, 2020.

Chou, Grace Ai-Ling. *Confucianism, Colonialism, and the Cold War: Chinese Cultural Education at Hong Kong's New Asia College, 1949–76*. Leiden: Brill, 2012.

Kan, Flora K. L. *Hong Kong's Chinese History Curriculum from 1945: Politics and Identity*. Hong Kong: Hong Kong University Press, 2007.

Luk, Bernard Hung-Kay. 'Chinese Culture in the Hong Kong Curriculum: Heritage and Colonialism'. *Comparative Education Review* 35, no. 4 (1991): 650–68.

Morris, Paul, and Anthony Sweeting. 'Education and Politics: The Case of Hong Kong from an Historical Perspective'. *Oxford Review of Education* 17, no. 3 (1991): 249–67.

Sweeting, Anthony. *Education in Hong Kong, 1941 to 2001: Visions and Revisions*. Hong Kong: Hong Kong University Press, 2004.

Sweeting, Anthony, and Edward Vickers. 'Language and the History of Colonial Education: The Case of Hong Kong'. *Modern Asian Studies* 41, no. 1 (2007): 1–40.

Vickers, Edward. *In Search of an Identity: The Politics of History Teaching in Hong Kong, 1960s–2002*. New York: Routledge, 2003.

Wong, Ting-Hong. *Hegemonies Compared: State Formation and Chinese School Politics in Postwar Singapore and Hong Kong*. New York: Routledge, 2002.

8
The Arts

Reynold K. W. Tsang[1]

The arts, which broadly encompass visual arts, performing arts, and literary arts, are an essential part of our social, cultural, and recreational life. Scholars across disciplines have examined various creative works in Hong Kong's past, especially popular music and cinema.[2] Meanwhile, there are increasing studies on the history of specific arts genres and arts institutes, such as Liu Ching-chih's work on Hong Kong's music industries, policies, and education, David Clarke's and Zhu Qi's studies on the transformation of Hong Kong's visual arts, and both academic and anecdotal research on the Hong Kong City Hall.[3] Moreover, studies on local municipal councils and politicians have touched on the arts administration of Hong Kong.[4] However, the general

---

1. I would like to express my gratitude to John M. Carroll, Allan Pang, Jodie Cheng, and Haider Kikabhoy for their kind assistance.
2. See, for example, Yiu-wai Chu, *Hong Kong Cantopop: A Concise History* (Hong Kong: Hong Kong University Press, 2017); Klavier J. Wang, *Hong Kong Popular Culture: Worlding Film, Television, and Pop Music* (Singapore: Palgrave Macmillan, 2020); Poshek Fu and David Desser, eds, *The Cinema of Hong Kong: History, Arts, Identity* (Cambridge: Cambridge University Press, 2000).
3. Ching-chih Liu 劉靖之, *Xianggang yinyue shilun: Yueyu liuxingqu, yansu yinyue, yueju* 香港音樂史論粵語流行曲, 嚴肅音樂, 粵劇 [Hong Kong music history: Cantonpop, serious music, Cantonese opera] (Hong Kong: Commercial Press, 2013); Ching-chih Liu 劉靖之, *Xianggang yinyue shilun: wen hua zheng ce, yin yue jiao yu* 香港音樂史論：文化政策・音樂教育 [Hong Kong music history: cultural policies, music education] (Hong Kong: Commercial Press, 2014); David Clarke, *Hong Kong Art: Culture and Decolonization* (Hong Kong: Hong Kong University Press, 2001); Qi Zhu 朱琦, *Xianggang meishu shi* 香港美術史 [Hong Kong art history] (Hong Kong: Joint Publishing, 2005); Fan Fu Chow, *Where Modern Hong Kong Began: The City Hall and Its 50-Year Story* (Hong Kong: Hong Kong City Hall, 2012); Tai-lok Lui, *Shimin de dahuitang: Yanliang liushinian weiguang* 市民的大會堂：延亮六十年微光 [People's City Hall: shining for sixty years] (Hong Kong: Chung Hwa Book Co., 2022).
4. Y. W. Lau, *A History of the Municipal Councils of Hong Kong 1883–1999* (Hong Kong: Leisure and Cultural Services Department, 2002); Hilton Cheong-leen, Gary Cheung, and Oliver Chou, *Hilton Cheong-leen: First Chinese 'Mayor' of Hong Kong* (Singapore: World Scientific, 2022).

development of the arts in Hong Kong, namely the changes in the arts landscape and arts policies, have received little attention. Liu Ching-chih and Chin Wan are two of the few researchers who study the evolution of arts and cultural governance in Hong Kong and organise it into distinct historical periods.[5]

This chapter scrutinises the overall progression of the arts sector in Hong Kong from 1945 to 1997. It focuses on the field of fine arts, which is generally considered to be 'high art'. The selected primary sources reveal the forces both advancing and restraining the arts sector. They are of varying forms and origins, representing the standpoints of different stakeholders, including the public, the municipal councils, and the colonial government. They illustrate the motives and actions of respective stakeholders in fostering, directing, and manipulating the arts. Other than the development of the arts, they also shed light on public leisure, public education, municipal politics, and colonial governance. While this chapter touches on the broader cultural policies and the politics embedded in them, it mainly deals with the provision and administration of arts amenities. The politics of culture are examined in a wider scope in the next chapter.

The arts landscape in late colonial Hong Kong was the product of negotiation, collaboration, and contestation between civil society, arts communities, the municipal councils, and the colonial government. After the Second World War, the colonial government maintained a laissez-faire attitude towards arts and cultural development. This prompted the Hong Kong community to unite and pressure the government to provide cultural amenities, which resulted in the re-establishment of the Hong Kong City Hall in 1962. This was a watershed for Hong Kong's arts sector, as it marked the beginning of official patronage for the arts and saw the Urban Council taking charge of the city's cultural amenities. The Urban Council, together with the Regional Council founded in 1986, were the two semi-elected municipal councils in colonial Hong Kong. They directed and delivered recreational and cultural services and oversaw the city's sanitation. Following the 1966 and 1967 riots, the Urban Council and the colonial government worked closely together to expand arts provision, as they sought to appease the public and foster their sense of Hong Kong identity through cultural programmes. Their collaboration led to a 'cultural boom' in Hong Kong in the 1970s and 1980s, which was marked by the erection of multiple cultural infrastructures and the birth and professionalisation of various arts organisations.

5. Liu, *Xianggang yinyue shilun: wen hua zheng ce, yin yue jiao yu* 香港音樂史論：文化政策・音樂教育; Chin Wan 陳雲, *Xianggang you wenhua: xianggang de wenhua zhengce* 香港有文化：香港的文化政策（上卷） [Hong Kong's cultural policies. Vol. I] (Hong Kong: Hua Chien Hsu Publications, 2008).

This chapter is organised thematically and roughly follows the chronological order of events. Section 1 reveals the arts and cultural scene of Hong Kong immediately after the Second World War. Document 8.1 shows its grim situation and the unofficial efforts in arts provision. Document 8.2 showcases the public's dissatisfaction with the local arts and cultural scene and their calls for change. Document 8.3 reflects the challenges faced by private organisations and individuals in sustaining the arts sector. Section 2 discusses the formation of the new Hong Kong City Hall, the first and only civic centre in Hong Kong at that time. Document 8.4 illustrates the collective community support for the re-establishment of the City Hall. Document 8.5 indicates the colonial government's commitment to arts and cultural development, which began with the inauguration of the City Hall. Section 3 focuses on the municipal administration of the arts. It explores the goals of the Urban Council in expanding arts and cultural services (Document 8.6), the Urban Council's dispute with the colonial government over the priority of cultural provision (Document 8.7), and the municipal councils' rising investment in the arts (Document 8.8). Section 4 inspects the objectives and contents of the arts programmes. Document 8.9 exemplifies how the promotion of local arts helped cultivate a Hong Kong identity. Document 8.10 displays how the colonial government employed the arts to its advantage. Section 5 illustrates the official arts policies of the colonial government. Documents 8.11 and 8.12 reflect the maturing of arts administration and the arts landscape at the end of Hong Kong's colonial era.

Section 1. 'A Cultural Dark Patch on the World'

In the immediate post-Second World War years, Hong Kong's arts and culture suffered from the absence of official patronage and the lack of cultural infrastructure. The following text is taken from the Hong Kong Annual Report for 1948, which was the first Annual Report to review the arts and cultural landscape of the city. In the report, the colonial government admitted the gloomy appearance of the local arts scene but tried to defend its minimal support for the arts by citing the various cultural activities conducted by interest societies and non-governmental cultural organisations.

Document 8.1: Government's review of the local arts scene, 1948. Extracts from 'The Arts', in *Annual Report on Hong Kong for the Year 1948* (Hong Kong: The Government of Hong Kong, 1949), 133–38.

The casual visitor to Hong Kong may easily believe that the citizens of Hong Kong are not devotees of the Arts, since he finds in the Colony no art gallery, no English-language theatre, no public concert-hall, no museum, no public library and few ways therefore in which during his stay in the Colony he can engage in that particular artistic activity in which he is most interested. Such an indictment would not be wholly fair to the Colony, since although there is little public patronage of the Arts there is a wide variety of clubs and societies, too numerous to chronicle in detail in this Report, whose members follow with enthusiasm one or other of the Arts, whether it be music or painting, photography, dancing or the drama. Most of these societies from time to time provide public performances of plays or concerts or exhibitions of paintings or photographs. . . .

Apart from clubs and societies devoted to the patronage of one particular muse there are organisations which aim at promoting generally the cultural activity of the Colony. Prominent amongst these is the Sino-British Club, formed during the period of Military Administration, with the object of providing a common meeting place for British, Chinese and other communities in the Colony for intellectual, musical and other activities. During the past year lectures on a variety of subjects have been delivered, a debate, a quiz, six orchestral concerts and various meetings of the Gramophone Group of the Club have been held. Within the Club various Groups have been formed whose members are interested in such subjects as history, philately, drama, literature and music.

The Y.W.C.A. and Y.M.C.A. have also had an active year and have included amongst their varied activities talks on a wide variety of subjects, classical gramophone recitals, "Brains Trust" sessions, orchestral concerts, Cantonese Classes, debates, the showing of travelogue films, folk dancing and production of full length and one-act plays.

A notable addition to the cultural organizations of the Colony is the British Council, an Office of which was opened in Hong Kong in September. Even before the establishment of the local office facilities provided by the London headquarters of the Council had been available to the Colony. Books had been presented to the University; gramophone records had been supplied to Radio Hong Kong; British Council publications had been distributed to schools; scholarships tenable at Universities in the United Kingdom had been awarded to a doctor, a social welfare worker and an engineer; and four persons were sent on visits to the United Kingdom. Much of the local British Council's work up to the present has been preparatory but it has succeeded in spite of cramped accommodation in illustrating the character and scope of its future plans. A library is being established; an exhibition of 18th and 19th century paintings is being prepared; lecture courses on painting and the British Constitution and a series of weekly documentary film shows accompanied by lectures are being arranged. Films on education, nursing, industries etc. have been shown to schools, societies and other groups; arrangements have been made for the publication of feature articles in leading Chinese newspapers; two scholarships are being awarded for the academic year 1949/50; these illustrate some of the many activities of the British Council.

Founded in 1949, the Reform Club of Hong Kong was one of the oldest political organisations in Hong Kong. While demanding political reform, the club also sought to improve the social and cultural life of the Hong Kong community. The following news article reported the Reform Club members' frustration with the dearth of cultural amenities in Hong Kong and their appeal for a civic centre. It indicates the public's desire to improve the bleak scene of the arts in Hong Kong.

Document 8.2: Reform Club's call for a civic centre, 1949. Extracts from 'Reform Club – Inauguration of Kowloon Branch – Cultural Needs', *South China Morning Post*, 22 April 1949, 7.

Views on the need for a civic centre in Hongkong, representation by election, the Municipal Council and the importance of the Reform Club were expressed by various speakers at the inaugural dinner of the Kowloon Branch of the Hongkong Reform Club held at the Peninsula Hotel last night with Mr. F. E. Skinner presiding, assisted by Lt-Col E. B. Braiser-Creagh as table topics master.

During dinner snap questions, dealing, among other things, with beach 'huts,' the Defence Force, co-operative systems, civic centre and the inadequacy of salaries, were replied to by Mrs Brasier-Creagh, Messrs George Yip, D. O. Silver, E. L. Tong, Harry Odell, Macintyre, R. Pestonji and Karel Weiss.

Speaking on the lack of cultural amenities in Hongkong, Mrs H. L. Dekker said that there was little regard paid to a meeting place. Any town in the United Kingdom, however small, had some place where people could meet to discuss public affairs, it was a peculiar thing that in Britain even in time of great stress and in time of poverty, things cultural seemed to flourish. Culture had been driven out by force in the Continent by the Nazis and the Fascists but here it was being driven out by apathy. We should see that Hongkong was not a cultural dark patch on the world.

Mrs Dekker said that it was a matter for regret that the British Council stage players and artists had to more or less beg for accommodation and expressed the hope that if we do have a civic centre it would be available for hire to all races who live in Hongkong to put forward the culture of their various communities.

The speaker suggested that a philanthropist should offer a prize for architects to submit designs for a civic centre which would include a theatre, concert hall, museum, debating and committee rooms.

Throughout the 1950s, interest societies and private organisations continued to shoulder the responsibility of organising arts and cultural activities in Hong Kong. In 1952, Jewish impresario Harry Odell founded the Empire Theatre in North Point, showing popular movies and hosting classical concerts and dance performances. In the absence of a proper performance venue in Hong Kong, the Empire Theatre became the city's cultural hub. However, as outlined in Odell's interview below, such private initiatives struggled to sustain themselves. The necessity for 'a suitable hall' to support the performing arts was evident.

Document 8.3: Harry Odell sells the Empire Theatre, 1957. Extracts from '"Retire? Who Me?" Harry Odell Gives His Answer', *China Mail*, 12 June 1957, 10.

Harry Odell, who, with International Films, was the main owner of the Empire cinema, has now sold his interest in it and the new owners, Charles Gray and partners, who bought the theatre for $3 million, plan an $18 million building development scheme there. . . .

Unfailing Optimist

In a pessimistic world, Harry Odell is an unfailing optimist. When the Empire struck lean times, through failure to obtain money-making pictures he felt that by hanging on, times might get better and the Empire not only pay her way but show a handsome profit.

When it became obvious that the type of films available to the Empire were not going to make her fortune, Harry Odell began bringing in internationally famous artists, but still the Empire did not come up to expectations and reluctantly he has now decided to relinquish his interest in her. . . .

He [Odell] told me that a young baritone will be his next artist and music lovers will be pleased to hear that two big names have been booked for August and October. First will be Luigi Infantino and October star will be the contralto Marian Anderson.

One Problem

The main difficulty in bringing these artists to Hongkong is the lack of a suitable hall in which they can be heard to their best advantage, but again, in his customary optimistic fashion, Harry will cross that bridge when he comes to it.

Many of the artists Harry Odell has brought to Hongkong have arrived here as complete strangers to him but most of them have gone away firm friends and his office walls are covered with autographed photographs bearing witness to the success of his efforts to make them happy while they have been performing here.

Section 2. Re-establishing the City Hall

Hong Kong's old City Hall was closed in 1933. In 1950, the Sino-British Club launched a campaign for a new City Hall. The club formed the City Hall Committee to coordinate the efforts of the wider Hong Kong community. The following list details the membership of the committee. Apart from arts and cultural societies, the sub-committee consisted of business chambers, trade unions, religious associations, charitable groups, and political organisations. Its diverse composition showcases the collective resolve of the Hong Kong community to re-establish a civic centre. The City Hall Committee would lobby the colonial government to undertake the new City Hall project and take charge of its early planning.

Document 8.4: The City Hall Committee, 1950. Extracts from 'New City Hall – Public Committee Formation – Meeting Friday', *South China Morning Post*, 18 July 1950, 6.

Up to the present, 39 different Institutions have accepted the Sino-British Club's invitation to join the Committee. . . .

The following are the institutions which have joined the Committee to date – The Association of Chartered Accountants in Hong Kong (represented by D. Black), Chinese General Chamber of Commerce (Tse Yue-chuen), the Chinese Manufacturers' Union (U Tat-chee), the Chinese Club (Mok Hing-wing), Chinese Young Men's Christian Association (Matthew Fong), the Choral Group (Dr. H. Talbot), Club Lusitano (A. de O. Sales), the Engineering Society of Hong Kong (S. E. Faber), the Garrison Players (Capt. E. C. Sarler), Hong Kong and China Branch of the British Medical Association (Dr. F. I. Tseung), Hong Kong and Kowloon Residents' Association (M. H. Tsui), the Hong Kong Art Club (A. E. Nobbins), the Hong Kong Chinese Medical Association (Dr. K. D. Ling), Hong Kong Chinese Reform Association (Ma Man-fai), the Hong Kong Council of Social Service (Fr. T. F. Ryan, SJ), Hong Kong Family Welfare Society (Mrs M. Allison), Hong Kong Federation of Labour Unions (Chan Man-hon), Hong Kong Light Orchestra (H. V. Ardy), the Hong Kong Stage Club (R. Oblitas), Hong Kong Teachers' Association (Rev- Bro. Cassian), Hong Kong University Alumni Association (Y. C. Kwan), Hong Kong University Union (Peter C. Wong), the India Association (Mr J. Kima), the Jewish Recreation Club (Dr H. Talbot), the Kennedy Town Kai-Fong Welfare Advancement Association (Messrs Lee Hin-leung and Lee Chik-lol), the Kowloon Chamber of Commerce (Mr Robert Der), the Kowloon Residents' Association (Mr J. Moodie), the North Point Kai-Fong Welfare Advancement Association (Mr Tsai Ching-yan and Kung-che Chen), the Photographic Society of Hongkong (Mr Kenneth A. Watson), the Reform Club of Hongkong (Dr Raymond Lee), the

Rotary Club of Hongkong (Mr Hugh Braga), the Rotary Club of Kowloon (Mr R. H. Jones), the Sino-British Club of Hongkong (Dr S. M. Bard), Stanley Sea & Land Citizens' Association (Mr H. de V. Booten), Toc H (Mr R. Holmes), Tung Wah Hospital (Mr Harry King), Wah Yan Dramatic Society (Mr Joseph Lim), the Western District Kai Fong Welfare Advancement Association (Mr Chan Pak-sing), the Young Women's Christian Association (Mrs G. W. Miller), and Y's Men's Club of Hongkong (Mr Wellington Hsie).

The colonial government initially hesitated to take on the new City Hall project, but it eventually agreed to finance and build the new City Hall upon the lobbying of the City Hall Committee. The new City Hall was officially opened on 2 March 1962. It encompassed a concert hall, a theatre, a museum and art gallery, a library, several exhibition halls and lecture rooms, and a memorial garden. The following speech was given by Governor Robert Black at the opening ceremony. Black highlighted the importance of providing a culture-rich 'good life' to the public. It reflects the end of the government's laissez-faire attitude towards arts and cultural development.

Document 8.5: Governor Robert Black's opening speech for the City Hall, 1962. Extracts from 'Hongkong City Hall – Governor's Opening Speech', *South China Morning Post*, 3 March 1962, 25.

Here, in these buildings which I am opening today, there will be a welcome for the citizen not as a bearer of his rates and taxes, but as a partner in the artistic and social life of the city; he will come not to beard one of his obedient servants in his lair, but to share in whatsoever is beautiful and available in this building.

Shelley wrote of Athens as:

> ". . . a city such as vision
>
> Builds from the purple crags and silver towers
>
> Of battlemented cloud."

Here in this Colony, upon barren rocks, through the joint labours of people of many races, one of the great metropolises of the world has risen, and surely no-one, a hundred years ago, even when dreaming dreams or seeing visions and with all the purple crags and silver towers of the clouds to inspire him, would have dared to prophesy such a transformation; Hongkong in its present form is indeed a city of towers. . . .

But there is only one building designed and erected to fulfil its own particular function as a place where the citizens of this city may receive the undoubted pleasures of the arts in their most varied forms, a centre of culture and a place of meeting, a desk for quiet reading or a restful spot for the contemplation of what is beautiful and refreshing to the mind.

Hongkong, like all large communities in the modern world, has many problems all pressing for attention and solution; perhaps in some respects, Hongkong has more than its fair share of these problems; but it must surely be a matter for pride that this city, while facing its material problems, can yet, without relaxing its energy to find their solutions, have the vision to carry through to completion a project of this kind intended not for commerce, not for the daily business of government administration, not for the healing of the body, but for the development of what philosophers call the "good life."

Here, in this new City Hall, as time passes and the project matures, our citizens will be able to draw on the treasury that is the heritage of all free men; they will enjoy the fruitful engagement of leisure in the Library, in the Museum, in the Art Gallery and Exhibition Rooms, in the Concert Hall, in the Theatre, and in the Lecture Rooms.

It may be said, indeed I know it has been said, that if it is really expensive to house these things, we could regard them as luxuries and postpone the provision for their enjoyment to a more fitting date when the times are more propitious.

But I am convinced that most citizens share with me the belief that these are things that we ought not shelve.

As Professor Butterfield, a former Vice-Chancellor of the University of Cambridge and a Doctor of Laws, honoris causa of our own University has written:

"It is not open to any of us to say that we will postpone what philosophers call 'the goodlife' – postpone any of the higher purposes of mankind – until the world is more happily placed or the environment more congenial."

"Some people have become accustomed to arguing, for example, that we must not pretend to have any art today – for how can a man write poetry when society is still so disjoined?"

"I have even heard it said that we must put aside all thought of the arts until the world has been made safe for democracy."

"If men had taken that attitude in the past there never would have been a civilisation or a civilised ideal for us to inherit; and I do not know that Providence has ever promised to men either the Arcadian bliss or the reign of justice which this argument seems to have in view. . . ."

That seems to me to be forceful and to the point and so apposite in this occasion that I make no apology for quoting it at length. . . .

In Hongkong we pride ourselves in swiftly adopting modern machinery and materials and designs, harnessing them to work alongside the undoubted skill and ingenuity of our local artisans and craftsmen, and this is precisely what this building demonstrates and will continue to exemplify to residents and visitors alike; within these walls will be shown something of the arts and craft both of the East and of the West, an amalgam of great interest and in microcosm of striking significance.

We in Hongkong are the beneficiaries of two great estates of culture, and all in Hongkong should share the beauty, should experience, or at least not be denied the means to experience, the eternal rhythm that moves below the turbulent surface of the waters of day-to-day perplexities and pre-occupation with getting. . . .

I am confident that, under the care of the Urban Council, this City Hall will bring light and pleasure to the people of Hongkong, to the enrichment of their lives and the lives of their children.

Section 3. The Municipal Councils and the Cultivation of Arts and Culture

The following manifesto was written by Hilton Cheong-Leen, the leader of the Hong Kong Civic Association and a long-time Urban Councillor. Cheong-Leen served in the Urban Council from 1957 to 1991 and held the council's chairmanship between 1981 to 1986. In the manifesto, Cheong-Leen urged the colonial government to further expand cultural services, with the aim of fostering a Hong Kong identity among the young population and disciplining them. It reveals the political motives behind the democratisation of the arts by the Urban Council.

Document 8.6: Hilton Cheong-Leen's appeal for more arts and cultural services, 1969. HKPRO, HKRS 41/1/10205/3, 'Decade of the 70's – Culture for Hong Kong People', 28 November 1969.

There is a vital and expanding need for more cultural services in Hong Kong, as indicated by the very high level of usage of the facilities of the City Hall. In order to strengthen the cultural heritage of our community and to cultivate a sense of Hong Kong identity, the Civic Association proposes that the Government should establish a long-term policy for the development of the cultural and artistic services.

Hong Kong, like any other city, needs its own culture. In a modern, industrial and sophisticated city such as Hong Kong, cultural activities should no longer be regarded as a luxury belonging to the rich only. As expressed in the report of the Round Table Discussion on Cultural Policy prepared by UNESCO, "cultural and economic development are closely linked," and "physical resources are not enough in themselves and equipment serves no purpose if it is not backed up by the necessary personnel and administrative machinery." Thus if Hong Kong is to have its own character and identity, the development of culture services should keep pace with economic and social growth. . . .

In several local newspapers, it has been said that many residents, especially young people, regard Hong Kong as a mere temporary address rather than a permanent home. Therefore, they are most unwilling to do anything to improve their surroundings. Hong Kong stands at the confluence of two cultures, the Chinese and the Western. While traditional Chinese ideas and values are not always suitable for modern Hong Kong and regarded as being more of a hindrance to progress, our people, especially the younger generation, would do well to develop the critical faculty of selectively discarding the obsolete and integrating what is new and constructive. This critical attitude has to be cultivated in order to develop a Hong Kong sense of identity.

Since 1967, the Government has recognised the importance of our two million young people to the future for Hong Kong. There is public concern about the increasing number of crimes by young people which is daily reported in the press. Although not a complete solution, cultural activities can provide a major outlet for the aspirations and energies of the young. Cultural activities will not only uplift the spirit, but will also promote self-discipline, creativity, and more community pride and responsibility. The future of Hong Kong lies in the ways of thought and the "commitment to live" of the new generation, who will in the coming decade take up their share of keeping Hong Kong alive and ticking as one of the great international cities of the world.

According to the Urban Council Annual Departmental Report for 1968/69, the usage of City Hall facilities available for hire to the public continues to increase and for the most important units it has virtually reached the maximum possible level, namely, the Concert Hall, Theatre and the Exhibition Hall of the Low Block. The City Hall Popular Concert Programme, a remarkable achievement, was started to encourage the appreciation of good "live" music, both Chinese and Western, particularly among young people. The warm acceptance of this programme by the public can be shown by the fact that 42 concerts and dramatic performances were given with a total attendance of over 50,000 people, representing 93% of the maximum capacity. The future plan is to increase the number and widen the scope of the cultural presentations and to encourage more overseas artists of high calibre to perform.

Last year, the Urban Council's Public Libraries Section had 31,448 new borrowers which meant an increase of 20% over the past year. Over 200,000 persons are using the two Public Libraries. Issues in the Adult Lending Library last year also indicate an increase of 10% in the Hong Kong City Hall Library and 15% in the Kowloon Library, i.e. a total of 695,270. Students' Reading Rooms proved to be extremely popular as they also conveniently served as study places. It is estimated that over 70% of the users of the Urban Council libraries are students seeking material to supplement their formal studies. Apparently, the libraries have now virtually reached maximum possible level of usage with respect to premises, staff and stocks of books.

The Urban Council's Museum and Art Gallery has in recent years made a significant contribution in uplifting the cultural awareness of the local population. It therefore seems logical for the Urban Council to proceed with plans to find a new and separate museum building of which the people of Hong Kong can be proud. Meantime steps should be taken to convert the two Whitfield Barrack buildings as premises for Museum and Art Gallery extension services to cater for the large number of people living in Kowloon and New Territories.

The cultural services and facilities provided by the Urban Council are mostly used by educated people. Regrettably, a large portion of our population are not yet using these facilities due to lack of leisure time or insufficient educational standard. The Hong Kong Government has the responsibility to give a reasonable level of education to the new generation and to help them develop a well-balanced personality. Wider educational opportunities including compulsory primary education and more vocational and technical education are matters of first priority.

It has been estimated that 242,800 Hong Kong people go to the cinemas every day, which highlights the need for a wider variety of entertainment and relaxation. By encouraging more educational and cultural programmes, and making greater use of the mass media, such as radio and television, the Hong Kong public, and in particular the young people, can have more choice in the development of their cultural life.

. . .

It would be advisable for a list of cultural projects to be prepared in order of priority so that a proper allocation of public funds could be made to give our young people an ever widening opportunity to study and appreciate both Chinese and other cultures so that they may become more responsive and responsible citizens of Hong Kong.

In fear of an economic recession at the end of the 1970s, the colonial government froze the funding for the new cultural complex at Tsim Sha Tsui. Arnaldo de O. Sales, the chairman of the Urban Council from 1973 to 1981, was deeply dissatisfied with the decision and delivered the following statement at the Urban Council meeting on 11 December 1979. Sales criticised the government for its parsimonious attitude and for reneging on its promises to the public. The statement shows that the Urban Council and the government had different levels of commitment to the development of arts and culture.

Document 8.7: A. de O. Sales's criticism of shelving the new cultural complex, 1979. HKPRO, HKRS 1074/1/39, Official Record of Proceedings: Meeting of 11 December 1979.

The call for proper physical conditions for the performing and creative arts can admit of no challenge in an affluent city. It should not be a case that needs to be argued vigorously in an enlightened society. It is even vindicated here by the consistently heavy use of the City Hall for a variety of community purposes and evidently reinforced by the growing aspirations of progressive people. Yet, there are reactionary elements who might sound the death knell of planned cultural progress by thoughtless though well-meaning action. There may not be a genuine appreciation of the true place of the arts in the life of a modern community for there appears to be only recognition of their political value in the education of young citizens. . . .

More than a decade ago it was recognized that Hong Kong needed additional and complementary auditoria, adequate in quality and sufficient in capacity, and also proper museums instead of the existing make-do-and-mend arrangements in cramped conditions. The concept of putting all these separate projects logically together in one place took root early on. The magnificent site bordering on the harbour at Tsim Sha Tsui was chosen. Feasibility studies were carried out and detailed planning was put in hand as work in committee began in earnest while experts were engaged and pertinent information gathered far and wide. All ideas were thought through and conscientiously worked out if warranted. For as bold and simple as is the concept, the translation of this combined project into practical terms to be implemented in well-regulated phases is an involved and specialist exercise.

A flying start was made at once by this Council when it came into its own. It initiated work resolutely with the ambitious space museum. Furthermore, the increased cost of its part of the whole scheme was accepted with resignation. Why should not the Government do likewise in inflationary times?

On the contrary, the Government is suddenly beset with doubts. Have they political or economic motives? If political, they are unworthy of a mature administration;

if economic, they seem penny-wise, proud-foolish upon reflection. Costs rise with little restraint, so he who hesitates is lost. Hence, even to pause in such predictable circumstances shows a false sense of values.

The ratepayer pays the piper but does not call the tune. He pays more when the authorities dilly-dally out of habit or design instead of taking decisive action promptly. Now, it is rumoured, the Government is thinking of reducing standards and requirements arbitrarily. There is the risk that a poor second-best may be foisted on the people as a result. It is likely to cost far more in the end. It will also not utilize the prominent site to best advantage. To be sure, such a complicated project as the cultural complex does not lend itself to being chopped down here and there in the misguided belief that savings would be made by scaling down the facilities. This mammoth project cannot be messed about by philistines. Without actually employing experts at enormous cost to start from scratch again. The faint-hearted wielders of power will make Hong Kong the laughing stock of Asia. Precious time will be lost by this absurd procrastination. The inferior product will probably cost more without pleasing anybody but the nagging mediocrity. And, the Government will surely fall between two stools. The present concept is not extravagant. The proposals are eminently suited to Hong Kong's need as determined by those most capable of judging the issue without pre-conceived notions in a political climate of make-believe.

The promise was made. The Government is a prisoner of its obligations to the people. They were encouraged to believe that in a short time a fine set of buildings would be going up there. The whole project would not only do Hong Kong proud in its splendid location but, more important, it would serve the needs of a dynamic community in evolution, particularly beneficial for the education of the young citizen in a society so deeply conscious of the need to advance on all fronts all the time. There is the real danger of loss of credibility if, in the midst of plenty in the public coffers, the Government should deny the people the means to enjoy the better things of life.

There must be the vision of a new Hong Kong in the coming century. It will not be achieved by a negative attitude. The people deserve better in every way in fair return for their daily effort to make the place what it is. A good government should boldly create a city which meets the just expectations of its successful people in the exacting years that remain in this century. Let the Government not disappoint the public and be found wanting by the generation now standing in the wings. They are just waiting for their cue to come on stage. Be it so, for how much longer can the Council hold the curtain for the Government?

The Urban Council and the Regional Council oversaw the arts and cultural development in the urban (Hong Kong Island and Kowloon) and rural (New Territories) areas respectively. Their arts expenditure was mainly for programme presentation, infrastructure development, and maintenance of professional performing groups. While the municipal councils were financially independent, they still relied on government financial support for large capital projects. The following tables record the capital, recurrent, and total expenditure of the Urban Council, the Regional Council, and the government in the 1980s and the early 1990s. The tables demonstrate a continuous increase in arts funding, which resulted in the rapid expansion of arts and cultural services in the period.

Document 8.8: 'Arts Funding by the two Municipal Councils and Government', 1981–1993. Recreation and Culture Branch. *Consultation Paper: Arts Policy Review 1993* (Hong Kong: Government Printer, 1993), 56.

I. Capital Expenditure

Year	Urban Council ($m)	Regional Council ($m)	Government ($m)	Total ($m)
81/82	23.5	–	53.0	76.5
82/83	6.0	–	116.0	122.0
83/84	17.7	–	86.2	103.9
84/85	96.0	–	159.1	255.1
85/86	91.6	–	172.3	263.9
86/87	81.1	0.2	129.1	210.4
87/88	97.0	0.6	161.9	259.5
88/89	29.7	1.4	178.2	209.3
89/90	216.6	2.2	178.2	397.0
90/91	30.6	1.2	107.5	129.3
91/92	23.2	1.5	48.2	72.9
92/93	20.5	23.1	7.8	51.4

II. Recurrent Expenditure

Year	Urban Council ($m)	Regional Council ($m)	Government ($m)	Total ($m)
81/82	67.7	–	14.3	82.0
82/83	90.3	–	29.0	119.3
83/84	104.1	–	28.0	132.1
84/85	121.0	–	45.7	166.7
85/86	116.0	–	65.1	181.1
86/87	139.4	44.8	81.8	266.0
87/88	158.9	71.5	93.6	324.0
88/89	188.1	71.4	114.1	373.6
89/90	300.2	85.8	130.3	516.3
90/91	315.6	114.0	148.1	577.7
91/92	374.8	133.9	155.9	664.6
92/93	395.8	143.3	163.4	702.5

III. Total Expenditure (Capital + Recurrent)

Year	Urban Council ($m)	Regional Council ($m)	Government ($m)	Total ($m)
81/82	91.5	–	67.3	158.5
82/83	96.3	–	145.0	241.3
83/84	121.8	–	114.2	236.0
84/85	217.0	–	204.8	421.8
85/86	207.6	–	237.4	445.0
86/87	220.5	45.0	210.9	476.4
87/88	255.9	72.1	255.5	583.5
88/89	217.8	72.8	292.3	582.9
89/90	516.8	88.0	308.5	913.3
90/91	346.2	115.2	255.4	717.0
91/92	398.0	135.4	204.1	737.5
92/93	416.3	166.4	171.2	753.9

Section 4. The Arts Programmes

Under the supervision of the Urban Council, public museums in Hong Kong actively nurtured local artists and promoted their artworks. The following brochure introduced the 'Young Artists of Hong Kong 1970' exhibition at the City Museum and Art Gallery (formerly known as the City Hall Museum and Art Gallery). It was authored by Lui Shou-Kwan, a prominent Hong Kong painter and the father of the 'New Ink Painting Movement'. Lui commended young Hong Kong artists for shaping a distinct artistic identity for Hong Kong and affirmed the museum's role in exhibiting it. This brochure manifests the Urban Council's scheme to foster a Hong Kong identity through arts and cultural activities.

Document 8.9: Exhibition brochure of 'Young Artists of Hong Kong 1970', 1970. Extracts from *Young Artists of Hong Kong 1970* (Hong Kong: City Museum and Art Gallery, 1970).

This group exhibition represents the younger generation of Hong Kong artists of today. Here contemporary art has emerged, just as Hong Kong today has emerged, from the past – through a process of deliberate growth.

Originally it would not be an exaggeration to say that Hong Kong was a cultural desert. Even after the war, Hong Kong was sterile as far as artistic innovation was concerned. Although the artistic circle was bustling, it was very fluctuating and variable. This was due to the fact that life in the post-war years lacked stability, and the inhabitants tended to regard themselves as temporary residents or mere passers-by. . . .

On March 2nd, 1962, when the City Hall opened, the responsibility of educating the public and establishing a cultural image of Hong Kong, began to rest with the City Museum & Art Gallery. In April the same year, an exhibition entitled "Hong Kong Art Today" was held. It stressed the need for art in Hong Kong to go beyond photographic realism and distinguished intelligent experiment and originality from outworn cliché, and dull technical skill from cheap imitation. While a small segment of local artist might have been dissatisfied with this attitude, a good many were immediately influenced and started to pursue a more creative and personal path of expression. . . .

Among the main work of the City Museum & Art Gallery is the attempt to establish Hong Kong on the international art map. If this is to be successful, the art of Hong Kong must have its own identity and should not imitate any international style. The collections of the City Museum & Art Gallery should and does begin to reflect this identity.

In the development of Hong Kong from a small trading port to a city of productivity and growth, much difficulty has been overcome. Similarly to change this once barren cultural desert into a fertile domain of creativity, immense courage and sustained effort are called for. This spirit should be particularly reflected in art which is still neglected by the public at large. The City Museum & Art Gallery have opened up this land for the cultivation of art, and it is on this land that the modern spirit takes root, grows and bears fruits.

Furthermore, the advancement of art also requires a system of new educational methods, to be established and put into practice. It is pointless to have vague ideals or just to wait for miracles. Obviously Hong Kong still lacks well-equipped art school. Even so, extramural classes in Chinese ink painting and design organised by the Chinese University since 1965, have produced encouraging results which contributed significantly to the Design Exhibition and the Chinese ink painting section of the Exhibition of Contemporary Art, both held by the City Museum & Art Gallery in 1969. "If we educate properly", Dr. Sun Yat-sen once said, "no talents will be born and undeveloped; if we stimulate properly, no men of ability will be left in dejection." Perhaps these words are worthy of our attention and speculation.

The artists participating in this exhibition represent, not only the generation that grew up after the war, but also the generation that has been educated locally. It is delightful for us to see them brought together for the first time. Unlike artists of the older generation who, educated elsewhere, have carried the tradition on their backs, the young artists cultivate the soil on which they stand firmly. They wish to confirm the existence of the generation to which they belong, and want to fulfil the responsibility which they have assumed. Although Western art seems distant, Oriental art obscure, and local art uncertain, they are right inside the space and time of the most conspicuous cultural interchange of East and West and their inner necessity for art is not lost. With genuine conviction, each of the artists tries to do what he/she can do or wishes to do. They explore a variety of ways of communicating their feelings and ideas; they attempt to create new forms to embody their personalities and zeal. Their discoveries signify a breakthrough in art.

This new breakthrough strongly reflects that the young Hong Kong artists, especially those who are classified as Chinese ink painters, have come to realise that they can no longer live in seclusion like hermit painters of the past, although they have a deep affection for tradition. Therefore, they either try to penetrate into philosophy and life, or seek to experience the mystery of nature, using their imagination to create new forms and contents. Or they adopt design concepts and mathematical structure to fuse together the Chinese "gold-and-blue" style with the contemporary "hard-edge" style. Or they look into Nature for its sculptural configurations. Between the tip of an ivory tower and the top of a skyscraper, they are like tight-rope-walkers, balancing design and art on their shoulders. Their work may be difficult for general understanding, but this is because few people try to understand it. In any case, we must accept this new generation which we see before our eyes. Let the past remain the past. Every generation of new talents has to be discovered, and each new generation should be given freedom, unbound by time-worn habits and rules. These artists must fully express their own individuality. In the domain of total spiritual freedom, they have to present, not only themselves, but also a new vision, a new order of reality, a new ideal, and a new harmony. We have to understand and respect this young generation, or else we shall age and decline.

Looking back over the twenty years of Hong Kong art, from the "Society of Hong Kong Artists", via many individual artists, the "Circle Group", to the young artists of this exhibition, we should be amazed at what has really happened. All these artists belong to Hong Kong, and are to be recognized internationally as Hong Kong artists. We have to thank all those who have sweated and shed blood for the establishments of Hong Kong art. In future we will need more artists to represent the many facets of artistic creation in Hong Kong. I sincerely hope everybody can deeply realise this, and be encouraged and stimulated by the exhibition.

LUI SHOU-KWAN (Translated by Wucius Wong)

Officially launched in 1973, the Hong Kong Arts Festival remains a major cultural event in Hong Kong today. Despite its magnitude, the festival was organised by the Hong Kong Arts Festival Society, a non-government body. Nonetheless, both the Urban Council and the colonial government actively supported and engaged in the festival. The following report on the first Hong Kong Arts Festival was presented by Governor Murray MacLehose to the Foreign and Commonwealth Office. MacLehose underlined the festival's boost to Hong Kong's tourist industry and international image. He also envisaged future festivals in cultivating a Hong Kong identity. This report reflects the political values that the government attached to arts and cultural events.

Document 8.10: Governor Murray MacLehose's report on the Hong Kong Arts Festival, 1973. TNA, FCO 40/458, Hong Kong's First Arts Festival, 19 April 1973.

Hong Kong has just completed its first Arts Festival. It was a striking departure for Hong Kong as well as a particularly happy event, and I hasten to report. Hong Kong has for the past few years had a festival of its own. But this has been in the tradition of Mardi Gras or the Lord Mayor's Show – a riot of colour and noise but essentially low-brow. This year, for the first time, an Arts Festival was held similar to that in, say Edinburgh. It lasted for four weeks from 26 February to 24 March. . . .

The high proportion of Chinese in the audiences was immensely satisfactory and encouraging for the future. It was also a tribute to the work of the Education Department which has been so active in interesting schools in music and drama.

Great efforts were made to entertain the artists and make them feel at home and welcome. Against the novelty of the occasion and the exotic setting the treatment took, and many of them were nice enough to become involved and to identify themselves a little with Hong Kong.

There was method in all this artistic madness – indeed from the start I regarded the Festival as of great importance for the Colony. Hong Kong needed a boost for its fast-growing tourist industry (12% of exports). It needed something to counter the Lancashire-cultivated but now out dated image of the sweat-shop and the slum. It has become a great enough city to need something more for relaxation for residents and visitors alike than restaurants and shopping, mahjong and night-clubs and the open air sports. I hope that some of this was achieved. Certainly the overseas publicity, particularly in America and Japan, was good, and even some English papers were pleased to print a few Hong Kong stories about subjects other than the stock exchange, drugs, or crime. Certainly in the artists Hong Kong now has some new ambassadors. Certainly a lot of people in Hong Kong, albeit a tiny minority, enjoyed themselves in a new way and took pride in their city being able to attract such a galaxy of talent, and this sort of impact was spread by the donation of many thousands of seats to students. The tourist industry seems satisfied that it has started something of real long-term value. So the Festival closed with a sigh of self-congratulation – which I think was justified. . . .

It was a first time, and the organisers had concentrated on getting the Festival off the ground, but many lessons were learned. There were the usual administrative snags which should be overcome next year. There will be adjustments to make in the balance of programmes. A basic deficiency was that in the performing arts there was too little of a regional flavour. Apart from the Royal Classical Javanese Dancers, the New Japan Philharmonic and Fou Ts'ong the performers were Western in their origin. It is accepted that next year more items from the region must be injected, and that there must be of a specifically Chinese nature – preferably from China itself. Somehow also the organizer must include some local Chinese performers, so as to produce a sense of local identity.

But all in all it was a good first try in introducing something of gracious living in Hong Kong, and it was particularly noticeable that the community's interest and support increased as the month progressed and people became accustomed to the idea of this form of relaxation. It will undoubtedly develop a demand for more cultural facilities – I certainly hope it does. As an example of what one may expect, during the Festival private donations for an Arts Centre, which have long been sought, suddenly became available and assured that the Centre will be built within two years. I imagine that a further biproduct will be a new determination to provide a second auditorium bigger than the City Hall.

Section 5. The Official Arts Policies

Although the colonial government had encouraged and supported the development of the arts since the early 1960s, it did not formulate any clear policy for the arts until the early 1980s. In 1981, the government drew up its first official arts policy, which aimed to promote the performing arts. The policy is outlined in the following memorandum for the Executive Council. It defines the role of the government in advancing the performing arts, along with clear objectives.

Document 8.11: Government's policy on promoting performing art, 1981. HKPRO, HKRS 934/7/50, Memorandum for Executive Council: Promotion of the Performing Arts, 9 June 1981.

Introduction

The purpose of this paper is to propose a policy for Government's role in the promotion of the Performing Arts, which are here defined as music (including singing), dance, drama and opera, with equal emphasis on both Chinese and Western forms.

. . .

Proposals

The increase in Government's involvement, and the growth of private performing arts organisations which has led to increasing demands for Government support, has drawn attention to the need to draw up objectives to ensure the orderly development of Government policies. Accordingly, preparation of the Programme Plans for Music and the Performing Arts commenced in 1978, and has recently been completed. Through the Programme Plans and professional advice received, an overall review has been conducted, with a view to drawing up a policy for promotion of the performing arts.

The review has taken into account the role of the Urban Council, the Urban Services Department in the New Territories, and the programme of construction of cultural complexes referred to in paragraph 6 above. As the work of the Urban Council and the Urban Services Department in the New Territories concentrates on the management of public cultural venues and the presentation of performances therein, the intention is that the new Recreation and Culture Department should concentrate on other areas not already provided for, such as provision of training in the performing arts and the development of community activities. Thus the activities of the Urban Council and the Urban Services Department in the New Territories will complement the work of the Recreation and Culture Department. The present proposals therefore do not cover the activities of the Urban Services Department in the New Territories or the building programme of cultural complexes which are already covered by existing policies, but refer to other areas of the performing arts. The proposed policy will be carried out by the Recreation and Culture Department.

As a result of this review, it is proposed that, in addition to the provision of cultural complexes and their management in the New Territories the following policy objectives should be adopted for the promotion of the performing arts:

(a) The development of community activities for the general public;

(b) The provision of training in the performing arts at the pre-vocational and vocational level;

(c) The development of professional performance groups; the advancement of the highest standards possible within the constraints of finance and available resources;

(d) The establishment of an Advisory Council for the Performing Arts; and

(e) General support and encouragement of performing arts organisations

Established in 1995, the Hong Kong Arts Development Council (HKADC) is a statutory body tasked by the government to support the development of the arts in Hong Kong. It replaced the Council of Performing Arts, which had only an advisory role. The formation of the HKADC marked the professionalisation of arts administration in Hong Kong. Upon its establishment, the HKADC issued a '5-Year Strategic Plan', which was until then the most comprehensive policy document on arts development. The following is the executive summary of the strategic plan. Its ambition and broad scope denote the advancement of arts administration and growing vibrancy of the arts in Hong Kong by the time of the handover in 1997.

Document 8.12: Strategic Plan of the Hong Kong Arts Development Council, 1995. Extracts from *Hong Kong Arts Development Council: 5-Year Strategic Plan* (Hong Kong: Hong Kong Arts Development Council, 1995), 4–5.

Hong Kong is at a critical moment in its history. The speed and scope of social, economic, political and technological change is breathtaking. The arts are a part of that change.

Over the next five years the Hong Kong Arts Development Council (HKADC) aims to make significant progress towards realising its vision of a dynamic and diverse arts scene in Hong Kong to improve the quality of life for the whole community.

In this, the first 5-Year Strategic Plan (the Plan) of the HKADC, the HKADC proposes a significant increase in the level of support for arts development in Hong Kong.

The HKADC plans to undertake an ambitious programme of arts development activities. To a large extent, the HKADC achieves its own objectives through its funding support of many different individuals and organisations. In this way the HKADC can work on a very broad front. When HKADC funding support helps others to meet their arts development objectives, it also helps the HKADC to meet its own.

The HKADC will be involved at almost every point in the process of Creation – Presentation – Communication – Appreciation in all art forms.

The HKADC has identified a range of key tasks for achieving its vision. These tasks are centred on four broad goals.

1. Access

For widening the base for arts appreciation and participation through promotion, information and formal and community education.

2. Excellence

For recognition and professional development of artists and arts workers.

3. Resources

For opening up opportunities for audiences and artists and art workers' development through the provision of support services and public and private funding.

4. Advocacy

For enhancing the public visibility of the arts and contributions of artists and arts workers to society and for mobilising community support from all levels and sectors.

Detailed action steps have been drafted for each of the following art forms:

Dance

Drama

Film and Media Arts

Literary Arts

Music

Traditional Performances

Visual Arts

For 1996–97, the first year of the plan, the HKADC proposes a 44% increase in arts development funding to $130 million. The HKADC anticipates that the full impact of the plan will be felt in the following financial year.

The existing budget of the HKADC is a notional figure based on the limited role of its predecessor, the Council for Performing Arts, and best guess estimates of the funding needs of the new areas of responsibility – including visual arts, literary arts, film, arts education, arts criticism and arts administration. The new budget is based on qualitative and quantitative assessments of the development needs of different sectors undertaken by the HKADC in close consultation with the community.

The HKADC will always listen to its key stakeholders – the arts community and the public – to ensure that it is always able to respond best to the changes in and demands of development in the arts. In this way it will endeavour to make the most creative use of the opportunities that arise from the interaction between itself, the artists, arts organisations and the community.

Suggested Readings

Chin, Wan 陳雲. *Xianggang you wenhua: xianggang de wenhua zhengce* 香港有文化：香港的文化政策（上卷） [Hong Kong's cultural policies, Vol. I]. Hong Kong: Hua Chien Hsu Publications, 2008.

Chow, Fan Fu. *Where Modern Hong Kong Began: The City Hall and Its 50-Year Story*. Hong Kong: Hong Kong City Hall, 2012.

Clarke, David. *Art and Place: Essays on Art from a Hong Kong Perspective*. Hong Kong: Hong Kong University Press, 1996.

Clarke, David. *Hong Kong Art: Culture and Decolonization*: Hong Kong: Hong Kong University Press, 2001.

Ho, Hoi Yin. 'Orchestrating Hong Kong: The Establishment of the Hong Kong Chinese Orchestra'. MPhil diss., University of Hong Kong, 2019.

Lai, Victor Ming-hoi 黎明海, and Eva Kit-wah Man 文潔華. *Yu xianggang yishu duihua 1980–2014* 與香港藝術對話1980–2014 [Speaking with Hong Kong art 1980–2014]. Hong Kong: Joint Publishing, 2015.

Lai, Victor Ming-hoi 黎明海, and Lau Chi-pang 劉智鵬. *Yu xianggang yishu duihua 1960–1979* 與香港藝術對話1980–2014 [Speaking with Hong Kong art 1960–1979]. Hong Kong: Joint Publishing, 2014.

Lau, Y. W. *A History of the Municipal Councils of Hong Kong 1883–1999*. Hong Kong: Leisure and Cultural Services Department, 2002.

Liu, Ching-chih 劉靖之. *Xianggang yin yue shi lun: wen hua zheng ce, yin yue jiao yu* 香港音樂史論：文化政策・音樂教育 [Hong Kong music history: cultural policies, music education]. Hong Kong: Commercial Press, 2014.

Tsang, Kai Won. 'Museums in Late Colonial Hong Kong'. MPhil diss., University of Hong Kong, 2020.

Zhou, Guangzhen, ed. *Xianggang yinyue de qianshi jinsheng – xianggang zaoqi yinyue fazhan licheng (1930s–1950s)* 香港音樂的前世今生——香港早期音樂發展歷程 [The past and present of Hong Kong music – early development of Hong Kong music (1930s–1950s)]. Hong Kong: Joint Publishing, 2017.

Zhu, Qi 朱琦. *Xianggang meishu shi* 香港美術史 [Hong Kong art history]. Hong Kong: Joint Publishing, 2005.

9
Cultural Policies

Allan T. F. Pang[1]

Culture in Hong Kong history has attracted scholarly attention across disciplines. Not only historians but also sociologists and cultural studies scholars have devoted countless works to analysing cultural products in Hong Kong's past, ranging from literature to artworks, and music to films.[2] Works on these various forms of cultural texts are abundant. Instead of focusing on the texts, this chapter follows the predecessors in this volume and examines the relationship between culture and governance in Hong Kong history.[3] It is not about the development of culture, but about how colonial administrators used culture as part of their techniques for controlling and attracting public support. The era from 1945 to 1997 witnessed the colonial government shifting its policies from imposing tight control to understanding what the people preferred. In later decades, official cultural products and events prioritised

1. I thank the Editorial Board (Session 2022), *Undergrad*, Hong Kong University Students' Union for the permission to reprint one of the documents.

2. See, for instance, Tong King Lee, 'Hong Kong Literature: Colonialism, Cosmopolitanism, Consumption', *Journal of Modern Literature* 44, no. 2 (2021): 62–75; David Clarke, *Hong Kong Art: Culture and Decolonization* (London: Reaktion, 2001); Yiu-Wai Chu, *Hong Kong Cantopop: A Concise History* (Hong Kong: Hong Kong University Press, 2017); Poshek Fu and David Desser, eds., *The Cinema of Hong Kong: History, Arts, Identity* (Cambridge: Cambridge University Press, 2000).
3. Recent examples of secondary literature on cultural policies and colonial governance include Poshek Fu, *Hong Kong Media and Asia's Cold War* (New York: Oxford University Press, 2023); Florence Mok, 'Disseminating and Containing Communist Propaganda to Overseas Chinese in Southeast Asia through Hong Kong, the Cold War Pivot, 1949–1960', *Historical Journal* 65, no. 5 (2022): 1397–417; Allan T. F. Pang, 'Entertainment, Chinese Culture, and Late Colonialism in Hong Kong', *Historical Journal* 67, no. 1 (2024): 124–47.

local Chinese elements over British ones.[4] These cultural policies were not signs of pure benevolence but strategies to secure public trust due to the political changes illustrated in earlier chapters. In other words, this chapter is also about the politics of culture in late colonial Hong Kong.

This chapter adopts a thematic approach. The first section focuses on the control measures imposed during the early Cold War years. Leftists attempted to spread their ideologies through cultural products such as films and literature. Documents 9.1 and 9.2 illustrate how colonial officials assessed, responded to, and censored this cultural threat from the communist world. Document 9.3 demonstrates Hong Kong's strategic importance for both the United States and mainland China in the cultural Cold War. Sections 2–4 proceed to show how colonial officials utilised Chinese, British, and local elements to achieve their aims in different eras of Hong Kong history. The second section focuses on the use of Chinese culture. The Chinese language (Document 9.4), festivals (Document 9.5), and entertainment (Documents 9.6 and 9.7) became part of official efforts to build social cohesion and secure support. Not all sections of society, however, agreed with the government's cultural policies. Document 9.6 reveals how local activists opposed these colonial cultural products. Section 3 demonstrates how colonial officials cooperated with British officials and institutions to showcase their care for local culture. Examples include postage stamps (Documents 9.8 and 9.9) and commemorative coins (Document 9.10) that featured Lunar New Year celebrations in Hong Kong. The process was not always a smooth one. Documents 9.8 and 9.9 reveal the differences between Hong Kong and London officials in understanding local (Chinese) culture and the resulting quarrel in their correspondence. Section 4 focuses on the use of local popular culture from the late 1980s to the 1990s. Document 9.11 exemplifies how a semi-official campaign utilised the appeal of top Cantopop stars to mitigate the crisis of confidence over Hong Kong's future. Document 9.12 shows the government's delayed support for the local film industry.

This chapter addresses different issues compared with the previous chapter on the arts. It focuses primarily on cultural policies directly under government departments, instead of those under the municipal councils. The interaction between culture and the broader political context is the primary theme. This chapter selects documents from diverse viewpoints to illustrate not only the official perspective on planning and implementing the policies but also the views and agency of the people, including students and social leaders. Similar to other chapters in this volume, it also

---

4. See Law Wing Sang, *Collaborative Colonial Power: The Making of the Hong Kong Chinese* (Hong Kong: Hong Kong University Press, 2009); Mark Hampton, *Hong Kong and British Culture, 1945–97* (Manchester: Manchester University Press, 2016), chapter 6.

emphasises the role of Hong Kong in transnational networks (especially Documents 9.1 and 9.3).

Section 1. Cold War Censorship and the Flow of Culture

Like the situation shown in earlier chapters, the colonial government also suppressed local communists in the cultural domain. The cultural side was more complicated, however, because of the transnational networks involved. After 1949, Hong Kong became a base for exporting communist propaganda, such as films, magazines, and plays, to Chinese overseas communities. Colonial governments across the territories cooperated to control these communist networks. The following document includes various extracts of correspondence within the Colonial Office. It focuses on the spread of communist propaganda and the role of Hong Kong in these networks.

Document 9.1: TNA, CO 1030/188, Colonial Office's Views on Communist Cultural Products, Extracts from Minutes on ISD 105/01, 1956.

. . . The Survey opposite shows one increasingly dangerous common factor, the growing importation of Communist literature. This began to be a large problem in 1950, constant exhortations have been sent to Colonial Governments and, with a few notable exceptions, all seems to have legislation which, if strictly administered, could stop much of this literature. The Communists, like the Roman Catholic missionaries before them, now know the value of pictographic propaganda among Africans, and there is nothing ostensibly subversive in glossy pictures of Communist youth dancing in the gardens and the like. The only answer is, I think, blanket banning by sources. (But, if I may draw on my own experience, what real good does it do to ban reading matter to the book-starved – to peoples who believe that to read and to write is the only European superiority – and to put nothing in its place? Surely we could reverse the position at no great expense by translating standard works into a few main languages. The Bible is not enough.) . . .

(sgd) Juxon Barton
27 February, 1956

I have only one comment. I think we should state quite frankly that although there is no Communist Party in the political sense in Hong Kong there can be no doubt that the Chinese Communist Party operates within the Colony on an organised and clandestine basis. Most of the trade unions in public utilities are Communist-controlled and their power represents, in my view, a potentially very grave internal danger to the Colony. We should perhaps also make some mention of the fact that Hong Kong is one of the main centres for the dissemination of Communist literature throughout not only South East Asia but all Colonies where a Chinese community exists.

2. I think we are altogether too complacent about Hong Kong which in my view (and I spent four years in the Far East dealing with Communism) is more Communist-penetrated than any other Colony.

S.I.A.

2.3.56 (sgd) A. M. MacDonald.

I agree with Mr. MacDonald's view of the danger in Hong Kong; but, given the composition of her population and her geographical situation, it is difficult to see what can be done about it. We owe more than is immediately obvious to the wisdom of the present Governor. Perhaps the file could later be returned to Mr. MacDonald for his comments as to any action we might consider to reduce the danger or safeguard against it.

I entirely endorse Mr. Barton's comment about the importance of providing suitable literature to compete with the glossy Communist publications.

(intd) J.M.M. 17/3

Sir John Martin

Reference your minute of March 17, I agree that it is easier to diagnose the disease than to prescribe a remedy. I have just been out to Singapore, Hong Kong, Sarawak and North Borneo and there can be no doubt that Chinese Communist literature sent from Hong Kong is one of the main spearheads of propaganda directed at the overseas Chinese communities. I have had the same experience in Fiji, British Guiana, Jamaica and Trinidad and I know it to be true of Mauritius as well. The problem is of steady and continuing subversion of overseas Chinese who tend, as always, to take the colour of their politics from China. The effect on the generation now growing up is, in my view, serious in the extreme, and in a very short time when this generation attains to manhood we will find our problems have greatly increased.

2. I know and appreciate how adroitly the Governor of Hong Kong has held his delicately-balanced scales. In Hong Kong with its 100% Chinese population we must give battle as best we may and the large and imaginative schemes for resettling and rehabilitating refugees must compel anyone's admiration. But that does not alter the fact that from the British Colony of Hong Kong a steady stream of C.P.G. propaganda goes out to contaminate the overseas Chinese communities in other British Colonies. I have the following suggestions for consideration:-

(a) I think we need from Hong Kong a detailed appreciation of the volume of Chinese propaganda coming into the Colony in the shape of books, periodicals, pamphlets, newspapers, films, gramophone records, etc.

(b) We require to examine the C.P.G. machinery for receiving and reprinting Communist propaganda in Hong Kong and the organizations, commercial or subsidised, which are responsible for disseminating this propaganda to other Colonial territories.

(The Hong Kong Special Branch, the S.L.O. [Security Liaison Officer], the Secretariat for Chinese Affairs and the Information Department might co-operate in producing the above appreciation. If necessary they might set up a small working committee to examine the problem.)

(c) Having secured such an appreciation, we might consider possible measures, including legislation to:-

(i) cut down the volume of propaganda imported into Hong Kong from China;

(ii) control the reprinting and export of C.P.G. propaganda from Hong Kong;

(iii) control the importation of Chinese Communist literature into the various Colonies affected.

4. I am not sanguine regarding the possibility of producing alternative pabulum for the young Chinese mind in Colonial territories. The thirst is for news and views from the "homeland", China. I doubt whether any substitute will command attention, at least until the flow from China via Hong Kong has been substantially reduced.

5. It is obvious that Hong Kong is a battleground of ideas. Its position and population make that inevitable. I am not convinced that because of this we should tolerate Hong Kong being used as a base for the production and dissemination of C.P.G. propaganda to other Colonial territories which are not so near to China and not so exposed to subversive infiltration.

S.I.A. (sgd) A. M. MacDonald

25.4.56

Instead of completely banning Chinese communist culture, the Hong Kong government censored and allowed some performances to take place. The following letter from Hong Kong's Colonial Secretariat to the Colonial Office illustrates how colonial officials strategically assessed, approved, and limited the flow of troupes from mainland China to Hong

Kong. It reveals the contexts in which the colonial government both censored and communicated with these cultural groups.

Document 9.2: TNA, CO 1030/1108, Discussion on Chinese Communist Performance Groups in Hong Kong, E. G. Willian to J. D. Higham, 17 October 1962.

[1.] You will have seen references in the LIC Monthly Reports to visits to Hong Kong by various troupes of theatrical and musical performers from China. The pressure to admit these "cultural manifestations" has increased this year and it seems clear that the C.P.G. and their supporters in the Colony are making up for their relative inactivity here on the political front by launching something of a cultural offensive. Their principal motive is presumably to enhance their prestige and standing in the eyes of the Chinese population of the Colony in a field in which they have something of wide popular appeal to offer (in which virtually the only competition comes from Formosa), and to do something to retrieve the damage done to their reputation by reports of economic difficulties and by the refugee influx of last May. We know that Communist circles attach great importance to the success of these visits, which also of course bring in useful foreign exchange.

2. Since June, 1956, troupes from China have visited Hong Kong on seven occasions:-

(i)	Chinese Folk Artists	-	18.6.56 to 19.7.56
(ii)	Swatow Opera Group	-	26.5.60 to 21.6.60
(iii)	Shanghai Shaoshing Opera Group	-	20.12.60 to 1.2.61
(iv)	Kwangtung Acrobatic Group	-	4.6.61 to 2.7.61
(v)	Shanghai Youth Opera Group	-	21.12.61 to 24.1.62
(vi)	Shanghai Vocalist Troupe	-	3.7.62 to 24.7.62
(vii)	Young Chinese Musicians	-	10.9.62 to 28.9.62

With the exception of the last, a talented group of young Western-style musicians, all of these were traditional Chinese-style performers. Their performances reached a high standard and enjoyed considerable popular support (the Kwangtung Acrobats to a slightly less extent than the others) and must certainly be regarded by their sponsors as a propaganda and a financial success.

3. While there can be no question of preventing these Communist ventures in the entertainment field altogether, it is not in our interests that they should be too frequent and successful or that the Communists should secure a monopoly of popular culture. There is also the danger that if such performances became too regular a feature in Hong Kong they might become a target for right-wing demonstrations.

It has therefore been the policy of the Hong Kong Government to set limits to the number of visits to which they are prepared to agree. When the application for the Kwangtung Acrobatic Group was under consideration, the sponsors gave an assurance that in the future applications for visits by troupes from China would be restricted to two per year and they have observed the various conditions laid down by the Commissioner of Police regarding the approval of scripts, avoidance of propaganda, sale of tickets through Box Offices and Agents and not through political organizations, etc. However, this summer applications were received from the sponsors for no less than three more visits; the Young Chinese Musicians, already mentioned, an Oriental singing and dancing troupe, in November, and a Mandarin Opera company in January, 1963. It was clear that they were anxious to break away from the limit of two visits per year: however, after discussion they agreed to drop the application for the second of the three times. It was decided to admit the Young Chinese Musicians even though this made the number of visits this year exceed two, because it was felt that this small Western-style group would appeal to a strictly limited audience.

4. We shall no doubt come under further pressure to permit an expansion of imported Communist cultural activities, but we intend to try to continue to limit visits by major troupes from China to two per year. We shall also no doubt see further cultural activities by local left-wing organizations such as the variety show staged by the Hong Kong Chinese Reform Association on August 25 and 26 referred to in paragraph 13 of the LIC Monthly Report for August.

5. I am sending copies of this letter to de la Mare in the Foreign Office and Morgan in Peking.

Cultural policies formed part of the Cold War battle to secure Chinese support in Southeast Asia. Both the People's Republic of China (PRC) and the United States valued Hong Kong's close linkages to Chinese overseas in Southeast Asia. Instead of relying on the Hong Kong government, the United States devised its own policies to combat communist propaganda. The following document, prepared by the Operations Coordinating Board of the United States, illustrates the precarious and transnational role of Hong Kong in the cultural Cold War.

Document 9.3: Guidelines for United States Programs Affecting the Overseas Chinese in Southeast Asia, 11 December 1957.

<u>Motion Pictures</u>. Push action at Hong Kong, Taiwan and SEA [Southeast Asia] posts, in cooperation with concerned other American and British agencies, toward meeting the drive Peiping is making to capture Hong Kong's existing film producing

industry, as the largest supplier of films for SEA, and to dominate production, distribution and showing of Chinese motion pictures in that area. Possible courses of action might include:

(1) Helping Hong Kong producers and distributors of anti-Communist Chinese films through direct subsidy methods and through indirect assistance in improving quality of technique and story content and in supporting projects for keeping and developing effective actors on the free world side.

(2) Influencing the Chinese motion picture output of Hong Kong by purchasing U.S. or certain foreign distribution rights, through private American agencies.

(3) Increasing filmed interviews of refugees from mainland China for showing in SEA.

(4) Providing advice, financial assistance and technical aid to the GRC [Government of the Republic of China] in improving its motion picture production as a means for reaching and selling itself to SEA countries including the overseas Chinese. . .

<u>THE ROLE OF HONG KONG AS A FIELD OF OPERATIONS AFFECTING OVERSEAS AND FREE CHINESE</u>

. . . Hong Kong has importance from the overseas Chinese standpoint, partly because of its population as a Chinese target per se, but mainly because of circumstances which give the colony strategic operational significance for the support of activities directed toward the overseas Chinese:

A. <u>Hong Kong Chinese as an Operational Target Per Se</u>

112. Despite the fundamental differences noted, many of the problems created in SEA by the presence of overseas Chinese are also found in Hong Kong. Although the Chinese Communists call the Chinese residing in Hong Kong "compatriots" rather than overseas Chinese, the policies and programs they adopt for overseas Chinese are also generally applicable to the Hong Kong Chinese. In particular, Chinese living in Hong Kong also constitute a target for Peiping's propaganda and for its infiltration activities in such fields as labor, education, the press, film studios, and business organizations. The fact that the population includes target groups which control and operate important facilities for reaching and influencing overseas Chinese in SEA increases the danger potential of this effort for us.

113. Thus, from the standpoint of Communist activities, Hong Kong's Chinese must be considered a part of the overseas Chinese complex; and it is much to the interests of the U.S. to minimize the Communist influence among them. . .

B. Hong Kong's Primary Importance as a Supporting Base for Activities Directed Toward Overseas Chinese and SEA

116. While Hong Kong's Chinese thus constitute in themselves a not unimportant target in the broader overseas Chinese complex, the colony's real significance as to overseas Chinese lies in its special potentialities for operations in support of activities directed toward the overseas Chinese and SEA. Factors contributing to this include:

a. Hong Kong is a "window" into Communist China and provides much of the information about the mainland which can be utilized for propaganda among overseas Chinese and SEA populations in general.

b. Being a haven for refugees from Communist China (who form about half the colony's population), Hong Kong is important both as a symbol of popular dissatisfaction with the Peiping regime and as a reservoir of intellectuals to help meet the need of trained personnel in SEA.

c. Hong Kong is a center of Chinese activities in such fields as the press, films, publications, education, fashion and art. As such, it not only provides a living contrast to the regimentation of mainland life, but also constitutes a rich source of physical equipment and human talent for production of American-sponsored materials in many informational media distributable in SEA. Particularly noteworthy are the facilities for producing printed matter and motion pictures for Chinese and other audiences in SEA.

d. Hong Kong is the home of anti-Communist organizations such as the Union Press, which, not being identified with the GRC, can be particularly effective in cultural and counter subversive work among overseas Chinese groups in SEA which may not respond to the GRC approach. . .

117. In the context of U.S. policy towards overseas Chinese as discussed in this paper, therefore, Hong Kong's major role is that of serving as a base of operations and a source of information, materials and qualified Chinese personnel that can assist importantly in the implementation of the programs developed to deal with the overseas Chinese problem in SEA.

Section 2. Chinese Culture and Festivities

While the colonial government was suppressing communist propaganda, it was also trying to meet the cultural preferences of local Chinese. In terms of language, it tailored its radio policy to cater to the colony's major dialect groups. At the same time, officials also attempted to integrate migrants into local society by promoting the use of Cantonese. The existence of different communities based on items such as hometown, clan, and dialect prompted the government to further promote social cohesion in the late 1960s. The following is a memo from T. C. Cheng (for the Secretary for Chinese Affairs John Crichton McDouall) to the Director of Broadcasting D. E. Brooks in 1962.

Document 9.4: HKPRO, HKRS 41/1/8524, Radio and Dialect Policies in Hong Kong, 22 June 1962.

Radio Hong Kong – Chinese Service

I am in general agreement with your proposals as summarized in para. 9 of your memo. I suggest, however, that information broadcasts need not be provided in –

(a) The Sze Yap dialect, because this group is not significantly large and because most natives of Sze Yap have an adequate knowledge of Cantonese; or

(b) the Shanghai dialect because the great majority of this group understand Kuoyu.

2. In other words, I advise that information broadcasts should be provided only in the following dialects –

(i) Cantonese;

(ii) Chiu Chow: I consider that Chiu Chow should be the representative dialect for the Hoklo Group. Thus Chiu Chow may be used, in addition to Cantonese, for specialized information programmes on fishing;

(iii) Hakka: The natives of the New Territories would prefer broadcasts to be made in Tai Po Hakka, but I think broadcasts made in either of the following (in order of priority) should be acceptable to Hakka listeners, without having to augment it with another dialect.

(a) Tai Po Hakka, or

(b) Waichow Hakka, or

(c) Meihsien Hakka; and

(iv) Kuoyu

3. I endorse your policy of using Cantonese as much as possible in your broadcasts, as it is the lingua franca of the Chinese in Hong Kong, and should therefore be promoted as soon as possible among the new-comers, hereby assisting their integration into our society. In any case the younger generation growing up in Hong Kong should all be able to use Cantonese as a tool of communication, as Cantonese is the medium of instruction in Chinese schools.

4. However, the above should not rule out, whenever occasions warrant it, the broadcast of special entertainment programmes in any of the major dialects (Chiu Chow, Hakka or Kuoyu).

5. Subject to the views of D.C.N.T. [District Commissioner, New Territories], I agree with your proposal for the splitting of transmission.

James Hayes joined the Hong Kong government in 1956 and later served as the District Officer of Tsuen Wan from 1975 to 1982. In the following account by Hayes, he recalls his participation in various local celebrations in Tsuen Wan. The account demonstrates how government officials viewed and joined traditional Chinese entertainment as part of their duties. It also illustrates the communication and interaction between the people and officials via cultural festivities in the New Territories.

Document 9.5: James Hayes's Recollection as a Tsuen Wan District Officer [James Hayes, *Friends and Teachers: Hong Kong and Its People, 1953–87* (Hong Kong: Hong Kong University Press, 1996).]

In the early years of the Tsuen Wan District Office, in the 1960s, it had been usual for senior staff to make new year calls on all the villages of the district over the festival period, but this had been discontinued as the town grew in size. However, such visits would have revealed the more serious side of the festival in the yearly round of village life, for this was also a time for worshipping in the ancestral temples and at the earth-god shrines.

In lieu of the new year visits to the villages, the District Officer and senior officials made ceremonial calls on each of the three rural committees at its office premises, and always attended the combined yearly celebratory dinner arranged by them for the village communities. The practice had also grown up of accompanying the Tsuen Wan Rural Committee and district leaders to two important local religious institutions, the Western Monastery and the Yuen Yuen Institute, at this season, to pay a new year call and eat a vegetarian lunch with their leading personnel...

Despite the fact that the Lunar New Year was a general holiday, the local officials still had ceremonial duties to perform. District Office staff, together with other government officers and many local leaders were expected to attend the opening and closing ceremonies of the community activities arranged over the period. On such occasions, it was our duty to make speeches of recognition or exhortation and to present tokens of appreciation for financial and other contributions or services rendered, on behalf of the organizers. It was the practice for various local bodies to join together to provide colourful entertainment and recreational programmes for residents in the various parts of the district. The three Rural Committees, with many other organizations and agencies, worked together with the District Office and other government departments to provide better programmes every year; and our staff, in particular, helped to coordinate the arrangements.

The Tin Hau Festival falls on the twenty-third day of the third lunar month every year. In Tsuen Wan District, as elsewhere, most of the older temples are dedicated to Tin Hau... The Tin Hau Temple on Tsing Yi Island was the most popular venue over this period. Besides the usual opera performances, its main feature was the yearly competition for the best floral shrine... The judging of the entries was done by local and New Territories' community leaders together with invited senior government officials, among them (as a permanent fixture) the District Officer, Tsuen Wan and some of his staff. The weather on this occasion was usually hot and humid. We assembled in the school playground, and exchanged courtesies. The committeemen placed millboards in our hands, on which the necessary judging forms were placed ready for us to fill out. We then walked slowly around, scrutinizing each altar in turn and entering marks for the different qualities that would, when aggregated, produce the winners. The design, subject, materials, colour, workmanship, originality of treatment, all counted. Besides judging. we had the usual speeches and presentations to make, shared out (as was usual on all such occasions) among the principal guests...

The next festival of local importance in which district office staff took part was the Dragon Boat Festival. This commemorates the suicide of Ch'u Yuan (Wat Yuen in Cantonese), a virtuous official of the third century BC who ended his life by drowning himself in the Milo River in protest against an imperfect ruler. The dragon boat races are said to represent the search for his body. The races are always most exciting competitions, made more so by the continuous drumming which pushes each boat's straining crew to a hoped-for victory.

In Tsuen Wan District, the three rural committees combined to organize races to which teams from other places were invited. However, they were essentially local events, small in scale compared to the major races held elsewhere. There were never the crowds that thronged to Tai Po in the NT [New Territories] or to Yaumati, Aberdeen and Shaukeiwan in the old urban area, where it was the tradition for the Governor, the Commander British Forces or some other high official to be the guest of honour and to present the main prizes and banners to the winning teams. However, in like fashion, these duties were carried out by the local officials from the different government departments, and by community leaders from Tsuen Wan and other places. Every year, I spent several hours watching the races and then helped to present banners to the winning crews...

The celebration of local festivals could sometimes involve us in confrontations with their organizers and followers... Sites for large theatrical matsheds were often very hard to find in the fast developing town. Due to the civil engineering schedules, land allocated for several years might not be available the next time round, and there was always keen competition between the several groups which needed to find a site for their matsheds. If one group received approval to use a particular spot, this could lead to harassment or even attacks by the other party, whose members might occupy the site regardless. Even government staff, seeking to recover the disputed ground and hand it over to the successful applicants, might find themselves opposed. This, I have been told by local leaders, was more often the case in the 1960s than later...

After the disturbances of 1966 and 1967, the colonial government modelled its Festival of Hong Kong on the Hong Kong Week organised by the Hong Kong Federation of Industries to foster a local sense of belonging. While the festival was not a Chinese one, the government filled the programme with traditional Chinese entertainment. However, part of the younger generation did not appreciate this official free entertainment. The following article, published in Undergrad *magazine of the Hong Kong University Students' Union, criticises the government for holding the festival. Readers may note how the article assesses the festival's cultural programme at the end, despite its attack on the government.*

Document 9.6: Criticism against the Festival of Hong Kong [*Undergrad*, vol. 20, 1 January 1970], 1 (translated).

The Festival of Hong Kong lasted for ten days, costed over four million Hong Kong Dollars, and mobilized a huge number of people and their time.

Relevant government departments expressed that they would repeat the Festival of Hong Kong next year. Chairperson of the Festival Preparation Committee Arnaldo de Oliveira Sales said, 'this is just a small beginning'. We can imagine that, if the festival is repeated next year, the cost would definitely exceed four million dollars. The time and human resources required would only increase, but not decrease. From the perspectives of time and space, we must ask: what are the purposes and significance of holding the Festival of Hong Kong?

Councillor de Sales writes in the preface of the festival's programme booklet 'let us enjoy the joy! Starting from next week, Hong Kong will be back to its normal and busy life again. Our society and its achievements are known to the world. Let us show off Hong Kong's achievements to the world once again!'

The view of de Sales should represent that of the Hong Kong government. According to him, the reason of organizing the festival was, based on my observation, to celebrate the achievements of Hong Kong. The Hong Kong society and its achievements are known to the world. We should let 'people from all parts of Hong Kong, whether they are in urban areas or rural villages, participate in and celebrate this festival in the ways they prefer'. . .

If the major factor leading to this Festival of Hong Kong was the city's achievements, we will have to ask: what are our achievements? . . .

What Hong Kong lacks was not a sense of belonging, but real democracy, a relatively equal allocation of income, more healthcare, housing, education, welfare, and infrastructure. Residents in Hong Kong have been working hard to develop Hong Kong and bring prosperity to the city since 1840. Without the hardworking Chinese people in Hong Kong, the city would have collapsed long before. Hong Kong residents have always loved Hong Kong, the place where they live, and they will always love Hong Kong in the future. Forcefully instilling a sense of belonging to them is an utmost mistake.

There is one thing that should be praised about the Festival of Hong Kong. That is the systematic time arrangement and comprehensive content. The festival included over four hundred items from the four aspects of entertainment, exhibitions, music, and sports. The successful organization and management are gratifying. They illustrate the cooperative spirit and cautious attitude of Hong Kong residents. However, we have to remind the Hong Kong government that, if they think that a Festival of Hong Kong can resolve local social problems, they will be making a big mistake!

The colonial government later provided more traditional Chinese entertainment via the Urban Council. The first example was the lantern carnival that celebrated the Mid-Autumn Festival in 1974. In the following speech by the carnival committee chairperson (and merchant) Yu Lok-yau, he expresses his identification with Chinese culture. Apart from participating in traditional Chinese entertainment, as described in Hayes's account, the government also organised its celebrations in urban areas to suit the local population's preferences.

Document 9.7: Opening Address by Yu Lok-yau in the Mid-Autumn Lantern Carnival, 1974 [*Wah Kiu Yat Po*, 29 September 1974, 3.2] (translated).

We hope that this year's Mid-Autumn Festival can be the happiest one in everyone's memories.

This is because we are holding this unprecedentedly huge lantern carnival in Victoria Park.

This grand event is organized by the Tsim Sha Tsui Kaifong Association, Causeway Bay Kaifong Association, City District Office of the Eastern District, Urban Council, Hong Kong Tourism Association and many other associations. The aim is to provide more recreation programmes locally in Hong Kong, and to promote the joyous atmosphere of our country's traditional festivals. The day after the Mid-Autumn Festival is a public holiday in Hong Kong. Hope all participants can play hard in the carnival.

Although the carnival was organized in a rush and had an inadequate budget, it was fortunate to receive sponsorship from the Hong Kong Tourist Association, Pentax, Hoe Hin Pak Fah Yeow Manufactory Limited and other associations. Therefore, we can organize this unprecedentedly huge lantern carnival in Victoria Park on 29 September (Sunday, the eve of the Mid-Autumn Festival) and 30 September (Monday, the Mid-Autumn Festival) 1974. We feel very delighted.

We also receive the support of various stars of the Shaw Brothers, Commercial Radio, artists of Radio Hong Kong, all members of the society, and many commercial organizations.

The programme will introduce each item in detail. However, please let me introduce it briefly. It includes lantern displays, huge Chinese archways, gongs and drums performance by the Chiu Chow Guild Hall, dance performances, lantern parade, demonstration of handicraft production, fortune-telling, fashion show, Cantonese opera, pop music appreciation, magic shows, acrobatics, and so on. Hope everyone can enjoy the festival cheerfully.

Section 3. British Symbolism and Networks

Colonial officials also promoted local Chinese culture through British networks. From 1967 onwards, the Hong Kong government issued postage stamps to commemorate the Lunar New Year. It cooperated with the Foreign and Commonwealth Office (FCO) and Crown Agents to design and produce the stamps. The stamps became significant cultural products in the colony, as illustrated by the correspondence between Governor David Trench and Secretary of State for Foreign and Commonwealth Affairs Alec Douglas-Home below. Trench insisted that the Hong Kong government issue the stamps despite disagreements from the FCO.

Document 9.8: HKPRO, HKRS 1082/1/3, Telegram from Douglas-Home to Trench, 13 August 1970.

Arts work for two denominations commemorating the Year of the Pig has been received from Crown Agents. The design features a pig and incorporates the Royal Cypher. As it would be considered to be in bad taste both here and in other (particular Muslim) countries, I regret I cannot submit for Her Majesty's approval. Grateful if you would inform the Postmaster General and arrange submission of fresh designs.

Document 9.9: HKPRO, HKRS 1082/1/3, Reply from Trench to Douglas-Home, 18 August 1970.

Your telegram 529. My Saving Despatch 698 dated 6th April 1967 proposing commemorative issues for each Chinese New Year of the current 12-year cycle named the animal symbols for each year including the pig. Yours Saving Despatch 432 dated 24th April, 1967 approved these issues.

2. Regret I do not consider it feasible to produce a satisfactory design commemorating the Year of the Pig without incorporating a pig and I also do not consider it possible to explain the absence of a 1971 commemorative issue without causing much comment and some ridicule. It could probably be argued that rats and snakes would not normally be singled out for portrayal in this way, but they appear in this series of symbols to which we are committed.

3. I would not have thought that the portrayal on a stamp of a pig in proximity to the Royal Cypher could reasonably be construed as being disrespectful. I am informed that in the new definitive issue for British Honduras made in 1968, there is a 2-cent stamp bearing a wild pig and the Royal Cypher.

4. I am advised that the Chinese Muslim community would see nothing incongruous or offensive in this design. It is perhaps relevant also that one other territory at least (Taiwan) has followed our lead in producing Lunar New Year issues and can be expected to incorporate the pig this year.

5. In the circumstances I would be grateful if the matter could be reconsidered.

Later in the 1970s, the Hong Kong government cooperated with the Royal Mint to further showcase its care for local (Chinese) culture by producing gold coins to commemorate the Lunar New Year. The following brochure not only introduced local Chinese traditions in Hong Kong but also demonstrated the remaining imperial linkages in an era when much of the world had experienced political decolonisation.

Document 9.10: TNA, MINT 34/TL/Z, Commemorative Coin Brochure, 1981.

HONG KONG HK $1000 GOLD COIN.

Newest In Series

The Government of Hong Kong has commissioned the British Royal Mint to strike a strictly limited issue of HK $1000 gold coins celebrating the Chinese Lunar Calendar Year of the Dog. Struck in 22 karat gold, this is the seventh coin in an attractive series of gold coins depicting the 12 animals of the Chinese Lunar Calendar.

Based on a 12-year cycle, each Chinese Lunar Calendar year is represented by an animal. The first coin in this series was issued in 1976 to commemorate the Year of the Dragon, followed by a Snake coin in 1977, a Horse coin in 1978, a Goat coin in 1979, Monkey coin in 1980 and a Cockerel coin in 1981. The Dog, Pig, Rat, Ox, Tiger and Rabbit complete the cycle.

To the Chinese this ancient system is much more than a calendar; rather, it embraces mythology and folklore thousands of years old which is used as the basis for determining traits of character. Very much like the signs of the Zodiac in astrology, each animal in the cycle symbolizes special characteristics and qualities.

People born in the year of the dog are said to have a strong moral sense and are regarded as loyal and trustworthy. They are generally quiet and show little emotion, yet they are always quick to help others. January 25, 1982, is the first day in this Year of the Dog, which ends on February 12, 1983.

The coin for the Year of the Dog is available in both Proof and Bright Uncirculated condition. Struck with highly polished dies on specially prepared coin blanks, the proof coins are extremely sharp in detail with a delicately frosted relief on a mirror-like background.

The bright uncirculated coins are mint-conditioned coins which have never passed into circulation.

Worldwide mintage is absolutely limited to 22,000 for the proof and 33,000 for the b.u. Only a small number of these have been allocated for North American collectors.

Struck in 22 karat gold, each coin measures 28.4 mm in diameter and weighs 15.98 grams.

LEGAL TENDER GOLD

These coins are legal tender in Hong Kong with a face value of HK $1000. There are no exchange control restrictions in Hong Kong and Hong Kong dollars may be freely sold for other currencies.

Each coin comes to you in an individually hinged presentation case, with a leaflet explaining the significance of the animal in the Lunar Calendar.

The Chinese dog's most common role throughout the ages has been that of house guard. However, the smaller varieties also hunted with the nobility and, as a result, have enjoyed a high place in Chinese society for many centuries. Today, in Hong Kong, dogs of all sizes and shapes have the status of "man's best friend," regardless of whether or not they guard property. Championship dog shows have been held regularly in the country for the last 40 years.

In Chinese mythology, the dog holds the place of the Heavenly Hound. Folklore has it that the coming of a stray dog into the home brings good fortune. The dog is featured as the central design on the reverse of this coin.

The obverse bears Arnold Machin's famous portrait of Her Majesty Queen Elizabeth II.

ORDER 1982 Hong Kong HK $1000 gold coins by completing the form which accompanies this brochure. Terms and conditions of sale are set forth on the order form. The British Royal Mint reserves the right to limit the number of coins on any order.

British Royal Mint

The British Royal Mint is a department of the British Government and is the Official Government Mint of the United Kingdom. The coins offered in this brochure have been struck by the British Royal Mint under the authority of the Government of Hong Kong and the prices which appear on the accompanying order form are the official issue prices for North America.

Section 4. Localness and Popular Culture

The Sino-British Joint Declaration confirmed Hong Kong's retrocession to the PRC in 1997. However, the Tiananmen Square Massacre in 1989 shook the confidence of many Hong Kong people towards the post-1997 era. A year later, former Chief Secretary David Akers-Jones initiated the Dreams of Hong Kong campaign to spread the idea that 'Hong Kong is our home and we should not leave'. This idea matches the one proposed by the government: there would be a smooth transition, and Hong Kong people should not leave. On 21 August 1990, the campaign climaxed with a concert featuring top Cantopop singers. It utilised the popular appeal of these singers and their Cantopop to spread the official messages. The campaign featured a theme song titled 'Lights of the City' 凝聚每分光, with lyrics written by Cheng Kok-Kong 鄭國江, a renowned lyricist and teacher in Hong Kong, and the melody composed by local musician Chris Babida 鮑比達. The song ends with four English lyrics reinforcing the official message: 'This is our home. This is our place. This is our dream. We love Hong Kong.'

Document 9.11: The Dreams of Hongkong Gala Concert, *South China Morning Post*, 22 August 1990, 3.

HONGKONG did its *We Are the World* impression last night in a massive display of on-stage enthusiasm at the Coliseum.

The programme for the Dreams of Hongkong Gala Concert read like a Who's Who of the recording industry with 12 leading local warblers performing as individuals then *en masse* before an audience of more than 11,000.

The whole Dreams of Hongkong project, organised by RTHK and sponsored by the International Bank of Asia, is a gung ho affair aimed at "expressing our feelings for Hongkong and encouraging every citizen to participate in the development of a better Hongkong through music and songs" . . .

Perennial favourite Alan Tam kicked things off with the Cantonese version of the World Cup theme song. Helping him out were members of the celebrity football team.

Next came Anita Mui herself, followed by Roman Tam and then a group of "younger" stars comprising Sandy Lam, Andy Lau, Jacky Cheung, Prudence Liew and Alex To.

Then came Sally Yeh, George Lam, Paula Tsui accompanied by kindergarten children and finally Sam Hui, who performed two interesting-titled songs, *Who Cares About 1997* and *In the Same Boat*. The latter song mentioned neither creeks nor lack of paddles.

To round it all off appropriately, all 12 singers got together for a version of *Lights of the City*, the theme song for the whole project.

The local film industry was another source of pride for many Hong Kong people. The industry had urged the government to support it by building a Hong Kong Film Archive. As the following newspaper article reveals, this proposal failed to win warm support from the government for years. The proposal appeared in Urban Council documents in the mid-1980s. The San Wan Ho building mentioned below, however, was only opened in 2001, after Hong Kong's retrocession to China and the dissolution of the Urban Council. To some extent, this development reveals the official priorities in cultural policies.

Document 9.12: Local Film Industry's Support towards the Establishment of a Hong Kong Film Archive, *South China Morning Post*, 18 May 1995, 6.

THE territory's film industry is hoping for a shot in the arm with the opening of a $116 million Hong Kong Film Archive.

The industry hopes the archive will be a vital research tool for local movie-makers and students and help maximize the quality of Hong Kong films.

After years of red tape, the archive is being set up by the Urban Council to acquire, conserve, catalogue, document, research and exhibit local films and related material.

Actor Chow Yun-fatt said yesterday that the delay to the archive had been disappointing. It would greatly benefit the industry in the long-term.

"We have tried to push the Government for the archive for many years and now it is coming together it is very exciting as it is very important for the future of Hong Kong's film industry," he said.

"It will help to increase the quality of films here, particularly in terms of authenticity of period films. They can check in the archive and be sure their props and sets are just like the real thing was in 1940 or whenever."

A veteran of almost two decades in Hong Kong film and television, Chow is as widely known in the international film community as fellow Hong Kong actors Jackie Chan and Tony "The Love" Leung Ka-fai...

Chow called on the industry to donate such valuable pieces for preservation in the archive rather than allowing them to be thrown out.

Suggested Readings

Fu, Po-Shek. *Hong Kong Media and Asia's Cold War*. New York: Oxford University Press, 2023.

Hampton, Mark. *Hong Kong and British Culture, 1945–97*. Manchester: Manchester University Press, 2015.

Law, Wing Sang. *Collaborative Colonial Power: The Making of the Hong Kong Chinese*. Hong Kong: Hong Kong University Press, 2009.

Lee, Joanna Ching-Yun. 'All for Freedom: The Rise of Patriotic/Pro-democratic Popular Music in Hong Kong in Response to the Chinese Student Movement'. In *Rockin' the Boat: Mass Music and Mass Movement*, edited by Reebee Garofalo, 129–47. Boston, MA: South End Press, 1992.

Mok, Florence. 'Disseminating and Containing Communist Propaganda to Overseas Chinese in Southeast Asia through Hong Kong, the Cold War Pivot, 1949–1960'. *Historical Journal* 65, no. 5 (2022): 1397–417.

Pang, Allan T. F. 'Stamping "Imagination and Sensibility": Objects, Culture, and Governance in Late Colonial Hong Kong'. *Journal of Imperial and Commonwealth History* 50, no. 4 (2022): 789–816.

Roberts, Priscilla, and John M. Carroll, eds. *Hong Kong in the Cold War*. Hong Kong: Hong Kong University Press, 2016 (especially chapters 4, 6, and 7).

Taylor, Jeremy E., and Lanjun Xu, eds. *Chineseness and the Cold War: Contested Cultures and Diaspora in Southeast Asia and Hong Kong*. New York: Routledge, 2021.

Wang, Xiaojue. 'Radio Culture in Cold War Hong Kong'. *Interventions* 20, no. 8 (2018): 1153–70.

Yeung, Jessica Siu-yin. 'Hong Kong Literature and the Taiwanese Encounter: Literary Magazines, Popular Literature and Shih Shu-Ching's Hong Kong Stories'. *Cultural History* 12, no. 2 (2023): 224–50.

10
Migration

Doris Y. S. Chan

Hong Kong had become an important transit port in East and Southeast Asia since its establishment as a British Crown Colony in the mid-nineteenth century. The free trade port policy adopted by the colonial government allowed freedom of movement of people, and economic opportunities in Hong Kong and beyond facilitated a steady flow of population entering and departing Hong Kong.[1] The colony's population thus grew rapidly from a few thousand in the early 1840s to 1.6 million on the eve of the Japanese invasion.[2] The population fell during the Japanese Occupation (1942–1945) to 600,000, but it quickly recovered to the pre–World War II level because of the resumption of cross-border movement between Hong Kong and China. The establishment of the People's Republic of China (PRC) further intensified the influx of Chinese immigrants, and by 1954, Hong Kong's population had already reached 2.25 million. The constant cross-border population movement has been a popular theme to explore in recent scholarship in order to understand not only the colony's domestic development but also its transnational connections with the outside world in the past century.

Recent scholarship on the post–World War II migration history of Hong Kong has adopted an international perspective and paid close attention to the role of factors related to the Cold War and China in shaping inward migration into Hong Kong.[3]

1. For pre–World War II Chinese migration via Hong Kong, see, for example, Elizabeth Sinn, *Pacific Crossing: California Gold, Chinese Migration, and the Making of Hong Kong* (Hong Kong: Hong Kong University Press, 2013).
2. Saw Swee Hock, 'Population Growth and Redistribution in Hong Kong', *Southeast Asian Journal of Social Science* 4, no. 1 (1975): 124, 126.
3. For the post-1949 immigration restrictions controlling the influx of Chinese immigrants and its Cold War connection, see John P. Burns, 'Immigration from China and the Future of Hong Kong', *Asian Survey* 27, no. 6 (1987): 661–82; Chi-kwan Mark, 'The "Problem of People": British

However, besides revisiting the development of Hong Kong's immigration policies since the late 1940s, this chapter seeks to draw attention to the history of emigration from Hong Kong after World War II. Emigrants are often forgotten in local histories as they no longer reside in their 'homelands'. Nevertheless, it is important to highlight their history in the broader field of migration history to reconsider the role of Hong Kong as a transit port instead of a city that merely received immigrants after 1945. This chapter also highlights how the Hong Kong and British governments responded to changing migration trends, including overpopulation due to the influx of immigrants and the loss of talents due to emigration.

The following is divided thematically into three sections, each of which is organised chronologically. Section 1 shows the implementation of major immigration policies in Hong Kong. Documents 10.1–10.4 demonstrate how the government responded to the two major waves of population influx into the tiny colony – namely, the influx of Chinese immigrants from mainland China from the late 1940s to the early 1970s and the influx of Vietnamese refugees (or boat people) in the 1970s. Sections 2 and 3 focus on the 'outward' movement of Chinese from Hong Kong. The influx of Chinese immigrants after World War II led to overpopulation and the deterioration of living conditions in Hong Kong. Documents 10.5–10.7 reveal the policy discussion on exporting Hong Kong's excess population to colonies and countries facing labour shortages. Document 10.8 shows the number of Hong Kong Chinese emigrating to Britain in the mid-1960s. Building on the migration of Chinese labourers from Hong Kong in the 1950s and 1960s, section 3 demonstrates, however, a more pressing concern faced by Hong Kong: the 'brain drain', a rapid loss of skilled labour as a result of external opportunities. Documents 10.10–10.12 depict a more recent trend of mass emigration in the late 1980s and 1990s, while Document 10.9 shows that the 'brain drain' had already been a political and economic concern of Hong Kong since the 1960s.

Section 1. Immigration Restrictions since the Late 1940s

The Chinese Civil War broke out between the Chinese Communist Party (CCP) and the Nationalist Party (Kuomintang, or KMT) immediately after the end of World War II. This led to the influx of Chinese immigrants from China to Hong Kong (together with the return of immigrants who had been repatriated under Japanese rule during the war). By

Colonials, Cold War Powers, and the Chinese Refugees in Hong Kong, 1949–62', *Modern Asian Studies* 41, no. 6 (2007): 1145–81; Laura Madokoro, 'Borders Transformed: Sovereign Concerns, Population Movements and the Making of Territorial Frontiers in Hong Kong, 1949–1967', *Journal of Refugee Studies* 25, no. 3 (2012): 407–27; Florence Mok, 'Chinese Illicit Immigration into Colonial Hong Kong, c. 1970–1980', *The Journal of Imperial and Commonwealth History* 49, no. 2 (2021): 339–67.

1947, Hong Kong's population had recovered to the pre-war level of 1.5 million. Their arrival severely affected supplies in the colony. Nevertheless, the following telegram from Hong Kong Governor Alexander Grantham partially explains the slow implementation of border controls in Hong Kong.

Document 10.1: TNA, CO 537/4802, Hong Kong (Sir A. Grantham) to the Secretary of State for the Colonies, 19 December 1949.

...

Immigration Control and Refugees.

[1.] Need for control depends on circumstances which vary from day to day and week to week. Our policy is to avoid controls as far as possible and consistent with security in order to preserve free port character of colony and permit maximum trade contacts. Am grateful for discretion you have already accorded to me in deciding when further control measures are necessary.

2. Position at present is under control. Influx of recent months has been absorbed although congestion is admittedly heavy. There is however still some leeway. It is difficult to be tied down to an absolute figure.

3. I would in any event consider control over immigration from Canton inopportune at this juncture. Bad impression would be created if announcement of recognition of Peking Government and closure of the frontier synchronised. Closure of frontier might give the communists impression that we were nervous.

4. It is difficult to forecast immigration trends in coming months. Recognition would create better atmosphere for efflux. Conditions in Canton have deterred many from returning but if things settle down many should go back. Relaxation of Nationalist blockade would undoubtedly be strongest factor in starting outward movement.

5. Large influx is most likely from Taiwan and Hainan, the remaining areas under Nationalist control, if conditions there suddenly deteriorated. Hence the necessity for the visa requirements now applied to those two places which can if necessary be intensified. No sudden influx is likely from other areas. I will undertake to keep you fully advised if further control measures are contemplated.

Border controls were implemented to slow down population growth. These legislations included the Immigration Control Ordinance, the Registration of Persons Ordinance, and a quota system from the spring of 1950, in which only fifty entries daily were allowed. However, they were not exercised strictly due to political constraints faced by the Hong Kong government and thus the effectiveness of the policies varied year by year. In 1974, the Touch Base Policy was introduced to further curb the influx of Chinese immigrants. It allowed immigrants to stay in Hong Kong if they reached the urban area and applied for a Hong Kong identity card; otherwise, they would be repatriated to China. This was met with criticism from the British public, who condemned the government's antagonistic and unhumanitarian approach towards the so-called refugees fleeing from the communist regime during the Cultural Revolution (1966–76). The following reply was a standard response and justification from the Hong Kong and Indian Ocean Department to British domestic criticisms.

Document 10.2: TNA, FCO 21/1274, Bruce Dinwiddy, Hong Kong & Indian Ocean Department to Reverend J. B. Casson (a constituent), 18 December 1974.

I have been asked to reply to your letter to Mr Wilson of 2 December about the return of illegal immigrants to China.

The arrangements you read about are not new; they represent a return to the situation that applied up to 1967, when they went to abeyance in the wake of the cultural revolution. Those who are now being turned back after trying to enter Hong Kong illegally are, for the most part, young people who are seeking to improve their economic situation, and who often have an exaggerated impression of the economic opportunities which would be open to them in Hong Kong. You will also wish to know that before a decision on the return of any individual is reached in Hong Kong, each case is carefully examined on an individual basis. Full account is taken of any special circumstances or cases of genuine hardship.

You may wonder why, having accepted these people for the last seven years, Hong Kong cannot do so any longer. The reason is that immigration from China has now built up to a rate which Hong Kong simply cannot cope with. Estimated figures for total Chinese immigration into Hong Kong were 74,000 in 1973, compared with 37,000 in 1972 and less than 13,500 in 1971 (they have to be estimated because, of course, not all illegal immigrants are detected). Translated into UK terms this is the equivalent of about a million new immigrants a year. And Hong Kong already has one of the highest population densities in the world. In certain districts this rises to 400,000 to the square mile, which is ten times greater than in Tokyo.

Moreover there are already huge problems of housing, health, social services and education in Hong Kong; as well as under-employment arising from current world economic conditions. The Government are [*sic*] tackling these problems energetically; for example enough new public housing will be built over the next ten years to rehouse almost half the present population of four million. But they cannot cope with a new influx on the scale of recent immigration.

I hope you will agree that this is a problem which needs to be tackled with humanity, but also bearing in mind the interests of the overwhelming Chinese population of Hong Kong. They are asking for a better life and they are entitled to get it.

The fall of Saigon in late April 1975 marked the ultimate withdrawal of the United States from the Vietnam War. Vietnam falling under communist rule soon led to a new wave of refugee crises in Southeast Asia, including in Thailand, Malaysia, Singapore, the Philippines, and Indonesia. In early 1975, a Danish ship, Clara Maersk, *rescued about 3,700 Vietnamese refugees and arrived in Hong Kong on 4 May 1975, marking the beginning of the influx of Vietnamese boat people to Hong Kong. In 1979, the arrival of* Huey Fong, Sky Luck, *and many other vessels and small boats fuelled the population crisis faced by the Hong Kong government. The following telegram shows the draft of passage from Governor Murray MacLehose for the United Nations Conference on the change of policy from the United Nations High Commissioner for Refugees (UNHCR). MacLehose was also present at the conference as part of the British delegation and argued for a fair distribution of resettlement from the countries of first asylum.*

Document 10.3: TNA, FCO 40/1104, Murray MacLehose to Foreign and Commonwealth Office, 12 July 1979.

M.I.P.T.: Draft Passage on Hong Kong Resettlement Pledge.

1. The UNHCR has suggested that Hong Kong should contribute to his policy of partial resettlement within the region by absorbing 10,000 boat refugees. This came as a surprise since the territory is so small and over-crowded, has already accepted since 1975 14,000 persons from Indo-China with some Hong Kong connection, and has now given temporary asylum to 65,000 boat refugees. Moreover in addition to the Vietnamese refugees Hong Kong has had an influx of well over 200,000 persons from China in the last 18 months. The latter flow has now happily been substantially reduced, but the problems it has created remain.

2. However the Hong Kong Government's main concern is that an effective and complete resettlement plan for the region should emerge from this conference which will lift from Hong Kong the burden of these refugees from Vietnam who lack affinity or connection with the territory. The Hong Kong Government therefore agrees to the UNHCR's suggestion, and will accept 10,000 of these refugees for permanent residence, on the understanding that the UNHCR will accept responsibility for the maintenance and resettlement of all other Indo-Chinese refugees who are in, or who come to, Hong Kong.

MacLehose

Governor MacLehose's appeal to the United Nations Conference did not significantly alter the refugee situation in Hong Kong. The following telegram shows the growing concern of the Hong Kong government about the slow rate of resettlement of its Vietnamese refugees compared with those in other Southeast Asian countries. At the end of the telegram, MacLehose points out that the open-centre policy might be the cause of the slow resettlement rate, which was a prelude to the implementation of the 'humane deterrence' policy in 1982.

Document 10.4: TNA, FCO 40/1193, Murray MacLehose to Foreign and Commonwealth Office, 29 January 1980.

Vietnamese Boat Refugees.

1. We now have UNHCR resettlement figures for 1979. These show that of the 135,000 boat refugees resettled from all places of first asylum in 1979, only 24,700 (18.2 percent) were from Hong Kong, compared to 68,000 (50.6 percent) from Malaysia, 18,500 (13.6 percent) from Indonesia, 9,300 (6.9 percent) from Thailand, 4,400 (3.2 percent) from the Philippines and 3,700 (2.7 percent) from Singapore. These figures must be seen against the past and continuing burden of boat refugees in Hong Kong compared to other countries of first asylum . . .

4. The problem of boat refugees in Hong Kong must be seen against the background of serious immigration problems from China. Hong Kong has already been hard pressed to absorb an estimated 280,000 legal and illegal immigrants from China over the last two years. (Incidentally, this is equivalent to some 12.5 million immigrants from Mexico into the US – about 4 times the US estimate for 1978-79). Despite measures taken by China, new arrivals are still coming in at a rate of about 300 a day. This massive addition to the population is seen by Hong Kong residents as a threat to their present standard of living, their future aspirations and it has already noticeably affected the quality of life. These latest immigrants, unlike earlier waves in the 1950s and 1962, have little to offer as they come from a background of poor educational standards and eroded respect for social discipline during the Cultural Revolution. In the past two years, the strain imposed by absorbing such large numbers has to some extent been masked by the coincidence of a period of low unemployment in Hong Kong. This may not last for long. Should there be an economic downturn (and protectionist pressures of industrialized countries are important factors) this will generate social tension; and refugees from Vietnam, if they remain in significant numbers, could well be a target for discontent.

5. In asking that the disparity in allocation of resettlement quotas in 1979 should be rectified in 1980, Hong Kong is representing the interests of the refugees as much

as its own interests. If fair allocations are not made refugees in Hong Kong would lose hope and patience, as would Hong Kong's long-suffering residents. The fact that refugees are allowed to live relatively freely in the community and to take up employment pending their resettlement elsewhere is good for the morale of refugees and equips them better for resettlement. But it also means that the problems caused by a slow rate of resettlement could be greatly exacerbated, especially if the inflow should resume.

MacLehose

Section 2. Post–World War II Overseas Employment of Hong Kong Chinese

Hong Kong faced severe land and population pressure in the post–World War II era due to the influx of immigrants from China and the local baby boom. In the meantime, surrounding countries lacked essential skilled and unskilled labourers for their economic reconstruction and development. Among them was the British Colony of North Borneo (today's Sabah, in East Malaysia), in which the problem of labour shortage had been an obstacle to the development of its industries since the end of World War II. After reaching a regional agreement to import Chinese labourers in 1955, the North Borneo government started to negotiate labour recruitment schemes with the Hong Kong government. The following is a meeting summary written by Chief Assistant Secretary for Chinese Affairs of Hong Kong, J. T. Wakefield.

Document 10.5: HKPRO, HKRS 934/9/98, J. T. Wakefield to Hon. S. C. A. [Honorary Secretary for Chinese Affairs], 9 November 1957.

At the request of Mr. R.A. Joscelyne, Managing Director of Gibb Livingstone and Co., I met Mr. J.H. Macartney this morning to discuss emigration labour problems. Mr. J.H. Macartney is the Commissioner of Labour for North Borneo. . . .

3. Mr. Macartney is now in Hong Kong to explore the possibilities of arrangements for such emigrants to go to North Borneo from Hong Kong. It is intended emigrants in the first place will be confined to farmers or cultivators only, and H.E. [His Excellency] the Governor of North Borneo was considering the suitability of permitting farmers now in North Borneo to bring down their relatives who may be in Hong Kong. . . .

4. Land is there for the asking and there are no restrictions at all on the erection on that land of what would be called squatter buildings in Hong Kong. These emigrants would go down as emigrant-labour in the first place for three years, their

employment etc. being in accordance with the appropriate I.L.O. [International Labour Organization] Conventions; their wives and families would, of course go,[*sic*] with them at the same time. . . .

5. From Mr. Macartney's conversation it was apparent that the Governor of North Borneo is keen to get a scheme working as soon as possible and for as many as possible to go down there, although the present permission is, I think, for a maximum of 5,000.

6. Mr. Macartney enquired whether, in the absence of suitable farmers with relatives already in Borneo, we could find suitable cultivator families in Hong Kong. I assured him that we could, either from the New Territories (in which case that would be a matter for the District Commissioner to discuss with him), or better still from this Secretariat's point of view, for them to be prepared to accept displaced cultivators from the urban area. It was explained that the rapid expansion of the urban area into the rural districts around Kaitak, Lyemun and Chakwoling would inevitably displace several hundred cultivators in the next year or two and in fact this displacement is going on every day at present in connection with the large resettlement area at Wong Tai Sin. I said that most of these cultivators have their roots in Hong Kong and many have been here for several generations. I also pointed out that it is a virtual impossibility to resettle these cultivators on any land in the New Territories since there is none available, and the only thing that can be done is to make facilities available for them to change their occupation such as becoming shop-keepers in resettlement areas. . . .

9. Mr. Macartney spoke highly of the several thousand labourers who have been recruited as temporary emigrant labour to North Borneo in skilled trades in the building and oil industry, and said that it was expected that the opportunity to become citizens of North Borneo would be offered to many of these labourers if they wished to bring their families down with them.

10. I said that as far as possible we would try to see that any farmers selected had no known political bias then I impressed on Mr. Macartney that his proposition and my subsequent suggestions were of importance to the Hong Kong Government and that the whole subject will require further consideration by Government. . . .

In 1959, the United Nations launched the World Refugee Year to raise attention and support for refugees across the globe. Taking the opportunity, British Conservative Party Member of Parliament Robin Turton proposed the recruitment of Chinese 'refugees' from Hong Kong to work in Britain as a gesture to show British commitment while encouraging international contributions to Hong Kong. The following excerpt shows the proposed conditions of non-British Chinese taking up employment in Britain, in which the 'returnability' of the Chinese labourers back to Hong Kong was the main concern.

Document 10.6: TNA, CO 1030/787, Richard F. Wood, Aliens Department, Home Office to J. C. Burgh, Colonial Office, 27 October 1959.

Dear Burgh,

As you know, in reply to a House of Commons Question on HMG's [Her Majesty's Government's] policy towards the admission of Chinese refugees in Hong Kong who desire to take up employment in the United Kingdom, the Home Secretary said on 23rd July that he was prepared to review the established practice in this matter in consultation with the other interested Departments. . . .

The question facing us in the Aliens Department is accordingly whether there is any sufficient ground for continuing a policy of discrimination against such Hong Kong Chinese, as would be likely to apply for permission to enter the country for employment, our provisional view is that there is none.

One of our Assistant Chief Inspectors of Immigration, who has recently returned from Hong Kong after advising the Government there on immigration methods, says that the number of applications for United Kingdom visas by Hong Kong Chinese for employment over the past year or so is insignificant. It may be that the restrictive policy of the past few years has had something to do with the lack of applicants, but this is speculation. At all events there is nothing to show that an easing of the restrictions would give rise to an appreciable increase in applications, although with the steady flow into the country of British Chinese it is possible that a few more jobs would be available here with Chinese employers, who are known to prefer Chinese as employees, and some slight increase is likely on that account.

To bar the entry of a few Hong Kong Chinese for employment when we have no option but to accept numbers of British Chinese who are entering the United Kingdom, seems however a rather ridiculous policy to attempt to maintain. The number of British Chinese coming here at present is not large, probably due to the restrictions on the issue of British passports which we understand are imposed by the Governor of Hong Kong. The point which arises is whether any relaxation of policy relating to the admission of alien Chinese from Hong Kong would be likely to make it difficult for the Governor to maintain those restrictions. No doubt you could advise us on that point.

Subject to Ministry of Labour concurrence, and to any comments you may have, it is our provisional view that we should in future authorise visas for those Hong Kong Chinese, in whose favour the Ministry of Labour, on the basis of their ordinary rules, are prepared to issue a permit, subject to the following provisos: -

(a) that the applicant has not less than four years residence in Hong Kong and is personally acceptable;

(b) that he/she has a valid travel document with ample return facilities to the Colony;

(c) that the prospective employer in the United Kingdom is willing to give a guarantee of responsibility for the expenses of repatriation if the employment fails or the employee is required on any other ground to leave the country; and

(d) that there is no security objection to the individual. . . .

We should not propose to extend these facilities for employment to Chinese holding Nationalist or Chinese Republican passports or to stateless aliens living in China; nor would we as a general rule extend them to Chinese holding Hong Kong affidavits, who were out of the Colony unless we were all satisfied that there would be no difficulties over documentation, and that the other provisos referred to above were met. Exceptions could, of course, always be made on the merits in a particular case. . . .

The proposal of the labour recruitment plan, however, raised concern from the Colonial Secretary of Hong Kong, C. B. Burgess, as shown below. It is likely that he (and possibly other colonial bureaucrats) had in mind the impact of the arrival of the 'Windrush Generation' (Citizens of the United Kingdom and Colonies (CUKCs) from former British colonies and the Commonwealth) and the outbreak of racial riots in Britain in the previous decade, including the most recent Notting Hill Riots in 1958.

Document 10.7: TNA, CO 1030/1319, C. B. Burgess to W. I. J. Wallace, 13 February 1960.

My dear Ian –

. . .

2. In the first place we wonder if you are right in assuming that the number of applications for entry under the proposed scheme would be small. This would depend on various factors, and in particular on the comparative economic conditions here and in the U.K., but for our part we believe that a scheme of this sort might well snowball

into something of significant proportions. We therefore wonder whether the Home Office and the Ministry of Labour have really considered the implications of sizeable Chinese communities springing up in the U.K., composed of persons with no real British roots even in Hong Kong, and no experience of or any sense of attachment to the British way of life? . . . We wonder whether this proposal might not lead to a problem similar to that presented by the West Indians, except that the claim on the U.K. of the Chinese concerned would be harder to define or justify.

3. . . . But we fear that, as the problem posed by the influx of Hong Kong Chinese into the U.K. developed, the Chinese immigrants might become the object of criticism of one sort or another. One of the results of such criticism might be that voluntarily or compulsorily they would return to Hong Kong. Here their return would, in itself, be an embarrassment and their experience of entirely different economic, social and political conditions and influences in the U.K., and perhaps disgruntlement at their failure to remain there, might represent a real security risk. This risk could no doubt be accepted in prosperous or normal times, but we fear that a reverse movement would be most likely to develop at times at which the economic and security danger which these migrants represented to the U.K. would be most evident, namely, in times of slump or political tension with China, and these would be precisely the times at which we would be most reluctant to have them back. . . .

8. To sum up, we are grateful for the intention behind this proposal and would naturally be glad enough if it could be seen through successfully as a means of ridding us permanently of significant numbers of our population. But, in the first place, we do not think the relief would be permanent, and secondly, we would see real damage to the Colony's interests if the scheme were adopted and then proved unacceptable or became a target for criticism in the U.K., and above all if it were abandoned under pressure. We wonder if the scheme could expect any other fate if it should in fact develop sufficient to benefit the Colony; on the other hand, if it is to make no appreciable difference to the present situation, we wonder if it is worth considering. Finally, we do not know if there is political pressure behind the proposal, but we have very much in mind the need to avoid taking up a position which might lead itself to misrepresentation. Perhaps in due course you would let me have your comments.

Since the 1950s, an increasing number of Chinese (skilled) workers from Hong Kong had sought employment abroad, including in British Southeast Asia (Singapore, Malaya, and later Malaysia, Borneo, etc.). Migration from Hong Kong to Britain was also supported by the British Nationality Act (from 1948 to 1962), Commonwealth Immigrants Acts, and Immigration Act of 1971 (up to 1973). The statistics below indicate the number and sectors of British Chinese and non-British Chinese participating in the British labour market in the mid-1960s.

Document 10.8: TNA, FCO 40/130, Employment Statistics of Hong Kong Chinese in Britain, 1966–1967.

Immigration from Hong Kong to the UK

October, 1966 – September, 1967

(Figures reproduced in the half-yearly reports of the Labour Department of Hong Kong)

Under the Commonwealth Immigrants Act

A Vouchers 172

B Vouchers..5

Total of Commonwealth citizens holding employment vouchers who actually left for the U.K. during the year...146

Aliens

Aliens from Hong Kong holding U.K. Ministry of Labour permits who left for employment in the course of the year...653

of these, 130 were nurses,
463 restaurant workers,
28 domestic servants,
16 trainees,
16 miscellaneous.

The Contracts for Overseas Employment Ordinance did not apply to all these. The number of contracts attested during the year in respect of aliens to take up employment (or to be re-engaged for employment) in the U.K. was....................553

of these, 510 were hotel and restaurant workers,
25 domestic servants,
7 launderers,
4 shop assistants,
2 tailors,
2 barbers,
1 secretary.

In the same period, the total number of persons leaving Hong Kong for employment elsewhere, coming under the Contracts for Overseas Employment Ordinance, i.e. excluding those to whom the Commonwealth Immigrants Act applies, was . . . 2,251.

Section 3. Confidence Crisis and Brain Drain

The post–World War II economic boom and the rise of industrial economies led to a global surge of labour shortages. During this period, many Chinese from Hong Kong also sought opportunities to work overseas, with the prospect of earning higher incomes to support their families. The following extract is a speech by Fung Hon-chu, appointed member of the Urban Council, calling for the Hong Kong government to introduce better measures to preserve manpower and open up opportunities for local talents.

Document 10.9: HKPRO, HKRS 70/2/136, Extract from the Budget Speech by Mr Fung Hon-chu on 10 March 1966.

There is another matter which I would like to raise for the urgent consideration of Government and that is the "Brains drain" that is apparently affecting Hong Kong. The impression one gets is that there is a steadily increasing number of Hongkong youngsters who do not come back at the conclusion of their studies abroad. One also hears increasingly of able local people migrating elsewhere in search of greater opportunities. I wonder if Government has made any assessment of this problems [*sic*] and of the likely effects of such loss of trained talent on our future economic growth and development. We need all the talent we can get and if there is a "brains drain" measures to remedy it should be adopted without delay.

There are of course many reasons why Hong Kong people settle abroad. In some instances there is probably nothing we can do to deter them but in others there would appear positive measures that we can take. For example, I know of cases where Hong Kong people are forced to stay abroad because they have become over-specialized in their studies and there are no suitable job openings for them in Hong Kong. Some of this can be avoided, if students can go to some organization for advice as to what are the likely skills needed and employable in Hong Kong at the present stage of development. If a person were so advised, he might well embark on a line of studies which would be of more immediate benefit to Hong Kong. To be able to offer sound advice implies the availability of organized information and the ability to determine reasonably the general directions of our development. I should be interested to know whether Government has made assessments of our man-power needs at all levels and whether it is in a position to offer career advice to our young people.

Another reason why able people migrate may be that they feel that Hong Kong does not offer enough opportunities for satisfactory careers. It occurs to me that a comprehensive programme for localization may open up more opportunities. In Malaysia, their Government requires foreign business firms to localize their top posts within given time limits. In Hong Kong we need not go so far at the moment but Government, as the largest employer, can and should take the lead.

My Honourable friend Mr. Dhun Ruttonjee, has spoken at some length on localization in the public service. I fully support his views and Government is urged to give this matter the consideration that it deserves.

In referring to localization, I should make it clear that I am not hinking [*sic*] along narrow racial lines. Hong Kong is a cosmopolitan city and there is no thought in my mind of chasing out people who are not Chinese. What I mean by a "local" is a person who stakes his future with Hong Kong, whatever his race. We need talent from whereever [*sic*] we can find it and if Englishmen, for example, wished to be identified with Hong Kong and to share a common future, then they are welcome as "locals".

These are some of the measures which can be taken to stem the "brains drain" and no doubt Government can think of many others. With the liberalization of immigration laws in certain countries, I think the temptation to migrate will increase among people in search of greater opportunities for advancement. If Government does not devote immediate attention to this problem, I think our future development will be seriously and adversely affected.

British Chinese in Hong Kong had enjoyed a different extent of freedom to migrate to the United Kingdom since the passing of the British Nationality Act of 1948. However, the creation of an 'imperial citizenship' – CUKCs – led to the influx of Commonwealth immigrants to the United Kingdom and prompted the British government to make several attempts to stop the flow, including the implementation of the Commonwealth Immigrants Acts of 1962 and 1968 and the Immigration Act of 1971. In 1981, the British Nationality Act was amended and revoked the right of abode of the CUKCs, including 2.6 million in Hong Kong. This raised concerns and debates in Hong Kong, including, as shown below, among the Hong Kong Observers, a Hong Kong affairs concern group established in the 1970s.

Document 10.10: 'We Belong to Hongkong . . .', *South China Morning Post*, 10 August 1981, 2.

THE issue of nationality and citizenship is not of great interest to the general public because it does not directly affect our daily lives and most people are not aware of its significance.

However, the Hongkong observers are preoccupied with this subject in the context of Hongkong's history and Hongkong's future. While we do not want to gripe about what is past, we do take an active interest in Hongkong's future – our future. . . .

We are not asking for British citizenship. However, we don't remember having been asked at any stage whether we would prefer a separate and distinct Hongkong identity. We object to Mr Raison's claim that we want British citizenship.

We are ethnic Chinese and regard Hongkong as our home, where our future lies. We would like to be able to look forward to a happy life here.

The Hongkong Observers for one have no desire to settle in the United Kingdom. To have a separate Hongkong identity now might lead nervous "belongers" to think Britain is abrogating its "responsibility" for its dependent territory.

We, the Observers, think not. Given Britain's "unshakable commitment" to Hongkong (as expressed by the Foreign Secretary, Lord Carrington) it is the only constitutional door through which Hongkong belongers can enter the Peking-London negotiations about this territory's future.

We have no such right at the moment. The CBDT [Citizens of British Dependent Territory] tag does not provide such a right. In fact, it raises the question what happens when Hongkong is no longer "dependent" on Britain?

Twice Britain has taken away rights without consulting fully the people affected. In 1962 those people in Hongkong with full British citizenship rights were not informed about the immigration laws about to be passed to restrict those rights.

The second time was when the Green Paper on British Nationality was publised [*sic*] two years ago: the Hongkong Government did not disclose the views it forwarded to the British Government. . . .

Where does all this leave the people of Hongkong? What about the other 2.5 million who were never CUKCs?

The rest of Hongkong people cannot claim to be CUKCs because they were not born here and have not taken the trouble to naturalise, which is a cumbersome (and costly) procedure quite unnecessary if one does not travel.

For these people it makes no practical difference to their daily activities what citizenship or nationality they hold. If needed they wish to travel, a Certificate of Identity [CI] will suffice although they may encounter more obstacles than a passport holder.

A CI is a document issued by the Hongkong Government stating "This certificate is issued for the sole purpose of providing the holder with identification paper in lieu of national passport. It is without prejudice to and in no way affects the national status of the holder."

The Hongkong Government and the British Government obviously regard these people as more than just ethnically Chinese. In the section under "nationality claimed" on their Hongkong identity cards, these people have to fill in "Chinese."

However, it is also doubtful if these people can legitimately claim to be People's Republic of China nationals abroad.

Certainly they see themselves as ethnically Chinese but do not identify themselves with the PRC.

Many of them have spent a greater part of their lives here and would like to continue to do so in Hongkong under the present social, economic and political infrastructure.

Perhaps these people would also like to have a distinct Hongkong citizenship. We don't know because the Government never bothered to ask them.

There is little different between them and CBDTs in that whatever happens in 1997, it will affect all of us. We are all residents of "Chinese territory under temporary foreign administration."

We would like to continue to lead a happy life here and there is no reason to believe we will all not be better off with a Hongkong citizenship.

Having a Hongkong identity at this time will at least foster a sense of belonging. We may be Chinese but we belong to Hongkong.

With the approach of 1997, the people of Hongkong must think about their future and what they want, not in terms of security for their investments alone but in terms of a place to bring up a family, where they would like to be buried.

The passing of the British Nationality Act in 1981, the signing of the Sino-British Joint Declaration in 1984, as well as many other incidents that took place in the 1980s caused an increasing number of Hong Kong Chinese to consider emigrating to other countries because of the lack of confidence in Hong Kong's future. By the end of the decade, several countries, including Australia, Canada, and Singapore, introduced schemes to attract Hong Kong people to settle in their country. Seeing the potential impact of the 'brain drain', the following two extracts show multiple measures launched by the British and Hong Kong governments to restore public confidence and to alleviate the situation caused by the loss of talent.

Document 10.11: 'Loss of talent puts HK's future at risk: The full text of British Home Secretary Douglas Hurd's statement to the House of Commons on the right of abode package', *South China Morning Post*, 21 December 1989, 7.

With permission, Mr Speaker, I should like to make a statement about our proposals to improve confidence in Hongkong.

The confidence of the people of Hongkong is at a low ebb. My Right Honourable and learned friend the Lord President told the House on June 6, about the traumatic effect in Hongkong of what happened in Beijing in June, and reported to the House on July 5 after he had paid a visit to the territory.

Many Honourable and Right Honourable members have themselves visited Hongkong since June. The House Select Committee on Foreign Affairs gave a lucid account of the problem in Hongkong in their report of June 28.

We must do all we can to build a secure future for Hongkong on the basis of the Sino-British Joint Declaration of 1984.

We have a continuing responsibility which will involve us in many difficult decisions over the next eight years, and in particular we must provide for those whose services are necessary for the prosperity and effective administration of Hongkong in the years up to 1997. . . .

After careful and detailed consideration over several months we have concluded that the assurance to be given should take the form of full British citizenship which would be awarded to recipients without their having to leave Hongkong. The scheme will cover a maximum number of 50,000 households.

Not all of the assurances would be distributed initially in order to spread the administrative load and to give opportunities for those who may move into key positions in Hongkong in later years. We shall hold back a proportion of the allocation for later in the life of this scheme. . . .

Beneficiaries will be selected on the basis of a points system which will embrace people from a wide range of walks of life in Hongkong. It will cover professional and business people, people working in educational and managerial skills, as well as those in the public and disciplined services.

The decisive criteria will be the value of the individuals' service to Hongkong and the extent to which people in the category of employment are emigrating. Provisions will also be made within the overall total for those who, by virtue of their position, may find themselves vulnerable in the years ahead. . . .

Although this is a British responsibility, and one which we don't shirk, Hongkong is an international centre, with huge international investment, its major trading partners have a strong interest in Hongkong's continuing stability and prosperity.

Some countries have already found ways to give Hongkong people assurances without their having to leave Hongkong.

It is clearly for us to take the lead, and I have set out our specific commitments. We shall now be asking our partners and allies to follow this lead. I emphasise two final points.

First, our proposals will be restricted to Hongkong and the unique problem which we face here. They will have no relevance to other people elsewhere, and the principles of the 1981 British Nationality Act will remain intact.

Second, they are designed not to encourage immigration into this country but to persuade to remain in Hongkong those whom we need to retain there if our last substantial colony is to pass successfully through the final eight years of British rule.

Document 10.12: TNA, FCO 40/3466, Emigration from Hong Kong, March 1991.

Emigration 1980–90

4. Taking the sources of information together, it has been established that emigration in the years 1980–1990 was as follows:

1980–86	1987	1988	1989	1990
Average 20,600	30,000	45,800	42,000	62,000

The figures relate to the total number of people and include all members of the family. In recent years, more than 90% of Hong Kong emigrants have gone to Canada, U.S.A. or Australia.

Reasons for Emigration

5. People have been emigrating from Hong Kong for at least 100 years. The most usual reasons, at least up until the early 1980s, were family reunion and economic advancement. In the period 1986–7 there were two significant developments: -

(a) the "honeymoon period" enjoyed after the coming into force of the Sino-British Joint Declaration came to an end. Some Hong Kong people began to doubt whether their lifestyle could be maintained after 1997 when China resumes sovereignty.

(b) the immigration policies and quotas of the most population destination countries were changed in ways that had the effect of providing more opportunities for Hong Kong people to go.

. . .

Insurance Policy

9. One recent development has been the emergence of "insurance policy" type immigration schemes whereby Hong Kong people secure the right to enter another country at some future time, either without time restriction at all or with very liberal time restrictions. The U.K. Nationality package, for example, will provide full British passports for 50,000 heads of households (up to 225,000 people) without requiring a period of U.K. residence. The two Singapore schemes, one for professionals and one for technicians, the latter for 25,000 households, provide approval in principle to move to Singapore valid for 5 years, renewable for a further 5 years. France has introduced a more modest scheme to benefit employees of French companies in Hong Kong, and other countries are considering similar packages. The combined effect of such schemes is to retain in Hong Kong large numbers of well qualified people content to stay because they have the insurance policy of assured departure at any time if this becomes necessary. . . .

Measures to Alleviate the Problem

13. On emigration generally, there is no question of the Hong Kong Government restricting the freedom of movement of Hong Kong people. This has been made clear in the most unambiguous terms by the Governor. The right to come and go freely is guaranteed in the Joint Declaration and the Basic Law. The emphasis must therefore be on encouraging people to stay by maintaining those aspects of Hong Kong life which are most attractive (economic lifestyle, low tax rates etc.) and further improving quality of life in Hong Kong (environment, social programmes etc.)

14. Specifically on "brain drain", the Government has developed a strategy for addressing the situation in the short, medium and long term.

15. For the long term, the best way to make good any shortfalls is to train up young people so that they have the education and skills required to enable Hong Kong to continue to prosper. In his Annual Address to the Legislative Council in 1989, the

Governor announced a firm commitment to increase the provision of first degree places from 7,000 to 15,000 a year by 1995, while at the same time maintaining or even enhancing standards. The number of new first degree graduates from Hong Kong's own institutions was 3,000 in 1987, and will reach 5,900 in 1991. By 1996, the number will be over 17,000.

16. Obviously it will take time before the community is able to enjoy the full benefits of this expansion. In the medium term Hong Kong Government will try to secure an increase in the return flow of former Hong Kong residents. Already there are many thousands of former Hong Kong residents who have come back here to live and work after studying abroad. But the surge in emigration did not easily get underway until 1988. And the residence requirements of the destination countries mean that those people will not for the most part be eligible to return until 1991 or even later. Hong Kong Government will ensure that potential returnees have ready access to information on the up-to-date situation in Hong Kong, including job opportunities. Another major factor affecting decisions to return is availability of suitable educational opportunities for children bearing in mind part of their education will have been overseas. In other words, on their return, they are likely to require an international-type education. In preparation for an increasing number of these returnees, provision has been made for the construction of a third secondary school on Hong Kong Island under the auspices of the English Schools Foundation. The Hong Kong Government welcomes any bona fide proposals to construct new international schools. Without creating special incentives to return (which would in effect become indirectly incentives to go) Hong Kong Government will see whether disincentives to return can be reduced or eliminated.

17. In the short term, the Government has undertaken to continue to be flexible in allowing immigration of highly skilled personnel to fill the gaps. Every application by employers to bring in professionals and managers is being considered efficiently and sympathetically. There is no restriction on numbers or sources but prospective employees must be suitably qualified and their employers must pay the going wages in Hong Kong. There is also a special scheme to import skilled workers at the technical and craftsman level to relieve the pressure in those areas.

18. Hong Kong Government is aware that in recent years confidence in the future has become a major factor in many people's decision to emigrate. Hong Kong Government will play a full part in restoring confidence. At the same time it looks to other Governments which share a responsibility for Hong Kong's future to do their part.

Suggested Readings

Benton, Gregory, and Edmund Terence Gomez. *The Chinese in Britain, 1800–Present: Economy, Transnationalism, Identity*. Hampshire: Routledge, 2008.

Chan, Yuk Wah, ed. *The Chinese/Vietnamese Diaspora: Revisiting the Boat People*. Oxon: Routledge, 2011.

Hambro, Edvard. *The Problem of Chinese Refugees in Hong Kong: Report Submitted to the United Nations High Commissioner for Refugees*. Holland: A. W. Sijthoff, 1955.

Madokoro, Laura. *Elusive Refuge: Chinese Migrants in the Cold War*. Cambridge, MA: Harvard University Press, 2016.

Mark, Chi-kwan. 'Decolonising Britishness? The 1981 British Nationality Act and the Identity Crisis of Hong Kong Elites'. *The Journal of Imperial and Commonwealth History* 48 (2010): 565–90.

Peterson, Glen. 'To Be or Not to Be a Refugee: The International Politics of the Hong Kong Refugee Crisis, 1949–55'. *The Journal of Imperial and Commonwealth History* 36 (2008): 171–95.

Skeldon, Donald, ed. *Reluctant Exiles? Migration from Hong Kong and the New Overseas Chinese*. Armonk, NY: M. E. Sharpe, 1994.

Watson, James L. *Emigration and the Chinese Lineage: The Mans in Hong Kong and London*. Berkeley: University of California Press, 1975.

Watson, James L. 'The Chinese: Hong Kong Villagers in the British Catering Trade'. In *Between Two Cultures: Migrants and Minorities in Britain*, edited by James L. Watson, 181–213. Oxford: Basil Blackwell, 1997.

11
Medicine and Healthcare

Kelvin Chan

In recent years, a growing body of literature has begun to examine the post-war medical history of Hong Kong. Most of these works have been written by physicians from a professional perspective, orbiting around the development of 'modern medicine' in Hong Kong. This body of literature fundamentally centres on the modernisation and professionalisation of Western medicine, offering practical analysis of medical education, hospital development, and epidemic management.[1] Building upon these works, this chapter suggests a new interpretation of post-war medical history by situating the development of medicine in the changing colonial welfare policies. It offers a comprehensive account of colonial medical policies from the 1950s, when the colonial state invested in medical services to integrate Chinese refugees as healthy and productive workers, to the 1970s, when social reforms were introduced to legitimise colonial governance and therefore emphasised previously overlooked medical problems, such as rehabilitation of the mentally and physically disabled. This chapter also examines well-established themes, such as outbreaks of various epidemics and the regulation of medical personnel, as well as underexplored topics such as drug addiction, mental health, and disability.

Second, this chapter engages with a recent turn in the history of medicine by examining the globalisation of traditional Chinese medicine during the Cold

1. Faith C. S. Ho, *Western Medicine for Chinese: How the Hong Kong College of Medicine Achieved a Breakthrough* (Hong Kong: Hong Kong University Press, 2017); Yip Ka-che, Wong Man-kong, and Leung Yuen-sang, ed., *A Documentary History of Public Health in Hong Kong* (Hong Kong: The Chinese University Press, 2018); Chan-Yeung, Moira M. W. *A Medical History of Hong Kong, 1942–2015* (Hong Kong: The Chinese University Press, 2019).

War.[2] It reveals how the colonial government strategically prioritised biomedicine in government-funded hospitals and, at the same time, avoided regulating traditional Chinese medicine. The ambivalent colonial attitude towards traditional Chinese medicine led to an unintended consequence:[3] it turned Hong Kong into an 'in-between place' for circulating Chinese medical materials, personnel, and technology to Southeast Asia and North America. Adding Chinese medicine to the broader history of medicine raises critical questions about the meanings of 'healthcare'.

This chapter focuses on four interconnected perspectives to examine medicine and healthcare in post-war Hong Kong. The first section looks at colonial medical policies from the 1950s to the 1970s, highlighting the growing importance of medicine in colonial governance. It selects major policy documents to stress the purposes and financial implications of medical policies. The second section touches upon diseases and public health, while the third section focuses on the regulation of unlicensed doctors in the 1950s and 1960s. These two sections offer a broad overview of governmental attempts to maintain good health standards in Hong Kong. The last section explores the underexamined aspect of traditional Chinese medicine, which played an important role in healthcare.

Section 1. Medical Policies

Before 1957, the colonial government was reluctant to invest in social welfare for Chinese refugees. To colonial officials, welfare would only attract more refugees to Hong Kong. Medical policies were confined to epidemic control to safeguard public health. In 1957, Governor Grantham acknowledged a "problem of people" in the Legislative Council and accepted the fact that the refugees would not return to mainland China. The government was compelled to take action to deal with the refugees who would now remain in Hong Kong. Despite the primary focus on housing and resettlement in his speech, Grantham also highlighted that the Medical Department would draw up a 15-year plan to increase

2. Helen Tilley, 'Medical Cultures, Therapeutic Properties, and Laws in Global History,' *Osiris*, 36 (2021): 1–24; Emily Baum, Acupuncture Anesthesia on American Bodies: Communism, Race, and the Cold War in the Making of 'Legitimate' Medical Science. *Bulletin of the History of Medicine*, 95, 4 (2021): 497–527; She Yunchu, 醫學霸權與香港醫療制度 *Biomedical Hegemony and Hong Kong Medical System* (Hong Kong: Zhonghua Book Company, 2019).
3. Rance P. L. Lee, 'Interaction between Chinese and Western Medicine in Hong Kong: Modernisation and Professional Inequality', in *Medicine in Chinese Cultures: Comparative Studies of Health Care in Chinese and Other Societies*, ed. Arthur Kleinman (Washington, DC: US Department of Health, Education and Welfare, 1975), 219–40; Marjorie Topley, 'Chinese and Western Medicine in Hongkong: Some Social and Cultural Determinants of Variation, Interaction and Change', in *Medicine in Chinese Cultures: Comparative Studies of Health Care in Chinese and Other Societies*, ed. Arthur Kleinman (Washington, DC: US Department of Health, Education and Welfare, 1975), 241–71.

the hospital accommodation in the colony to cater the expanding population. The selected document briefly evaluates the medical facilities and estimated cost for future medical policies in 1960. This attempt at planning departed from earlier government's dependence on voluntary organizations to provide medical care to the population.

Document 11.1: TNA, CO 1030/1219 Memorandum for Executive Council, Development of Medical and Health Services, 1960–1965, 12 July 1960.

The Aim

2. It must be accepted that the medical facilities at present provided in Hong Kong, not only by the Government but also by voluntary agencies and private practitioners, are far from sufficient to meet the need. In present circumstances it is clearly out of the question for the Government to attempt to provide adequate facilities for the whole population. It is suggested that the aim should be to provide hospitals and clinics appropriate to that part of the population that cannot afford to pay for the services provided by non-Government agencies. Even the acceptance of this limited aim will involve a very large commitment. . . .

Cost

14. A rough estimate of the cost of these proposals, so far as they concern institutions not already included in the Estimates or undertaken by the Jockey Club, is given at Appendix 'D'. While the acceptance of this plan would clearly involve the acceptance of a larger financial commitment, the Director of Medical and Health Service has pointed out that even to maintain our inadequate facilities at their present standard, 267 hospitals beds and 23 doctors must be provided for every increase of 100000 in the population. 100000 is not very much more than the rate of natural increase. At the present time there are less Government hospital beds for each 1000 of the population than at any time since the war. This illustrates the urgency of the problem; but the difficulty in recruiting and/or training the necessary staff, particularly nursing staff, makes it impossible to recommend a more extensive programme than the one outlined.

In 1957, the Medical Department submitted an outline for a fifteen-year plan. But the plan was rejected by the government due to lack of population data. In 1964, the colonial government published the Development of Medical Services in Hong Kong as the first White Paper on medical policies. It targeted providing subsidized medical services to the poor and viewed a general standard of health as "an economic asset" to the community. The Appendix table included important data of government's expenditure over medical care.

Document 11.2: Hong Kong Government Printer, *Development of Medical Services in Hong Kong* (Hong Kong, 1964).

Forward Planning of Medical Services, 1957–1962

17. In 1957, an outline of a 15-year plan of development of medical and health services was submitted to Government. This plan was largely a statement of what was generally needed and desirable to provide as modern and comprehensive a service as possible within the limitations of finance, architectural and building capacity and staff training programmes. On examination of this outline plan, it was realized that, in the absence of factual census data upon which population projections could be based, the detail of planning was best undertaken into five-year phases. Further, uncertain economic trends and changing patterns of demand for medical and health services would require the maximum of flexibility in any long-term programme.

18. When the staff for a small planning unit within the Medical and Health Department became available in 1959, a detailed plan covering the years 1960–65 and representing a segment of the 15 year outline proposals was prepared. In the preparation of this plan, it was accepted that medical facilities existing at that time and those planed for the immediate future by Government, voluntary and private agencies were far from sufficient to meet the need. At the same time, Government did not possess the resources to provide comprehensive medical services for the whole population. It was therefore recommended that the aim should be to provide additional hospital and clinic facilities for that part of the population that could not afford to pay economic charges for the services provided by private agencies. Even this limited aim would involve a very large commitment of public funds. . . .

Population requiring subsidized medical services

23. As stated in the Annual Report of Hong Kong for the year 1962, 'the policy of Government is to provide, directly or indirectly, low cost or free medical and personal health services to that large section of the community which is unable to seek medical attention from other sources.' This policy decision was taken by Executive Council when the 1960-65 segment of the development plan was approved. It is in the light of this policy ruling, that the 1963 to 1972 Medical Development Plan has been prepared. . . .

27. In view of the nature of Hong Kong's economy, it would be unrealistic to plan future medical services to standards equivalent to those provided now in Western countries quite apart from the fact that such equivalence, even if the finance were available, would in any event be physically impossible to achieve within ten years. It is necessary, therefore, to plan *ab initio* from such basic data as is at our disposal.

28. Until 1961 there was no factual knowledge concerning the size or structure of the population. However, the census taken during that year has provided a firm foundation upon which to analyse current information and to make projections into the future. For the purpose of this report, the following estimates of size and structure of the population are used.

	Mid-year 1961	Mid-year 1971
Total	3,184,300	4,812,700
Age group		
0–14	40.9%	37.3%
15–29	20.1%	24.4%
30–44	22.2%	18.1%
45–60	12.0%	13.6%
60+	4.8%	6.6%

29. As is the case in almost all other countries, morbidity data in Hong Kong are scanty, except for certain circumscribed groups of diseases such as the notifiable diseases of which a fairly accurate assessment can be made. On the other hand, mortality is well-documented and, although of very limited value in the detailed assessment of morbidity, it can be of assistance in the establishment of certain disease trends in the comparison of data from other countries.

Premises for Forward Planning

30. In the light of the considerations set out in paragraphs 23-29 above, planning has been undertaken on the following premises:

(a) that the population trends will be as forecast;

(b) that 50 percent of the population are unable to afford unsubsidized outpatient medical care and that 80 percent are unable to afford unsubsidized inpatient treatment

(c) that the aim should be over the next 10 years to provide, within the limitations imposed by the Colony's financial and economic circumstances, augmented clinic and hospital services designed to meet the most urgent medical and health needs. These will have to be related to the physical capacity to finance, build and staff the institutions required.

31. Minimal ratios of provision will have to be set and a continuing attempt made to meet them if significant easing of the pressure created by the increasing demands

is to be achieved. If this is not done then there will be a progressive deterioration of the present unsatisfactory situation. These minima have been based on the local circumstances and we believe they are realistic. . . .

Review

89. A good general standard of health throughout a community is an economic asset to it and helps to condition the levels of energy and initiative which determine productivity, particularly in a free enterprise economy, such as Hong Kong. It has been stated earlier that 50% of the community cannot afford to pay economic charges for out-patient treatment and that 80% cannot afford economic charges for hospital care, and it is unlikely that living standards will improve so materially as to make full economic charges for health service realistic within the period under review. Some increase in fees may be possible but the resultant revenue is unlikely to be significant in relation to the total cost of the services. If the prevention and control of disease and the restoration of the sick to health and productivity are to be continued at present levels of efficiency, increasing subsidy from public funds will therefore be required unless the standards of the services are reduced. . . .

Appendix IV

Expenditure (c) – Medical and Health Department 1947–48–1963–64 [Extracted] (Figure in $ million)

Year	Recurrent	Non-recurrent	Total
1947–48	8.2	Unknown	8.2
1948–49	12.7	0.3	13
1949–50	14.2	0.3	14.5
1950–51	15.2	0.6	15.8
1951–52	19.4	1.1	20.5
1952–53	25.3	0.8	26.1
1953–54	28.1	2.9	31
1954–55	30.1	5.6	35.7
1955–56	32.9	2.6	35.5
1956–57	37.1	2.1	39.2
1957–58	42.9	3.2	46.1
1958–59	47.7	12	59.8
1959–60	59.2	21	80.2

Year	Recurrent	Non-recurrent	Total
1960–61	73	17.6	80.2
1961–62	82.9	17	99.9
1962–63	89.8	33.4	123.2
1963–64 Estimates	107.7	36.4	144.1

The 1970s has often been seen as a Golden Era of Hong Kong with expanding social welfare for housing, education and medicine. These policies, to a large extent, were an extension from the 1960s. The selected document is the second White Paper that outlines an ambitious plan for medical reform. It departed from the focus in the 1960s in offering medical services to the poor and expanded to offer a comprehensive medical care system to the public. This move was part of the broader social reform to legitimatize colonial governance and solicit public support after the 1967 Riot.

Document 11.3: Hong Kong Government Printer, *The Further Development of Medical and Health Services in Hong Kong* (Hong Kong, 1974).

Chapter 1 Introduction

1.1 The two main principles of Government policy underlying this White Paper are, and will continue to be, the need to safeguard and promote the general public health of the community as a whole and the need to ensure the provision of medical and personal health facilities for the people of Hong Kong, including particularly that large section of the community which relies on subsidized medical attention. This White Paper is concerned primarily with the action needed to expand the major areas of the Government's medical and health services, that is to say, with the maintenance and expansion of the general public health services (including the prevention and control of disease) and with the development of additional facilities and services for in-patients and out-patients. . . .

1.5 As the needs of the community change and develop, it is incumbent on the Government to introduce new services. For example, the Government has recently started to participate directly in the provision of family planning services and to take a more active part in the treatment of drug addiction. In the future efforts will be made to promote consciousness in the community of the importance of dental health, even though the introduction of a dental service on the lines of the medical service is impracticable at this stage.

1.6 The proposals are therefore designed to maintain and improve existing services and to consolidate and establish new services, in each case against the background of the growth of the population and the changing pattern of its distribution between the urban area and the New Territories. . . .

Chapter 4

Summary of the Proposals

4.1 The following chapters set out the Government's proposals towards meeting the objectives described in Chapter 3; these will be carried out as fast as is permitted by the Government's capacity to build, staff and finance them. The main proposals are-

A regional organization.

(a) medical and health services will be organized on a regional basis;

(b) the aim will be to serve each region with all appropriate general and specialist facilities;

(c) Government, and some Government-assisted, hospitals will be brought together in an integrated (regionally based) structure with uniform charges for third class beds;

(d) the accident and emergency services will be reorganized within the regional structure;

New hospitals and clinics

(e) the ratio of 5.5 hospital beds per 1,000 population should be regarded as a desirable standard for long term planning purposes;

(f) general hospitals will be built at Sha Tin and Tuen Nun and then in East Kowloon; further psychiatric facilities will be provided in the psychiatric wing of the Princess Margaret Hospital at Lai Chi Kok and later a hospital at Shau Kei Wan;

(g) "day" beds will be introduced on an experimental basis in selected clinics;

(h) polyclinics, besides the Tang Chi Ngong Specialist Clinic on Hong Kong Island, will be opened in East Kowloon, South Kwai Chung, Shatin, Tuen Mun and Kwun Tong;

(i) clinics will be provided at Ngau Tau Kok, Lam Tin, To Kwa Wan, Ha Kwai Chung, Lei Muk Shue and Sha Tin;

(j) the Violet Peel Clinic, Central Dispensary and the clinics at Sham Shui Po and Sai Kung will be reprovisioned;

(k) provision for medical rehabilitation will be expanded and further requirements will be reviewed in the context of services to the disabled;

Medical training

(l) a second medical school will be established at the Chinese University of Hong Kong;

(m) a third nurses training school will be built;

The health services

(n) a Health Education Unit will be established;

(o) action will be taken to increase public awareness of the need to reduce accidents of all kinds;

(p) family planning services will be expanded;

(q) the Government will play the leading role in the medical treatment of drug addiction;

(r) further consideration will be given to the development of community nursing;

(s) a school dental service will be introduced; and

(t) a dental school will be established at the University of Hong Kong.

4.2 These proposals involve the following modifications of the recommendations made by the MDAC [Medical Advisory Committee]:

(a) a revised distribution of the 1,000 psychiatric beds, originally planned for the proposed hospital at Shau Kei Wan;

(b) priority being given to the hospitals at Sha Tin and Tuen Mun;

(c) the hospital proposed for Tuen Mun to be planned for 1200 beds; and

(d) the ratio of 5.5 beds per 1000 population to be achieved over a longer period . . .

Financial Implications

13.1 The implementation of the proposals described in this White Paper will involve major capital expenditure and, on completion of the various projects, heavy additional recurrent cost. Clearly it is possible to do no more than estimate the total expenditure tentatively at this stage. However, it is calculated that the capital expenditure, which includes construction, furniture, equipment and related quarters, for those medical and health development items which are already in the Public Works Programme, and for the additional items proposed in this White Paper, would be about $914 m. at mid-1974 prices. . . .

13.6 The ambitious programme which is described in this White Paper will make substantial demands upon the resources of the community. If achieved, it will provide a substantial expansion of medical and health services in the New Territories, will ensure better facilities in the urban areas and give a more effective coverage of clinics throughout Hong Kong. The ratio of beds to people, in spite of the problems arising from a fast rising population, will be maintained and, when the full programme is achieved, will be improved. All these measures should go far to provide medical services of a quality and quantity which the people of Hong Kong would like to see.

From 1976, the Foreign and Commonwealth Office (FCO) began to pressure the colonial government for more radical social reform, largely focusing on labour right and social security. To accelerate social reforms in Hong Kong, the FCO drafted a grand scheme of social reform in the Hong Kong Planning Paper. The acceleration of social reforms was a crucial tactic for Britain in negotiating the future of Hong Kong with the PRC in the 1980s.

Document 11.4: TNA, FCO 40/702, Planning Paper on Hong Kong, 1976.

Summary

1. Hong Kong is a difficult political problem which is likely to become more acute as 1997 approaches. There are some advantages and some disadvantages to Britain in the present connection. The British interest in the long term is to disengage but the overriding consideration is that without careful handling disengagement could risk a mass exodus of Chinese/British subjects with humanitarian, if not legal, claims to entry to Britain. There is also the risk of the collapse of one of the world's leading financial centres.

2. There is an element of political embarrassment for the CPR [Chinese People's Republic] in the Colony's existence but it is of great practical value to them. They have publicly declared that Hong Kong is Chinese territory and that the problem will need to be settled when the time is ripe. They are likely to be satisfied with the status quo for the foreseeable future. This could change as a result of political events in China but, in any event, we shall need to discuss the future of the Colony with them well before 1997. This presupposes a well

ordered government in China in succession to that of Mao Tse-tung and we cannot determine the best negotiating posture for us until the new government emerges and its character is assessed. This points to a date in the mid-1980s and we cannot at present speculate on the best options for us. There is no advantage, and real disadvantage, in seeking to engage the CPR in discussion of internal policies in Hong Kong meanwhile.

3. On these assumptions the paper suggests a policy for institutional, fiscal and social reform, some aspects of which have been suggested by the Governor and some of which need further discussion with him. On institutions the paper suggests an enlargement of Legislative Council and a broadening of its social base (by the appointment not the elective process), and a greater differentiation of its functions from those of the Executive Council. On fiscal reform the paper argues in favour of a more broadly based and progressive system of direct taxation and an expansion of public sector spending to 25% of GDP. On social and labour questions the paper argues in favour of further acceleration of development in the housing, educational and health fields; a contributory social security system and improvements in terms and conditions of employment.

4. This policy presupposes a greater degree of direction from London and accountability from Hong Kong which may create friction between Britain and the Colony. There is a need for more dialogue over a greater surface of policy, partly to relieve the burden on the Governor. There is also a need for a greater British information effort in Hong Kong; greater effort to reduce friction over matters where British and Hong Kong interests clash; and a need to continue strongly to advocate Hong Kong's case publicly here.

Following the Hong Kong Planning Paper, the colonial government issued a new White Paper Integrating the Disabled into the Community: A United Effort in October 1977, which centred on the rehabilitation on the physically and mentally ill. Rehabilitation, a concept that straddled between social welfare and medicine, meant the medical treatment and social integration of the disabled. The selected document is an extract from a memorandum for the Executive Council that discussed the plan and financial implication of the social welfare reform. It indicates a dramatic expansion of treating and supporting the physically and mentally disabled.

Document 11.5: TNA, FCO 40/756, Memorandum for Executive Council, Programmes for the Development of Social Welfare Services, 20 September 1977.

Introduction

During August 1977 Honourable Members discussed proposals to expand the provision of social welfare services in the areas of:

(a) Rehabilitation;

(b) The Elderly;

(c) Personal Social Work Among Youth; and

(d) Social Security....

This memorandum draws together the total demands on financial and manpower resources required for the proposed programmes and indicates the time-tables proposed for the implementation of each one.

Annex C

Financial Implications

A. Recurrent Expenditure ($ million at March 1977 prices)

	1977/78	1978/79	1979/80	1980/81	1981/82	1982/83	Total 78/79–82/83
1.Services for the Elderly	2.3	8.8 (6.5)	15.3 (13)	22.3 (20)	30.3 (28)	36.3 (34)	113 (101)
2. Personal Social Work Among Youth	4.5	18.57 (14.07)	23.29 (28.79)	27.55 (23.05)	28.97 (24.47)	30.31 (25.81)	128.69 (106.19)
3. Rehabilitation	122.28	140.33 (18.05)	158.32 (36.04)	172.8 (50.52)	184.03 (61.75)	197.22 (74.94)	852.7 (241.3)
4. Social Security							
(a). Public Assistance	180	229 (49)	226 (46)	230 (50)	233 (53)	235 (55)	1153 (253)
(b). Community Allowance Scheme	97.7	107.7 (56)	153.7 (56)	181.7 (84)	202.7 (105)	219.7 (122)	865.5 (372)
Total	406.78	504.4 (97.62)	576.61 (169.83)	634.35 (227.57)	679 (272.22)	718.53 (311.75)	3122.89 (1078.99)

Note: Figures in parenthesis indicate the additional expenditure for these four programmes i.e. a total of 1078.99 over the 5 year period.

Section 2. Diseases and Public Health

Post–Second World War Hong Kong faced several challenges to public health, including the influx of refugees, lack of medical infrastructure, poor housing conditions, and an unsanitary environment. Yet the colonial government focused largely on combatting communicable diseases in the late 1940s and 1950s, with positive results. Hong Kong maintained a good record of public health until the outbreak of cholera in 1961. Document 11.6 highlights the excellent public health conditions in Hong Kong in the early 1950s.

Document 11.6: TNA, CO 129/624/2, Tour Notes by Dr E. D. Pridie on his visit to Hong Kong, 16 July 1951.

1. I was much impressed by the medical and health services of Hong Kong and consider that they are among the best in the British Colonial Empire. The high morale and excellent personal relationships among staff reflects great credit on all concerned.

2. The Queen Mary Hospital is one of the finest hospitals I have ever visited and is magnificently sited. The fact that it is a teaching hospital ensures the highest possible standards and it is adequately staffed with doctors and nursing sisters. It is very well-planned and is efficiently run.

3. The Ruttom Joe Tuberculosis Sanatorium, with its fine new clinic, is a magnificent voluntary effort and must have given a most useful stimulus to anti-tuberculosis work in Hong Kong after the war. Excellent work under less pleasant surroundings is being done at the Harcourt Road Clinic and the new Tuberculosis dispensary in Kowloon is first class. The new X-ray lorries presented by U.N.I.C.E.F. should be a useful addition to the anti-tuberculosis organization. Tuberculosis is being more thoroughly dealt with in Hong Kong than in most Colonial Territories.

4. Venereal Diseases are being tackled in a thorough and systematic manner and I was impressed by the amount of work being done in the venereal diseases centres.

5. The organization of the Child Welfare Centres and training of staff is excellent.

6. The Lai Chi Kok hospital with 200 beds for tuberculosis, 200 beds for clinical cases from other hospitals and 80 beds for infectious diseases serves a most useful purpose.

7. Kowloon Hospital: The amount of work done in the out-patient department of this hospital, as well as in other out-patient departments – particularly the Polyclinics in the city, is almost bewildering and it is impressive to see the long queues of out-patients, each paying a dollar if he can afford it, waiting for attention. The out-patient department of Kowloon hospital has 400000 attendances a year. Kowloon hospital has 200 beds at present, but an extension of 70 beds is nearly completed. It has a fine maternity block. The usual specialist facilities are provided in this hospital.

8. Port Health Work: This is well organized and efficient.

9. The Tung Wah Charitable Hospital: This long-established charitable institution does very fine work. The hospital admits every kind of patient without discrimination and has a great name throughout the territory. It was a pleasure to have an opportunity of visiting it and meeting the Chinese Authorities responsible. It was overcrowded as might be expected, but had a happy cheerful atmosphere.

10. Housing: The sudden influx since the war, which has trebled the population of Hong Kong, has created an appalling housing problem both by gross over-crowding of existing houses and by squatters in shanty towns on the ill sides. It is to the great credit of the health authorities that they have managed to maintain public health under such very adverse conditions, but there is likely to be a grim legacy of tuberculosis later.

11. Health Education: The medical services have done excellent work in health propaganda including the production of films and posters and have attracted the attention of the W.H.O. [World Health Organization] authorities by the excellence of their work.

12. Tsam Tuk [Tsan Yuk] Maternity Hospital: This hospital of 100 beds does excellent work under rather crowded conditions. It is popular and 5000 maternity cases a year are delivered there. It serves as a teaching hospital for the medical school. The maternity organization of Hong Kong is excellent under an energetic Supervisor of Midwives.

13. Medical Laboratories: These laboratories carry out all the routine work for Hong Kong and produce T. A. B. [for typhoid], Cholera and anti-rabies vaccine. They require more suitable and more modern accommodation.

14. Leper Settlement: I thought the present site of the leper settlement most unsuitable, and to put it mildly, depressing. The sooner they can be moved to their new island settlement, the better.

15. New Territories: This area is adequately served by the static and travelling dispensaries and dressing stations. The accommodation for the dispensary at Yuemlong

[Yuenlong] was poor, but excellent work was being done. I formed the impression that the people both in the New Territories and the rural areas of Hong Kong were provided with adequate dispensary facilities for treatment. Malaria has been eradicated on Hong Kong Island but remains a difficult problem in part of the New Territories. Fortunately, the people have a considerable acquired immunity to the disease. I was horrified by some of the village water supplies in the New Territories and suggest that the problems of rural water supplies should receive special attention.

16. Personnel: The Hong Kong medical services very wisely have made use of the best of the displaced Chinese doctors, many of whom are men of high professional standard and great experience, who have left posts in the Chinese Medical Schools or Government. As a result the service is well staffed at present. It should be remembered, however, that when China becomes more normal again many will return to their posts and also that the large number of medical students qualifying at Hong Kong in the near future will have to be absorbed. For both reasons it would be unwise to consider these displaced doctors as being other than very temporary. They should not be registered or taken on the permanent establishment.

17. Finally, I should like to say again how impressed I was with the health and medical services of Hong Kong. The people of Hong Kong have every reason to be satisfied and proud of their medical service.

One of the most serious public health crises in the 1950s and 1960s Hong Kong was drug addiction. The colonial government followed the international regulatory tide to prohibit opium and faced the immediate consequence: surging number of heroin offenses and consumption. The escalating heroin crime rates alarmed the Colonial Office. The Secretary of State for the Colonies Alan Lennox-Boyd ordered the colonial government to investigate the problem. The selected document is a private investigation report written by Brian C. K. Hawkins, Secretary for Chinese Affairs. This report revealed the horrifying conditions about drug addiction and signalled as the first official account that led to the beginning of the anti-narcotics war in 1959.

Document 11.7: HKPRO, HKRS 163/1/2041, B. C. K. Hawkins, 'The Drug Problem in Hong Kong', 7 May 1957.

...

3. The Problem

The problem of drug trafficking in Hong Kong is an enormous one and possesses several facets which become dominant according to the line of approach. There is, for example, Hong Kong's position in the overall international network of drug distribution in which the Colony undoubtedly acts to some extent as an entrepot for breaking up and forwarding consignments to Japan, Canada and the U.S.A. Then there is evidence that Hong Kong is moving beyond the role of distributor pure and simple, and is starting to manufacture heroin for export as well as local consumption. Finally, there is the problem of the spread of drug addiction in the Colony itself. All these are facets of the same big problem and cannot be divorced from one another, but the first two have been covered in a separate report by the Commissioner of Police and I do not propose to consider them in detail but shall only refer to them incidentally as and when they impinge on our own local problem. . . .

This in itself is a very serious state of affairs indeed because heroin addiction bears about the same relation to opium addiction as the drinker of wood alcohol bears to the drinker of beer. Heroin, which is of course a derivative of opium extracted from morphine, is thought to be about five times as strong as morphine and is far more habit forming. The habit is not only acquired more quickly but is also more difficult to break both in the withdrawal period and in the convalescent stage. There is no hope of effecting a cure after the withdrawal period except by continuous – rigid total denial of the drug over a long period of time and, even when this has achieved a break in the craving, relapses are frequent particularly when the addict returns to his former mode of life.

A particularly deadly aspect of heroin addiction is the speed with which the drug takes hold of its victims. Dr. Lee of the Prisons Department estimates that a man will become completely addicted in three months but medical opinion varies on this point and some doctors put the habit forming period as low as two weeks. One thing is certain, once the drug takes hold mental and moral degeneracy is extremely rapid and the customary restraints imposed by upbringing, education, honour and family affection are swept away by the craving for the drug. There is ample evidence from the Family Welfare Society case workers and from our own experience in family cases in this office that every cent the addict can obtain by any means will be spent on satisfying his craving. It is impossible to help him and very hard to help his family because food, clothing, bedding, anything on which he can lay his hands will be converted into money to continue his supply. In the family cases which come before this department the wife often pays a lump sum of money in order to secure a promise that the husband will leave her and the children to fend for themselves; separation is the only hope of maintaining their own livelihood.

While it would be absurd to contend that opium smoking was not a harmful vice, compared with the heroin habit it is relatively innocuous. Any officer with long service in this Colony must have had plenty of experience of opium smokers of many years standing who could maintain their regular consumption at a moderate level without apparent difficulty and without appreciable detriment to their physical and moral standard. The real opium addict was comparatively rare and, unless there was the complication of organic disease, it took years for an opium smoker to deteriorate to the abject slavery that heroin imposes on its devotees in a matter of months. It is a sobering thought that our efforts to suppress opium have been largely instrumental in putting heroin in its place. . . .

56. In conclusion may I again stress the fact that even my casual investigation of this problem has confirmed me in my previous opinion that it is deadly serious and must be tackled urgently. I believe that the seriousness of the situation has been rather obscured for us in Hong Kong owing to the fact that drug addiction has always been with us. It is so easy to think in terms of the past and to feel that a substantial increase in drug offences is only to be expected when one takes into account the enormous increase in the total population. This is quite true and if the increase was in opium smoking I should not regard the present situation with any great alarm. It is the introduction on a large scale of the far more deadly vice of heroin smoking that changes the whole picture. From such figures that we possess it is obvious that the increase in the use of this drug is leaping upwards at an alarming speed and our figures do not begin to tell the whole story. The Police have estimated, though it is little more than a guess, that we probably have 30000 confirmed drug addicts in the Colony. If the spread of heroin smoking continues at no more than its present rate I would estimate that this figure will be doubled in two to three years, and the effect on Hong Kong will be all the more appalling because it will be concentrated in such a small area. It is going to cost a great deal of labour and money to cope with this problem but unless we really do tackle it now with all our resources we will find that in a few years time it will be too big to tackle at all.

B. C. K. Hawkins
Secretary for Chinese Affairs
7th May 1957

Caused by environmental hygiene and sanitation, cholera was associated with water supplies and contamination of food and water. The Urban Council was in charge of the inspection of sanitary conditions in the colony. In August 1961, a new subtype of cholera, Cholera E1 Tor, broke out in Hong Kong. The colonial government immediately responded to the epidemic and implemented multiple measures, such as cleansing food stalls, markets and water supplies, to contain the epidemic. Two months later, Hong Kong successfully combatted the epidemic and made it free from cholera.

Document 11.8: Hong Kong Government Printer, *Report on the Outbreak of Cholera in Hong Kong Covering the Period 11 August to 12 October 1961* (Hong Kong, 1961).

Recommendations

140. Following on the experience gained in this outbreak of cholera, it is recommended that:

(i) An inoculation campaign against cholera should be carried out in February, March and April 1962 aimed at protecting 70% or more of the population, using vaccine produced in the Government Institute of Pathology.

(ii) Consideration be given to advancing the priority of certain projects concerned with water supplies, reclamation and resettlement. These are a piped water supply to the North East Kowloon area, the reclamations at Aldrich Bay, Aberdeen and Tai Kok Tsui with resettlement of the boat people concerned.

(iii) Action should be taken to deal with illegal piggeries in the urban areas.

(iv) The duties and responsibilities of the Health Inspectorate should be reviewed, particularly with regard to routine house inspections and any modifications in the system of training that this would entail.

(v) The future use of the Chatham Road Camp should be considered in the light of the value of the Camp as a quarantine centre until such time as adequate quarantine facilities have been provided at the proposed New Lai Chi Kok Hospital.

(vi) A regional liaison should be established, either direct or through the World Health Organization, with the neighbouring territories affected by cholera this year. These territories include the Kwangtung Province of the Chinese Peoples Republic, Macau, Sarawak, Indonesia and the Philippines. How this liaison should be established is a matter for further discussion.

(vii) The Secretary of State should be requested to enter a reservation, in request of Hong Kong, with the World Health Organization in Geneva regarding the 1958 resolution passed by the World Health Assembly which does not regard an infection with EI Tor as being cholera for the purposes of the application of the International Sanitary Regulations.

(viii) Meantime, urgent consideration requires to be given to the continuation of the chlorination of wells, the measures against dangerous practices amongst hawkers and the use of insecticides to control fly breeding.

In 1968, an influenza pandemic outbreak took place in Hong Kong and quickly spread to the entire world, killing over one million people in total. Wai-Kwan Chang, a medical officer at the Queen Mary Hospital, isolated the virus subtype immediately after the discovery of the first case in Hong Kong. Hong Kong's effort in virus surveillance was praised by the WHO. The Hong Kong Flu in 1968 also indicated an emerging global consensus about China as an epicentre of viral threats.[4]

Document 11.9: W. K. Chang, 'National Influenza Experience in Hong Kong', *Bulletin of the World Health Organization* 41, no. 3 (1969).

In 1968, our first intimation of a possible new epidemic strain of influenza virus was a report in The Times of London for 12 July that a widespread outbreak of acute respiratory disease was occurring in south-eastern China. Five days later the health authorities in Hong Kong and Dr Chang, Director of the Influenza Centre there, reported a sudden increase in influenza-like illness and, most important, the isolation of viruses which by preliminary tests appeared to be similar to influenza virus A2. The strains were despatched as infected tissue-culture fluids on wet ice to the World Influenza Centre, where strain-specific sera were prepared in ferrets, and by this means it was determined that the antigenic pattern of the Hong Kong strain differed markedly from previous strains of virus A2. Similar findings were obtained in the International Influenza Center for the Americas to which Dr Chang had also sent specimens.

Origin of the Epidemic

We are dependent on a single newspaper report that the outbreak in Hong Kong was immediately preceded by an epidemic of acute respiratory disease in south-eastern China. There is no information on the etiology of this outbreak in China but its close temporal relationship to subsequent events makes it possible that it was due to the Hong Kong strain. It will have escaped none of the members of the Conference that the 1957 pandemic first came to light in southern China, and the experience in 1968, though very tenuous, adds a little more information to the often-expressed hypothesis that strains of influenza virus which have the capacity to spread widely and rapidly often arise in that part of the world. Unfortunately contact between health authorities in China and other countries is even more difficult than in 1957 and it is impossible to obtain information on the possible origin or behaviour of the epidemic prior to its appearance in Hong Kong. However, it is known that in Hong Kong about half a million cases occurred by the end of July.

4. For more on Hong Kong Flu, see Robert Peckham, 'Viral Surveillance and the 1968 Hong Kong Flu Pandemic', *Journal of Global History* 15, no. 3 (2020): 444–58.

By mid-August quantities of virus were prepared at the 2 international centres and were made available to research and vaccine production laboratories wishing to have them. The national influenza centres were informed of the emergence of the strain and of the possibility of widespread epidemics. . . .

Efficacy of the WHO Programme

The main purpose of this presentation has been to describe in general outline the origin and progress of the epidemic. In conclusion we should, however, like to mention again the WHO influenza programme. So far as the isolation and characterization of the virus were concerned, the programme fulfilled its objective and thanks to the efforts of the national reference centre in Hong Kong and the 2 international centres, the strain was isolated, identified and distributed to vaccine producers with all possible speed. It is difficult to imagine circumstances in which the interval from arrival of specimens in a national influenza centre to the characterization and distribution of the strain could be shortened. Contact between the national influenza centres on the one hand and the international reference centres and WHO in Geneva on the other hand is improving each year. The number of national centres has increased from 59 in 43 countries in 1962 to 85 in 55 countries in 1969. However, there are still large areas, especially in Africa, where no centres exist.

In contrast to the precise information obtained about the viruses, the quantity and quality of the epidemiological information is variable. This is partly because different countries use different methods of assessment.

In the United States of America much emphasis is placed on excess deaths from pneumonia and influenza; the United Kingdom relies mainly on claims for sickness-absence made to the Ministry of National Insurance, on increased demands by doctors for urgent admission of their patients to hospitals, and on reports of the occurrence of influenza-like disease received from members of the Royal College of General Practitioners; in Czechoslovakia information from serological surveys and clinical data from a variety of sources is collected and analysed regularly throughout the winter.

These are examples of different approaches in 3 countries in which ascertainment is practised fairly intensively. There are many countries in which the occurrence of influenza-like disease receives much less attention - which is scarcely surprising when the other important health problems which face them are taken into account.

In the past year we have introduced a scheme by which national influenza laboratories provide us with regular information on a special form. The scheme has been taken into use by most of the national centres and is beginning to work smoothly. But the separation between laboratory and epidemiological services in so many countries still hampers the free flow of information nationally and internationally.

The current interest in epidemiological surveillance and the resolution adopted by the 22nd World Health Assembly on the importance of developing national and international surveillance for specified diseases provides us with an opportunity to establish simple methods of obtaining from as many countries as possible reliable information on which valid comparisons can be made. We have already begun the pursuit of this objective.

Section 3. Medical Personnel

In 1957, the colonial government passed the Medical Registration Bill 1957 to prohibit the practice of unregistered doctors completely. The government invited the Society of Apothecaries to conduct examinations of these doctors. However, Sir Alexander Grantham was worried about the political repercussions because the left and right wings considered medical care as an ideological battlefield to provide medical services to the poor. Regulation faced opposition from the right wing, which had the most unregistered doctors.

Document 11.10: HKPRO, HKRS 163/1/2119, Savingram, from the Governor to the Secretary of State for the Colonies, 11 June 1957.

Please refer to my dispatch no. 1035/57, with which was enclosed the Medical Registration Ordinance 1957, a revision and re-enactment of the Medical Registration Ordinance, cap. 161.

I now seek your assistance in the matter of arranging examinations locally which would enable doctors at present unregistrable to obtain a registrable qualification, i.e. one recognized by the General Medical Council. It seems advisable to explain fully the background to this request and the sequence of events since the draft legislation was published.

Section 27 of the new Ordinance provides that any person who not being registered or provisionally registered or exempted from registration practices or professes to practise or publishes his name as practising medicine or surgery shall be guilty of an offence and on summary conviction liable to a fine of $2,000 and to imprisonment for six months . . .

It is estimated that of the doctors at present in the Colony, who possess only qualifications that are registrable neither here nor in the United Kingdom, between 150 and 200 (many of them refugees from China) nevertheless support themselves by practising their profession in the many cheap medical clinics that have sprung up in recent years. Such people are in fact still coming into the Colony from China.

Many do in fact practise for gain but evade the law by representing themselves, with the co-operation of some trade union or other organisation, as practising only as an act of charity . . . it is almost impossible to initiate a successful prosecution because of the difficulty of obtaining willing witnesses. Experience has shown that by no means all these people have received adequate instruction in medicine and surgery, but it was, under the old Ordinance, impossible to control them.

It consequently became necessary, in order to safeguard the poorer sections of the community who patronise these clinics because they cannot afford the charges of the registered private practitioners, to provide in the new Ordinance for complete prohibition of and practice by unregistered doctors, as has already been done in Singapore. It would otherwise, become impossible to maintain the standards necessary for safeguarding the health of the people . . .

In order to allow time for the clinics to be staffed with registered doctors and/or for the unregistered doctors to become registrable, Clause 1 of the Bill was amended to provide that Clause 27 should, instead of coming into force on a fixed date, be brought into operation at the Governor's discretion. At the same time an assurance was given that efforts would be made to arrange an examination in the colony so that unregistered doctors might have an opportunity of acquiring a registrable qualification . . .

I should therefore be grateful if you would, on my behalf and as a matter of urgency, approach one of the examining bodies in the United Kingdom – it is thought that the Society of Apothecaries of London, or the Royal College of England, Scotland or Ireland would be the most appropriate bodies – and enquire whether any of them would be prepared to send examiners to Hong Kong or to depute persons here to hold an examination in the Colony . . . If a proportion of these doctors could qualify for registration this would assist towards raising the number of registered doctors to a level more fully commensurate with the Colony's needs, and would enable some refugees to continue to earn their living in their profession. In addition to those already mentioned there are 115 unregistrable doctors in Government service, who are exempted from registration but who it is expected would also wish to sit the proposed examination . . .

I should add that this matter has potentially embarrassing political aspects. Medically, the control envisaged is necessary. But the opposition was widespread. It was on the whole ill-informed. It has died down since the Director's speech referred to. It is however very necessary that this Government should not be open to a charge of reducing unnecessarily the medical facilities available to the poor, and it is consequently most important that this examination should be held, so as to demonstrate that the Government is prepared to go as far as possible to help – while maintaining our stand that, for the benefit of the community, we are determined to preserve the standard already set for registration.

A political complication is that the majority of the clinics connected with the right-wing Trades Union Council have unregistered doctors while the left-wing Federation of Trade Union clinics have registered doctors. Opposition came therefore particularly strongly from the right wing, which is afraid of losing politically if all the unregistered doctors are put out of business. In consonance with the present Communist tactics here of seeking on the one hand to befriend, attract and then engulf neutral and right wing personalities and organizations and on the other to embarrass and discredit the Government, the Federation of Trade Unions, although itself largely unaffected by this change in the law, has supported the campaign – with the facile but effective cry that the poor are being deprived of medical aid – and has encouraged the Trades' Union Council in its opposition to clause 27 of the new Ordinance.

The Medical Registration Bill 1957 left a legal loophole and failed since unregistered doctors could continue practicing under the name of charity clinics. Also, only a few doctors attended the examination in the late 1950s. In 1964, the government passed another act, the Medical Clinics Ordinance, to tighten the regulation and offer another examination to unregistered doctors. It found that almost half of the doctors who attended were not qualified, even though the examination standard was "extremely low."

Document 11.11: Hong Kong Government Printer, *Report of Advisory Committee on Clinics* (Hong Kong, 1966).

Subsequent to 1949, a considerable number of medical practitioners who qualified in medical colleges in China and were engaged in medical practice there came to Hong Kong. In order to assist such persons to obtain a registrable medical qualification, the Society of Apothecaries of London responded to the Hong Kong Government's invitation to conduct examinations in Hong Kong in 1958, 1959 and 1960. 177 candidates sat for these examinations and 126 were successful. The training provided prior to 1953 in 12 selected medical colleges in China was recognized as conferring eligibility to sit for the examinations . . .

The law of Hong Kong at that time was that anyone other than a registered medical practitioner or a medical practitioner deemed to be registered, might not practice medicine for gain. It was, however, open to an unregistered medical practitioner or indeed to anyone, to practise medicine provided that he did not do so for gain. As there were many unregistrable doctors available and as this legal loophole existed the result was the establishment, during the 1950s and early 1960s, of so-called charity clinics. These were opened by missionary societies, residents associations, trade unions, and other bodies; their stated object was to provide low cost medical attention for the sick poor; and they were staffed in the main by unregistered doctors with Chinese qualifications who claimed that they gave their service in an honorary capacity.

The Medical Clinics Ordinance which came into force on January 1st, 1964, provides for the registration, control and inspection of clinics employing registered medical practitioners . . . thus it is an offence for anyone to practise medicine unless he is a registered doctor or an unregistered doctor approved to practise in an exempted clinic . . .

A total of 697 applications for registration or registration with exemption were received in the period 1st January to 30th June, 1964. A total of 33 further applications were made up to 31st December, an overall total of 730 applications . . . it was discovered that many persons practising medicine in clinics and claiming to be graduates of various medical colleges in China and elsewhere were not in possession of medical diploma or certificates of any kind. Some produced photostatic copies, but were not the originals, of medical diplomas and certificates; some were in possession of testimonials as to their medical competence, identity documents stating that they were doctors, and other similar documents. Other were in possession of medical diplomas which they stated had been issued to them in China and elsewhere, but, in the absence of fully reliable information as to the recent organization of medical education in China, it was in general impossible to determine whether or not these diplomas were genuine, and if they were genuine, whether or not the holders of them had undergone a comprehensive medical education . . .

Eight hundred and twelve persons claiming to be unregistrable medical practitioners employed in clinics as on 30th June, 1964, were invited to attend for interview and 801 (614 males and 187 females) attended. 482 candidates gave satisfactory answers but the remaining 319 failed to satisfy the Panel of Specialists that they were competent to practise medicine at clinics . . . It is therefore apparent that medical students, and indeed competent and intelligent nurses and dressers, could quite easily have passed the clinical interviews and have been permitted to practise medicine at clinics. In other words the standard set by the Panel was extremely low . . .

In our view it is impracticable to make any sudden change in the control of clinics and of unregistrable medical practitioners practising medicine at them at the end of 1966. There is need for time to allow unregistrable medical practitioners an opportunity to raise their standards of medical practice, and fully to assess them as to their competence. It is also necessary, or at least very highly desirable, to give those persons at present permitted to practise medicine at clinics, but found unsuitable to continue to do so at the end of the interim period which we now recommend, time to make arrangements to earn their livelihoods in some suitable occupation . . .

Section 4. Colonial Regulation of Chinese Medicine

In 1958, the Pharmacy Board discussed the amendments to the existing Ordinance to tighten the control over regulated drugs and poisons and suggested regulating Chinese medicine. However, the Board members were concerned about the political repercussions of regulating Chinese medicine. Before the Pharmacy and Poison Ordinance, the colonial government already exempted Chinese medicine practitioners and proprietary medicine from the Undesirable Medical Advertisements, giving them a considerable edge in marketing Chinese medical products. Document 11.12 highlights the government's limited control over Chinese medicine.

Document 11.12: HKPRO, HKRS 49/1/15, Minutes of the 21st Meeting of the Pharmacy Board, 15 October 1958.

Members were informed that the Pharmaceutical Society of Hong Kong had submitted a number of amendments to the Pharmacy and Poisons Ordinance and had suggested that, after amendment, the Sections of the Ordinance be re-arranged to render it more readily comprehensible. The Chairman pointed out that it had taken the Society some four years to complete this valuable work and that acceptance of these proposals need not necessarily bring the Ordinance completely up-to-date. Members were asked to consider whether or not it was now opportune to rewrite the whole of the Ordinance and Regulations.

At this point Mr. Rowan[5] laid before the Board the following memorandum:–

"After reading through the suggested amendments to the Pharmacy and Poisons Ordinance, my impression is that it would require many more Pharmacists than are at present available to implement fully the various changes proposed. Should they be adopted by the Board and passed into law by Government, the medicine companies and manufacturers of Chinese Proprietary Medicine affected would plead that there are not enough Pharmacists to "go round" and petition His Excellency the Governor to that effect. If they can prove their case, His Excellency the Governor would wonder what the Board meant by recommending changes which could not

5. Arthur Rowan, the first president of the Hong Kong General Chamber of Pharmacy in the 1950s.

be implemented . . . to go thoroughly into the matter and consider it from all angles, since various other interests are affected by the proposed changes.

For instance, the following classes of business are vitally affected:–

1) Manufacturers of Chinese Proprietary Medicines, who have been manufacturing their products from secret recipes handed down through successive generations for countless years, without the aid of registered pharmacists. Their products are exported to various countries in South East Asia and elsewhere, earning for Hong Kong large sums of foreign exchange.

2) The large number of medicine companies, not employing pharmacists, which have been in existence for fifty years of less, to be found scattered all over Hong Kong Island, Kowloon, and the New Territories, supplying a larger proportion of the public than the dispensaries.

3) The very large number of native medicine shops, which, in their own way, do more dispensing and compounding than dispensaries, and whose art and skill are not understood by pharmacists trained in the Western style of dispensing.

The above-mentioned three classes of people have invested, in total aggregate, a huge sum of money in their undertakings and I feel sure that they will resist any changes, which are too drastic and with which, in the circumstances, they are unable to comply." . . . Mr. Rowan felt some concern . . . which would prohibit the word "drug" in connection with any business carried on unless a registered pharmacist is employed on the premises. Most of the native medicine shops are identified as "drug shops".

During discussion a member expressed the view that the Pharmacy and Poisons Ordinance related to "Western" drug and not to "Native" drug and it was intended to cater for this category only . . . Prof. Driver thought that as most of the objections appear to be applied in relation to traditional Chinese medicine, would it not be possible to provide for some kind of exemption.

Between 1972 and 1974, the colonial government received at least twenty letters from different medical agencies and individuals in Canada, the United States, South Africa, and Australia for consulting advice on acupuncture and conducting study tours of Chinese medicine in Hong Kong. Document 11.13 highlights how Hong Kong became one of many sites for foreigners to learn about Chinese medicine.

Document 11.13: HKPRO, HKRS 1394/1/47, Letter from New Zealand to the Superintendent of the Hong Kong Medical Centre, 23 November 1972.

23rd November 1972.
The Superintendent,
Hong Kong Medical Centre,
Kowloon

Dear Sir,

Just over a year ago, and two years after a hysterectomy, my wife . . . was rushed to hospital for an emergency investigation of her spine as she was in great pain. After diagnosis . . . a team of doctors . . . decided not to operate. It was their opinion that my wife showed all the signs of having had a tumor which apparently had dissolved itself. As well as her back pains which continued unabated she had a reaction to the lumbar punctures experiencing severe head noises which to this day have not abated – she has just learnt to live with them. (They are noticeable only during quiet as environment noise seems to balance out the head noises.)

For the following months after the initial investigation various doctors tried to help her, but to no avail. For instance for six weeks she attended daily by ambulances a Civilian Rehabilitation Centre which specializes in physiotherapy and physical medicine generally. There she learnt exercises for hydro therapy too. Daily swimming in a tepid pool has been part of the treatment all this year. She had traction and chiropractic treatment. Everything was done except an operation . . .

Now my reason for writing this letter is to ask your professional opinion as to whether acupunctures would seem to offer hope of recovery. I could, if you wish, arrange for Xray's to be forwarded to you and if necessary send my wife to you for treatment, because I am sure that there must be something that can be done further than our form of medical science has managed to achieve. Physically, apart from the book trouble my wife is very well and if she hadn't been strong mentally I consider that by now she would have degenerated psychologically, for believe me for the past 12 months she has endured constant and considerable pain almost without complaint . . .

I would be grateful for your advice. If you want to really show orthodox medicine that there are other ways of treatment available, this is an opportunity for my wife's case history file is sufficiently documented to show that normal treatment methods have plainly failed . . .

I will be extremely grateful if this matter is given urgent attention, and will await your reply with interest.

The 1970s marked a turning point in the history of Chinese medicine, when acupuncture became popular globally and sparked immense interest in North America. During his travels to China and Hong Kong in 1972, Arthur Steinberg, a real estate developer from the US, and his wife visited Lok Yee Kung to seek treatment for her headaches. Steinberg later invited Lok to open a temporary clinic in Nevada for treating the state legislature and eventually convinced legislators in Nevada to pass the first bill to allow the practice of Chinese medicine in the United States. The State of Nevada passed the first legislation to allow the practice of Chinese medicine in 1973.

Document 11.14: 'American Rush to Try Acupuncture', *South China Morning Post*, 5 August 1973.

Acupuncture, once regarded with heavy scepticism by American doctors, is being used widely in the western United States – particularly in California, the experimental state.

Twelve months ago, there was hardly a doctor in the country who would have agreed that acupuncture could become a popular and open practice in the United States.

Today, scientists in scores of medical schools and research institutes are exploring its uses, health insurance companies are including it in their coverage and, inevitably, a number of charlatans with long needles and dubious credentials are turning willing, wincing victims into human pincushions to small purpose.

In this highly controversial new field of medicine, the experts appear to agree on one point: that acupuncture, when properly performed, does work.

Since the Chinese have been using the technique for some 5,000 years, there should be little surprise over that – but there is, and now even state legislatures are declaring this ancient art of alleviating pain by inserting thin needles in certain parts of the body to be "a learned profession".

Those were the words used by Nevada lawmakers when, by an almost unanimous vote, they legalised acupuncture, herbal medicine and other medical practices from the East.

The State Medical Association had lobbied hard against the law, but the legislators were convinced by the expertise of Professor Lok Yee-kung of Hong Kong, warmly supported by the Madison Avenue skill of Mr Arthur Steinberg, a real estate developer from Las Vegas who is the founder and president of what he calls the American Society of Acupuncture.

Mr Steinberg says he was converted to belief in needle therapy by Professor Lok in Hong Kong last year, when treatment improved his hearing and stopped his wife's migraine headaches. But when Mr Steinberg tried to interest American physicians, he got the cold shoulder. He hired a Las Vegas advertising firm which used television commercials to such effect that the society swelled its membership to 10,000 with dues at $10 a year.

Mr Steinberg brought Professor Lok to Nevada, installing him a clinic across the street from the State Capitol in Carson City, where he treated more than 100 sufferers including half the state's 60 legislators.

"People were falling over themselves to get treatment," says a local doctor. "It was like a miniature Lourdes." Indeed, some of the reported cures did border on the miraculous. State Senator Mahlon Brown, who says Professor Lok's needlework cured an old muscle pain in his shoulder, tells of a woman who had been bed-ridden for years, yet started walking again after treatment.

"The look in that lady's eyes when she stood was enough to convince anyone."

Another state assemblyman was cured of a 20-year-old sinus condition and his delighted wife reported that it had stopped him snoring. A Bill to allow unlicensed people to perform acupuncture under the supervision of licensed doctors was vetoed recently in California by Governor Ronald Reagan; but it is perfectly legal for a physician with only the most minimal acupuncture training to use the technique as part of treatment.

Many are, and medical authorities say even more laymen are practising it illegally here.

Horror stories abound. Of the retired bank manager turned acupuncturist whose patients wince as the needle goes in (it's supposed to be painless, who gives out handbills indicating the cost of treatment (a U.S. $50 minimum), and who scratches his head with his antiseptic surgical gloves on. Or the specialist who has hired a well-known theatrical agent to advertise his newly-learned accomplishment. Or the doctor who is trying to sell an electrically-operated needle machine, allegedly smuggled out of China.

On the other hand, there is no lack of reports about acupuncture's sunny side. A score of operations have been performed at a Los Angeles clinic, including a leg operation, and a gall-bladder removal. At the University of California's Los Angeles hospital an obstetrician has used acupuncture to ease labour in a dozen difficult deliveries. Now the possibility that stimulation of certain acupuncture points may be used to induce abortions is being studied . . . American doctors also report considerable success in using acupuncture to relieve conditions like arthritis, migraine headaches and back pains.

Dr. Morton Barke, head of a Los Angeles group that runs two acupuncture clinics, says that many of his patients are "medical failures" — i.e. conventional treatments have had little result.

Suggested Readings

Barnes, Linda L. 'A World of Chinese Medicine and Healing'. In *Chinese Medicine and Healing*, edited by T. J. Hinrichs and Linda L. Barnes, 284–380. Cambridge, MA: Harvard University Press, 2013.

Baum, Emily. 'Acupuncture Anesthesia on American Bodies: Communism, Race, and the Cold War in the Making of "Legitimate" Medical Science'. *Bulletin of the History of Medicine* 95, no. 4 (2021): 497–527.

Chan, Kelvin. 'Therapeutic Governance in Hong Kong's Anti-Narcotics War, 1959–1980s'. *China Information* 38, no. 1 (2024): 44-67.

Chan, Kelvin. "Commercialising Everyday Distress: Neurasthenia and Traditional Chinese Medicine in Colonial Hong Kong, 1950s to 1980s," *Medical History*, Online First, 2024: 1-16.

Chan-Yeung, Moira M. W. *A Medical History of Hong Kong, 1942–2015*. Hong Kong: Chinese University of Hong Kong Press, 2019.

Cheung, Fanny M., Bernard W. K. Lau, and Sai-wo Wong. 'Paths to Psychiatric Care in Hong Kong'. *Culture, Medicine and Psychiatry* 8 (1984): 207-28.

Ho, Faith C. S. *Western Medicine for Chinese: How the Hong Kong College of Medicine Achieved a Breakthrough*. Hong Kong: Hong Kong University Press, 2017.

Lee, Rance P. L. 'Interaction between Chinese and Western Medicine in Hong Kong: Modernisation and Professional Inequality'. In *Medicine in Chinese Cultures: Comparative Studies of Health Care in Chinese and Other Societies*, edited by Arthur Kleinman, 219–40. Washington, DC: US Department of Health, Education and Welfare, 1975.

Peckham, Robert. 'Viral Surveillance and the 1968 Hong Kong Flu Pandemic'. *Journal of Global History* 15, no. 3 (2020): 444–58.

She, Yunchu. 醫學霸權與香港醫療制度 [*Biomedical hegemony and hong kong medical system*]. Hong Kong: Zhounghua Book Company, 2019.

Sinn, Elizabeth. *Power and Charity: The Early History of the Tung Wah Hospital, Hong Kong*. Hong Kong: Oxford University Press, 1989.

Tilley, Helen. 'Medical Cultures, Therapeutic Properties, and Laws in Global History'. *Osiris* 36 (2021): 1–24.

Topley, Marjorie. 'Chinese and Western Medicine in Hongkong: Some Social and Cultural Determinants of Variation, Interaction and Change'. In *Medicine in Chinese Cultures: Comparative Studies of Health Care in Chinese and Other Societies*, edited by Arthur Kleinman, 241–71. Washington, DC: US Department of Health, Education and Welfare, 1975.

Yip Ka-che, Wong Man-kong, and Leung Yuen-sang, eds. *A Documentary History of Public Health in Hong Kong*. Hong Kong: Chinese University of Hong Kong Press, 2018.

12
Environment and Natural Disasters

Jack Greatrex

The history of post-war Hong Kong's environment is told less often than that of its miraculous economic growth, its knotty geopolitical standing, or its own political dramas. Yet environmental issues played essential roles in shaping Hong Kong in the second half of the twentieth century and as it exists today. Hong Kong's environment has been the inescapable accompaniment of economic, social, and even political developments. Hong Kong's miracle economy entailed both environmental depredation and preservation. Amid Cold War antagonism, the decline and end of the British Empire, and transforming political consciousness, questions such as whose land was disrupted by development, where drinking water came from, and even which animal species ought to be protected carried domestic and even geopolitical weight. This chapter, therefore, intersects with, and provides background to, each and every other chapter in this volume.

This chapter explores the environmental history of post-war Hong Kong through six themes. It is designed in a deliberately expansive but thematically linked manner, proceeding via the transformations of Hong Kong's city- and sea-scapes; environmental despoliation and environmental conservation; the management of water; and the ecology of infectious disease. Environmental history is best told not through government documents alone, and so this chapter therefore includes an array of different types of sources, including visual ones such as maps and photographs. The historiographical literature on Hong Kong's environment is more scattered and diverse than for many other subjects, in-keeping with the diversity of environmental issues themselves. But in recent years important work has been written exploring such questions as land use, biodiversity, and disease ecology. This chapter serves to highlight some of these texts and their concerns, including that of Timothy Choy on 'endangerment' and Frédéric Keck on avian influenza and

Hong Kong's standing as a 'sentinel' site. Selecting sources to illustrate such a broad and diverse topic entails partiality and this chapter aims less to be comprehensive, therefore, but rather to provoke consideration of key themes and, perhaps counter-intuitive, connections.

Environments cannot be fitted easily within political borders. Hong Kong was part of a region spanning southern China and Southeast Asia which witnessed massive environmental change across these decades. Moreover, Hong Kong has long been interconnected with global systems of trade and their imbricated transformations of environments and ecosystems. The discovery by archaeologists of Persian trade goods during the construction of High Island Reservoir during the 1970s, for instance, illuminates how the area was tied into maritime trade links for centuries, witnessing movements of natural products in, out, and across the varying Chinese dynasties.[1] In the eighteenth and nineteenth centuries, the Pearl River was tied into a network of trade which fundamentally reshaped the environments of Southeast Asia and the Pacific through the exchange of such goods as sandalwood, sea cucumbers, and opium.[2] More recently, harvesting exotic fish to fill water-tanks at Hong Kong's seafood restaurants has entailed severe ecological damage in the waters of Indonesia, the Philippines, and as far as the Maldives to the west and Palau to the east.[3] This chapter is focused on Hong Kong, but this regional and global context ought to be borne in mind throughout, not least for reasons made clear at the chapter's closing.

This chapter begins with the observation that the way Hong Kong looks has undergone fundamental change across its history. Its urban space and land use have experienced repeated transformation, though often still shaped by the legacies of earlier forms. Many of the most consequential changes happened in the nineteenth century, or in the pre-Japanese Occupation decades of the early twentieth. But it was in the post-war decades that many of the most profound alterations occurred and the cityscape of Hong Kong as it exists today emerged. Three maps of the Bowrington Canal area are used to illustrate these changes and legacies.

Profound transformation characterised the urban cityscape, and so too the seascape – that is, the physical form of the city's coastline and the cultural, economic, and social activities undertaken there. As with Hong Kong's urban form, these changes come through most clearly in maps which testify in visual form to the

1. 'Archaeologists Unearth HK–Persian Connection', *South China Morning Post*, 8 May 1977. For more, see Timothy Brook, *The Troubled Empire: China in the Yuan and Ming Dynasties* (Cambridge, MA: Harvard University Press, 2010), 226–28; Thomas T. Allsen, *The Steppe and the Sea: Pearls in the Mongol Empire* (Philadelphia: University of Pennsylvania Press, 2019), 108.
2. On this trade, see John R. McNeill, 'Of Rats and Men: A Synoptic Environmental History of the Island Pacific', *Journal of World History* 5, no. 2 (1994): 320–22.
3. Greg Bankoff, *Cultures of Disaster: Society and Natural Hazard in the Philippines* (London: Routledge, 2002), 27; Celia Lowe, *Wild Profusion: Biodiversity Conservation in an Indonesian Archipelago* (Princeton, NJ: Princeton University Press, 2007), 139–41.

transforming character of the territory. The second section again, therefore, provides maps – this time of Tsing Yi and the western Kowloon coast – providing a window onto the profound transformation of Hong Kong's seascape, paralleling that of the city, as well as the shifting energy demands of Hong Kong's economic life, displacing junks for oil tankers.

Through the transforming city- and seascapes of Hong Kong, this chapter traces a history of fundamental economic transformation and growth. Yet economic growth is simultaneously a history of many consequences, which the third section begins to explore. Histories of economic growth are often histories of environmental destruction and loss at the same time. This becomes clear by turning to a site just west from Tsing Yi, along the northern Lantau coast: at the two islands, known as the Brothers (大小磨刀), just north-east of the island Chek Lap Kok (赤鱲角), now the site of Hong Kong International Airport. The Brothers are today a marine park, created in 2016 to protect the remaining population of Hong Kong's Indo-Pacific humpback dolphin (*Sousa chinensis*), often known as "pink dolphins". This attempt to protect the dolphins of the Brothers followed from public awareness that dolphins in Hong Kong were disappearing and dying, due, it was suspected, to the massive construction work on the new Airport, which had begun in 1991, amidst broader issues of coastal pollution.[4] This section, then, presents not a map but a photograph: of a beached dolphin, with a crowd looking on, amid discussion regarding the environmental costs of Hong Kong's transformations.

The founding of the marine reserve to protect these dolphins followed in the wake of extensive efforts to preserve Hong Kong's nature, which in many ways were catalysed in 1965, though with important differences between the two moments. Before 1965, there had long been enthusiastic naturalists in Hong Kong who wrote accounts of its flora, fauna, rocks, and hikes in both English and Chinese, such as Geoffrey Herklots and Yip Linfeng (葉靈鳳).[5] But there had been few sustained attempts to protect the colony's natural areas until the visit to Hong Kong of Lee and Martha Talbot, who arrived in March 1965 and produced a report for the

4. Timothy Choy, *Ecologies of Comparison: An Ethnography of Endangerment in Hong Kong* (Durham, NC: Duke University Press, 2011). This section is heavily indebted to the work of Choy, who has explored the symbolic status of the disappearing dolphin.

5. For two examples, respectively in English and Chinese, see Geoffrey Alton Craig Herklots, *The Hong Kong Countryside* (Hong Kong: South China Morning Post, 1951); Yip Linfeng 葉靈鳳, *Xianggang Fangwuzhi* 香港方物志 [Hong Kong Local Annals] (Hong Kong: Zhonghua Publishing House, 1958). For nineteenth-century reforestation efforts, albeit undertaken for very different purposes, see Robert Peckham, 'Hygienic Nature: Afforestation and the Greening of Colonial Hong Kong', *Modern Asian Studies* 49, no. 4 (July 2015): 1177–209. On Yip and other naturalists, subject of a recent exhibition in Hong Kong organised by Maxime Decaudin and others, see Ethan Paul, 'Hong Kong Owes Much of its Understanding of its Flora and Fauna to Amateur Naturalists,' *South China Morning Post*, 8 April 2021.

government in June, despite the distraction of a plane crash into the sea waters around Ma Wan island (close to Tsing Yi) in-between.[6] A system of country parks would develop in Hong Kong after the publication of the Talbots' report. The fourth section therefore presents an extract from the Talbots' work, inviting consideration of motivating forces behind natural conservation.

One key concern of the Talbots' report is hydrology: that is, water and its storage and distribution. Conservation in Hong Kong was here being driven forward by a practical concern with water and its supply to residents, businesses, and factories. Since at least the 1860s, Hong Kong suffered perpetual problems of drought during dry seasons, reaching crisis levels in 1963. Attempts to solve this problem transformed Hong Kong and its landscape. The fifth section, therefore, presents a government document produced by the Water Resources Development Committee, providing insight into the extensive works undertaken to ensure a reliable and relatively secure source of water for Hong Kong, spanning a broad array of measures – from reservoirs to desalination to water importation.

The sixth and final section is concerned with 'disease'. This may be surprising in a chapter dedicated to the 'environment and natural disasters', especially as there is already a separate chapter on health and medicine within this volume. But inclusion of this theme is well merited. Diseases do not emerge and spread in isolation: they are the products of specific environments. Infectious diseases emerge within ecological contexts – in relation to different types of animals, landscapes, and economies, that is. As many schools of medical thinking – both ancient and new – have emphasised, disease too can often be understood as a 'natural disaster' of sorts, though as much social phenomena as natural ones.[7] Hong Kong in the late twentieth century became significant to investigations of the ecology of disease. Its specific ecological context – as a hyper-connected modern city, linked simultaneously to the rest of the world and to rural and then rapidly urbanising southern China – made it so, especially in the case of epidemic influenza.

In one sense, the six themes of this chapter are disparate. Histories of dolphins are rarely simultaneously histories of flyover roads, reservoirs, and flu. But tied together, they help trace the contours of post-war Hong Kong's environment, a story of miraculous transformation, devastating loss, paradoxical preservation, and possibilities for the ecologically unexpected.

6. 'Scientists Study H. K. Wildlife', *South China Morning Post*, 10 March 1965; 'Conservation Study Completed', *South China Morning Post*, 25 June 1965.
7. One way into the rich literature on ecological understandings of disease is Linda Nash, *Inescapable Ecologies: A History of Environment, Disease, and Knowledge* (Berkeley: University of California Press, 2006).

Section 1. Cityscape

Examining a range of maps from the 1840s to the 1980s helps show the changes which occurred to Hong Kong's cityscape. Three extracts from two maps and one aerial photograph showing the Bowrington Canal area are provided here. This area sits between Wan Chai and Causeway Bay on Hong Kong Island. The first map is from 1843, in the very earliest years of the colony. At this time, the area was flat land marked for possible reclamation, though a few buildings had begun to appear around its edges. The Wong Nai Chung (黃泥涌) River, which flowed through this area to the sea, was especially consequential at this moment. This was used as a source of fresh water, encouraging early British colonisers to establish one of the island's earliest settlements close by, though disrupted by intense outbreaks of malaria.[8]

Document 12.1: Map of the Bowrington Canal Area in 1843, National Archives (United Kingdom) via hkmaps.hk, 1843, https://www.hkmaps.hk/viewer.html.

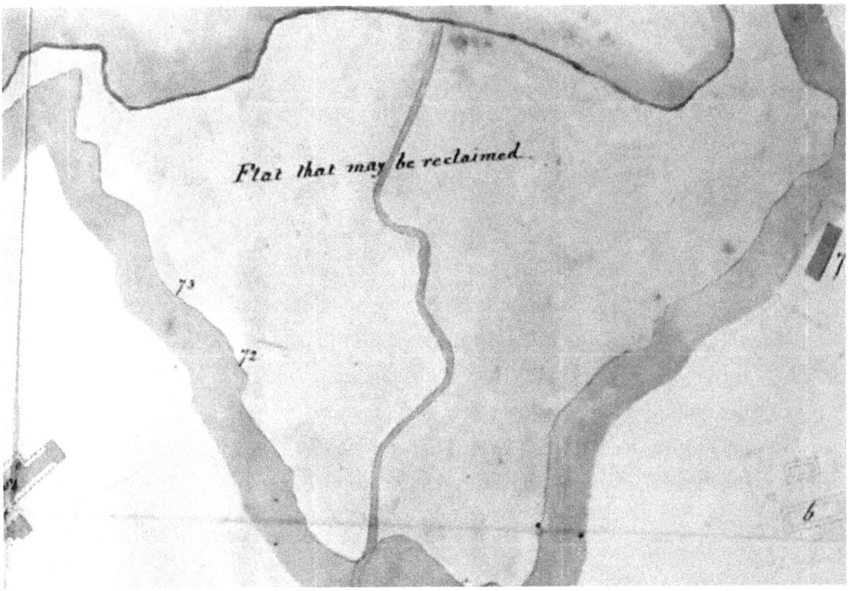

8. Christopher Cowell, 'The Hong Kong Fever of 1843: Collective Trauma and the Reconfiguring of Colonial Space', *Modern Asian Studies* 47, no. 2 (2013): 340-342.

The second map, from 1913, demonstrates the extensive changes which had already occurred by the end of the nineteenth century. The river had been canalised by 1864, with a bridge spanning it. The Hong Kong tram would pass over this bridge and be powered by the generating station close by, which burned coal provided to it by boats travelling along the canal. The earlier emptiness of the seafront flats has been replaced by dense blocks of buildings, and the snaking river has been disciplined into the rigid line of the canal.[9]

Document 12.2: Map of the Bowrington Canal area in 1913, National Library of Australia via hkmaps.hk, 1913, https://www.hkmaps.hk/viewer.html.

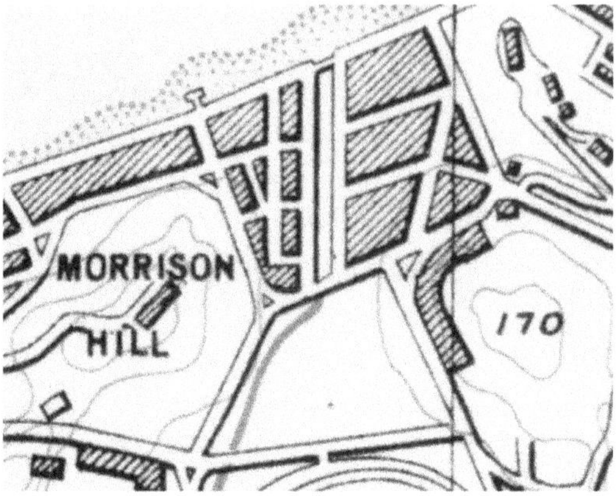

By the 1980s the area had transformed fundamentally once again. By the time this aerial photograph was taken in 1982, the Bowrington Canal had been decked over due to pollution in 1964 and turned into a subterranean conduit.[10] *The Canal Road Flyover, opened in 1972 and connecting to the cross-harbour tunnel, now runs along the path of the former canal. Dense buildings line the streets and even the shoreline has changed, the area having been reclaimed from the sea and claimed for automobiles. Though the very name 'Canal Road' points to how older versions of the city continue to be layered into the current-day urban form.*

9. For more on the Bowrington Canal, see Hugh Farmer, 'Hong Kong Tramways—Bowrington Canal Depot', Industrial History of Hong Kong Group, https://industrialhistoryhk.org/hong-kong-tramways-bowrington-canal-generating-station/. A new wave of Hong Kong history is being written online, on websites such as that of the Industrial History Group. Their inclusion in this chapter is deliberate, pointing to this emerging resource for historians.
10. "How Canal Road Got Its Name," *South China Morning Post*, 8 July 1972.

Document 12.3: Aerial photograph of the Bowrington Canal Area in 1982, 1982.1 map, gov.data.hk via hkmaps.hk, https://www.hkmaps.hk/viewer.html.

Section 2. Seascape

Here are two excerpts from maps which together show a seascape in flux. The first dates from 1945, just after the Japanese Occupation. It depicts the island of Tsing Yi (青衣) and the coastline of Kwai Chung (葵涌) in western Kowloon. In one sense, the image is deceptive. Though it appears empty here, Tsing Yi was inhabited. Oral histories explain that those living there engaged in many traditional trades, involving the harnessing of mostly organic and local forms of energy. As early as the Song dynasty, Tsing Yi had possibly hosted coastal salt-farming.[11] *Around the time this map was produced, patches of forest were maintained on the island, while hillsides were used for the collection of grasses to burn, including by grass harvesters visiting from Hong Kong Island and Kowloon.*[12] *On Tsing Yi, grass was sometimes burned at night to attract fish, which were then caught from the boats on the water.*[13] *So too was grass employed in the major local industry lime production, in the island's probable three to five limekilns.*[14] *Along with the grass harvested from the island, the lime was produced from the clam shells, oyster shells, and coral*

11. Cecile Kung, 'Guanfu Salt Farm and Hong Kong in the Song Dynasty (960–1279), *Social Transformations in Chinese Societies* 17, no. 1 (2020): 59.
12. W. Schofield, 'The Islands Around Hong Kong', *Journal of the Hong Kong Branch of the Royal Asiatic Society* 23 (1983): 94; David Faure, 'Notes on the History of Tsuen Wan', *Journal of the Hong Kong Branch of the Royal Asiatic Society* 24 (1984): 82.
13. Faure, 'Notes on the History of Tsuen Wan', 81.
14. Schofield, 'The Islands Around Hong Kong', 94–96; Tak-yan Wong, 'Lime-Making on Tsing Yi', *Journal of the Hong Kong Branch of the Royal Asiatic Society* 24 (1984): 295–96 and 299.

heads, transported to the island from off the coasts of Yuen Long and Sai Kung.[15] *Junks would have travelled historically past Tsing Yi as they transported the sewage from public latrines in Hong Kong from a collection point on Stonecutters Island, immediately to its south, to Shun Tak, further along the Pearl River Delta, for use manuring the mulberry trees on which silkworms fed.*[16]

By switching from Tsing Yi across to the other side of the Rambler Channel, however, portents of massive change are to be seen. The traditional economy of Tsing Yi had been characterised by the use of low-carbon-intensive natural products: grass, shells, lime, fish, corals, and nightsoil. But across the channel, new infrastructures of carbon-intensive forms of energy were being inaugurated. A depot for the American oil company Texaco was founded at Kwai Chung, in the harbour leading out to Tsing Yi, at least as early as 1931, with its opening greeted with the promised arrival of the largest-ever diesel tanker delivering petroleum to the site.[17]

Document 12.4: Excerpt of map from 1945 showing Tsing Yi and the Rambler Channel, Map 1945.1, hkmaps.hk, https://www.hkmaps.hk/viewer.html.

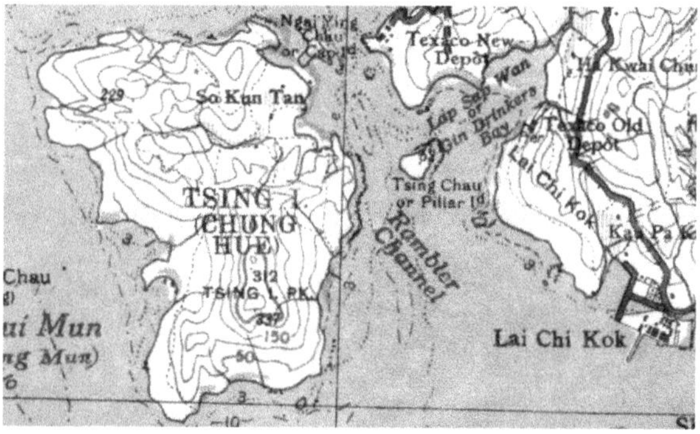

Whereas the map from 1945 shows a seascape in flux, the map from 1974 shows it completely transformed. The most extensive transformation had by this time occurred on the Kowloon coastline. Extensive land reclamation had been undertaken, wholly destroying Tsing Chau island in the process. The area had begun to emerge as a port for container shipping – a process which by this time had transformed shorelines around the world,

15. Wong, 'Lime-Making on Tsing Yi', 296.
16. Yuk-sik Chong, *Toilet as Business for the Hygiene of the Chinese Community in Colonial Hong Kong* (Singapore: Springer, 2022), 94.
17. 'Texaco's New Oil Installation', *South China Morning Post*, 7 May 1931.

revolutionising port cities.[18] *Note here how the curved line of the coast has been disciplined into the straight line of the port. The Tsing Yi and Kwai Chung of lime and junks has been supplanted by a new era of oil and container ship.*

Document 12.5: Excerpt of map from 1974 showing Tsing Yi and the Rambler Channel, 'Map 1974', available online via hkmaps.hk, https://www.hkmaps.hk/viewer.html.

Section 3. Loss

From the early 1990s, photographs of dead dolphins began appearing in Hong Kong's newspapers. The remains of the deceased animals were washing up on beaches or floating dead in the sea. In a photograph published in the South China Morning Post *in the summer of 1994, reproduced here, the beached mammal lies on the sand of Big Wave Bay, while a crowd has gathered to examine it – in the foreground, a girl points at the dolphin's corpse, left incongruously stranded on the summertime beach. Though not itself specifically one of the Pearl River pink dolphins, the photograph symbolises this moment of public concern with the beached animals. In other photographs, dead dolphins float belly-upward near Tai O (1995) and lie open-mouthed in a patch of grass on Lantau (1996).*[19]

18. 'The Development of Containerization at the Port of Hong Kong', Industrial History of Hong Kong Group, https://industrialhistoryhk.org/development-containerization-port-hong-kong/.
19. 'Corpse on Beach Sparks Fears for Pink Dolphins', *South China Morning Post*, 22 May 1996, 5; 'UN Seeks Report as Dolphin Found Dead', *South China Morning Post*, 5 May 1995, 5.

Photographs like these sharpened public awareness of the fate of Hong Kong's dolphins and, by extension, of Hong Kong's changing nature. Deceased dolphins found stranded on beaches helped make immediately visible how Hong Kong's success was paralleled by pollution and environmental despoliation. The cause of the dolphins was taken up by environmental pressure groups in Hong Kong, especially the World Wildlife Fund (WWF). Activism led to the government of Hong Kong consulting experts in 1993, commissioning studies undertaken by the Swire Institute of Marine Science, and, in 1996, founding Hong Kong's first Marine Park.[20] *The deaths of the dolphins, revealed to the public in discomforting fashion via newspaper photographs such as this one, thereby helped catalyse environmental activism, symbolising public anxiety over 'a threat to something uniquely Hong Kong'.*[21]

Document 12.6: 'Dead Dolphin Washed Ashore at Big Wave Bay', *South China Morning Post*, 18 July 1994, 6.

Section 4. Conservation

What follows is text from the report of the Talbots, beginning with the end of their document – wherein the naturalists stress the urgency of nature conservation in Hong Kong, on the eve of what they warned would be irreparable loss.[22] *For readers of this chapter, this urgency ought to be unsurprising in light of the profound transformations to the cityscape and seascape described above. The document is worth paying close attention to, however, not least in hinting at all the different motives for why nature would be conserved in Hong Kong.*

20. Choy, *Ecologies of Comparison*, 28–29.
21. Choy, *Ecologies of Comparison*, 31.
22. Lee Talbot and Martha H. Talbot, *Conservation of the Hong Kong Countryside: Summary Report and Recommendation* (Hong Kong: Agriculture and Fisheries Department, 1965), 23.

Document 12.7: Excerpt from Lee Talbot and Martha H. Talbot, *Conservation of the Hong Kong Countryside: Summary Report and Recommendation* (Hong Kong: Agriculture and Fisheries Department, 1965).

The impression one gains from many meetings with those concerned with development in Hong Kong is one of urgency and pressure. Flying over the Colony, and driving through it, one is struck by the apparent rapidity of development—new factories, roads with ribbon development, houses, shacks—and with the disorganization apparent in the development. Considering the rate of population increase, the limited land, and the political and economic pressures, it is apparent that if the open space values of the countryside are to be realized to establish an organized system of parks, reserves and recreation areas, the action will have to be taken promptly. Further, development plans are now being made for the Colony. Consequently, if something is not done quickly to establish a park system, the opportunity may be lost forever.

Starting at the end, it is then worth flipping forward in the Talbots' report, to the description of the conserved areas which they wished to see established in Hong Kong. Here is the Talbots' list as follows:

(a) **Hong Kong Island.** One or more relatively small areas in the better wooded catchments, especially in the Tai Tam system for strict nature reserves. These could be bounded on the lower edge by limited access reserves for school children, and such a reserve is appropriate above Aberdeen.

(b) **Stonecutters' Island.** Careful protection from fire and cutting has resulted in the growth on this island of the richest flora and fauna we have seen in the Colony. As such it is of great value and deserves recognition as a strict nature reserve—one of the most valuable such in Hong Kong—although the protection afforded it by the military is doubtless the most complete it could receive.

(c) **Mai Po Marshes** and the associated fish ponds contain a rich bird life. An area of mudflat and mangrove swamp should be protected as a strict nature reserve, and an adjacent and larger area of the fish ponds could be a limited access, no hunting reserve.

(d) **Mountain peaks.** Several of the taller mountains in the Colony are of significant ecological interest, and have a distinct and interesting flora and fauna. At the same time there is relatively little competition for these areas from other forms of land use, except for the R.A.F. station on Tai Mo Shan, which can be a positive influence in limiting visitor access. The outstanding peaks which deserve

reserve status include Tai Mo Shan, Ma On Shan (the north and east faces especially) and Lantau Peak, although other lower peaks are also appropriate.

(e) **Jubilee catchment.** The Fung Shui grove at the head of present reservoir. Also the upper part of one of the valleys running into the head of the reservoir from Tai Mo Shan.

(f) **Tai Lam Chung catchment.** A study area could be established including one of the afforested slopes and an adjacent eroded one.

(g) **Other areas** that deserve consideration include some of the secluded highlands north of Tolo Harbour, between Kowloon and Ma On Shan, and on the Sai Kung Peninsula; an unoccupied beach-bay on the south east side of Sai Kung Peninsula or on an adjacent island; an appropriate marine area in Port Shelter or Rocky Harbour; — possibly Sharp Island and the water around it; a part of the western end of Lantau Island, and Basalt Island.

This list testifies to the multiple pressures driving nature conservation in the mid-sixties. One was a genuine concern with ecology and nature. The Talbots convened with Patricia Marshall at the University of Hong Kong, a zoologist and expert on the ecology of Hong Kong. So too they consulted John Dudley Romer, a Pest Control Officer who wrote with intense enthusiasm about Hong Kong's snakes and frogs and even made early records of its dolphins. This desire for natural and scientific conservation might be seen in the Talbots' recommendations to preserve Stonecutters Island and the Mai Po marshes.

Simultaneously, this document fitted the need to mitigate the political pressures of mid-sixties Hong Kong. Nature preservation might be conceived here almost as a safety valve for a colony with a growing population potentially threatening to its politically inequitable status quo. Note in this context the emphasis on recreation – such as the reserve at Aberdeen. At the same time, the document here exposes its different historical moment to that of the activism regarding dolphins in the 1990s. It was hardly the case that there were no popular protests regarding Hong Kong's changing landscape prior to the 1990s. The transformation of the landscape of Tsing Yi, which we have seen above, sparked protests regarding the destruction of feng shui woods, for instance.[23] *Yet the list of those consulted for the Talbots' document comprised largely expatriates in governmental service. The contrast between the 1965 work of the Talbots and the 1990s dolphin activism tracks the changing political nature of Hong Kong.*

Alongside the ecological and political considerations of the Talbots' report, another important theme runs throughout. Note the prevalence of hydrological concerns in the

23. James Hayes, 'Local Reactions to the Disturbance of "Fung Shui" on Tsing Yi Island, Hong Kong, September 1977 – March 1978', *Journal of the Hong Kong Branch of the Royal Asiatic Society* 19 (1979): 213–16.

Talbots' recommendations. The Tai Tam, Tai Lam Chung, Aberdeen, and Jubilee (Shing Mun) reserved areas were all relatively green spots surrounding reservoirs and catchment areas. At the same time, the Talbots consulted with P. R. Helliwell and A. S. Robertson, both of whom worked for the Water Authority, the former as the colony's hydrologist. Conservation in Hong Kong was here being driven forward by a practical concern with water and its supply to residents, businesses, and factories. Since at least 1953, afforestation work had been undertaken at such sites as the Tai Lam Chung Reservoir in order to protect the supply of water. Concerns with water—following on from concerns for industry, and for popular unrest—were here driving concerns to make Hong Kong greener.

Section 5. Water

In May 1978, the Governor of Hong Kong approved the recommendations of the Water Resources Development Committee (W. R. D. C.) for an eight-pronged approach to Hong Kong's supply of water. The list of eight recommendations appears in Document 12.8.

Document 12.8: HKPRO, HKRS 394/29/94, Excerpt from 'Preliminary Appraisal on Future Increase of Supply from China', W.R.D.C. Water Resources Development Committee, Hong Kong Public Records Office, 1–12.

(a) Water from China should no longer be considered as "unreliable",

(b) Chinese authorities should be approached to establish the extent to which they were prepared to meet Hong Kong's future demand for water, and

(c) the feasibility of

— joint production of water and electricity,

— re-use of water of sub-standard quality,

— desalting by reverse osmosis processes,

— construction of bulk storage reservoirs,

— maximisation of the potential capacity of the extension to Lok On Pai desalter, and

— transformation of Tolo Harbour into an enclosed lake as a water resource should be investigated.

This eightfold set of measures was extraordinary by world standards. Some of the recommendations, such as desalination by reverse osmosis and the transformation of a coastal

harbour into a reservoir, were at the cutting edge of technological feasibility at the time. They came after decades of transformative change to Hong Kong's hydrology – dating back to the construction of Pokfulam Reservoir (1860) and passing through the founding of Aberdeen, Tai Tam, Kowloon, Shing Mun, Tai Lam Chung, Shek Pik, Plover Cove, and High Island reservoirs, with enormous catchwater systems, some of which would become the basis for the later country parks.

What explains the array? Desperation, in part. Hong Kong's seasonality threatens droughts during dry periods, with potentially devastating effects on industry and the threat of popular unrest. Serious droughts struck in 1963 and 1967, as Florence Mok describes in an earlier chapter. Extensive and expensive infrastructural systems followed on from the desperate need to avoid future droughts. Hedging serves as the second explanation: the array of measures is explicable through a desire to avoid dependence on any single source. Especially, Cold War tensions made importation of water from across the mainland Chinese border from Guangdong potentially vulnerable in the eyes of Government. While water was imported systematically from 1960, and especially after the East River Scheme agreement in 1964, the colonial state hedged against geopolitical risk with a profusion of other measures – reservoirs, such as at High Island, and even desalination.[24]

This specific source comes from a very particular moment. By the late seventies, after the immediate tensions of the Cultural Revolution period had come to an end, the uncertainties of importing water from Guangdong were decreasing, leading first to the recommendation to the Governor that mainland water was no longer to be considered 'unreliable' and, a few years later on, to the dissolution of the Water Resources Development Committee itself in 1982. This source was created at a moment of transformative change, in which the array of measures for obtaining water were being reassessed after decades in which Cold War tension had played a decisive factor.

If this source prompts consideration of the reasons for the broad array of measures taken to ensure Hong Kong's water supply, then so too does it help reveal the deep transformation of postwar Hong Kong. In order to service the city's residents, businesses, and factories, even remote areas of Hong Kong had been transformed — as with Sai Kung for the High Island

24. By contrast to other neglected areas of Hong Kong's environmental history, there is now excellent literature on its water, to which this section points. In particular, see Dorothy Tang, 'Local Reservoirs and Chinese Aqueducts: The Politics of Water Security in Hong Kong', *Infrastructure and the Remaking of Asia*, ed. Till Mostowlansky and Max Hirsh (Honolulu: University of Hawai'i Press, 2022), 110–33 on Hong Kong's connections with Guangdong and infrastructural transformation; David Clayton, 'The Roots of Regionalism: Water Management in Postwar Hong Kong', in *From a British to a Chinese Colony?*, ed. Gary Luk (Berkeley: University of California Press, 2018), 166–86; and Jack Greatrex and Florence Mok, 'Catchwater Colonialism: Reshaping Hong Kong's Hydrology, Infrastructure, Metabolism and Landscape, 1937-1968,' *Urban History* (2024), on intra-Hong Kong transformations and the links spanning city-reservoir-country park-and-prison.

Reservoir. Salt water had become a manipulable resource for the city via the desalter. Distant rivers and catchments had become sources too, including those of Guangdong. The conjoint imperatives of desperation and hedging in the search for domestic, commercial, and industrial water transformed Hong Kong's use of water, connecting even distant reaches to the industrial centre in important ways.

Section 6. Disease

Document 12.9 is a selectively edited excerpt from the 1982 Lancet *article 'An Influenza Epicentre?', published following a conference held at the University of Hong Kong on the subject of influenza in southern China. Quotations are included here, to be explored in greater depth below. This text was written by Kennedy F. Shortridge and Charles Stuart-Harris. Shortridge was based at the University of Hong Kong for three decades between 1972 and 2002, working in the Department of Microbiology and, in 1981, becoming a chair professor of virology.[25] In the influential work of Shortridge and Stuart-Harris, Hong Kong came to occupy a prominent and very specific position. Hong Kong served as a 'sentinel', in the words of one scholar. Its specific ecological position, linking together the transforming agrarian ecology of southern China and the broader world, made it a site where pandemics might emerge and spread, but also where they might be identified and described.[26]*

Document 12.9: Excerpt from Kennedy F. Shortridge and C. H. Stuart-Harris, 'An Influenza Epicentre?', *Lancet* 2, no. 8302 (October 1982): 812–13. Reproduced with permission of Elsevier.

INTERESTED workers in virology, animal husbandry, veterinary medicine, and public health met in April, 1982, in Hong Kong to consider the ecology of influenza. The group examined some features of human and animal life in Hong Kong and the southern regions of China where epidemics of influenza A caused by viruses with novel surface antigens… have arisen and have spread as pandemics throughout the world. Such outbreaks include the Asian pandemic of 1957 (H2N2), the "Hong Kong" epidemic of 1968 (H3N2), and possibly the recirculating H1N1 outbreaks of 1977 onwards…

25. For an overview of Shortridge's career, see Robert G. Webster, Yi Guan, and Malik Peiris, 'Kennedy F. Shortridge PhD (April 6, 1941 to November 8, 2020): Obituary', *Influenza and Other Respiratory Viruses* 15, no. 3 (May 2021): 324.
26. Frédéric Keck, 'Liberating Sick Birds: Poststructuralist Perspectives on the Biopolitics of Avian Influenza', *Cultural Anthropology* 30, no. 2 (25 May 2015): 224–35, https://doi.org/10.14506/ca30.2.05.

The densely populated, intensively farmed area of southern China adjacent to Hong Kong is an ideal place for events such as interchange of viruses between host species. The diversity of avian influenza viruses that circulate in the domestic poultry of this region suggests that it may be important as a point of origin of pandemic viruses.

FARMING SYSTEMS IN CHINA

Much of the vast area of China is mountainous, and the small proportion of arable land has to support a huge human population, which is particularly great in coastal areas such as Guangdong province next to Hong Kong. Thus, only 7% of the world's arable land supports 23% of the world's population. The agricultural practices in China . . . have developed from the need to feed the people as efficiently as possible, using all available resources, and with little recourse to modern farming methods . . .

The population of the southern areas of China is approximately 1000 per square kilometre even in areas of intense cultivation. To satisfy the need for rice, the main cereal of the south, farmers rely on age-old techniques to reduce effort and cost. They make use of the food preferences of domestic ducks which help protect the growing rice from insect and shellfish pests and carry out weeding, intercultivation, and manuring. This practice reduces farmers' dependence on chemical insecticides, herbicides, fertilisers, and mechanical farming aids and provides a close bird/water/rice/man association that varies with the seasons of rice-growing. Ducks are raised chiefly in the summer in association with rice-growing, and the greatest number of influenza-virus isolations have been made from domestic poultry of the region during summer also. Most of these viruses were isolated from ducks rather than from land-based chickens and partially aquatic geese.

THE FUTURE

The remarkable advances in molecular biology have given us the ability to detect antigenic and genetic variation of influenza viruses with precision, but even a technique as sensitive as oligonucleotide mapping merely underlines the genetic complexity and diversity among the avian isolates from the region. Meanwhile, an important issue that remains to be resolved is whether the clue to influenza variation really does lie in domestic animals. If it does, is the closeness of man and animals in the long-established ecosystems of southern China the important factor in the emergence of pandemic strains? Continued efforts to understand these inter-relations are clearly justified if the hypothesis that southern China is an influenza epicentre is to be supported.

Shortridge's specialism was influenza – in particular, he studied the emergence of different strains of influenza from zoonotic reservoirs into the human population, with the potential to become pandemics.[27] *'Zoonosis' refers to diseases which transmit from animals to humans. 'Reservoirs' in this sense refers to animal populations in which a disease circulates. 'Pandemics' hardly needs defining for readers of this sourcebook who have lived through the three years of the Covid-19 pandemic which preceded its publication. Shortridge's career was concerned with the specific ecological relations – the 'bird/water/rice/man association', as described in this article – which allowed influenza to emerge as a zoonotic danger from bird and pig populations, threatening human life and wellbeing both in Hong Kong and in the wider world. In particular, Shortridge in this document is explaining how influenza potentially emerges from the specific agricultural practices of southern China. Ducks, as he describes, are used in rice farming to control pests. Their close proximity to humans, other poultry, and domestic pigs creates opportunities for viruses to switch between these different species, in the process mutating and swapping genetic material and developing new strains with greater capacity to infect animals and people.*

This document is written in part with an eye to the past. It references the influenza pandemic of 1968, which became known as the 'Hong Kong Flu'. The disease had reached Hong Kong from southern China in the summer of 1968, infecting an estimated 15 per cent of the population, before travelling elsewhere in the world – including the United States, where by February 1969 it had killed some 100,000 people.[28] *So too did it express a concern with the future. In 1997, avian influenza did appear in Hong Kong. An initial outbreak occurred from late March to early May, just prior to the handover in August. A second outbreak occurred shortly after, in November and December.*[29] *Eighteen people were infected across the year, with six dying.*[30] *The infections posed the threat of another worldwide outbreak, such as that of 1968: as Shortridge wrote in 1999, 'the question arose after the fatal index case in May whether a new pandemic was in the offing'.*[31] *Infectious disease in this manner entailed attention to the ecology of Hong Kong and its region: thinking about disease meant thinking about ducks, pigs, farms, markets, people, airports, and more.*

---

27. Webster, Yi, and Peiris, 'Kennedy F. Shortridge', 324.
28. Robert Peckham, 'Viral Surveillance and the 1968 Hong Kong Flu Pandemic', *Journal of Global History* 15, no. 3 (November 2020): 448–51, https://doi.org/10.1017/S1740022820000224.
29. Kennedy F. Shortridge, 'Poultry and the Influenza H5N1 Outbreak in Hong Kong, 1997: Abridged Chronology and Virus Isolatio', *Vaccine* 17 (30 July 1999): S26.
30. Shortridge, 'Poultry and the Influenza H5N1 Outbreak', S26.
31. Shortridge, 'Poultry and the Influenza H5N1 Outbreak', S26.

Conclusion

Across these six themes, the environment of post-war Hong Kong has been seen in profound transformation. The 'Great Acceleration' is a term often used to describe changes to the world economy and environment post-1945. It fits Hong Kong perfectly. Transformation was deep and extensive: a mudflat became the Bowrington Canal then a flyover for automobiles. Oil terminals and container ports at Tsing Yi and Kwai Chung replaced the older lime kilns, grass fires, and nightsoil junks. These are only two examples which could be replicated across almost all of Hong Kong in one manner or another.

Profound transformations entailed extensive effects. Profit, wealth, and lifespans grew drastically alongside environmental transformation. But there was destruction too – environmental loss, pollution, contamination. If maps show the transformation of the seascape, then photographs of the beached dead dolphins show possible devastating effects.

Loss drove protection too, however. Photographs of dead dolphins galvanised activism to save them. Popular concerns in the 1990s would culminate in the founding of marine parks to defend dolphin habitat. The marine parks themselves followed in the train of attempts since the mid-1960s to conserve Hong Kong's green spaces through country parks and reserved areas. Not discounting losses, counter-intuitively Hong Kong in 1997 was likely greener than in 1945.

Massive change drove both loss and protection. At the same time, just as the Great Acceleration galvanised the movement of capital and commodities, so too did it open up rapid velocities for other, less expected things. Hong Kong across this period was hyper-mobile – think of the connections on the map from the Kwai Chung container port, for instance. But mobility for containers meant simultaneous mobility for microorganisms. Influenza, as we saw in the last source, and later other pathogens were part of Hong Kong's post-war environmental story, unwelcome attendants to the flows of people and goods. Hong Kong's post-war Great Acceleration, traced here through the work of cartographers, photographers, waterworks officials, and scientists, created miraculous accomplishments, devastating loss, paradoxical preservation, and openings for the unexpected.

Suggested Readings

Boyden, Stephen, K. Milar, and B. O'Neil. *The Ecology of a City and Its People: The Case of Hong Kong*. Canberra: Australian National University Press, 1981.

Choy, Timothy. *Ecologies of Comparison: An Ethnography of Endangerment in Hong Kong*. Durham, NC: Duke University Press, 2011.

Ho, Pui-yin. *Making Hong Kong: A History of Its Urban Development*. Cheltenham: Edward Elgar Publishing, 2018.

Keck, Frédéric. *Avian Reservoirs: Virus Hunters and Birdwatchers in Chinese Sentinel Posts*. Durham, NC: Duke University Press, 2020.

Owen, Bernie, and Raynor Shaw. *Hong Kong Landscapes: Shaping the Barren Rock*. Hong Kong: Hong Kong University Press, 2007.

Peckham, Robert. 'Viral Surveillance and the 1968 Hong Kong Flu Pandemic'. *The Journal of Global History* 15, no. 3 (2020): 444–58.

13
Gender and Family

Carol C. L. Tsang[1]

Debates revolving around gender equality in Hong Kong have always intersected with family politics. The early colony was overwhelmingly male.[2] According to the census of 1853, there were 876 European men and 28,928 Chinese men in Hong Kong, but only 411 European women and 8,608 Chinese women.[3] By the late nineteenth century, Hong Kong had transformed from a transient to a more stable colony. As more women settled there and had children, family welfare became a vital subject of effective governance. Maternity institutions including the Victoria Hospital for Women and Children (founded in 1903), the Alice Memorial Maternity Hospital (founded in 1904), and the Tsan Yuk Hospital (founded in 1922) sprang up to provide obstetric and gynaecological services.[4] Chinese elites established the

---

1. I would like to thank Alison So, Allan Pang, Henry Choi, Phoebe Tang, and Yeung Chuk for their feedback on the earlier draft of this chapter. My thanks also go to the Family Planning Association of Hong Kong (FPAHK), the Hong Kong Family Welfare Society (HKFWS), and the Hong Kong Society for the Protection of Children (HKSPC) for granting permission to reproduce their publications.
2. Gender and family are important concepts that illuminate social relations. Gender roles and stereotypes are often acquired in the domestic sphere. The family serves as a critical site that drives gender equality. Gender refers to the attributes associated with women and men. A social construct, gender can vary across time and cultures. Family refers to people sharing a household who are usually connected by blood, marriage, or adoption. In most societies, the family is a basic unit of organisation. Major scholarship on gender and family in Hong Kong adopt anthropological and sociological approaches to advocate fair treatment of the sexes. See, for example, Jane Lewis, 'Regulation: Family and Gender', in *International Encyclopedia of Social and Behavioral Sciences*, ed. N. J. Smelser and P. B. Baltes (San Diego, CA: Elsevier Science & Technology, 2001); Scott Coltrane and Michele Adams, *Gender and Families* (Lanham, MD: Rowman & Littlefield Publishers, 2008).
3. 'Hong Kong', *Hong Kong Government Gazette* (Hong Kong: Government Printer, 1853), 89.
4. Moira M. W. Chan-Yeung, *A Medical History of Hong Kong* (Hong Kong: Chinese University of Hong Kong Press, 2018).

Po Leung Kuk (founded in 1878) and the Hong Kong Society for the Protection of Children (founded in 1929) to support destitute children and mediate family disputes.[5] By the end of the Second World War, the issues of gender relations and family welfare were too important to be ignored. Hong Kong's reconstruction depended on restoring family ties and advancing gender equality.

The early literature on gender and family depicts women as underprivileged subjects, specifically in debates over mui-tsai, concubinage, and prostitution.[6] Recent works have shifted their lens to women's growing agency in education and paid work and its contribution to their improved family status.[7] Above all, scholars in anthropology and sociology have demonstrated how colonial politics and Chinese patriarchy intersected in the family, generating multiple levels of privileges and inequalities.[8] Marriage, childbirth, and childrearing were major sites in which women and men negotiated pre-existing gender norms.[9] Adopting a mix of quantitative and qualitative methods, scholars have shown how the changes in political and legal infrastructures led to a paradigm shift in women's position after the Second World War.[10]

5. Elizabeth Sinn, 'Chinese Patriarchy and the Protection of Women in 19th-Century Hong Kong', in *Women and Chinese Patriarchy: Submission, Servitude and Escape*, ed. Maria Jaschok and Suzanne Miers (Hong Kong: Hong Kong University Press, 1994), 141–70.
6. See, for example, Maria Jaschok and Suzanne Miers, *Women and Chinese Patriarchy: Submission, Servitude and Escape* (Hong Kong: Hong Kong University Press, 1994); James L. Watson and Rubie S. Watson, *Village Life in Hong Kong: Politics, Gender, and Ritual in the New Territories* (Hong Kong: Chinese University of Hong Kong Press, 2004).
7. See, for example, Patricia Chiu, '"A Position of Usefulness": Gendering History of Girls' Education in Colonial Hong Kong (1850s–1890s)', *History of Education* 37, no. 6 (2008): 789–805; Staci Ford, 'Women, Gender, and HKU', in *An Impossible Dream: Hong Kong University from Foundation to Re-establishment, 1910–1950*, ed. Kit-ching Chan Lau and Peter Cunich (Hong Kong: Oxford University Press, 2002), 119–38; Anita Kit-wa Chan, 'From "Civilising the Young" to a "Dead-End Job": Gender, Teaching, and the Politics of Colonial Rule in Hong Kong (1841–1970)', *History of Education* 41, no. 4 (2012): 495–514; Elizabeth Sinn, 'Women at Work: Chinese Brothel Keepers in Nineteenth-Century Hong Kong', *Journal of Women's History* 19, no. 3 (2007): 87–111; Eliza Wing Yee Lee, *Gender and Change in Hong Kong: Globalization, Postcolonialism, and Chinese Patriarchy* (Vancouver: UBC Press, 2003); Janet W. Salaff, *Working Daughters of Hong Kong: Filial Piety or Power in the Family?* (New York: Columbia University Press, 1995); Helen F. Siu, *Merchants' Daughters: Women, Commerce, and Regional Culture in South China* (Hong Kong: Hong Kong University Press, 2010).
8. Anita Kit-wa Chan and Wong Wai-ling, *Gendering Hong Kong* (Hong Kong: Oxford University Press, 2004).
9. See, for example, Veronica Pearson and Benjamin K. P. Leung, *Women in Hong Kong* (Hong Kong: Oxford University Press, 1995); Max W. L. Wong, *Chinese Marriage and Social Change: The Legal Abolition of Concubinage in Hong Kong* (Singapore: Springer, 2020).
10. See, for example, Fanny M. Cheung, *Engendering Hong Kong Society: A Gender Perspective of Women's Status* (Hong Kong: Chinese University of Hong Kong Press, 1997); Fanny M. Cheung and Eleanor Holroyd, *Mainstreaming Gender in Hong Kong Society* (Hong Kong: Chinese University of Hong Kong Press, 2009).

This chapter builds on existing scholarship and shows how gender and family overlapped, complemented, and contested each other at critical moments in Hong Kong history. Population policies, land reforms, and wage laws substantially altered gender roles and family dynamics.[11] Poverty relief reallocated family resources and generated new expectations for women and men in the household. The notion of gender equality that legislators upheld was often rejected to 'preserve family tradition'.[12] The dynamic influence of gender and family provides unique insights into marital relations, fertility preferences, and the division of household labour in Hong Kong.[13] Using primary sources, this chapter explores how the government, elites, and ordinary people regulated and redefined gender roles and family structures in response to population explosion (see Chapter 10, 'Migration'), the economic boom (see Chapter 4, 'Economy and Trade'), and changing geopolitics around Hong Kong after 1945. The government and non-governmental organisations (NGOs) provided daily necessities to families, specifically working-class Chinese households. In so doing, they promoted and sustained the heteronormative nuclear family structure, which remains prevalent in Hong Kong today. Meanwhile, legislators and feminists strove to advance women's status in the family and at work by pursuing reforms. Ordinances for equal pay, maternity leave, monogamy, and expansion of female inheritance rights in the New Territories are shining examples. Men were asked to do their share of housework and childcare. Ordinary people, as the chapter shows, were not passive recipients of welfare. Many confronted and negotiated the family ideals promoted by the authorities as they constructed their desired version of family.

The chapter is organised thematically. Section 1 examines how the government and NGOs rebuilt the notion of family amid the refugee influx after 1949 and the increased contact between Hong Kong and the mainland before the handover. Documents 13.1–13.3 show how the Hong Kong Family Welfare Society (HKFWS), the Hong Kong Society for the Protection of Children (HKSPC), and the Family Planning Association of Hong Kong (FPAHK) offered food, shelter, contraceptives, and counselling services to Chinese refugee families entering Hong Kong in the early post-war years. Document 13.4 explores how cross-border families, mostly

11. See, for example, Annie Hau-nung Chan and Lawrence Ka-ki Ho, *Women in the Hong Kong Police Force* (London: Palgrave Macmillan, 2017).

12. See, for example, Sally Engle Merry and Rachel E. Stern, 'The Female Inheritance Movement in Hong Kong: Theorizing the Local/Global Interface', *Current Anthropology* 46, no. 3 (2005): 387–409.

13. See, for example, Deborah Davis and Sara Friedman, *Wives, Husbands, and Lovers: Marriage and Sexuality in Hong Kong, Taiwan, and Urban China* (Hong Kong: Hong Kong University Press, 2014); Carol C. L. Tsang, '"The Limits of Fertility": Birth Control in Hong Kong, 1945–1997' (MPhil thesis, the University of Hong Kong, 2008); Carol C. L. Tsang, '"Two Is Enough": Class, Gender, and the Nuclear Family Ideal in Cold War Hong Kong' (to be published, 2025).

results of marriage between Hong Kong resident husbands and mainland Chinese wives, faced new opportunities and challenges in the run-up to the handover in 1997. Section 2 inspects social reforms. Elites and professionals addressed gender inequality by fighting against discrimination in marriage, wages, and property rights, thus promoting women's position within the family. Some advocated male participation in the domestic realm. Documents 13.5–13.8 look at the Marriage Reform Ordinance, the principle of equal pay for equal work, statutory maternity leave, and amendments to the New Territories Land (Exemption) Bill respectively. Document 13.9 urges men to shoulder more responsibilities in pregnancy, childbirth, and childcare. All these reforms coincided with the rapid expansion of the feminist movement in Hong Kong between the early 1970s and the mid-1990s. Section 3 considers medical technologies. The availability of and easier access to both old and new medical procedures (see Chapter 11, 'Medicine and Healthcare') changed how ordinary people maintain families. Document 13.10 shows that most pregnant teenagers sought 'backstreet' abortions across the border in the 1980s when they were denied access to abortion in Hong Kong. Document 13.11 demonstrates how, on the one hand, the availability of in-vitro fertilisation (IVF) allowed many infertile couples to expand their households. On the other hand, IVF generated deep-seated conflicts among politicians, medical professionals, and religious communities on how individuals should build families. The NGOs and legal infrastructure discussed in all three sections are still up and running today, demonstrating their lasting influence in shaping gender and family dynamics in Hong Kong.

Section 1. Rebuilding Families

In 1949, the Hong Kong Social Welfare Council was renamed and reorganised as the Hong Kong Family Welfare Society (HKFWS) that is still in operation today. In one of its earliest Annual Reports, the HKFWS explored how it relieved distress among families who entered Hong Kong during the refugee influx. The report shows how HKFWS caseworkers strove to help the lowest strata of the population – those who were poor, sick, and illiterate. The HKFWS collaborated with government departments and other relief organisations to rebuild families in a recovering colony.

Document 13.1: Hongkong Family Welfare Society, Annual Report for 1949, 1–8.

The aims of the Society as laid down in the Constitution are as follows:–

- To relieve distress by promoting family and social welfare among the citizens of Hong Kong.

- To investigate problems of poverty individual and general.
- To cooperate with other organisations and institutions also engaged in any form of family welfare.
- To receive, administer or distribute such funds or supplies as are entrusted to it.
- To provide a Family Casework Service at the disposal of other organisations or persons requiring help with particular cases.
- To assist in the maintenance of an adequate standard of training for Social Workers.

The Caseworker

Much of the success of the Society's work depends on the caseworkers. Throughout the year we have maintained a staff of seven caseworkers or casework secretaries. They have dealt with an average of 650 persons per month. No relief is given without a thorough investigation of the case and this may involve several interviews and house visits. The caseworkers are trained professional workers who need to bring to their work, intelligence, patience and a deep understanding of human hearts and minds with an ability to be sympathetic yet firm. The course of investigating a case and solving a problem may bring the caseworker into contact with all kinds of people – official and unofficial, neighbours and friends of the applicants and sometimes those who would be hostile. All these they must handle with tact and friendliness. On the whole most people who come to our centres are in genuine need of help and more often than not the investigation reveals a deeper need than the applicant would lead the caseworker at first to suspect. Those not in genuine need are few comparatively but it is the caseworker's job to detect and deal with them.

Relief in kind or in money is given in cases of dire necessity but it is not the policy of the Society to hand out a dole but to try to put those people who come to us for help into such a position that they can help themselves.

Poverty is invariably due to ill-health with consequent loss of employment. A great many cases of destitution have TB (i.e. tuberculosis) as the root cause, while a few are due to moral weakness and instability of character.

While trying to put a family on its feet it is often necessary to give temporary relief in money or in kind – but the main task of the caseworker is to put the client into touch with those agencies which can best help. Many illiterate and other clients do not know how to go about getting assistance for themselves, so the caseworker, in the case of sickness will introduce the applicant to a clinic; in the case of unemployment she will try to find a job. Often she is able to help eligible applicants to secure hawkers' licenses. Sometimes there is the problem of children whom the mother is unable to care for while she is working and the caseworker will try get the children into school or orphanage. The caseworker may help a family to obtain pensions and gratuities which are due to them and in some cases to hold money in trust for such people. Occasionally the Society will provide repatriation expenses.

In all this work the Society's caseworkers are in close touch with the Social Welfare Office, the Government Medical Department, the Labour Office and voluntary relief organisations.

The Hong Kong Society for the Protection of Children (HKSPC) was founded in 1926 and officially registered in 1929 at the request of the Secretary of State, Lord Passfield. He aimed to form an institution similar to the National Society for the Prevention of Cruelty to Children (NSPCC) to tackle the mui-tsai question in Hong Kong. By the end of the Second World War, the HKSPC focused on providing food and shelter for babies and children in need. In one of its earliest Annual Reports, the HKSPC outlined its work in supporting families of the poorest classes and appealed to the public for support.

Document 13.2: The Hong Kong Society for the Protection of Children, Annual Report, 16 April 1946 to 31 October 1946, 1–9.

The aims and objects of the Society shall be:–

(1) To protect children and young persons by preventing, removing or mitigating any wrongs or injustices done to them; to safeguard their morals; to prevent any act which causes or is likely to cause them unnecessary suffering or injury to their health; and generally to protect the interests of children.

(2) To take all necessary steps for the enforcement of any existing law for their protection or in their interests, and to advocate and promote any amendment of any law which may be considered desirable for their protection or in their interests.

(3) To take such steps by personal, written or printed statement, public meetings, or otherwise as may be deemed expedient for the purpose of educating the public generally in the interests of the welfare of the young.

(4) To provide and maintain an organisation for the above objects.

(5) To do all other such lawful things as are incidental or conducive to the attainment of the above objects. . . .

- On the resumption of the Society's activities, it became apparent that the parents of many thousands of children could not afford to purchase milk for their families owing to the excessively high prices demanded on the black market; this essential food was then selling as high as $8.00 per tin. . . . the Society undertook responsibility for the sale by voluntary workers of condensed milk at the controlled price of 80 cents a tin. The work began in three depots – two in Hong Kong and one in Kowloon. . . .

- Another great boon to the Society and to the children for whom it cares has been the free supply of powdered milk from the stocks left in Hong Kong on the departure of the British Red Cross. Tinned meat and fish have also been made available from the same source for the sick and undernourished. . . .

- By October the Society was able to resume another part of its work, the support of children in suitable institutions. It is now responsible for the maintenance of two destitute, fatherless children in the Taipo Rural School and Orphanage, and for two orphans in the Babies' Home, Fanling, as well as contributing to the maintenance of twenty children in the Orphanage of the Convent of the Precious Blood, Shamshuipo, and five in the Po Leung Kuk.

- Your Committee views with apprehension the growing need for the expansion of the Society's work which can only be undertaken by securing suitable premises, staff, equipment, more voluntary workers, and above all, greater financial support. The immensity of the task can only be realised by visiting the densely populated districts of the poorer classes, or bearing in mind the distress amongst those thousands who are existing today in war ruins, endeavouring to improvise shelter against the coming winter. It will be readily realised that it is such derelict and neglected children who, unless they are cared for and given some help and guidance, may easily develop criminal instincts. This situation is a matter of grave public concern which must be faced and considered not only by your Society but by all citizens of the Colony.

- Before closing the General Report, your Committee wishes to place on record the Society's regret at the grievous losses it has suffered during the last five years; several of its former officers, one Inspector, and many Life and Ordinary Members are no longer with us. We take this opportunity of appealing to the public of Hong Kong by personal service as well as by financial contributions to make good the Society's losses and to ensure the continuance and expansion of their devoted work for the children of the Colony.

Formerly the Eugenics League, the Family Planning Association of Hong Kong (FPAHK) was renamed and founded in 1950. In the early post-war years, the FPAHK was the largest government-sponsored organisation in regulating reproductive health, specifically in promoting birth control in Hong Kong. The FPAHK defined the ideal family as nuclear and self-sustainable. Internationally, in 1952, the FPAHK became one of the eight founding members of the International Planned Parenthood Federation (IPPF). In this quarterly bulletin, the FPAHK highlighted how its activities prevented unwanted births and enhanced the well-being of families and the colony.

Document 13.3: The Family Planning Association of Hong Kong, *Quarterly Bulletin*, no. 17, 1st Quarter 1959.

The population of Hong Kong has increased by more than 1,700,000 in the last 12 years; nearly 700,000 through natural increase and over 1,000,000 through immigration, legal and illegal. The 1955 Annual Report commenting on an increase of almost 100,000 in a space of 6 months states that 'only a small percentage of this rise is due to any continued entry of refugees from China; the principal factor is an already high, and evidently still rising, birth rate. A large proportion of the newcomers who entered the Colony after the war were young men and women uprooted from their homes, coming in search of employment and security. Most of them have been absorbed into the economic life of the Colony, and, having found security, are marrying and raising families'. His Excellency the Governor in introducing the Annual Report for 1956 describes how the population has increased four-fold during the past ten years and explains that this has been the root cause of most of the problems which Government has had to face. At the present time, many thousands are still unemployed, and despite a fantastic building programme there are still over 300,000 people living as squatters, roof-dwellers and street sleepers.

In few places can the effects of population pressure be more apparent. The need for birth control is widely accepted, but doubt arises as to whether present contraceptive methods can prove an effective measure in the face of difficult local living conditions.

The Hong Kong Family Planning Association commenced its postwar activities in 1951 and accurate records have been kept of the 37,000 cases who have attended our clinics for birth control advice. From these we have attempted to evaluate our programme as a whole and to relate it to the Colony's total births and birth rate. . . .

The typical woman who seeks Family Planning advice has lived in Hong Kong for ten years and came originally from a village in Kwangtung province, China. She is 31 years of age and has been married 10 years with 4 children living. Her husband, 2 years older than she, is employed, with an income of less than $200 a month. She had only two years of schooling and is unable to read a newspaper. Her husband, on the other hand, completed primary school. The entire family including the mother-in-law live in one small cubicle in the urban area, paying $45 rent.

Our patient first learned of family planning from a neighbour who had been coming to our clinic. Her reasons for seeking family planning advice, like that of all our cases was financial; she would have come sooner had she known about our clinics earlier. As they have four children already, including two sons, they do not wish more children. When asked what she considered the ideal number of children, she said two to three including at least one son. Her husband both knew and approved of her visit to our clinic and there was no objection on the part of her mother-in-law or any of her other relatives.

CONCLUSIONS

These two studies point up several significant facts about Family Planning in Hong Kong:

1. It is already effectively helping to reduce the birth rate.
2. It is reaching the lowest income groups who are least able to support large families.
3. It is readily accepted by the Chinese; among the thousands of cases who have come to our clinics there is no evidence of prejudice against it.
4. It is now reaching less than 10% of the population and the chief problem is making Family Planning more widely known. As noted above, the majority of our interview cases said they would have come sooner had they known about Family Planning before.
5. The large spurt in attendance in the past two years has been made possible by the greatly increased financial assistance from Government and private contributors. This has made possible the establishment of 10 new clinics, raising the total number of clinics to 20.
6. The great increase in new cases in these two years, statistics show has been the direct result of the establishment of these new clinics.
7. Most people who come to Family Planning (some 80%) have learned of it from a personal contact: a friend, relative, doctor, nurse, or social worker whom they know and trust. One of the places where such contacts exist and can be utilized is in the Maternal and Child Health Centres; in each centre where the Family Planning Association has been permitted to share the premises our attendances have been significantly higher than in those established separately.

These studies should make it clear that Family Planning offers an effective and compatible answer to Hong Kong's growing population problem. With larger resources it could influence greatly the birth rate and through it, the well-being of the colony. This however cannot be achieved without the encouragement and active support of all those who feel Hong Kong's population problem must be taken seriously.

Facing the resumption of Chinese sovereignty over Hong Kong, in 1995, the daily quota on one-way permits increased from 105 to 150 per day. One-way permits were endorsed by Article 22 of the Basic Law and issued by the Public Security Bureau in the mainland. The policy is still in place today to regulate entry of mainland residents into Hong Kong, with a major aim to facilitate family reunion. The following news article, published on the eve of the handover, highlights the anguish of cross-border families, most of them the result of marriage between Hong Kong resident husbands and mainland Chinese wives. Some of these families suffered separation for over a decade.

Document 13.4: 'Illegal Mothers' Year of Anguish', *South China Morning Post*, 13 January 1997, 85.

It was a year of hope, desperation, tears and relief for thousands of mainland women and their Hong Kong resident husbands who became outlaws to have their babies born in the territory. Life is tough for the cross-border families. Husbands must live and work in Hong Kong where they can earn far more. But their wives – often brides chosen from the man's home village – must remain across the border.

Many women have applied to join their husbands in the territory but have found themselves still waiting in vain years later. So, when the pair decide to start a family, the last thing they want is for their child to spend years wading through bureaucracy for the chance to live and study in Hong Kong.

If a child of a Hong Kong-resident father is born in the territory, he or she automatically gains the same rights as the father: permanent residency or the right to remain until the expiry of a temporary visa. If father and child have Hong Kong residency, many hope it will be merely a matter of time before the mainland mother can stay permanently.

The year began with a groundswell of sympathy for the desperation of pregnant women who risk their lives on tiny speedboats, ancient fishing skiffs or in the back of old delivery vans to give their child a Hong Kong birthright.

Mr Justice Joseph Duffy, presiding over the prosecution of several illegal immigrant mothers, called for the women to simply be returned to China, rather than be forced through the Hong Kong courts and jails. A 'too rigid' adherence to sentencing guidelines was seeing young mothers raise their newborn infants in jail, he said.

By February, Justice Duffy was stepping up his campaign, declaring he would keep releasing illegal immigrant mothers who crept across the border to give birth until the Immigration Department changed its policy.

On July 1, cross-border families displayed quiet pragmatism to the announcement of a rise in the daily quota of migrants from China. The number of one-way permits, allowing the bearers to live in Hong Kong, rose from 105 to 150 a day. Thirty of the extra were earmarked for children who would have the right of abode under the Basic Law after July 1, 1997, and 15 were for spouses who had been separated from their Hong Kong partners for more than 10 years.

On Mother's Day last year, it was estimated there were more than 400,000 mainland mothers married to Hong Kong men with no right to live here, many living a secret, underground life.

By late last year, it was becoming obvious that more and more mothers were arriving to give birth ahead of the handover. Indignation over the number of mainland births in Hong Kong hospitals prompted much discussion between China and Hong Kong authorities. A crackdown made it more difficult for pregnant women to obtain the three-month permits which would allow them to come to Hong Kong during their final weeks of pregnancy.

The new policy saw a fall in births to visiting permit holders – 4,139 in 1995 to 2,324 for the first nine months of last year. Conversely, the number of births to those who placed their lives and savings in the hands of snakeheads was rising.

In February last year, Immigration Department figures showed an inexorable rise in the number of illegal immigrants giving birth at Hong Kong's hospitals. About 240 such babies had been born in each month of the previous year, ending with a total of 2,886 infants – a rise of 24 per cent on the 1994 figure of 2,324. In the first nine months of last year, the figure stood at 2,193.

The Preparatory Committee's legal sub-group, charged with the task of deciding how to handle the status of Hong Kong–born children of illegal immigrant mothers, spent much of the year deadlocked. Debate suggests the status quo will continue, allowing residency rights to the children of Hong Kong fathers.

Meanwhile, the pain, hope and tortured emotion of the issue are never far from the minds of those whose families are split by border control points.

Section 2. Social Reforms

The enactment of the Marriage Reform Ordinance in 1970 and subsequent legislation in 1971 were important landmarks in achieving equal status of married couples and raising women's status in families. The Ordinance abolished concubinage and upheld monogamy in all marriages. In 1971 Woo Pak-chuen (P.C. Woo) (1910–2008), eminent lawyer, unofficial member of the Executive and Legislative Councils, and grandson of thinker and translator Woo Lai-woon, explained the legal changes and their repercussions on marriage and family dynamics at the Rotary Club.

Document 13.5: 'The Objects of the New Reform Legislation of Family Law in Hong Kong', Mr P.C. Woo's Speech at the Luncheon Meeting of the Rotary Club of Hong Kong Island West, 23 July 1971.

Within a period of not more than 12 months a series of legislation to amend the family law in Hong Kong had been enacted by the Legislative Council. They are –

(1) Marriage Reform Ordinance 1970 following up with

(2) Intestates' Estates Ordinance 1971,

(3) Deceased's Family Maintenance Ordinance 1971,

(4) Married Persons Status Ordinance 1971,

(5) Matrimonial Causes Ordinance 1971,

(6) Legitimacy Ordinance 1971,

(7) Affiliation Proceedings Ordinance 1971,

(8) Law Reform (Miscellaneous Provisions) Ordinance 1971.

The objects of these new legislative measures are –

First, to abolish as far as possible the dual system of family law in Hong Kong, namely, the Chinese law and custom which has been regarded by many of us as obsolete and unjust to Chinese females, particularly with regard to the rights between husband and wife and the question of succession.

Secondly, to recognize the universal principle of equality between the sexes.

Thirdly, to bring the law as near as possible as regards family law with the laws of England, and

Fourthly, to tidy up the family law in Hong Kong.

Because of the time available I cannot deal with all these Ordinances at length and I have to confine my remarks to the most important changes in the law effected by these Ordinances.

First, with regard to the Marriage Reform Ordinance 1970, the most important point is the abolition of concubinage in Hong Kong. The subject matter has been mooted and debated many times and I can only remark that as from the 7th October 1971 the status of concubines can no longer be recognized in Hong Kong. However, all the concubines taken before this date, if they are lawfully taken, are regarded as lawful spouses.

Secondly, all marriages in Hong Kong whether registered marriages or otherwise will be regarded as monogamous that is to say, the marriage is between one man and one woman to the exclusion of all others.

Thirdly, the modern Chinese marriages or the Chinese customary marriages can be registered and regarded as valid marriages if registered in accordance with the provisions of the Ordinance. . . .

The Married Persons Status Ordinance 1971 is to clarify the law in relation to the status of husband and wife. First, a married woman is no longer restrained from alienating her property past, present or future. Secondly, subject to certain limitations either party to the marriage is entitled to sue the other in tort. Thirdly, the Court has power to decide in a summary way questions between husband and wife regarding property and the Court also has power to order payment of money and order the sale of the property belonging to the parties. Furthermore, a married woman whether an infant or not has power to appoint an attorney or attorneys on her behalf for the purpose of executing any deed or instrument or other acts. . . .

It is interesting to note that it takes nearly 130 years before we can substantially replace the Chinese law and custom which has been the family law of the Chinese community in Hong Kong and throughout these years, although with some improvements, the status of Chinese females, to put it in the mildest term, is inferior to that of the Chinese male population.

The principle of equal pay for equal work was passed in Hong Kong in 1969 for civil service, and in 1975 for all members of civil service and teachers. Maria Tam (1945–), prominent politician and lawyer, explained how, despite the enactment of equal pay, women across social classes and marital statuses still faced unequal treatment in the workplace. Citing examples from the United Kingdom, she urged the Hong Kong government and the public to build a fairer society for women by introducing equality legislations.

Document 13.6: 'Woman's Rights' and the Law, Lion's Club Luncheon Speech by Maria Tam, 7 October 1977.

"WOMANS RIGHTS" AND THE LAW

"Women's Rights" movement is a steadily progressing revolution by women all over the world to attain equality of the sexes. In order to explain the situation in Hong Kong I shall tell you a story about three women who come from different background and have different social status.

The case of the single woman: Ada

Ada is a single woman whose parents have left some properties to her on their death. She is also the sole proprietor of an import and export firm. She belongs to the 3.9% of privileged people in Hong Kong called "the employers". Her legal status and rights are exactly the same as a man because she is single. . . . Also Ada is self-employed. She needs not worry about sex discrimination in job opportunities.

The case of a married woman: Betty

For our purpose Betty is a married woman with a son. Her husband is an architect working for a firm of architects in town. Betty is a civil servant and she has attained the rank of an executive officer. She is a University Graduate. In order to give you some idea how the income of educated women compared to that of men I have listed out the February 1977 figures of the median earnings of the employed populations in Hong Kong by educational attainment and by sex.

Educational Attainment	Male	Female	Difference in HK$ per month
Matriculation or other post-secondary	1,567	1,035	532
University (non-grads)	2,045	1,500	545
University graduates	3,000	2,275	725
Technical or vocational training	2,024	2,121	97

It is clear from these figures that females receive less wages than males from the same education attainment. The issues here are: firstly there is sex discrimination against women in getting better jobs, and secondly, there is no equal pay policy in some private enterprises.

Take the case of Betty, if she finds that her male colleagues of the same rank are promoted one after the other, there is no way she can alter the position even if it is known that the reason is because she is a married woman. Here is where the inadequacy of our legislation lies. In England, ever since the passing of the Sex Discrimination Act 1975 a case like Betty's would be a fit one to be heard in the Industrial Tribunals. . . .

The case of a divorced woman: Kate

Kate, for our purpose, is a blue collar worker, divorced, with 2 daughters in her custody. Her status as a legal person is the same as Ada and Betty i.e. they are fully liable in civil, common and criminal law for their own act. They are not liable for their husband's debts or breach of contract or criminal acts, and vice versa.

It was practically impossible for a single blue collar worker to buy a little flat and so before her marriage Kate lived with her parents.

During marriage the couple successfully applied for a flat on the low costs housing scheme and although Kate contributed to the family piggy bank the flat was registered only in her husband's name. Then she gave birth to a son and 2 daughters and on and off she continued to work in an electronics products factory as an assembler. During marriage her husband could obtain a passport and take the children abroad without her consent, but she could not do so without his – not even to Macau.

After the divorce she was given custody of the daughters and her husband was ordered to give maintenance for the daughters. Kate did not ask for any for herself. However, her husband refused to give up the flat and so Kate and the 2 daughters moved out because she was not allowed to register as a joint tenant.

It is even more impossible now for her to get a mortgage to buy a flat and so she goes back to her parents and lives in a crowded home, like so many others of our population.

You see, if the Housing Authority would allow Kate to be registered as a joint tenant at least she can have a platform to discuss with her husband on who is to occupy the flat after the divorce. If their rights are equal as joint tenants she may be given a chance of staying on the ground that he suffers greater hardship.

Kate is doing well in her line of factory work because electronics and weaving factories pay their female workers similar wages to the male and sometimes even more. In order to make clear my point here is a list of average daily wage rates between male and female workers:–

Type of Industry	Type of Work		Daily wage rates HK$
Bleaching and dyeing	Lab worker	M	18.56
		F	17.58
	Printing designer	M	64.73
		F	46.15
Cotton knitting	Looping machine-operator	M	35.3
		F	30.77
	Packer	M	21
		F	17.69
Cotton spinner	Learner	M	14.16
		F	13.17
	Supervisor	M	25.94
		F	25.73
Cotton weaving	Pirnfeeder	M	18
		F	15
Woollen knitting	Examiner	M	21.38
		F	17.94
	Foreman	M	44.53
		F	39.03
Electrical appliances	Tester	M	21.54
		F	19.52
	Line-supervisor	M	39.62
		F	30.51
Garments	Cutter	M	26.15
		F	23.19
	Sewing machine operator	M	28.36
		F	23.84
	Button sewer	M	21.85
		F	19.71
Handbags	Assembler	M	22.67
		F	18.63
Plastic toys	Assembler	M	22.99
		F	22.47
	Painter	M	24.89
		F	22.61

All these jobs require similar skill, strength and intelligence from a male or a female worker, and yet male workers are better paid each day for working the same hours. If a female worker in U.K. meets with such a situation she will have no difficulty going to the Industrial Tribunals and put her case under the Equal Pay Act 1970. . . .

. . . Yet, in Hong Kong, no credit is given to female workers who form a less expensive but equally effective and productive work force in our industry. This is the 20th Century, we cannot expect the less educated females to work in a factory in the day time and take care of her children and husband at night and don't even bother to pay her a proper wage! There is every reason to bring equality legislations in Hong Kong especially when there is already strong criticism of part of our statute book remaining in the 19th Century!

May I conclude by referring to the various tables of statistics and suggest this: that both well-educated and less well-educated women are not properly paid for their efforts and ability. They constitute a cheaper labour pool which was and still is a source of our industrial and commercial prosperity – and yet women have only equal liability in paying tax and no equal rights to jobs, education and housing.

Gentlemen, the next time you open a car door for a woman, don't forget you are getting a lot more in return.

Statutory maternity leave was first introduced in 1970 under the Employment Ordinance but the leave was without pay. In 1981, a pregnant employee under continuous employment for not less than forty weeks was entitled for maternity leave pay equivalent to two-thirds of her daily wages. The following report shows how the Hong Kong Council of Women (HKCW, now disbanded) urged the government to provide women with paid maternity leave, defining it as a basic step to ensure family harmony and social stability. The HKCW was one of the leading women's organisations in raising women's status in Hong Kong after the Second World War.

Document 13.7: 'The Hong Kong Council of Women's Report on Maternity Leave', 15 February 1989.

In the statement, we [the Hong Kong Council of Women] referred to the backwardness of Hongkong in this area of social legislation, being one of the few places in Asia that does not legally entitle women workers to paid maternity leave. In this respect, we are even behind countries far less affluent than ourselves. This is unjustifiable, not only ethically, but also economically since women constitute 1/3 of the total labour force and over 1/2 of the industrial labour force. We also put forward the argument that the absence of paid maternity leave is against the personal welfare of the woman and her new-born, causing undue strain at this time and against the possibility of bonding parent and the child. We urged the government to give heed to this most vital issue and to consider our recommendations which were:

1. a. That maternity leave for women workers be paid leave.

   b. That the period of maternity leave of 10 weeks remain unchanged.

   c. That a worker who has worked continuously for the same employer for 6 months receive 2/3 of her daily wage, full wage if the employment period is one year or more, and pro rata if it is between 3 to 6 months.

2. a. That in no case can an employer terminate the contract with any woman worker simply because of her pregnancy.

3. a. That a pregnant worker be paid 2/3 of her wage for days off for medical check-ups.

4. a. That the husband of the woman worker who is in confinement be given one week off and 2/3 of his regular wage during the period.

Since the occasion, members of the Council of Women Committee have become more and more convinced that the issue of paid maternity leave does not concern women so much as their families. In fact, to see it solely as a woman's concern is chauvinistic and psychologically lacking in insight. We have seen the stresses and strains surrounding childbirth as one that works positively against bonding between parents and children and thus as being totally relevant to the growing incidence of child abuse in our community. Paid Maternity Leave is thus hardly a luxury as the quality of family life in our community is what is at stake. This is directly related to social stability. Thus we do well, socially and politically, to do everything in our power to arrest the forces that break up our families and paid maternity leave is a most basic way of doing this. . . .

In March 1994 amendments to the New Territories Land (Exemption) Bill were accepted, expanding the inheritance rights of female indigenous inhabitants of the New Territories from non-agricultural to agricultural land. The following news article shows how the fight over inheritance laws was more than a 'battle of the sexes'. The fight boiled down to a generational divide in understanding 'tradition' and 'women's rights'.

Document 13.8: Quinton Chan, 'Behind the Battle of the Sexes', *South China Morning Post*, 27 March 1994, 12.

Cheng Lai-sheung has every reason to be angry. When her father died 10 years ago, ancestral law prevented her from inheriting any of his property. As chairwoman of the Anti-Discrimination Female Indigenous Residents Committee, she does not want others to suffer the same fate and is in the forefront of the battle to allow inheritance rights to be extended to women in the New Territories.

'Things have to change now', Ms Cheng said. However, she does not see the controversy simply as a battle of the sexes. It goes deeper than that. If the inheritance laws are changed, the powerful rural lobby which has dominated the New Territories for decades risks losing its power and influence.

'They are not fighting for their tradition, but their privileges', she said.

Rural leaders desperate to cling on to the old ways of life have said if the amendment from legislator Christine Loh Kung-wai on the New Territories Bill is passed, their clans and families will be forced to disband. Those affected – the 300,000 indigenous residents comprise just over 10 per cent of the estimated 2.4 million residents of the New Territories – know that more than just handing over a piece of land to a female heir is at stake.

They fear that any change in the traditional laws that have long set them apart from their urban counterparts may mean an end to the many privileges they have enjoyed for the last 150 years. That is why, last Tuesday, so many gathered outside the Legislative Council chambers and why it ended in violence with the assault of liberal legislator Lee Wing-tat. . . .

Ma Tin village in Yuen Long is typical of the 740 villages affected by the proposed changes. It has about 1,000 villagers and sits oddly juxtaposed next to the bustling town centre of Yuen Long. It is serviced by the Light Transit Railway and its residents live in modern Spanish-style town houses and drive Japanese cars.

Once occupied solely by the Tang clan, other clans have moved in over the decades and today Ma Tin village is home to seven clans. The debate over inheritance has, not surprisingly, split the village, with older residents desperate to hang on to the past while the younger generation is more open minded.

'Females shouldn't have the right to property succession', said 78-year-old Tang Kin-po. 'Once a daughter marries, she is the wife of her husband but not a core member of the family. She shouldn't come back, she belongs to her husband, not the village'.

He freely admitted that males were the more important members within the clan and village. 'Males are different. My sons can inherit the family properties and develop them, and they will look after me', he said.

With three sons and two daughters, he said the customary inheritance law prohibits daughters becoming landowners because, on marriage, their land would be lost from the clan's shared wealth.

'If my daughter had the right to inherit properties, our family properties will one day fall into the hands of my son-in-law, a man with a different surname. Then my clan and family will be mixed with outsiders. If that becomes the case, our family will be disbanded after a few generations', he explained.

But villager Tang Siu-bor, 34, said: 'I will pass my properties on to my daughter. Why not?' The businessman, who inherited two houses from his father several years ago, admitted the notion of tradition was not so important among the younger generation.

Ms Cheng said tradition no longer exists in the villages. 'Many of the village houses are already rented to outsiders', she said.

Debates revolving around fatherhood took a new turn in the 1980s. Judith Mackay (1943–), a British-born and Hong Kong-based medical doctor, international anti-tobacco advocate, and feminist, urged men in Hong Kong to share responsibilities for pregnancy, childbirth, and childcare. In this news article Mackay prompted the public to reconsider a father's role without losing sight of deep-rooted Chinese patriarchal values and masculinity ideals in Hong Kong.

Document 13.9: Judith Mackay, 'Hints for Expectant Fathers', *South China Morning Post*, 16 December 1981, 34.

What is your role in pregnancy?

Some men feel that they have none, and are out of the limelight. Others are deeply involved with purchasing prams, attending ante-natal classes with their wives, and learning as much about pregnancy, labour and caring for the baby afterwards as they can.

She may feel sick and sleepy, and need sympathy, or she may remain in robust good health and resent being treated like a China doll. . . .

There is some controversy at present as to whether sex is completely safe in the last two to four weeks, and different medical authorities have different ideas about this, some believing it to be all right, while others believe it may lead to infection and premature labour. It is difficult to know at this point of time what to advise. . . .

Most men who do stay with their wives in labour, however, report it is as a profoundly meaningful experience.

If you decide to stay, see some pictures of newborns first, as they often look wrinkled, purple, covered in messy white "cream", with funny shaped heads, and do not, at the moment of birth, resemble TV ad babies!

After the baby, you may feel ecstatic, or have a sense of anti-climax. There are a lot of adjustments to make in the first few weeks both for yourself, but especially for your wife, and problems like depression or discomfort with her episiotomy stitches may be magnified by the loss of sleep you may both experience. . . .

In some parts of the world the man will get paternity leave, and stay home to look or help look after the children, but I have not heard of this arrangement in Hongkong. Men who have done this have written about their experiences and attitudes of others, which vary from amazement to hostility in what is seen as a subversive and abnormal act!

Perhaps we can hope for the future that fathers can contribute to the upbringing of their children without feeling it is "unmanly".

Section 3. Medical Technologies

A highly controversial medical procedure that ends a pregnancy, abortion is legal and accessible in Hong Kong today. In 1972 a law was passed to allow a woman to abort if two doctors considered that continuing the pregnancy would harm her. The law was revised in 1981 to include women under sixteen and victims of rape or incest. This news article shows that, despite the legalisation of abortion in Hong Kong, many teenage girls sought 'backstreet' abortions across the China border. They sought 'backstreet' abortions in order to reject the official surveillance of form filling, questioning, and interviews before receiving an operation. The article also reveals how the number of legal and illegal abortions greatly increased in the 1980s amid the rise of premarital sex in Hong Kong.

Document 13.10: 'More Seek Illegal Abortion in China', *The Star*, 21 October 1982.

More and more women are seeking illegal abortions in China.

According to a Guangzhou hospital for overseas Chinese, about 100 women a day go to Shenzhen for the termination of their pregnancies. During the past three years, about 10,000 women had been there for abortions, a spokesman for the hospital said yesterday.

In Hong Kong an abortion can only be legally performed if two doctors testify that the continuation of the pregnancy endangers the health of the woman. The hospital spokesman said most of their clients would not qualify for legal abortions under Hongkong rules.

They also had no confidence in "underground" clinics which performed such operations with no questions asked. He said this was because some "backstreet doctors" had been conducting operations in unhygienic conditions and often used equipment not properly sterilised. The cost of an illegal operation ranged from $3,000 to $10,000 depending on the condition of the women. The cost of the operation in China is about $350. Chinese hospital authorities said many of those seeking help were very young. In one case, it involved a 15-year-old girl who had got into trouble after having sex with her boyfriend.

The spokesman said most of the underaged women seeking help worked as "fishball" girls in Hongkong or those from the lower strata of society. In these latter cases, some had very little knowledge about sex. The spokesman said blue movies could be a factor in the increase in teenagers getting into trouble. According to a police report, only two illegal abortion cases were recorded in Hongkong this year compared with five cases last year. On the other hand, there were 10,617 legal abortions last year compared with 184 in 1973 – a fantastic increase of 570 percent.

Hong Kong's first test-tube baby (or baby born via in-vitro fertilisation, IVF) was born in December 1986. IVF has since allowed many infertile couples in Hong Kong to build their families. IVF stirred debates among members of the public when it first became available. Commentators were divided among those who hailed IVF as a 'cure' for infertility and those who considered it a human intervention in nature.

Document 13.11: Media Reports and Comments on In-Vitro Fertilisation, 26 May 1987.

The birth of HK's first test-tube baby in the UK Sanitorium in December was reported prominently by the local media. Most reports gave a detailed account of the IVF process and IVF centre at the hospital.

The director of the IVF centre, Dr Michael Tucker, was quoted by some papers as calling for the setting up of a committee to register and monitor the operations of medical institutions engaged in IVF. Dr Tucker also called for legislation to control the handling of embryos and to ban the use of embryos in experiments 14 days after fertilisation.

Mrs Peggy Lam of the Family Planning Association described the successful birth of HK's first test-tube baby as a "great leap forward" in the territory's medical history. She said that IVF was a good thing which would help infertile couples.

Exco member Chiu Hin-kwong said that IVF was in its initial stage of development in HK and that in this particular case, no donors were involved. Therefore, there should be no legal problem concerning estates and blood links. Dr Chiu admitted however that IVF would give rise to religious, legal and ethical issues. Laws in other countries should be used as reference if it came to a stage where legislative control was necessary, he said.

The IVF technology had understandably come under scathing attack from the Catholic Church and related religious bodies which described the process as tampering with nature.

A spokesman for the Catholic Church, the Rev Louis Ha, said that the position of the Church was quite clear – the act of procreation was sacred and that man should not interfere with this natural process. The Rev Ha said that the Church considered that life began when the egg was fertilised and that it should have its basic human rights.

The Rev Ha called on infertile couples to adopt children rather than resorting to IVF. In a similar vein, Sister Therese Howard of the Pro-life Action Association said that the group would press for legislation governing IVF and more stringent control over embryonic research. She said that embryos were human and could not be anything else. There were however people in the religious sector who adopted a more liberal view of IVF. The Rev Law Siu-hong of the Baptist Church said that according to the Bible, God allowed men to use their wisdom to develop many things. Therefore, he was not opposed to using IVF to help those in need of the service.

The birth of HK's second and third test-tube babies announced on May 2 received good coverage. A co-director of the IVF centre at the HK Sanitorium, Dr Milton Leong was quoted as appealing to the Government to urgently address the legal issues of artificial conception. Dr Leong said the Government needed to especially look at the status of children born from the use of artificial insemination by donors and IVF procedures using donor eggs or embryos. He said that these children would be illegitimate unless the law was changed. He said that a child conceived from donor eggs or embryos should in law be treated as the legitimate child of its social mother and social father. Another co-director of the centre, Clement Leung, said that a birth certificate should only be used to indicate nationality and the social relationship of parents and child, rather than the biological relationship.

On the introduction of laws to control IVF programmes, Dr Leong said that legislation would be a mistake. He said the code of practice would be effective in setting out the parameters of IVF practice. The SCM Post reported on May 14 that a revised code of practice covering IVF programmes and research in HK would ban surrogate motherhood and the transfer to a woman of any embryo used in laboratory experiments. The guidelines also proscribed the implantation of human embryos into animals and restrict cultivation of ova and embryos to 14 days – after which the cells must be destroyed. A spokesman for the Medical and Health Department was quoted as saying that the code of practice was not legally binding. . . .

Suggested Readings

Chan, Anita Kit-wa, and Wong Wai-ling. *Gendering Hong Kong*. Hong Kong: Oxford University Press, 2004.

Cheung, Fanny M. *Engendering Hong Kong Society: A Gender Perspective of Women's Status*. Hong Kong: Chinese University of Hong Kong Press, 1997.

Cheung, Fanny M., and Eleanor Holroyd. *Mainstreaming Gender in Hong Kong Society*. Hong Kong: Chinese University of Hong Kong Press, 2009.

Davis, Deborah, and Sara Friedman. *Wives, Husbands, and Lovers: Marriage and Sexuality in Hong Kong, Taiwan, and Urban China*. Hong Kong: Hong Kong University Press, 2014.

Jackson, Stevi, and Petula Sik Ying Ho. *Women Doing Intimacy: Gender, Family and Modernity in Britain and Hong Kong*. London: Palgrave Macmillan, 2020.

Lee, Eliza W. Y. *Gender and Change in Hong Kong: Globalization, Postcolonialism, and Chinese Patriarchy*. Hong Kong: Hong Kong University Press, 2003.

Pearson, Veronica, and Benjamin K. P. Leung. *Women in Hong Kong*. Hong Kong: Oxford University Press, 1995.

Salaff, Janet W. *Working Daughters of Hong Kong: Filial Piety or Power in the Family?* New York: Columbia University Press, 1995.

Siu, Helen F. *Merchants' Daughters: Women, Commerce, and Regional Culture in South China*. Hong Kong: Hong Kong University Press, 2010.

Wong, Max W. L. *Chinese Marriage and Social Change: The Legal Abolition of Concubinage in Hong Kong*. Singapore: Springer, 2020.

14
Race and Diasporas

Vivian Kong[1]

Hong Kong has always been a multiracial city. Despite the popular belief that the city was a barren rock before 1841, the reality was that it already had a diverse population at the time, with villages inhabited by Puntis, Hakkas, and Hoklos. Living around Hong Kong waters were also the Tankas, often referred to as the 'boat people' in earlier records.[2] When the British occupied Hong Kong Island in 1841, they estimated that the island housed 7,450 Chinese, of which 2,000 were the 'boat population'.[3] Despite being grouped under the umbrella category of 'Chinese', they had distinct cultural practices and spoke vastly different dialects. And Hong Kong's population further diversified as British colonisation began there. To build, rule, and make money, white Britons ranging from government officials and military officers to missionaries, traders, sailors, intermediaries, and engineers for the dockyards arrived. Many others also came to work and develop the colony. Among the earliest 'British settlers' were Portuguese from Macau (now more commonly termed 'Macanese') who worked as interpreters and clerks. The British also brought over several military regiments from India and recruited Sikh, Punjabi, and Muslim police. Alongside the Parsi and Bohra Muslim merchants drawn by the British trading network in South China, a sizeable Indian population established roots in the colony. From the social interactions that arose in such a multiracial port, a Eurasian community – a community of individuals of European and Asian ancestry – naturally emerged.

1. The author would like to thank Michael Ng for his generous advice and Steven Hon and the *South China Morning Post* for granting us the permission to reproduce the letters to editor included in this chapter, as well as Document 14.21, written by Jane Moir and published in *The Post*.
2. James Hayes, 'Hong Kong Island before 1841', *Journal of the Hong Kong Branch of the Royal Asiatic Society*, 24 (1984): 105–42.
3. *Hongkong Gazette*, 1841, 289.

Racism played an instrumental role in structuring social hierarchies in this multiracial colony. Because the premise of colonialism lies in an imagined racial superiority of the ruling class, colonial authorities were anxious to create and consolidate racial categories to distinguish themselves from the colonised others and assert their commanding power. Existing literature has therefore discussed the laws, policies, and social practices that were in place in Hong Kong to construct and enforce divisions, and more importantly to sustain a racial hierarchy that benefited the white British.[4] But underneath the pervasive racial division and distinctions were also subtle interactions between various segments of the colonial society. While earlier works tended more to dwell on the divides and divisions in colonial Hong Kong, today we are as likely to see the city as a place of complex, diverse cross-cultural interactions.[5] Of course we should not take these interactions at face value. Sometimes these interactions brought understanding and friendships. But at other times, as recent literature has also uncovered, they brought bitterness, tensions, and disappointment, as systemic racism prevented people of colour from receiving just treatment and protection.[6]

The sources presented in this chapter include official publications (such as census reports and minutes of Legislative Council meetings), news reports, and personal accounts, such as letters to the editor published in local newspapers and retrospective life writings. They convey the perspectives of state officials and several diasporic groups that called the city home. These accounts touch upon various topics of scholarly discussion on race and diasporas in colonial Hong Kong, including the prevalence of racial perceptions in colonial governance, the diversity of the colony's population, the role of the Second World War in disrupting racial hierarchies, and the enduring impact of systemic racism in late colonial Hong Kong.

4. Historians have, for instance, explored how and why residential segregation was enforced in certain areas of Hong Kong – most notably on the Victoria Peak. On this, see John M. Carroll, 'The Peak: Residential Segregation in Colonial Hong Kong', in *Twentieth-Century Colonialism and China: Localities, the Everyday and the World*, ed. Bryna Goodman and David S. Goodman (London: Taylor and Francis, 2012), 81–91. Carroll has also written about how social segregation was also practised in the European-style gentlemen's club. See John M. Carroll, *Edge of Empires: Chinese Elites and British Colonials in Hong Kong* (Cambridge, MA: Harvard University Press, 2005), especially chapter 4.
5. Elizabeth Sinn and Christopher Munn, eds, *Meeting Place: Encounters Across Cultures in Hong Kong, 1841–1984* (Hong Kong: Hong Kong University Press, 2017).
6. Vivian Kong, 'Exclusivity and Cosmopolitanism: Multi-ethnic Civil Society in Interwar Hong Kong', *Historical Journal* 63, no. 5 (2020): 1281–302.

Section 1. Census Reports and Official Perceptions of 'Races' in Hong Kong

To understand how racial hierarchies came about in post-war Hong Kong, we need to look further back to the years before the Second World War. The following excerpts from the 1901 and 1911 census reports provide us with not only demographic data on the multi-racial population in early twentieth-century Hong Kong, but also enlightening material on the prevalence of racial thinking in British colonial rule. In placing the population into different groups, racial categorisations of census work allowed officials to create and reinforce racial identities by engendering, altering, and strengthening traits of communities to distinguish one 'race' from another. At first glance, comments made in the 1901 census report tell us about the non-Chinese population in the colony. But a closer look reveals the underlying racial perceptions that officials had about the colonial population, and more importantly, their eagerness in highlighting the perceived racial differences between the people of colour and the white population there (as we can see in the comment on the Portuguese community in Document 14.1).

Of course, colonial officials could not always hold to the neat racial categorisation between the colonisers and the colonised. The ways in which Eurasians were presented in Document 14.2 under the overarching category of 'non-Chinese', but as a separate column after that for the total number of the non-Chinese population, gives us a solid example of how much Hong Kong officials struggled to classify the Eurasian community.

Furthermore, although the Chinese were always presented as one umbrella category in all census reports, a closer look at the tables listing their birthplace and dialect spoken at home (such as those selected in Document 14.3) also reveals the diversity of this community. The numbers of those born in Hong Kong and other British territories (including Australia, Penang, and Singapore) are also notable.

The first population census produced after the Second World War was conducted in 1961. Unlike those taken before the war, the 1961 census did not include a question on 'race' per se. Documents 14.4–14.6 include explanations for this decision as well as numbers recorded on local births, dialects spoken, and 'transients', offering us insights in understanding the city's diverse population.

Document 14.1: 1901 Census Officer's Remarks on the 'Non-Chinese Races' in Hong Kong.[7]

The European and American resident civil population numbers 5,808 as compared with 5,532 in 1897, and 4,555 in 1891. These figures include Portuguese. The

7. A. W. Brewin, 'Report on the Census of the Colony for 1901', *Sessional Papers Laid Before the Legislative Council*, 15 August 1901.

numbers of the latter community tend to decrease, and it is now composed of 1,948 persons as compared with 2,263 in 1897 and 2,089 in 1891.

The rest of the European and American population has increased by 591 since 1897 and by 1,394 since 1891. An accurate comparison cannot, however, be made with 1891 as the figures for that year do not include the European Police, some "temporary residents," or the inmates of the Gaol.

The British resident civil population numbers 2,708 as compared with 2,213 in 1897 and 1,448 in 1891. The larger number of military families, due to the strengthening of the British troops in garrison, the Naval Yard Extension works and those of Messrs. Butterfield and Swire at Quarry Bay, and other large undertakings are factors in this increase.

The Americans have increased from 93 in 1891 to 198, the Germans from 208 to 337, and the French from 89 to 103. The Spanish number 126 as compared with 88 in 1891. The cosmopolitan nature of the community can be realized from the fact that there is hardly a nationality on the face of the globe which is not represented.

The Portuguese population has again, for the reasons stated by Mr. Brewin in his Census Report for 1897, been separated in most of the Tables from the rest of the Europeans and Americans. It is mainly recruited from Macao, and only ten members of the community were born in Portugal. 1,095 or more than one-half were born in Hongkong, 746 in Macao and 60 in various ports in Portugal. Several members of this community described themselves as being of Asiatic race [*sic*]. The great majority of the Portuguese have returned themselves as Portuguese subjects. British nationality is claimed by a very few.

Of the British population of 3,007 (inclusive of those on board the shipping in the harbour) 1,777 claim to be English, 655 are Scotch, and 251 Irish. 2,053 were born in the British Isles, 574 in Hongkong, 140 in Australia, and 74 in India. The percentage of adult females to males is 55, taking all those over 15 years of age as adults. The percentage in 1891 was 38 and in 1897, 48.

The Non-Chinese races, other than European and American, number 2,607 as compared with 2,502 in 1897 and 1,439 in 1891. No separate return was made of the various races in 1891, so the present figures can only be compared with those of 1897. The Indians number 1,453, the increase over 1897 being 60. 345 or 24 per cent of this number are females. There are 484 Japanese as compared with 335 in 1897, and 266 Philippine Islanders as compared with 216 in the last Census. Of the remainder the Malays number only 66, there being 141 fewer than in 1897.

There are 2,139 Indian camp followers whom I have considered it advisable to include with the garrison. They are attached to that portion of the China Field Force, which is at present in garrison in this Colony.

The number of Eurasians was ascertained to be 267. This is 5 less than in 1897. It is a very difficult matter to obtain the true figures for this portion of the population. The large majority of Eurasians in this Colony dress in Chinese clothes, have been brought up and live in Chinese fashion, and would certainly return themselves as Chinese. Those who have called themselves Eurasians in this Census probably only represent the small minority who have been brought up as Europeans. Of the 3,589 Eurasians in the Singapore Census of 1891, the large majority were probably the children of Tamil, Malay or Indian mothers, and not of Chinese ones. They would most likely not have any objection to declaring themselves Eurasians. The Chinese consider the term one of reproach. If enumerators were instructed to find out the numbers of Eurasians themselves, it is obvious that this would inevitably lead to abuses, and would present great opportunities for the exercise of private spite.

Document 14.2: Racial Categories in the 1901 Census Table on 'Total Civil Population of the Colony'.

TABLE I.

TOTAL CIVIL POPULATION OF THE COLONY.

Locality.	Non-Chinese.																		Chinese.			Total.	
	Europeans and Americans other than Portuguese.			Portuguese.			Indians.			Races other than the before mentioned.			Total.			Eurasians.							
	Males.	Females.	Total.	Males.	Females.	Total.	Males.	Females.	Total.	Males.	Females.	Total.	Males.	Females.	Total.	Males.	Females.	Total.	Males.	Females.	Total.	Males.	Females.
Land Population.																							
Victoria, ...	1,646	1,092	2,738	794	1,007	1,801	847	328	1,175	474	417	891	3,761	2,844	6,605	91	166	257	129,396	45,660	175,056	133,248	48,670
The Peak, ...	231	182	413	5	5	10	9	4	13	2	...	2	247	191	438	...	...	...	1,672	114	1,786	1,919	305
Hongkong Villages, ...	134	33	167	6	5	11	54	...	54	3	1	4	197	39	236	...	...	...	9,805	3,628	13,433	10,002	3,667
British Kowloon, .	339	203	542	62	64	126	198	13	211	3	3	6	602	283	885	6	4	10	32,860	10,116	42,976	33,468	10,403
Stonecutters' Island, .	...	...	...	...	...	...	...	...	...	...	...	...	...	...	...	...	...	...	12	...	12	12	...
Total,......	2,350	1,510	3,860	867	1,081	1,948	1,108	345	1,453	482	421	903	4,807	3,357	8,164	97	170	267	173,745	59,518	233,263	178,649	63,045
Mercantile Marine,	631	7	638	8	...	8	95	...	95	257	2	259	992	9	1,001	1	...	1	1,180	...	1,180	2,172	9
Floating Population.																							
The Harbour, ...	...	...	...	...	...	...	...	...	...	...	...	...	...	...	...	...	...	...	18,932	9,597	28,529	18,932	9,597
Aberdeen, ...	...	...	...	...	...	...	...	...	...	...	...	...	...	...	...	...	...	...	2,940	2,311	5,251	2,940	2,311
Shaukiwan, ...	...	...	...	...	...	...	...	...	...	...	...	...	...	...	...	...	...	...	3,010	2,429	5,439	3,010	2,429
Stanley, ...	...	...	...	...	...	...	...	...	...	...	...	...	...	...	...	...	...	...	520	361	881	520	361
Total,......	...	...	...	...	...	...	...	...	...	...	...	...	...	...	...	...	...	...	25,402	14,698	40,100	25,402	14,698
Grand Total,...	2,981	1,517	4,498	875	1,081	1,956	1,203	345	1,548	739	423	1,162	5,799	3,366	9,165	98	170	268	200,327	74,216	274,543	206,223	77,752

Document 14.3: Diversity of Chinese Diasporas in Hong Kong, as shown in the Tables of the 1911 Census.[8]

Table VII

The Birth Places of the Chinese Population (other than inhabitants of the New Territories)

Provinces and Countries	Males	Females	Total
Provinces of China:–			
Chehkiang	209	79	288
Chihli	34	44	78
Fukien	1,021	281	1,302
Honam	10	4	14
Hunan	159	28	187
Hupeh	11	10	21
Kiangsi	57	39	96
Kiangsu	242	365	697
Kwangsi	406	304	710
Kwangtung	194,442	77,297	271,739
Nganhwui	16	14	30
Shansi	8	3	11
Shangtung	231	13	244
Shensi	10	4	14
Szchuen	8	7	15
Yunnan	32	6	38
Kweichau	11	12	23
Pekin	16	29	45
Kansu	1	...	1
Tibet	1	...	1
Hak Lung Kong	2	2	4
Total	196,927	78,541	275,468

8. P. P. J. Wodehouse, 'Report on the Census of the Colony for 1911', *Sessional Papers Laid Before the Legislative Council*, 23 November 1911.

Provinces and Countries	Males	Females	Total
Other Countries:–			
America	107	95	202
Corea	7	0	7
Formosa	23	8	31
Germany	2	0	2
Hongkong	28,773	24,740	53,513
New Territories	7,422	5,531	12,953
India	4	2	6
Japan	39	32	71
Philippines	2	2	4
Macao	1,057	820	1,877
Mongolia	1	0	1
Portugal	2	0	2
Siam	9	4	13
Singapore	52	59	111
Cuba	2	0	2
Burmah	1	0	1
Holland	1	4	5
Honolulu	6	12	18
Peru	2	0	2
Indo-China	54	50	104
Australia	55	45	100
Penang	6	0	6
Borneo	3	7	10
Canada	1	0	1
Guiana	1	0	1
Vancouver	1	1	2
Morocco	0	1	1
Sandakan	0	2	2
Not stated	105	6	111
Total	37,738	31,421	69,159
Grand Total	234,665	109,962	314,627

Table XI

Dialects spoken in the Home for Chinese population of the Colony (except New Territories, North, and South)

Dialects	Males	Females	Total
Punti	209,936	102,056	311,992
Hakka	16,394	6,428	22,822
Hoklo	6,353	596	6,949
Others	1,982	882	2,864
Not stated (Mercantile Marine)	5,551	240	5,791
Total	240,216	110,202	350,418

Document 14.4: Summary and evaluation of the 1961 Census.[9]

8.1 The 1961 census, the first in Hong Kong for thirty years, disclosed a total population, including transients, of 3,133,131 made up as follows:–

	Males	Females	Total
Non-transient	1,607,779	1,521,869	3,129,648
Transient	2,871	612	3,483
Total	1,610,650	1,522,481	3,133,131

8.2 The following are some of the most important totals:–

	Males	Females	Total	
Hong Kong born	760,683	425,493	1,482,887	(all ages)
Literate	1,024,489	617,861	1,642,350	(aged 10 and up)
Have received some education	1,177,479	743,348	1,920,827	(aged 6 and up)
Able to speak English	172,675	83,068	255,743	(aged 5 and up)
Able to speak Cantonese	1,296,479	1,197,808	2,494,287	(aged 5 and up)
Labour force	864,668	347,091	1,211,759	(aged 6 and up)

9. *The Hong Kong Census, 1961,* Vol. II (Hong Kong Government: Census and Statistics Department, 1961), accessed 3 January 2024, 8, https://www.censtatd.gov.hk/en/data/stat_report/product/B1129001/att/B11290021961XXXXE0100.pdf.

Document 14.5: The 1961 Census Officer's commentary on 'ethnic characteristics' in Section 20.6.3 of 1961 Census Report (emphasis in original).

By comparison with previous censuses the proportion of **Hong Kong–born** has **greatly increased**, the percentage being 47.7% as against 32.5% in 1931, 26.7% in 1921, and 31.5% in 1911. This increase is to Hong Kong, Kowloon, New Kowloon and the marine districts, the percentage in the New Territories having fallen. The increase in the proportion of Hong Kong–born has been almost entirely at the expense of those born in Kwangtung province: those claiming to have been born in some part of Kwangtung province total 45.6%, whereas in previous censuses they have always been about 60%. Those born in **other parts of China** total 4.9% as against 1.8% in 1931, 1.1% in 1921 and 0.9% in 1911. There is no significant change in the proportions of those born outside Hong Kong and China.

In a cosmopolitan centre like Hong Kong place of birth is not a sensitive indicator of **ethnic characteristics.** Since in the urban areas "race" and language do not operate as social barriers, many successful examples are found of what in many other places would be described as "mixed" marriages, and it was expected that the offspring of these marriages would give "Hong Kong" as their place of origin rather than claiming the origin of either parent. The only others who were expected to give "Hong Kong" as their place of origin were those few whose ancestors lived on Hong Kong Island or in Old Kowloon before their cession to the British Crown, the much greater numbers whose ancestors lived in New Kowloon or the New Territories before the lease, and of course the boat people who have been here from time immemorial.

Document 14.6: The diversity of languages spoken in Hong Kong, as shown in the 'Usual Language' Chart in *The Census and You*, which provides a more accessible account of the 1961 Census.[10]

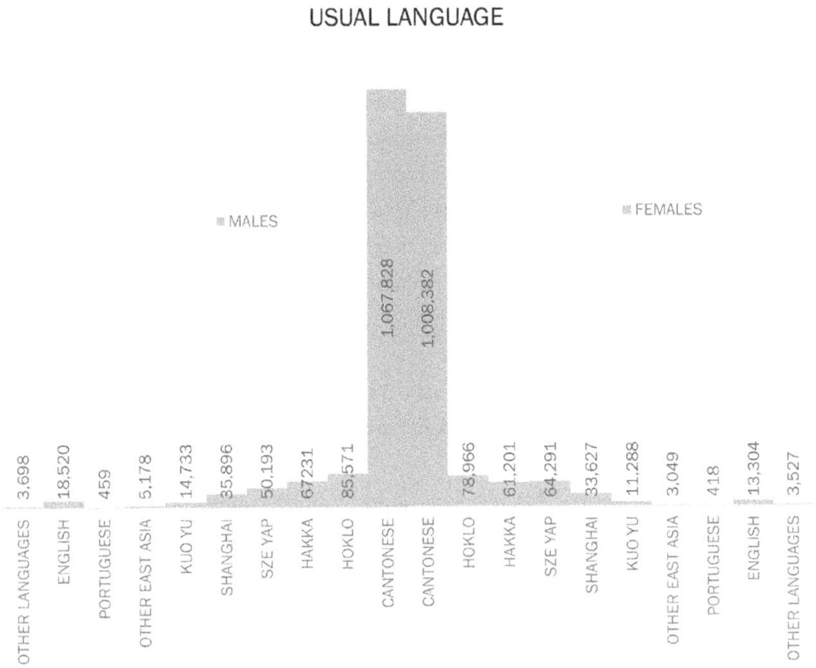

10. K. M. A. Barnett, *The Census and You* (Hong Kong Government: Census and Statistics Department, 1961), accessed 3 January 2024, 11, https://www.censtatd.gov.hk/en/data/stat_report/product/B1129004/att/B11290041961XXXXB0100.pdf.

Section 2. Personal Accounts on Being 'Eurasian' in Hong Kong

Document 14.7 features a short piece entitled 'We Eurasians', in which Jim Silva, a Portuguese born in Hong Kong in 1928, reminisced on how the community navigated the colonial hierarchies in British Hong Kong. His recollection also offers us a glimpse into the different peculiar positions that the Portuguese and Eurasian communities had in colonial Hong Kong. Born in 1918, Catherine Joyce Symons (neeé Anderson) spent much of her life in British Hong Kong. She was the first Eurasian to become headmistress of the Diocesan Girls' School, which itself had a long history of providing education for Eurasian girls in colonial Hong Kong, and the first woman to be appointed to the Executive Council. Document 14.8 is an excerpt from her autobiography published in 1996, in which Symons described to her readers the 'isolationism' that Hong Kong Eurasians, such as herself, experienced.

Document 14.7: Jim Silva's Account on being Portuguese in Hong Kong, in Frederic A. (Jim) Silva, *Things I Remember* (Frederick A. Silva, 2010), 12.

[Excerpt from the chapter 'We Eurasians']

We were comfortable with a lot that placed us on an economic level much lower than that of the European colonials, but also at the same time we were economically better off than the majority Chinese. There was never much in the way of dissent or rebellion against a system that was overtly racist, not to say inherently unfair and unjust. It was unjust because, regardless of education, experience or ability, the higher executive positions were exclusively reserved for Europeans. Hong Kong's biggest employer, the government services, in their varied departments initiated this racist hierarchy, and it was automatically followed by the big British hongs (trading houses) and banks. Needless to say, these higher executive positions brought along with them much higher pay grades, generous overseas leave and excellent living quarters.

Yet, despite this there was an unquestioning willingness to work within a system that seemed to have been natural and eternal. Perhaps this acceptance lay in the fact that we were the successors of our fathers, grandfathers, and great-grandfathers who had originally chosen to leave their Macau homes and opt for a better livelihood available in Hong Kong and Shanghai.

Knowing or not, we owed our strength and assurance to our culture and our community. There were enough of us in numbers to live within our own world. We could socialize and intermarry without ever going beyond the community. Most of us, and our fathers and grandfathers before us, appeared happy enough to conform and not feel those psychological hang-ups that other Eurasians may have felt in living the colonial life.

Because of our large community we always had our clubs, our names, our religion, our food, our patois and our Macau roots on which to anchor ourselves. We belonged, and we were secure in the knowledge that we did.

In contrast, the strain of being an English Eurasian in a British colonial society can take its toll. Many felt suspended between the two worlds, European and Chinese, and found it hard to fully belong to either. The British practiced discrimination and a subtle racism in both personal contacts and employment opportunities.

Perhaps a contributing reason for uncertainty among these other Eurasians was that they were smaller in number and, moreover, never considered or presented themselves as a cohesive and united group. There were the older established and monied families that intermarried among themselves. Many were well entrenched in professions or businesses. They formed a somewhat closed club that found little in common with the impecunious first generation offspring of English servicemen and their Asian wives. There certainly were hang-ups here: two worlds standing apart and divided by a snobbish English caste and racial system made unfair by employment opportunities.

By contrast, *filhos de Macau* ['sons of Macau', a phrase commonly used by the Portuguese to refer to themselves] were secure. We had our place, we knew our place, we accepted our place. Unfair or unjust as things may have been, we had no hang-ups. We had our own world and our own community. I am not writing of today, but rather reminiscing of a time and place where the good old days for some were the bad old days for others. All our *filhos de Macau* then lived in the midst of this colonial system.

It is part of our heritage.

Document 14.8: Joyce Symons on being Eurasian in Hong Kong, in Catherine Joyce Symons, *Looking at the Stars: Memoirs of Catherine Joyce Symons* (Pegasus Books, 1996), 2–3.

It was not long after I was born that the family moved back to Hong Kong. As a young couple with three children, my parents immediately noticed the tremendous difference between living in Hong Kong and Shanghai, so far as the status of Eurasians was concerned. In Shanghai, people were Chinese, or non-Chinese—foreigners—who included British, American, Irish, German, Filipino, or even Eurasians. But in Hong Kong throughout the colonial period, people were either expatriates or Chinese[.] [N]o-one mentioned Eurasians.

Because expatriates found themselves Chinese 'wives', the children born illegitimately could choose to take either the father's Western surname or the mother's Chinese name, which meant there were many "aliases"—many of which pepper this text.

The typical Eurasian lifestyle, food, and, certainly female dress, were mainly Chinese, but some expatriate ideas and habits were admired, and gradually assimilated when a family could afford to move up the social (and financial) scale. This pattern of grafting a Western culture onto the indigenous ethnic culture was evident for many decades in Hong Kong and the ports of Shanghai, Tientsin, Amoy, and Swatow, and penetrated even as far as Hankow, on the mighty Yangtsekiang river in the heart of central China.

I, like many other Eurasian children, was often bewildered and confused by trying to cope [with] vastly dissimilar languages, and contradictory codes of conduct or even table manners. There was never any discussion or explanation. Obedience was expected and indeed, willingly given, but as children we had to grow up bi-cultural, as well as bilingual. Children will often [choose] the easiest way of doing something, so honing a sharp sense of opportunism. Such adaptability applied to school life, often led to academic success, athletic distinction, and being awarded responsible positions at school. Expatriate teachers usually expected Eurasian children to do well and naturally enough, this apparent favouritism often made us detested by the Chinese children. Being in the middle was not easy. Even now, the "no-man's land" of Eurasian isolationism is still a hazard for those born into two cultures as they try to blend the different threads together. Today, at the age of 78, I am still painfully aware of them.

Section 3. Racial Pay Gap

Born and raised in Hong Kong, Eddie Gosano was a doctor trained at the University of Hong Kong. In 1997, he published an autobiography entitled Hong Kong Farewell, *in which he wrote extensively and candidly on the bitterness he felt about the unfairness of British colonialism. The passages below are from two different sections in his book, thirty pages apart from each other. But both are his recollections of the racial pay gap that was too formidable for anyone – let alone a highly educated Portuguese doctor like him – to miss. That Gosano wrote about the same issue in two different sections perhaps shows how painfully aware he was of the inequalities of colonial rule.*

Document 14.9: Eddie Gosano on Racial Pay Gap, in Eddie Gosano, *Hong Kong Farewell* (Greg England, 1997), 14 and 46.

[Excerpt from the chapter 'Doctor Eddie']

Finally, on 1 January 1939, at the age of 24, I achieved something a step beyond what Anglos might consider ordinary internship. I was appointed surgical medical officer of the Medical Department of HK in Kowloon Hospital. But mind you, there was a string attached. While of Portuguese ancestry and status as recognized in my native country, here in the British colony, I was still legally classified as Chinese. My compeer was Dr. G.A.V. Griffiths, a Britisher of 45 to 50 years of age. The two of us performed all surgery for this Government Civil Hospital. Our workload was measured in terms of free services for 100,000 people, 24 hours a day.

My salary was now $375 (HK) per month, or $62.50 U.S. Each year the stipend increased $25 (HK) monthly. We Chinese medical officers were given 2 weeks leave yearly. English medical officers were given 9 months leave every 3 years with passage to and from the United Kingdom for the whole family. This status was permanent in our contract during the pre-war period, irrespective of our years of service in the HK Government.

It was, as a doctor would be inclined to say, a bitter pill to swallow.

[Excerpt from the chapter 'I Resign from Government Service']

An anaesthetist at the Queen Mary Hospital, Dr. Esmonde, an Irishman, would apply the anaesthetic while I, as a local ("Chinese") surgeon, operated. Any lay person surely knows that a surgeon rates higher than an anaesthetist. But while we worked together for two years, Dr. Esmonde was paid roughly 4 times my earnings. He was given, in addition, a 5-room flat in the European sector. I had a 4-room flat in the Chinese sector. He was given 9 months' leave, passage paid, to England every 3 years. I was given 2 weeks once a year.

Two years after returning from England and living at the poverty level, on 23 May 1948, I resigned from the Government.

Section 4. The 1940 Evacuation and Racial Discrimination

In July 1940 the Hong Kong government carried out an evacuation to send away 'all British women and children' of 'pure European descent' as a precautionary measure against a possible Japanese invasion. The passages below are of very different natures, but all centre around the disappointment many felt about the racial discriminations involved in the scheme. Document 14.10 is a letter to the editor, presumably written by a Cantonese-speaking father to express his dissatisfaction that Chinese children in the colony were excluded from the policy. Document 14.11 is Joyce Symon's recollection in her autobiography of her attempt to register for the evacuation. Document 14.12 is an excerpt from an editorial in the South China Morning Post, *the editor-in-chief of which was a Chinese Australian, Henry Ching.*

Document 14.10: A Father's Letter, BA BA, 'Evacuation', *South China Morning Post*, 16 November 1940, 7.

Sir,

I agree with Safety First for Children [another anonymous writer of a letter to the editor] that Hongkong if attacked will be no place for the young. The noise, the destruction, the fright, the Starvation, the crime, the disease, etc. I suppose the Chinese children would also suffer similarly—unless they are hardened by heredity or something. But I forgot: it's the blue blood that matters. Excuse me.

BA BA.

Document 14.11: Joyce Symons on the government's refusal to evacuate Eurasians, *Looking at the Stars*, 23.

By the summer of 1941, the first signs of war reached Hong Kong when the Government decided to evacuate all expatriate women and children to Australia. This was a strong hint that Japan would soon declare war itself. Discrimination also came out into the open, with angry voices raised in the Legislative Council when the Government refused to evacuate other local groups—Eurasians and Portuguese—despite their possession of valid British passports. Marjorie and I tried to register for evacuation but were turned down by the authorities who said they didn't know what to do "with the likes of you". However, "the likes of us" were ordered to share in the war effort, with our young men conscripted into the volunteers and trained for battle, and everyone with a non-Chinese name having to take on some kind of war work. I was incensed when some Eurasians escaped all this, simply by adopting Chinese names.

Document 14.12: Editor of *South China Morning Post* on the unfairness revealed by the evacuation scheme, 'Being British', *South China Morning Post*, 1 July 1940, 10.

The Correspondence column indicates that the non-European part of the British community strongly resents the seeming discrimination in the official evacuation plan. For a "sheep and goats" division there is, we agree, no moral justification. It is conceded that, since the Imperial Government ordered it, the families of the regular forces should be sent away first. Thereafter, however, nothing can excuse inequality of treatment. Several thousands of British subjects not of pure European descent are serving in the defence of the Colony. They pay the same taxes as any other section: they will have to bear their share of the cost of the evacuation, whether they participate in it or not. If their wives and children cannot get away, they will naturally feel that they have been badly treated. Government announces, in what it conceives to be reassuring terms, that "schemes are under consideration for the evacuation, in due course, of the women and children of other sections of the population:" but this promise is obviously subject to a number of "ifs." We need not enlarge upon the effects of loss of confidence in the Government. For years we have striven to secure recognition for the Hongkong citizen, regardless of race—and we feel it will be a deplorable setback to British prestige if, even now, with the Empire in grave danger and every friend needed, Government is unable to divest itself of the old mentality.

Section 5. Two Recollections of Wartime Hong Kong

The Second World War challenged the racial hierarchy that the British had imposed in Hong Kong like never before. Multiracial British subjects undertook their obligation and contributed towards British war efforts: many fought courageously during the Battle of Hong Kong. Even after the fall of the city on 25 December 1941 – when Hong Kong was no longer British but a Japanese occupied territory – their service for the British Empire did not lapse. Many took crucial, irreplaceable roles in the British war efforts in South China and Macau, at great risk to their lives. They expected – for good reason – the British state to fulfil its imperial responsibility and give them the assistance they deserved as part of the empire. Many, however, were denied that and became profoundly aware that despite their service, racism still prevented them from being fully accepted by the British state.

Document 14.13 is an excerpt from the autobiography of Eddie Gosano, who, like many Portuguese in Hong Kong, had fled to Macau after the fall of Hong Kong. When in Macau, Gosano was the attending physician to the British Consul and ran his own medical practice, while also living a secret life as the head of the British Army Aid Group (BAAG) in Macau. Officially classified under the MI9, the BAAG was a British resistance network in wartime South China that involved relief operations and intelligence gathering. In his autobiography, Gosano praised the British Consul in Macau of the time, John Reeves, highly. His discussion of Reeves as a 'rare Britisher' who contrasted strongly with the impression that 'we second-class citizens' had of British authorities hinted at the prevalence of systemic racism at the time. He also lamented the little recognition that the British state had for the contributions that people of colour like him and his family made to the British war effort.

Their efforts, however, did earn the appreciation of some white Britons, especially those who fought and worked side by side with British subjects of colour during the war. These white Britons witnessed the perseverance of these subjects despite the racist, unfair treatment the latter had received from the British colonial regime. These include Selwyn Selwyn-Clarke, Hong Kong's Director of Medical Service, who found the 'conduct of Chinese, Eurasian, Portuguese, and other subjects of a none too generous British government [...] wonderfully inspiring'.[11] *In 1946, months after the liberation of Hong Kong, he wrote an article in a journal on how Hong Kong should adapt itself to the post-war world. Document 14.14 is an excerpt from this article, in which he also wrote about the 'moral and political necessit'y to offer more equal treatment to people of colour in the colony.*

Document 14.13: Eddie Gosano on the contributions and unequal treatment of people of colour during the war, in Gosano, *Hong Kong Farewell*, 33–34.

[Excerpt from the chapter 'Strained Relations']

Irrespective of our personal relationship, Consul J. T. Reeves remained, in my esteem, a rare Britisher. Had it not been for him being in Macao during the war, the Portuguese and other refugees including British affiliates from HK would have a different story to tell of the horrors of war on civilians. John Reeves redeemed much of the bad image we second-class citizens had of Colonial domination.

But from that time forward, my feelings towards the British turned more bitter by degrees. I could not help reflecting on how I volunteered to serve without pay in the prisoner-of-war camps aiding the wounding, whether Chinese or British nationals.

And it was still with me that I was volunteering without pay as head the Macao BAAG, risking my life daily [on] behalf of the British. What care did they show my brother Zinho, slaving in Japanese coal mines, or for two other brothers languishing in prison camps for the duration?

Document 14.14: Selwyn-Clarke on sacrifices made by the Chinese during the war, in P. S. Selwyn Clarke, 'Hong Kong Faces the Future', in *Health Horizon* (July 1946), 14 of 13–18. In MSS. Brit. Emp. s. 470, Box 7, Bodleian Libraries.

The war years in Hong Kong have done more than anything else to demonstrate the very real attachment of the local Chinese to the British. Scores of thousands

11. Selwyn Selwyn-Clarke, *Footprints: The Memoirs of Sir Selwyn Selwyn-Clarke* (Hong Kong: Sino-American Pub. Co., 1975), 88.

of Chinese (and a lesser number of Portuguese, Indians, and Eurasians) resident in Hong Kong willingly sacrificed themselves. Thousands lost their homes and property and were reduced to penury owing to serve as 'quislings' or to help Japan. To accord adequate recognition to these gallant people will be a difficult task. It is, however, morally necessary and politically desirable that no time should be lost in doing so. We are in the debt of those who relied upon Hong Kong as part of our Empire, and, consequently, as being entitled to such protection as that membership entailed. Politically, early action is desirable, because there is a small but vocal minority that seeks to substantiate the claim for the cancellation of the treaties ceding the territory to Great Britain.

Reports have been received that, earlier in that year, several thousand demonstrated before the British Embassy in Chungking asking for the return of the Colony to China.

Many thoughtful Chinese in Hong Kong would prefer to await the results of the policy of unity, freedom and democracy, which it is hoped will come from the discussions in the Political Consultative Council and National Assembly in Chungking. On the other hand, a vigorous programme of reconstruction by his Majesty's Government, in the execution of which the Chinese and other local elements are invited to serve as partners, should release the pressure on the safety valve and avoid the repetition of strikes and boycotts, which marred the earlier history of Hong Kong and from which the sister Colony of Singapore has suffered.

Section 6. Post-war Progress towards Eliminating Racial Divides

In many ways, Hong Kong was indeed becoming less racially segregated in the years immediately after the Second World War. The three sources below capture respectively the greater appetite for interracial interactions in the social world, the gradual removal of the glass ceiling in the civil service, and the removal of residential racial segregation in the colony.

Recent research has uncovered the emergence of multiracial social spaces in interwar Hong Kong. The opening of the Sino-British Club in 1949, as captured in Document 14.15, represents a continued determination by middle-class professionals to widen cross-cultural interactions in post-war Hong Kong. Compared with its pre-war counterparts, what was pioneering about the Sino-British Club was its founders' outwardly stated goal of eliminating racial discrimination in the colony. This perhaps has much to do with its members' wartime experience, which made many white Britons recognise the presence of racial inequality in the colony.

Document 14.16 consists of excerpts from two different chapters from the memoir of Florence Yeo, daughter of Sir Robert Hotung. In these two chapters, Yeo recollects her husband K. C. Yeo's promotions within the Hong Kong Government's Medical and Health Services. A Malayan Chinese born in Penang in 1903, K. C. (Kwok Cheang) Yeo received his medical training at the University of Hong Kong, and after his graduation in 1925 he stayed in the colony to practise medicine. The excerpts included here cover K. C. Yeo's promotion in 1947 as the Acting Deputy Director in the Medical and Health Services, and in 1952 as the Director of Medical and Health Services.

The most notable example of racial segregation enforced in Hong Kong was the Peak. In 1888, 1904, and 1918 respectively, the colonial government passed legislations to prohibit Chinese and Eurasians from living on the Peak to reserve it as effectively a white-only neighbourhood. Document 14.17 captures the historically significant Legislative Council meeting in 1946 where such legislations were removed.

Document 14.15: Excerpt from news report of a speech given by K. M. A. Barnett, Chairman of the Sino-British Club, at the Club's inaugural meeting in August 1949, 'Inaugural Meeting Held: Chairman of Sino-British Club Denounces Racial Distinctions', ***South China Morning Post,*** **27 August 1949, 3.**

The Chairman next drew the meeting's attention to the first three of the 21 objects for which the Club is declared to be established. These were (1) the promoting of cultural and social relations between all communities in Hongkong, (2) to devise ways and means of arousing and stimulating interest in the cultural heritage of different communities and (3) to do everything to eliminate racial prejudice, discrimination, disharmony and misunderstanding, wherever they may be found.

Continuing, Mr Barrett said: When I compare Hongkong with other places drawing their population from different parts of the world, I think we are fortunate in the fluidity and indistinctness of the lines of demarcation drawn around our component communities. To a visitor who comes here from Africa, India, or even Singapore it must appear that we have no racial or communal distinctions. But to one who comes here straight from England, and to any permanent resident, who keeps his eyes and ears open, it is evident that distinctions exist. Not, perhaps, very grave ones; nothing that could be fairly described as discrimination or racial barriers. But distinctions and misunderstandings there are.

It was the belief of the founders of this Club that while every community in Hongkong has something of its own to be proud of, some precious heritage to be treasured, nevertheless those precious heritages ought not to be guarded in jealous seclusion, but freely exchanged and handed round for general approbation and comparison.

By promoting interchange between our different communities they hoped not to obliterate the identity of each, but to promote understanding by each community of its neighbours; not to depreciate in the eyes of any community the value of the inherited culture of which everyone of that community is a trustee, but to enable each to see his own tradition as a part of the grand pattern of human civilization: and thereby, it was hoped, to observe in it virtues and beauties before unsuspected.

It was the belief of those founders that racial prejudice, discrimination and disharmony, hatred and suspicion between neighbours near and far, all had their origin in ignorance, in misunderstanding, in lack of friendly contact. It was and is the aim of the Sino-British Club, to such extent that opportunity shall offer, to enlighten that ignorance, to dispel those misunderstandings, by providing those opportunities for friendly contact which make possible actual understanding and knowledge.

I have spoken of communities in Hongkong. Advisedly, because I am not thinking only or principally of race. The divisions that divide us, and the bonds that unite us, are racial, national, social, religious, economic, educational—something of each of those and something more, of a more fortuitous nature, shall I say just propinquity. We have all made jokes at some time or other about The Peak, the Middle Levels, and Kowloon. Accidental divisions, but divisions none the less. I have remarked how few people I have met here who were educated at American universities; yet I know them to be numerous, more numerous perhaps than those from English universities. Here is another example of two sub-communities between which, evidently, some barrier exists. Some would say "Tear it down." It will be for the benefit of both. But like a fence between two gardens, both neighbours must be willing before it can be torn down. It is one of the functions of your Club to produce, by example and persuasion, that willingness.

Document 14.16: Florence Yeo on her husband K. C. Yeo's promotions in the Government's Medical Department in 1947 and 1952, Florence Yeo, *My Memories* (Words & Images, 1994), 124–25 and 143.

[Excerpt from chapter 13, 'K. C.'s Promotion']

K. C. reported back to work. Selwyn greeted him with, "So, you didn't want to come back when I sent for you. I had a good job for you as Acting Deputy Director of Health Services, but you didn't seem to want it," he teased. "However, Dr Graham, Cumming has been kind enough to keep it warm for you!" Selwyn continued.

K. C. could hardly believe it. Chinese were seldom promoted to the higher jobs, so he was really elated. His foot was placed on the first rung of the ladder towards success. It had been Selwyn all along that had faith in K.C.'s abilities and integrity.

K. C. did not let him down. From that day on, he devoted his whole life to his work. His diligence and honesty were outstanding. During this period, K. C. also held the post of Deputy Chairman of the Urban Council. This was the beginning of his period of innumerable meetings, especially after work. We, as a family, saw less and less of him as his responsibilities grew. At the top of his career, I think K. C. was in twenty-five separate committees and chaired nearly all of them.

K. C. chaired on as Acting Deputy Direct of Health Services for four months and still the post was not confirmed. This was rather unsettling as we felt anything could happen and he might lose the position.

So, one day, when I met the Governor of Hong Kong, Sir Alexander Grantham, I boldly went up to him and brought up the subject of K.C.'s promotion. He was surprised that the confirmation of K.C.'s post had not come through and promised me he would look into it. "I shall tie a knot in my handkerchief to remind me," he smiled and duly did so. We heard very shortly after this that the post had been confirmed and K.C. was definitely made Deputy Director of Health Services, receiving the same salary and house allowance as an expatriate for the first time. I felt justice had, at least, been done.

[Excerpt from chapter 18, 'K. C.'s Final Promotion: Father's 90th Birthday Celebration']

Activity stepped up yet again when K. C. was promoted to the very top job of Director of Medical and Health Services in January, 1952. He also became part-time Professor of Preventive Medicine in the Hong Kong University, and was made Official Justice of Peace in connection with his work. Of course, responsibilities mounted, as did the social commitments, many of which were in celebration of his promotion. The Chinese community, especially the doctors, were very proud of him. He was the very first Chinese to hold this top job. (Previous to this, all Heads of Departments were British). So, each section of the Chinese community feted him, e.g. the Chinese Medical Association, the Chinese nurses, the "Yeo clan", etc. This went on for weeks. It wore us out.

K. C.'s health was suffering from overwork and eating too much food. Often he would have tummy upsets and this caused him to lose weight. Once he went down with amoebic dysentery and had to go to hospital. After a few days, he discharged himself because, he said, the treatment was worse than the disease! Somehow, he recovered, but it left him weak and thin. It was sheer determination that enabled him to carry on with his work. But I was always worried about him.

It mattered to me very much that he would succeed. We both felt he was on trial. It was imperative for him to do well and not let the Chinese community down. He didn't.

Document 14.17: Minutes of the Legislative Council Meeting for the Second and Third Read of the Ordinance to remove the racial discrimination enforced on the Peak, 25 July 1946, *Hansard*, 77–78.

PEAK DISTRICT (RESIDENCE) REPEAL BILL, 1946.

The ATTORNEY GENERAL moved the Second reading of a Bill intituled "An Ordinance to repeal the Peak District (Residence) Ordinance, 1918."

The HON. MR. M. K. LO said. —Your Excellency, —The Bill which was passed into law as the Peak District (Residence) Ordinance 1918 by this Council on the 30th May, 1918 was introduced in this Council only one week previously. There was no time for making representations to Government between the First reading of the Bill and its passage into law. But after the enactment there was very strong and bitter opposition to this measure on the part of the Chinese Community, and in this opposition the Chinese General Chamber of Commerce took the leading part.

As a member of that Chamber I made my own humble contribution to the opposition, in which my friend Mr. J. M. Wong, J.P., among others, took a prominent part. The Chinese then had no particular desire to live on the Peak. Their opposition was based solely on the ground of racial distinction.

This Ordinance has been a source of resentment to the Chinese ever since its enactment and I feel sure the repeal of this Ordinance, which is being effected by this Bill, will give universal satisfaction to the Chinese and not the least to those who, like Mr J. M. Wong and others, tried in vain to obtain its earlier repeal.

Sir, I should like, if I may, to congratulate Government on its own initiative in bringing about the repeal of this Ordinance and of the Cheung Chau (Residence) Ordinance 1919 implying, as it does, Government's recognition that Ordinances of this nature are out of harmony with the spirit of the times.

The COLONIAL SECRETARY seconded, and the Bill was read a Second time.

On the motion of the Attorney General, seconded by the Colonial Secretary, Council then went into Committee to consider the Bill clause by clause.

Council then resumed.

The ATTORNEY GENERAL reported that the Peak District (Residence) Repeal Bill had passed through Committee without amendment, and moved the Third reading.

The COLONIAL SECRETARY seconded, and the Bill was read a Third time and passed.

Section 7. Persisting Racial Discrimination

Notwithstanding progress made towards eliminating racial divides captured in the sources above, it would be naïve to assume that racial discrimination disappeared overnight in post-war Hong Kong. Residents often voiced their disappointment that the government had not done enough on the matter, as we can see in the sources selected below. Documents 14.18 and 14.19 are letters to the editor of the South China Morning Post *from the late 1940s, and Document 14.20 is a news report of a talk given by Ma Man-fai in 1969 on the issue.*

Document 14.18: 'Disgusted Local', 'Equality for All', *South China Morning Post*, 23 December 1946, 5.

Sir,

Every day brings forth more complaints from the Police Reserve, HKVDC, ARP, Auxiliary Fire Service, locally engaged Government nurses, teachers, etc. Your columns are being continually filled with such letters. Yet nothing seems to be done and little has been achieved after 15 months of so-called rehabilitation.

The Government settled with Sterling paid Civil Servants soon enough; British Volunteers and other nationals as well as the few fortunate local born who did not return to the Colony from Japan camps, but were repatriated from Manila and elsewhere, were paid in full in England, received their demobilization clothing and enjoyed a nice holiday. Other Stanley internees have had their share of the spoils; for all of which the ordinary man in the street will be called upon to meet in the form of new and higher taxes for decades to come. And here again the Hongkong born will be affected most. For this is our home and we are here to stay. All this and yet, the poor local born, whether Volunteer, Auxiliary Services or Civil Servant must await the whims and condescension of the powers that be. Final Settlement cannot be made; your petition is under consideration; queries should be deferred; the matter is receiving consideration. What a waste of stationery and with such a large Budget deficit!

Talks and promises of more representation in the Government; chances for the Hong Kong born, no more discrimination. Mere talk, as our friends the Americans so very aptly put it. Nothing can be done and nothing will be achieved until official red tape, incompetency and sheer discrimination, are completely brushed aside. I am inclined to believe firmly in that old adage—the leopard never changes its spots.

Are we in any way different from that fateful year, 1941? The war matters little now. It is all over and forgotten. We were only useful when we were needed. Promises made to prisoners at Shamshuipo as to what was theirs by right; profusely worded letters from Stanley thanking those outside for their kindness and bravery in sending parcels that were the means of keeping many an internee alive; promises of better times and promotions for many. These are mere things of the past and of no importance. We fought side by side and risked our lives together: we went through the rigours of North Point, Shamshuipo and Japan; we were in the political section in Stanley Gaol; we were hounded by the Japanese and betrayed by the collaborators; but this is a new era and time eradicates everything. We are no longer needed; they can fend for themselves; our loyalty and work during the fighting and occupation means nothing.

One wonders whether there is still one recourse. Are the unofficial members of the Executive and Legislative Councils really looking after the interests of the Colony and its inhabitants. Short speeches and slight criticism carries but little weight. They must be followed up and relentless pressure applied. Remember we are dealing with the Government and everyone knows what that means. One need have no fears when fighting for a just cause.

The picture stands out clearly in my mind. I have no doubts at all about same. It only means one thing. We served, we suffered, and now we understand. We are local born, we just do not count. Justice and Equality. For many maybe, but not for us.

Document 14.19: Ralph Shaw's Letter on Racial Discrimination in 1949, 'Correspondence: Racial Discrimination', *South China Morning Post*, 20 December 1949, 10.

Sir,

Mr Ma Man-fai's recent talk on "Racial Discrimination" was a timely reminder of the immense task that lies before us in this so-called enlightened age if we are to preserve the precarious peace which followed the recent bloodfest. It is an amazing thing that, in time of war, a man's colour is no drawback to his dying with a bullet through his brain on some battlefield. Yet, in time of peace, colour of skin and place of birth appear to govern the conditions of a man's career, both in the business and social spheres. Why a fellow should be a "damned good sort" when he's firing a rifle, and a "rank outsider" when he isn't killing his fellow men, is a question I've never been able to answer satisfactorily to many of my friends in this part of the world.

I was amazed that, in Shanghai after the war, the staid, old Shanghai Club—with the longest bar in the world—admitted only white-skinned elbow benders and completely ignored the Chinese businessman and the potential gimlet fan. This, in view of the changed conditions in Shanghai, left me rather perplexed. Little harm would have been done had the Shanghai Club opened its doors to Chinese—a new gesture in a new world dedicated to the principles of the United Nations.

There is precious little sense in the outmoded method of giving the plums in business and Government organizations to the fellows from Home. The fact that a man is born in Hongkong should be no drawback in later years to his advancement. Nor should the colour of his skin, or the mixture of his ancestry have any influence on his fitness to hold an executive position.

As a matter of fact—if we are to hold on to this precarious peace—it might be a good idea for us all to get into the boiling pot and to do a little mixing of the races. If we are all of the same shape and approximately the same colour, it might bring out that old herd instinct and keep us from tearing one another to pieces on the obsolete platform of nationalism.

And the colonial Powers would do well to realize that a contented population is the best guarantee for internal peace and security. If the Chinese, or the Eurasian resident, feels that he is getting a raw deal compared with the man from Home, then there is a potential source of trouble when trouble comes.

The time of inferiority or superiority complexes has gone. We have much to learn from the Chinese—although we might not think so—and they have plenty to learn from us. Only by mixing together and scrapping the old prejudices on both sides can we iron out a path to the kind of future we all dreamed of when the world was in the throes of war.

To my way of thinking, I lose nothing by having a drink with a Chinese in my club, and I should be honoured if I could trot along to his and sample his particular brew.

This intense racial feeling—and it is intense, despite the United Nations—is shown in so many fields. Take Association Football. When a Chinese team plays a British side, there are two flags involved—a major war in which racial interests tower above those of the sporting element. Usually, the Chinese are at fault on this score. And it is a bad fault.

But we Europeans have our prejudices, too, and I don't blame our Chinese friends for feeling hurt in face of the many social injustices we foist on them.

If the world—it looks like a forlorn hope—is to be made a better place in which to live, let us pluck out one cancer—that of nationalism. Let us be one family in which colour of skin and ancestry have no influence on our feelings.

Ralph Shaw

Document 14.20: Ma Man-Fai criticizing the Government for Racial Discrimination in 1969, 'Govt Criticized for Racial Discrimination', *South China Morning Post*, 9 March 1969, 8.

The chairman of the United Nations Association of Hongkong, Mr Ma Man-fai, yesterday criticized Government for racial discrimination in the Colony.

"There is only one political party in Hongkong and that is the Government with 80,000 members," he said.

Racial discrimination, he said, could be weakened if Government became autonomous and less dependent on Britain.

"Many Government posts are given to those who speak good English. In many cases there are Government employees who speak better English than their native Chinese language," he added.

Mr Ma was one of four speakers at a University of Hongkong teach-in on social changes in Hongkong.

"If you speak a few words of English then you come further up the social ladder."

Mr Ma said that he would not serve as a juror in Hongkong because the local system violated British Law.

"In Hongkong it is difficult to find jurors of equal standing to accused persons because most of the accused do not speak English yet English is one of the qualifications for a juror."

Other speakers at the teach-in were Dr David Ho, from the University of Hongkong; the director of Hongkong Council of Social Service, Mr Murdock Keith; and the social work co-ordinator for Caritas, Miss Margaret Lam.

In the years prior to the handover, legislators had attempted to raise bills to outlaw racial discrimination in Hong Kong. These attempts were unsuccessful, and it was in 2009 that the city first enacted its Race Discrimination Ordinance. The news report below captures public reactions to a consultation paper that the government issued in February 1997 on a possible bill on racial discrimination, which provides us a glimpse of the stance that the colonial administration took on the issue, and the experiences of racial minority groups living in the city at that time.

Document 14.21: Minority groups speak out on racial discrimination, 1997. Jane Moir, 'Authorities "Blinkered" to Prejudice', *South China Morning Post*, 20 February 1997, 5.[12]

Minority groups and human rights activists yesterday accused the Government of donning "self-imposed blinkers" when claiming racial discrimination was not significant.

The claim—in a consultation paper on the topic in which the Government says it adopts the dictum "If it ain't broke, don't fix it"—sparked fears that legislation had been ruled out.

But Secretary for Home Affairs Michael Suen Ming-yeung was adamant the Government had an open mind. "We haven't taken any particular stance," he said, admitting it could look as if the Government appeared "forgiving" of discriminatory incidents in the report.

The Government responded to every claim of discrimination in the report. In all, more than 70 bodies—from academics to ethnic minority groups and consulates-general—made such a claim.

For example, complaints by nationals of Botswana that they had been verbally abused, refused service and ostracized could merely be "innocent reactions from persons meeting expatriates from a different culture for the first time," the paper says.

Indian Resources Group director Anita Gidumal said: "People do feel that discrimination is an issue in Hong Kong. We think there should be legislation. Even the Basic Law distinguishes between ethnic and non-ethnic Chinese."

A human rights law expert, Andrew Byrnes, said the paper showed "the Government has no genuine commitment to do anything about racial discrimination—they have self-imposed blinkers on."

12. I am grateful to Steven Hon and the *South China Morning Post* for granting me permission to include this source in the chapter.

The director of Human Rights Monitor, Law Yuk-kai, said: "Even if the problem is not serious, there's an obligation for the Government to enact a law to prohibit such discrimination."

The consultation paper lists complaints of racial discrimination in the spheres of education, employment, health and social welfare, and law and order.

A Pakistani said that, except for police and correctional services, no South Asian resident had been recruited into the civil service for 20 years.

Domestic helpers from abroad complained of being barred from residential lifts and clubs, being fired for having dark skin, being attacked physically, and being denied permission to have their families with them in Hong Kong.

Suggested Readings

Chan, Catherine S. *The Macanese Diaspora in British Hong Kong: A Century of Transimperial Drifting*. Amsterdam: Amsterdam University Press, 2021.

Chu, Cecilia. *Building Colonial Hong Kong: Speculative Development and Segregation in the City*. Abingdon: Routledge, 2022.

Chu, Cindy Yik-yi, ed. *Foreign Communities in Hong Kong, 1840s–1950s*. New York: Palgrave Macmillan, 2005.

Kong, Vivian. 'Exclusivity and Cosmopolitanism: Multi-ethnic Civil Society in Interwar Hong Kong'. *Historical Journal* 63, no. 5 (2020): 1281–302.

Kong, Vivian. *Multiracial Britishness: Global Networks in Hong Kong*. Cambridge: Cambridge University Press, 2023.

Lee, Vicky. *Being Eurasian: Memories across Racial Divides*. Hong Kong: Hong Kong University Press, 2004.

Snow, Philip. *The Fall of Hong Kong: Britain, China, and the Japanese Occupation*. New Haven, CT: Yale University Press, 2003.

Teng, Emma Jinhua. *Eurasian: Mixed Identities in the United States, China, and Hong Kong, 1842–1943*. Berkeley: University of California Press, 2016.

White, Barbara-Sue. *Turbans and Traders: Hong Kong's Indian Communities*. Hong Kong: Oxford University Press, 1994.

Index